Thomas Lahusen
Peter H. Solomon, Jr. (eds.)

What Is Soviet Now?

WHAT IS SOVIET NOW?

Identities, Legacies, Memories

edited by

Thomas Lahusen and Peter H. Solomon, Jr.

LIT

Cover Photograph by Tracy McDonald

Bibliographic information published by the Deutsche Nationalbibliothek
The Deutsche Nationalbibliothek lists this publication in the Deutsche Nationalbibliografie; detailed bibliographic data are available in the Internet at http://dnb.d-nb.de.

ISBN 978-3-8258-0640-8

A catalogue record for this book is available from the British Library

Auslieferung/Verlagskontakt:
Fresnostr. 2 48159 Münster
Tel. +49 (0)251–62 03 20 Fax +49 (0)251–23 19 72
e-Mail: lit@lit-verlag.de http://www.lit-verlag.de

Distributed in the UK by: Global Book Marketing, 99B Wallis Rd, London, E9 5LN
Phone: +44 (0) 20 8533 5800 – Fax: +44 (0) 1600 775 663
http://www.centralbooks.co.uk/acatalog/search.html

Distributed in North America by:

Transaction Publishers
New Brunswick (U.S.A.) and London (U.K.)

Transaction Publishers
Rutgers University
35 Berrue Circle
Piscataway, NJ 08854

Phone: +1 (732) 445 - 2280
Fax: + 1 (732) 445 - 3138
for orders (U. S. only):
toll free (888) 999 - 6778
e-mail:
orders@transactionspub.com

Contents

Introduction

Thomas Lahusen and Peter H. Solomon, Jr.

"Society is full of mush (*kasha*), and so are the heads of the teachers," said Vladimir Putin on June 27, 2007, at the National Russian Conference of Humanities and Social Sciences Teachers.[1] Leonid Poliakov, chair of the department of political science at the Higher School of Economics, and editor of a recent "social studies" textbook for the 11th grade,[2] agreed wholeheartedly—at least with the first part of the president's sentence. He lamented the general "ideological disarmament" that had befallen Russia after 1991, the fact that Marxism and communism had been replaced by "some kind of shaky, abstract ideology of universal values. We added words such as 'freedom,' 'democracy,' 'the market,' 'human rights,' and 'civil society' to our lexicon. When you're a child, you get little blocks with letters on them, but you don't get taught how to make them into words. It's as if we were given these blocks and we are still learning how to put them together."[3] President Putin, never shy of providing instruction, said the new history textbooks should "make our citizens, especially the young, proud of their country." And he added the hint of a warning: "Many school books are written by people who receive foreign grants. They dance to the butterfly polka (*pol'ka-babochka*) that others have paid for ... These books, regrettably, get into schools and universities." Putin admitted that there were problematic pages in Russia's history, such as the events "starting from 1937," a statement that is itself reminiscent of the historiography of the Secret Speech. He conceded that "we should not forget these moments of our past." At the same time he reminded his listeners:

> Other countries have also known their bleak and terrible moments. In any event, we have never used nuclear weapons against civilians, and we have never dumped chemicals on thousands of kilometers of land or dropped more

---

[1] Andrei Kolesnikov, "Ne zhdat' milostei ot istorii: Prezident proinstruktiroval prepodavatelei obshchestvennykh nauk." *Kommersant*, no. 107 (3683) (June 22, 2007). Online edition available at http://www.kommersant.ru/doc.aspx?DocsID=776927 (accessed September 8, 2007); Pavel Felgenhauer, "Kremlin Rejects 'Foreign' Approach to Russian History," *Eurasia Daily Monitor*, June 27, 2007, available at http://www.jamestown.org/edm/article.php?article_id=2372256 (accessed September 8, 2007); excerpts of officials transcripts of the conference can be found on http://www.kremlin.ru, June 21, 2007.

[2] L.V. Poliakov, ed., *Obshchestvoznanie: global'nyi mir v XXI veke*. 11 klass (Moscow: Prosveshchenie, 2007).

[3] http://www.kremlin.ru/eng/speeches/2007/06/21/2137_type82917type84779_135471.shtml (accessed September 8, 2007).

> bombs on a tiny country than were dropped during the entire Second World War, as was the case in Vietnam. We have not had such bleak pages as was the case of Nazism, for example.[4]

For the chronicler of *The Moscow Times*, Putin's intervention at the conference was "worthy of a true, old-time Soviet polemicist."[5]

A few days before the teachers' conference, the program *The Street of Our Destiny* aired on TV Tsentr. Viewers could witness a scene that also had an eerie feel of old. The hosts of the program, Alexandra Burataeva and Alexander Dediushko, had invited foreign teachers of Russian—a Czech, a Hungarian, an Afghan, and an African— to share their views about this "language of international communication."[6] And so we learned that Russian is extremely popular in Hungary nowadays, and that the Czechs remember with nostalgia the time when people were learning Russian. The backdrop changed to footage showing fields of red poppies; the Afghan representative said that when the Russians were in his country, schools were built, whereas today the United States and its allies support the drug lords. The African guest, a graduate of Patrice Lumumba Peoples' Friendship University in Moscow, waxed nostalgic about the bygone years of Soviet presence on his continent, but was interrupted by his hosts when he started to lament the disappearance of the USSR.

The hosts of *The Street of Our Destiny* understood only too well what parts of Soviet history should be remembered, and what not: the invasion of Hungary in 1956, of Czechoslovakia in 1968, and of Afghanistan in 1979 would not "make proud" its young viewers.

Almost two decades after the disintegration of the Soviet Union, the specter of its moral, social, economic, and cultural systems still haunts Russia and its successor states. The forceful return of Russia's economic and political presence in the world inspires pride indeed, and sometimes fear. And on the rise is the nostalgia for a world often perceived as simpler, more secure, or as some kind of "camp reunion" of the happy years of youth.[7]

---

[4] Ibid.

[5] Yevgeny Kiselyov, "Worthy of a True, Old-Time Soviet Polemicist," *The Moscow Times*, Wednesday, June 27, 2007, 9.

[6] "Govorite po-russki!" *Ulitsa nashei sud'by*, TV Tsentr, June 20, 2007.

[7] Alison Smale, "We All Live in a Red Submarine," *New York Times*, Sunday, August 26, 2007, 5.

The goal of the present volume is to contribute to the endeavor of "putting the blocks together," by asking "What is Soviet now?" Of course, the question forced the authors here to contend with what was "Soviet" then.

The book begins with two chapters on the nature of markets and market places in the late Soviet period and its implications for economic and social development in post-Soviet Russia.

Focusing on how society in the USSR related to markets, Robert Johnson observes that markets, in a physical and abstract sense, evoked ambivalence if not downright hostility among at least part of the Soviet citizenry. After providing a vivid portrait of the variety of physical markets he witnessed in late and post-Soviet Russia (legal versus illegal; trading food and necessities versus other things), Johnson seeks to explain the ambivalence of many Russians about markets. In the Brezhnev era, he contends, the problem was partly the need to operate in the shadows of the law, and partly one of disapproval of persons who profited through "speculation." But the lingering ambivalence to the market in post-Soviet times, Johnson concludes, reflects also nostalgia for socialism, in particular a world in which trade was regulated, and people did not have to worry about the risk of being cheated or dealing with the law of supply and demand. Even competition of ideas, another kind of market in the author's view, seems to make some Russians nervous, particularly those for whom a liberal market grounded in autonomy and free exchange seems foreign.

In contrast, James Millar provides an economic historian's perspective on markets in Soviet and post-Soviet experience. Starting from the vantage point of Marxist theory and the goal of eliminating markets from the socialist economy, he reminds us that despite the persistence of markets for consumption (kolkhoz and peasant markets), many crucial markets from the viewpoint of a capitalist economy were abolished or at least seriously diminished. These included markets in producer goods, markets in productive assets (faculties, stores, land), stock and bond markets, and markets in credit and financial instruments as well. Inexperience with such markets, he demonstrates, proved catastrophic for the development of post-Soviet capitalism. There was no problem developing new markets for consumer goods and service, which had effectively existed outside the official structures for decades, but it was a different story for "other markets vital to the capitalist economy." Difficulties reviving these markets led to such consequences as underinvestment in domestic productive assets, the weakness of commercial banks, and risk avoidance among entrepreneurs, as well as to the perverse and destructive saga of privatization of state assets. Millar goes on to explain how the post-Soviet Russian economy has come to resemble the pre-socialist Soviet economy of NEP), and to reflect on the failure of Russian leaders' attempt to substitute utopian capitalism for utopian socialism.

The post-Soviet era in Russia and other states has featured attempts to establish new institutions, economic and political, that do not fit with underlying social institutions and needs, and it is not surprising that the result has been the development of institutional facades, where underlying realities and informal practices do not correspond to the institutions' formal side and the institutions have a "Potemkin" quality. In her chapter Jessica Allina-Pisano starts by examining two such institutions, private ownership of land in rural areas and elections. First, she demonstrates how the apparently successful privatization of agricultural land in two neighboring regions of Russia and Ukraine constitutes a facade behind which commercial agriculture moved into the hands not of ordinary farmers but "of a small number of well-positioned individuals." Similarly, elections that were supposedly free and fair were guided in practice by public officials through the unfair distribution of advantages among the competitors, or the use of the "administrative resource." Then, Allina-Pisano goes on to analyze in depth how a "symbiosis of incentives" (including some that reflect more than personal interests) helped to bring about institutional facades, rather than a mere continuation of Soviet-era practices or the impact of tradition.

Part of the underlying social reality that shapes how new institutions turn out in practice is the informal social networks that continue from late Soviet times but whose nature and impact may also have changed. A further issue is how Russian networks resemble the social networks that matter for the global economy. Alena Ledeneva grapples with these questions by examining the social networks of Russia against the background of the comparative theory of social networks developed especially by Endre Sik and Barry Wellman. Her chapter offers a perceptive account of some key theoretical distinctions, including how personal relationships can become a form of social capital and even "enabling structures," and on this basis provides an exegesis of the various ways that such networks can interact, positively and negatively, with formal economic institutions. She comes to the conclusion that the nature and function of networks in post-Soviet Russia do not conform to the allegedly universal models of "network society" that connect to the global economy. At the same time, the networks in Russia have lost some of their traditional benefits by becoming monetarized, and in the process declined as vehicles of socialibility, lost their open character, and become less available to the poor.

Finally, to conclude Part One, Peter Solomon explores what kind of public administration characterized the Soviet experience and what legacy it left for post-Soviet rulers. What emerged in the USSR under Stalin, he argues, was a hybrid type of public administration, in which some rational or Weberian elements such as hierarchy and specialization coexisted with elements of patrimonialism, including network relationships and the dominance of informal norms and practices over formal law. After Stalin, Solomon argues, the patrimonial elements deepened, especially with the growth of the second economy, yet at the same time the Brezhnev era was marked by attempts to develop a rational approach to bureaucratic decision-making and greater attachment to law within administration. Overall, though, the bureaucracy of late Soviet times was more traditional than modern and is appropriately characterized as a form of "patrimonial rationality." It was left to the rulers of post-Soviet Russia to struggle to overcome the dominance of informal social relations over public administration and to try to separate the public and private realms.

Part Two of the book examines various ways history is conceived, written, and perceived from today's post-Soviet perspective.

Ben Eklof investigates the reception in Russia and abroad of Boris Mironov's monumental *A Social History of Imperial Russia: 1700-1917*, first published in 1999 in Russia, and a year later in English translation in the United States. Eklof was himself invested in the latter. According to him, only a handful of western reviewers fully appreciated the scope and depth of Mironov's work. Despite some positive responses, the overall reaction to the book in a 2001 *Slavic Review* forum and other western reviews was generally "polite, if tepid," and, at times, even condescending. In response to this almost "postcolonial setting," contends Eklof, one has to evaluate this work in its Russian context. *A Social History*, which was given extraordinary and unprecedented attention at home, is not only "the first serious grand synthesis of Russian history of the post-Soviet era," it also offers a synthesis that can contribute to finding "a usable past, combining the quest for truth, empathetic understanding, and pride in one's country." Mironov's work provides a "professional alternative" to the popular histories that have mushroomed all over Russia's book stalls. *A Social History* normalizes not only Russian history but also the Russian historical profession.

How "Soviet" are the templates, formulas, and clichés, inherited from the Soviet era, and do modern, post-Soviet writers of Soviet history actually employ them? Nikolai Krementsov tries to answer the question by comparing two biographies of the biologist and animal breeder Ilya Ivanov (1870–1932). The first one was published in 1964 and betrays "Sovietness" not only by what was highlighted on its pages, but also by what was omitted. The second biography, published in 2003, under the sensationalist title, *The Red Frankenstein: The Kremlin's Secret Experiments*, focuses on what was allegedly omitted in the first biography—Ivanov's expedition to French West Africa, which aimed to produce hybrids between apes and humans by means of artificial insemination. The post-Soviet biography seems to follow the well-known cold-war template of "unmasking." Only this time "Soviet," and not "bourgeois science," is the object of denigration. Having demonstrated the presence of such "reincarnations and permutations," Krementsov doubts whether the very question "What is Soviet now?" has any value. It is judged as "flawed, methodologically suspect, and ultimately unproductive." It may be productive, however, to ask if Krementsov's polemic itself is embedded in a context where "Soviet" still matters.

When templates, formulas, and clichés leave the pages of a biography and become part of life, perhaps they matter even more. Tracy McDonald explores the layers of narrative that have entwined themselves through and around a rebellion of February 1930 against the forced collectivization of the peasantry in the Pitelino district of Riazan province, in central Russia. These narratives were found in: daily state-security reports reacting to the rebellion; the memoirs of a party worker, written more than 20 years after the events; Boris Mozhaev's novel *Muzhiki i baby*; and interviews with surviving eyewitnesses. Mozhaev was born in Pitelino and "witnessed the events of collectivization through the frightened eyes of a child." So did several women in their eighties and nineties, interviewed by McDonald in 2004 and 2005. Seventy-five years after this history unraveled, was recorded, interpreted, written and rewritten, some of its participants are still "afraid of Joseph Stalin." For those who participated in the making of Soviet history, Soviet then is still very much Soviet now.

How does the state deal with this past? Kathleen Smith's chapter traces the development of official attitudes toward anti-Stalinism from the Gorbachev era to the present, which are part and parcel of the attempt to construct a new national narrative. A "popular litmus test" for those politicians committed to liberal change during perestroika and the early Yeltsin years, the condemnation of the Stalinist, and later the Soviet heritage, was not accompanied by the creation of new national myths to legitimize the new Russian state. Instead, the growing nostalgia for the Soviet past, endorsed and used by the Communist Party of the Russian Federation and other nationalists, triggered the redeployment by the Yeltsinites of Soviet patriotic symbols. This process was considerably reinforced during Putin's presidency, as shown by the celebrations of the sixtieth anniversary of Victory Day in 2005, a whole list of commemorative calendar additions, various patriotic appearances of the president himself, as well as Putin's "reluctance to spend much time on negative issues," an attitude that reflects not so much a return to Communist values than their use to strengthen state power.

Part Three explores different "continuities" in the realm of attitudes toward sexual minorities, welfare and medicine, and the penal system.

For Dan Healey, *Gays and Lesbians*, published in early 2003 by the mediatic "sexopathologist" Dilia Enikeeva, supplies a blueprint for the new, nationalist, and conservative antigay rhetoric that has been adopted and refined by political opinion makers of the Putin era. This rhetoric transforms Russia's "everyday homophobia" into something more politically powerful, drawing on reserves of nostalgia for the lost innocence and invented traditions of Soviet sexual life. Healey proposes a "slightly mischievous" model of "traditional sex" that draws on the conventions of Stalinist and Soviet discourse about gender, which he roots in the socialist realist formula of *beskonfliktnost'* (absence of conflict) and *zhizneradost'* (joie de vivre). Submission to the elemental force of masculine sexuality—the very definition of a "conflictless" relation between genders—is the condition of the (sexual) *zhizneradost'* of any "normal" woman. But the old Stalinist strategy of discursive silence, of a public blank spot marking "sex," argues Healey, is over. Challenged by the new market forces, the defenders of post-Soviet morality have come out of the closet and have transformed life significantly for the worse for Russia's citizens who wish to speak openly about their sexual preference.

President Putin in Tuva
August 15, 2007

Courtesy of the Official Web Portal
of the President of Russia

As Andrea Chandler demonstrates in her chapter, gender is likewise involved in the reforms of Russia's social welfare system. It has been much easier to make changes in Russian social welfare programs that primarily affected women, than to accomplish the monetization reform, which primarily affected veterans and pensioners. While many privileges enjoyed by the *nomenklatura* have been challenged, and in part abolished, during the erosion of socialism, the system of special social welfare benefits (the *l'goty*, *privilegii*, *skitki*, free transportation, etc.) has survived on the basis of an "emotionally resonant patriotism." Its beneficiaries are groups that gave active service to the nation. The conditional and provisional character of Soviet policies towards mothers' and child benefits has also survived the end of socialism, but not to the advantage of women. Since 2006, however, benefits for parents and children have become again a matter of higher priority for the state: healthy families symbolize a healthy nation.

Judging from what Michael Z. David writes in the next chapter, Russia is in dire need of better health. The number of new cases of multidrug resistant tuberculosis has doubled in Russia between 1990 and 1998, an era marked by a collapse of the infrastructure for social services, rising unemployment, malnutrition, internal migration, and alcoholism. Today, the disease continues to spread in an epidemic of thousands of cases often concentrated in penal institutions. Professional inertia and national pride have prevented post-Soviet medical experts from adopting drug-based western systems of treatment, and from reforming the infrastructure inherited from Soviet times. The Soviet system of care was derived from the pre-Revolutionary tuberculosis control program, which was built on the dispensary, a clinic that served the social and medical needs of impoverished TB patients. This structure, in turn, became part of a project of Soviet Medicine as a whole. Sixteen years after the fall of the Soviet Union, this large, crumbling, and underfunded system is no longer able to function as state-subsidized medical care and a source of social welfare for those most in need, which was its *raison d'être* from the very start.

As we know from Michel Foucault, the prison is never very far from the dispensary, and it is in a study of "Continuities in Penal Russia" that Judith Pallot concludes Part Three of the book. Once again, the subordinate status of women is confirmed. Although far more men than women are arrested and sentenced in Russia, women are more likely to be sent to isolated colonies, which removes—literally—the problem of female criminality from the center of debate. Moreover, it is women who travel to Russia's penal periphery to support tens of thousands of men. Pre-existing gender stereotypes are reaffirmed as women are expected to bring food, clothing, and solace. Thus, the Russian penal system uses their "domestic role" to overcome its own economic problems. Much of the chapter is devoted to the analysis of *Arestant*, a self-help internet site established in 2001 to support prisoners and their families. More than a practical guide of how to navigate penal Russia, *Arestant* is, according to Pallot, an attempt on part of the women to bring the debate about Russia's prisons into the public arena and contest their powerlessness.

Part Four explores the artistic and architectural geography of post-Sovietness from the vantage point of a series of contemporary art works from St. Petersburg, an "archaeological study" of Gorky/Nizhni Novgorod, and a journey through the ruins of real socialism.

"Post-communist nostalgia" cannot explain why an increasing number of artists and art critics turn in their work to Soviet topics and aesthetics, writes cultural anthropologist Alexei Yurchak. Late Soviet and post-modern cynicism have given way to a "new sincerity," observable in the paintings of St. Petersburg artists Dasha Fursei, Georgii Gurianov, and more generally in today's youth culture. Certainly, recovering the alleged idealism, romanticism, and futurism of Soviet culture has something to do with the collapse of state socialism and the provincialization of Russian culture on the world market. Fursei describes her turn to Soviet topics in her art as a reaction to "misconceptions of the Soviet past" in Western media and public discourse. Neither Soviet nor neoliberal, the utopian world that the discourse of these artists envision belongs to a different system altogether, to a yearning "for what [the Communist] past might have been," argues Yurchak. Looking at the "heroic masculinity" displayed in some of these paintings, one might ask the question to what extent this system is not another example of "submission," post-Soviet style, and all that it entails.

When, in the next chapter, Heather DeHaan excavates the post-Soviet city of Nizhni Novgorod, she uncovers not only the Soviet past, but the dialogue between the Soviet, pre-Soviet, and post-Soviet eras. It turns out to be an uneasy one. During Soviet times the Alexander Nevsky cathedral inherited from the tsarist era remained on a patch of land in the midst of loading cranes. This site was to be the new city center. A "subterranean conspiracy," that is, very real underground streams, undermined the project of relocating the city center altogether. The "socialist city" that was to arise near GAZ, the Gorky Automobile Factory, built 20 kilometers up the Oka River, never really came to life. The Soviet authorities inverted the spatial soteriological structure of the pre-Petrine city to replace it with a Soviet narrative of redemption through architectural closures, erasures, and renaming. As it turns out, they had inverted a defunct space, largely irrelevant to day-to-day life. When Gorky became Nizhni Novgorod again, much of the Soviet past was shed, but many Soviet artifacts remained, together with the legacy of Soviet industrial modernization.

It is precisely this legacy that Thomas Lahusen investigates in the last chapter of the book. Arguing that the building of the socialist project, in its concrete and metaphoric sense, was in a state of constant decay—in ruins—from the very beginning, he concludes that those who lived in these ruins had no other choice but to endure. This endurance explains the resistance, by both people and the landscapes in which they live, to the market. Nostalgia for socialism is different for those who inhabit these ruins of socialism than for those who suffer (on paper) from "leftist melancholia." Indeed, the decrepit-looking buildings made of precast concrete slabs are still the only home for many inhabitants of the former "second world"—half a billion square meters, out of the 2.8 billion square meters that constitute the entire housing space of Russia. To resolve the housing crisis, between 150 and 200 small cities have to be entirely rebuilt in the near future, or three times Moscow, according to some recent sources. Hopefully, Andrei Platonov's formula will not be repeated: "endurance exhaustedly went on in the world, as though everything living were located somewhere in the middle of time and its own motion: the beginning has been forgotten by everyone and the end was unknown, so there remained only direction."

Most of the articles published in *What Is Soviet Now?* were presented at a conference of the same title, held at the University of Toronto in April 2006.[8] The conference represented the conclusion of a three-year collaborative project, entitled "Real Socialism and the 'Second World'," funded by a University of Toronto Connaught grant for seed support for research clusters, and administered first by the Centre for Russian and East European Studies (CREES) and then by its successor the Centre for European, Russian, and Eurasian Studies (CERES). The goal of the project was to come to a better understanding of a world that long existed in the shadow of the "First" and "Third" worlds. We wanted to assess and discuss the perspectives that emerged after the disintegration of the Soviet Union and other "real-existing" state socialisms, and the previous framework of cold-war thinking. The first stage of the project aimed at a reconceptualization of Soviet socialism by looking at the everyday aspect of its history, at how the system functioned "behind the facade," how people operated within the system, and how the state coped with the facade and with its people, on as many levels as possible. A workshop devoted to this first phase took place in April 2003, followed by another workshop in 2004. At this second gathering scholars from other national areas and disciplines shared their work with scholars of the Soviet Union, in an effort to understand the twentieth-century history of the "Second World" and its importance for the present and the future.

When the organizers of the project started thinking about the concluding conference—events in what was once the "Second World" continued to transform this world by further shifting its geopolitical landscape to the West: part of the former socialist camp became "Europe," and the second most important former "SSR"—Ukraine—engaged in its "orange revolution." The focus on "what is Soviet now" can also be explained by these events and reactions toward them.

[8] For the full program, see http://www.utoronto.ca/ceres/realsocialism.html (accessed September 8, 2007).

The editors of this volume would like to thank the following persons for their help and involvement: the participants in all three meetings; the other co-investigators of the "Real Socialism" project, Robert Johnson, Susan Gross Solomon, and Lynne Viola; Steve Maddox, the conference and workshop coordinator; the staff of the Munk Centre for International Studies. Our gratitude goes to Jeffrey Kopstein, director of the CERES, for financial support to cover part of costs of this publication, as well as to Jana Oldfield, the business officer of the Centre. Additional funding has been drawn from the Canada Research Chair program. A special thanks goes to Janet Hyer, former CERES program officer and copy editor of this volume.

I. Markets and Facades

"I lost it at the market"

Some Thoughts on the Political Economy of Post-Soviet Russia

Robert E. Johnson

> Summing up, let us define the difference between the Russian and the West European in a single word: non-marketeer. The Russian national character was not formed on the basis of market activity. From this derives the essential distinction in the spiritual make-up. For the European, social significance lies in business, craftsmanship, and wealth. This is the source of the leading values of freedom and law. For the Russian, greater importance is attached to society, Motherland, glory and power.
>
> *From a prize-winning essay in a national competition on the theme "The Idea of Russia,"* Rossiiskaia gazeta*, July 1996*[1]

In the article that follows, I will examine some ideas about the market, or the market-*place*, in Soviet and post-Soviet Russia. My starting-point is not the abstract Market of economists, but the everyday space in which vendors and consumers exchange tangible goods. I will argue that this space was, in Soviet times, fraught with tensions and contradictions that are still in evidence fifteen years after the end of communism. Attitudes toward the local physical market may, I believe, carry over into the broader discourse of exchange, not just in the realm of economics but in the putative Marketplace of Ideas.

I will begin with some vignettes of market places and transactions, based upon personal observation. I will then explore some of the ambivalent or negative feelings that markets evoked in some part of the Soviet citizenry. After suggesting some explanations for those feelings, I will speculate on their wider implications for understanding Soviet and post-Soviet life.

Foreigners sometimes picture the USSR before Gorbachev as a monolithic planned economy in which the supply and prices of goods and services were entirely under state control. Even at the height of the Stalin era, however, the peasant or collective-farm market (*kolkhoznyi rynok*) operated on different principles. Under Soviet law each collective farm household was allowed to maintain a minuscule private plot of land and sell its produce at unregulated prices. As late as the 1960s, private

[1] As quoted in Robert Service, *Russia: Experiment with a People* (London: Pan Macmillan, 2002), 185.

producers accounted for most of the eggs, dairy products, and poultry consumed in the USSR, and as much as half of the red meat. In the summertime, peasants brought fresh fruits and vegetables to the city for sale. In the winter, inhabitants of the southern territories—the Caucasian and Central Asian republics—travelled great distances with suitcases full of fresh flowers and citrus fruits, which they hawked in the streets and markets of Moscow and other northern cities.

The typical market (*rynok*) of the Brezhnev era was a collection of outdoor stalls covered by tin roofs and surrounded by a high fence. Adjacent rows of tables would feature various products, by category: green vegetables in one place, spices, honey, cheeses or meats, and even exotic items such as herbal medicines or miracle kitchen gadgets, each in their own section or niche. Each vendor had a few square feet of table space and, where appropriate, a scale for weighing out the products. Larger urban markets included an indoor hall with more permanent counters, typically covered in tile, which were reserved for meat and dairy products. Apart from the tables and stalls, there were numerous free-lancers—typically elderly men and women—who stood or sat around the periphery of the market and along the adjacent streets, offering bunches of wildflowers or garden herbs, mushrooms, or small baskets of berries.

Often these markets were located only a few steps away from official, state-run shops, but to go from the latter to the former was like stepping into the another world. The shops were stocked, for the most part, with goods that no one wanted to buy, shelves lined with bottles of conserved fruit or vegetables, often of an unappetising grey-brown color. Service was generally slow and sullen. From time to time a shipment of more desirable products would arrive, and immediately a queue would form as consumers stocked up for themselves and their neighbors. Within a short time the "deficit" product would be sold out.

Lines in the market were short because the prices were high. You could always find a much wider array of goods, sold by people who actively sought your business by calling out the virtues of their own particular product. Each honey-seller would tempt the customer with a list of the particular wild flowers that her bees had favored. Taste it! she would declare, offering a fresh toothpick to dip into an open jar. Only wild forest flowers! Only clover! And every vendor's honey *was* special, each jar offering subtle gradations of shade and flavor.

To a North American accustomed to homogenized supermarket honey, the Russian product was a (possibly unhygienic) novelty, but the market offered still more exotic fare. In the meat section, what looked at first like chicken sometimes turned out to be rabbit or muskrat, recognizable because the feet had been left on for identification. Butchers who dealt in more familiar meats such as beef and pork would sell the head, feet, and tail, along with other parts that disappeared from North American meat counters two or more generations ago. I have never encountered fresh fish in a Russian market, even on the seacoast, but in the northern markets in summer one would sometimes see live crayfish for sale.

In another corner of a market, spice-vendors would measure out spoonsful of *suneli*, a Georgian equivalent of curry powder, which the customer carried home in a twisted cone of newspaper. Nearby, other Georgian traders sold *churdzhkhela* (candied hazelnuts dipped in grape juice) or salty *brynza* (goat cheese). In summer there were fresh herbs: parsley, coriander, purple basil. In winter, the array of fruits and vegetables was narrower, but still greater than in the shops: salted apples, dried boletus mushrooms, pink pickled garlic, and a salted green onion called *cheremsha*. After the first snow-fall, flower-vendors kept their wares in glass cases with burning candles to prevent freezing. In the afternoon dusk these outdoor corners had a glow reminiscent of icons in a church.

In principle, the *rynok* existed to enable ordinary peasants to sell foods that they had grown on their private plots of land. Although the vendors were all supposed to be peasants, many travelled great distances to sell their goods. In a provincial town that I visited in the winter of 1970, oranges were *defitsitnye* (hard to find) in the state-run shops, but were not scarce in the market. The picture that sticks in my mind is of a swarthy Caucasian vendor, with a thick moustache and gold teeth, who smiled almost tauntingly as he held out his fruits to passersby, then peeled one and ate it section by section, pantomiming the pleasure that it gave him. Shoppers, most of whom could afford only potatoes and cabbage, regarded him with suspicion and, I suspected, resentment.

Transporting perishable items—berries in the early spring, melons in summer, flowers and citrus fruits in winter—to northern cities from the remote places where they grew required more expense and coordination than most peasants could provide. The "second economy" was in fact dominated by wholesalers and middlemen. In June of 1983, in Moscow's Kiev railway station, I watched a line of strawberry-sellers board a southbound train after a day's trading. They were clearly country people, poorly dressed and seeming a bit bewildered at the city's bustle. Each carried an identical basket lined with a white napkin, stained from berry juice. Accompanying them was a woman who took a head count and handed out tickets. Her relationship to the group was unclear, but her speech and dress set her apart, and the others seemed to look to her for direction. A popular Soviet film of the period, *Railroad Station for Two*, put this behavior into context. In this romantic comedy, Sergei Mikhalkov plays a railroad conductor who uses his position to transport crates of melons and other deficit goods for sale in northern markets. Among his confederates is a formidable peasant woman known as Uncle Misha (sic), who organizes "independent" peasants to sell imported produce in the local market.

Ten years later I saw a truck unloading hundreds of melons onto the sidewalk in a plaza directly across the Moscow River from the Kremlin. A couple of young Azeri men were the vendors, selling to passersby over the next week or more and sleeping in shifts next to their wares, which were too bulky to be moved off the street for overnight storage. I had no doubt that this was a latter-day variant on the Soviet-era marketing system.

In a large city such as Moscow, the central peasant markets were well known even to foreigners. Other markets were less advertised. I tried to visit them all—not just the produce markets, but the places where other deficit goods could be found. In the dreariest Brezhnev years, for example, Moscow had a semi-legal Gray Market for books—a central street where bibliophiles would assemble on Sundays, close to one of the few shops that sold second-hand printed matter. Here one could find out-of-print classics of Russian literature, such as the works of Akhmatova or Tsvetaeva, or old issues of legally-published journals such as *Novyi mir*. More rarely, foreign publications—Solzhenitsyn's novels, under the imprint of the YMCA Press of Paris— were available in defiance of the censors, but in those cases the vendors were more circumspect. They did not hawk their wares, but whispered the titles to would-be customers or flashed them a glimpse of the cover-page. Transactions were furtive and often took place in the doorways of nearby side-streets. From time to time the militia would appear and the crowd of buyers and sellers would disperse, only to reassemble a few minutes later.

Moscow's Pet Market (*ptichii rynok*), located in what seemed to be a factory yard, operated only on weekends. Pets were a low-priority item in the Soviet planned economy, but the market offered animal-lovers an opportunity to pursue their interests. Dogs, cats, birds, fish, and small reptiles were all available, along with the foods appropriate to each, including birdseed and live worms and grubs. An elderly veteran once tried to sell me a lark in a cage, promising that if the bird wouldn't sing for me I could call him up and ... *he* would sing.

Despite official slogans about "completed socialism," those years saw enormous expansion of the country's Second Economy—not exactly a free market but a semi-legal one that ranged from grey to black and operated by its own rules. It existed not just in the stalls of the peasant *rynok* but in wholesale trade, and operated with the connivance of officials and functionaries of the planned economy. From time to time the Soviet press would present scandalous stories about the manager of some factory, restaurant, or shop who was caught selling goods through the rear door, or some opportunist who traded in bootleg jeans or auto parts. But where else could a consumer find those goods? So long as the official economy failed to satisfy consumer demand, someone was always ready to bend or break the rules to derive a profit. Though this "market" was freer than the official economy, its semi-legal or illegal status made it vulnerable to criminal infiltration and influence. Occasionally those accused of speculation received long prison sentences. A few were even executed, but their example did not seem to discourage others.

Like the peasant food market, the "markets" of the Second Economy operated informally. Transactions took place in open-air spaces or out-of-the-way corners—someone's apartment, a laneway behind some enterprise. Prices were rarely posted but were informally known. For these goods there existed no shops, no supervision, no consumer protection, but rather an atmosphere of subversion, defiance, and illegality.

During the Gorbachev era private or "cooperative" trade was encouraged within certain bounds, but at the same time many basic commodities became harder to obtain. The sale of alcohol was restricted, and when independent producers increased production of their own *samogon* (bootleg liquor) sugar and other fermentables disappeared from the shops. By the early winter of 1991-92, as the Soviet Union was breaking apart, the shelves of shops were literally empty and sidewalks were lined by independent "traders"—often elderly women—who huddled in the cold, offering minute quantities of goods: a single package of butter, a pair of woollen gloves, a chunk of sausage.

The years that followed brought a blur of changes. Retail trade passed rapidly into private hands, but concentrated mainly on a few commodities. Alcoholic beverages were in high demand, as were imported foodstuffs, but in both cases the soaring prices made many products inaccessible to most consumers. Over the course of a couple of years the street corner trade moved from upturned crates to kiosks, some of them reincarnations of Soviet-era ice cream stands, newspaper stalls, or smoke shops. New ones were built in rows or clusters, ten or more selling identical merchandise and keeping identical hours (some stayed open all night), as if seeking safety in numbers. The burned-out shells of a few such establishments testified to the need for security guards or other protection.

On successive visits to Moscow I saw small kiosks and stalls expand into shops and then into supermarkets, but in the first post-Soviet years their business was more in luxuries than in everyday staples; alcohol was disproportionately represented. Meanwhile, other would-be entrepreneurs continued to sell their wares off makeshift tables or from the backs of trucks. In a Moscow suburb one August, I was shocked to see people queuing up to buy potatoes, as they might have done in Soviet times. I was puzzled, because I knew that potatoes were abundant in the shops. It turned out that these particular potatoes were special—the leftover seed potatoes from the previous year, selling at a cheaper price that brought consumers running.

The older public markets continued to operate, spreading outward from their original locations. Imported items—bananas, pineapples, kiwi fruit—now appeared, along with a greater variety of packaged goods. Clothing, canned goods, and household appliances could now be bought in crowded bazaars, at prices that were rarely written down. Urban folklore whispered of price-fixing and *mafiya* extortion, of stolen and tainted goods being offered for sale, but still the crowds flocked to the markets.

And meanwhile the sidewalk trade expanded. Subway entrances were a favorite location, as were large boulevards and their underground crosswalks. No matter how many kiosks or shops appeared, the number of independent traders kept increasing. Many of these were the types of people who had formerly gathered outside the gates of the *rynok*—grandmotherly figures with a few small bunches of flowers or herbs spread out on a newspaper, grizzled old men with a small supply of forest mushrooms. When I remarked to a Moscow friend that there seemed to be more dairy products for sale on the street, she pointed out that many of the vendors were from Belarus or Ukraine. "Those could be Chernobyl products."

On a Saturday morning in May of 1999, I visited a peasant market near a small railway junction some 500 kilometres from the capital. At dawn, vendors and customers had already assembled, more than half of them coming by horse-drawn cart. Here I saw no painted dolls for sale, no bananas or kiwis—nothing but home-grown vegetables, staple foods, and, because I was there in late spring, a certain number of rooted plants, wrapped in wet newspaper for replanting. (These were for city-dwellers, "summer people" planting their gardens at the dacha.) This market, it seemed to me, was emblematic of post-communist Russia, in which millions of people struggled to adjust their lives to a new and difficult environment. In the old days of communism there was nothing in the shops, and everyone knew what it cost. Since the early 1990s the shops have been full, but only a small part of the population can afford to buy more than a minimal range of products. The rest rely on habits and institutions that helped their grandparents (and their remote ancestors) to survive and surmount far greater challenges than those of today. The market at the railway junction and the one on a city boulevard exist because people need them, because they offer goods and prices and opportunities that the more structured "modern" economy does not provide. If, in the midst of it all, they also shelter opportunism and corruption, these are in some ways more familiar and acceptable than the trendy shops and foreign goods that have flooded the capital city.

One of the most interesting, and ultimately (to my eye) disappointing market phenomena of the 1990s was the evolution of an arts-and-crafts flea market ("Vermissage") that appeared in Moscow's Izmailovsky Park in the Gorbachev years. I first visited it in the winter of 1989, when it operated free-form along the pathways of this large wooded park. Oil paintings and wooden toys, hand-carved implements, and plastic kitsch were displayed along a row of folding tables and benches that seemed to go on for miles. This was a flea market for samovars and other antiques, housewares, table and bed linen, and even printed matter. (I was startled to see Mandelshtam's poetry side-by-side with the *Protocols of the Elders of Zion* and Baltic pornography; the vendor was indifferent.) One retailer sold homemade papier-mâché masks of the Communist heroes and leaders, from Marx to Gorbachev, and another had joke buttons with slogans such as "I am KGB." Although the weather was bitterly cold, the crowd—vendors and customers and sight-seers—seemed cheerful and enthusiastic.

The next time I visited the Izmailovo flea market it had moved a short distance to an enclosed area around a nearby stadium. One entered through a gate, and paid a small fee for admission. The vendors were closer together, with hardly any trees or shelter. The amount of kitsch had increased exponentially, but not all the artists were of the con variety. One could still purchase oil paintings, ink drawings, or watercolors from the people who had created them (though a separate market just for artists was also operating along the banks of the Moscow River upstream from the Kremlin). I remember speaking with a young man who turned out to be a physicist with a PhD, who told me he was earning more from selling his paintings on Sundays than he earned in the rest of the week at his real trade. By now the Communist regime had given up the ghost, and Soviet-era military paraphernalia was one of the best-selling items. Antiques such as dinner plates and silver cutlery were also available, as well as books and tape cassettes of formerly hard-to-find artists such as Vladimir Vysotsky. The clientele, however, was speaking more English or German and less Russian.

On my most recent visit, the flea market's gates had been made over in the style of an old wooden fortress—a Disneyfied Kremlin. The ticket takers wore colorful folk costumes, and a similarly-attired array of buskers entertained the crowds, some singing, others juggling, and even one doing tricks with a trained bear cub. The prices, it seemed to me, had risen even faster than the ruble had fallen, and most of the banter with customers was in foreign languages. Like more than one North American or Western European market, Izmailovo had become—as I saw it—a tourist trap, losing the spontaneity that had originally attracted me.

Over the past decade years Moscow's city administration has been cracking down on the outdoor markets. Amid much publicity, the *ptichii rynok* was relocated to a remote suburb so that a new building could be erected on its original site. Many of the open-stall markets have been summarily closed, and sidewalk free-lancers chased away. But one new structure continues some of the street-market traditions in an unexpected realm. Gorbushka, a market for CDs, electronics, and computer software, operates indoors in a building not unlike a shopping mall. It is famous for operating outside the rules of copyright, but also for the enormous volume of business that is transacted. Gorbushka's annual turnover is estimated, unreliably, in the billions of rubles, and in the popular press it is frequently described with such terms as "pirate haven."

What all these examples have in common is a minimal level of formal regulation, shading over into illegality. These markets do—and this is a point that I will return to in a moment—follow unspoken rules of their own, but they often have had a transitory, almost furtive quality. Vendors often seem to be looking over their shoulders—whether for the militia or the supervisory eye of fellow-traders. Purchasers are often wary and mistrustful. The foreigner who comes looking for local color will not always be welcomed.

I have often tried to photograph markets, but in Soviet times I learned to expect trouble when I took my camera out of its case. Not all the vendors were camera-shy, but almost always someone would raise a fuss and arouse the others, even to the point of calling in the militia. I never personally had my film confiscated, but this was a common experience among foreigners. Visitors who thought they were photographing something charming and innocent found themselves accused of slandering Soviet society. In post-Soviet times, the reaction is likely to be more muted, but a foreigner may still feel unwelcome.

My Russian friends and acquaintances have often been unenthusiastic when I expressed a desire to visit markets. Why would I want to go *there?* Surely there were more interesting, and safer, places for a foreigner to visit. Perhaps understandably, Russians who have travelled abroad prefer the not-so-discreet charms of the supermarket. But this alone does not account for the disapproving tone that often comes into people's voices when I raise the subject of the *rynok*.

In Soviet times peasant markets were correctly regarded as a sign of official failure, of communism's inability to meet the population's needs. They were a throwback to earlier times—a compromise, not so much with capitalism as with a precapitalist peasant economy. The juxtaposition of old and new could be stark: One of my most vivid recollections of my first visit to Moscow, in 1970, is of the clop-clop sound of a horse's hooves on busy Kutuzovsky Prospect, at dusk on a Saturday evening—a peasant driving his wooden cart home from the Dorogomilovsky market. In a country that equated progress with mechanization and communal endeavor, such a sight was not a source of pride. Unsurprisingly, markets rarely appeared on the Intourist itinerary.

But the sensitivities of communists do not, it seems to me, account for all the negative feelings I have encountered over the years. Individuals who were otherwise critical of the Soviet regime and its proclivities were also uneasy on the subject of markets—suspicious of the traders and the surroundings, reluctant to carry out transactions under the eyes of an outsider. Markets were a necessary but not entirely welcome part of Soviet people's existence, and I wonder if some of the negative feelings can be traced back in history, perhaps to the very dawn of the capitalist era.

We might, for example, look back a few generations in North America, to a small-town society that was far more isolated and homogeneous than it is today. The arrival of a carnival, a family of "gypsies" or an itinerant peddler elicited some of the same responses that the Russian market does today. The Outsider spoke with an unfamiliar accent, appeared and disappeared unpredictably, and was liable to be blamed for all manner of misdeeds. Such individuals aroused curiosity and a craving for things unknown, balanced by suspicion and ethnic stereotyping—attitudes that help to shape the image of markets in Russia down to the present day.

Consumers in the Brezhnev era felt a similar ambivalence about dealing with the entrepreneurs of the Second Economy, and not just because of the risk that such transactions could entail. The regime's denunciation of "parasites" struck a responsive chord in some members of the public, whose hostility encompassed not only thieves and black marketeers but every kind of small-scale entrepreneur. I recall seeing angry shoppers in a peasant market berating a gray-haired grandmother who was selling strings of dried mushrooms. She had no stall, and carried her wares in her arms. The mushrooms were of better quality than could be found in any store, but she was charging a higher price. "Speculator! Somebody ought to call the police!"

Where more expensive and durable goods were traded—bluejeans or even automobiles—citizens' resentment sometimes extended from the sellers to the buyers, who were seen as corrupted by alien, material values.

Paradoxically, although markets evoked ambivalent feelings and even hostility among some Russians, citizens were just as likely to express a sense of proprietorship over the market, which may partly account for defensiveness in the presence of foreign visitors. The rapport between seller and buyer appears from some angles to be governed by unspoken mutual understanding that a true outsider—the foreign visitor, with or without camera—could not share. Even in the central kolkhoz markets of Moscow, where such visitors were a familiar presence, one heard the phrase "*ne nashi*"—"these are not our people"—not about vendors from the South, but about Europeans and North Americans who shopped there. I heard it about myself, when I was too quick to accept a vendor's price for flowers. A consumer who was "ours" would have haggled.

Let me suggest that there is more than xenophobia at work here. A market governed by customary rules and expectations may perhaps be analysed under the rubric of "moral economy." I don't mean to suggest by this that the *rynok* is inherently moral or economic, but that it shares some of the characteristics that Edward Thompson and others have described in early modern European society. The phrase evokes a set of assumptions that governed many aspects of everyday life, including the notion of a "just price," sometimes upheld by governments but also enforced through community action. Another fundamental tenet was the notion of economic exchange as a zero-sum transaction: Whatever one participant gains must necessarily entail a loss to the other participant(s). The moral economy stigmatized the charging of interest, and meshed with a society of ascribed status that valued social relations above purely economic calculations.

The Soviet Union, as many writers have depicted it, tried to leap-frog from a pre-capitalist peasant economy to socialism. Ideologically, this meant skipping over neoclassical liberal economics, giving short shrift to the visible or invisible hand of the Market. The *rynok* of the Soviet era, and even to some extent today, embodies some of the values, assumptions, and suspicions of much earlier times. Those same values make some post-Soviet consumers suspicious of the western-style supermarkets that have grown up since 1991, and nostalgic for the regulated trade of the Soviet *gastronom.* Is their nostalgia for socialism or for a still older social order where everyone knew their place and transactions were governed—or supposed to be governed—by more than the law of supply and demand?

It goes without saying that the markets of post-communist Russia are figurative as well as literal. Even before the collapse of the USSR in 1991 Western advisors, official and otherwise, were propounding a liberalism that saw unfettered exchange as the foundation of political as well as economic freedom. In practice, however, the "level playing field" of liberal theory has proved to be an elusive goal. Moreover, it is an ideal for which few ordinary citizens have shown enthusiasm. Political parties that put forth neo-liberal slogans were generally overwhelmed by those with nationalist and statist agendas. (Note in particular the pro-Putin youth organization *Nashi*, which presents itself as anti-fascist but lists the liberal Yabloko Party among its adversaries.)

Is it unreasonable to suppose that the market of ideas evokes, in many Russians, some of the same responses as the physical *rynok*? Polls throughout the Yeltsin and Putin eras have shown the citizenry to be at best ambivalent toward western-inspired politics and economics. Many prefer, or profess to prefer, security and stability over competition—in politics, in the workplace, and perhaps in the casual transactions of everyday life.

The suspicion or uneasiness that many Russians express toward liberalization has many sources. Not least among them is the rampant corruption that has flourished in the years since 1991. Closed-auction privatization and gangster capitalism have persuaded many Russians that capitalism and democracy are unrealistic, unattainable, or fatally flawed. In the early 1990s, many Russians who came of age in the Soviet era went through a period of infatuation with western practices, but the abuses of the early post-Soviet era led to widespread disillusionment.

I suggest, however, that disillusionment is not the whole story. If the attitudes toward markets that I have been sketching are as deeply rooted as I suspect they are, they may also have helped to condition Russians' reactions to the political values that they confronted after 1991. Russians do have a market tradition, but it is *sui generic*. It doesn't easily mesh with the markets pictured by Adam Smith or Milton Friedman, nor with the institutions or values of Western liberalism.

The post-Soviet polity has more than once been described as an illiberal democracy, but perhaps the causes of this go beyond Yeltsin's incompetence, the oligarchs' machinations, or Putin's authoritarianism. Classical liberalism in politics, as in the marketplace, gives priority to autonomy, rationality, and free exchange, unfettered by custom or an individual's ascribed status. In post-Soviet Russia's *rynok*, its macro-economy, and its political discourse, these principles all have very shaky support. Perhaps the causes lie in the legacy of an older "moral" economy that survived and, within its own sphere, flourished during the extraordinary experiment that was Soviet.

Markets, Money, and Private Property

The Persistence of Soviet Socialism in Russia Today

James R. Millar

> The ideas of economists and political philosophers, both when they are right and when they are wrong, are more powerful than is commonly understood. Indeed, the world is ruled by little else. Practical men, who believe themselves to be quite exempt from any intellectual influences, are usually the slaves of some defunct economist.
>
> Madmen in authority, who hear voices in the air, are distilling their frenzy from some academic scribbler of a few years back. I am sure that the power of vested interests is vastly exaggerated compared with the gradual encroachment of ideas. Not, indeed, immediately ... But soon or late, it is ideas, not vested interests, which are dangerous for good or evil.
>
> *John Maynard Keynes*

How Socialist Was Soviet Socialism? The Marxist Idea

It is a cliché that Karl Marx did not spell out the institutions and functional operation of the socialist state he expected to follow capitalism, but it is only partially true. Both he and Engels stated that socialism, or communism once capitalist vestiges had been eliminated, would be the *negation* of capitalism.[1] The "Manifesto of the Communist Party" lists the steps that would be taken immediately following the revolution to convert from a capitalist economy to a socialist.[2] Moreover, in the "Critique

---

Also presented as a seminar at the Davis Center, Harvard University, May 9, 2006.

[1] The conception of socialism (or communism) as the negation of capitalism is immanent in all of the writings of Marx and Engels as a direct result of their belief that history is a dialectical process, a conception that they borrowed from Hegel and inverted. See Frederick Engels, "Socialism: Utopian and Scientific," in *Karl Marx and Frederick Enges, Selected Works in Two Volumes*, vol. 2 (Moscow: Foreign Languages Publishing House, 1955), 93–166, especially section 2, 128–36. Marx's most explicit statement is found in the author's preface to the second edition of *Capital:* "In its rational form it [the dialectic] is a scandal and an abomination to bourgeoisdom and its doctrinaire professors, because it includes in its comprehension and affirmative of recognition of the existing state of things, at the same time also, the recognition of the negation of that state, of its inevitable breaking up." Karl Marx, *Capital. A Critique of Political Economy* (New York: Modern Library, 1906), 25–6.

[2] Karl Marx, "Manifesto of the Communist Party," in *Basic Writings on Politics and Philosophy. Karl Marx and Friedrich Engels*, ed. Lewis S. Feuer (New York: Doubleday &

of the Gotha Program" Marx spelled out how national income proceeds would be divided and implied a continuing role for government to administer what functions remain.[3] The Marxist socialist economy, at least in the transition from capitalism to communism, can be pieced together from these two conceptions.

First, as the negation of capitalism, the socialist economy would eventually have no markets at all. This includes both consumer and producer goods markets, the labor market, all financial markets, and all markets in ownership titles whether stocks and bonds or second-hand goods. Consequently, prices, money, and all financial instruments would also disappear. It follows that banks would not be necessary either. With the exception of individual consumption goods, all forms of private property would be abolished. Second, as Engels explained in "Socialism: Utopian and Scientific,"

> As soon as there is no longer any social class to be held in subjection … nothing more remains to be repressed, and a special repressive force, a state, is no longer necessary … State interference in social relations becomes, in one domain after another, superfluous, and it dies out of itself; the government of persons is replaced by the administration of things, and by the conduct of processes of production.[4]

What "things" would the state continue to administer in the transition from capitalism? In the "Critique" Marx points out that the "total social product" (which is an approximation to today's concept of gross national income) would be administered by the state and that workers could not, as the Gotha program stated, receive the "undiminished proceeds of labor." The following deductions would be required before distribution to workers: 1) capital consumption allowances; 2) new investment outlays; 3) insurance against accidents or natural calamities; 4) public administrative costs (much and increasingly reduced from capitalist days); 5) public consumption goods such as schools, health services, etc.; and 6) provision for those unable to work. These functions represent a rather extensive list of administrative activities that are subsequently to be carried out without repressive means under socialism.

Marx also made it clear in the "Critique" that in the transition period the distribution of the fruits of labor in the form of consumption could not adhere to the rule that would obtain after the establishment of full communism: "From each according to his ability, to each according to his needs." Marx envisioned each worker receiving "a certificate from society that he has furnished such and such an amount of labor

---

Company, Inc., 1959), 28–9.

[3] Marx and Engels, "Critique of the Gotha Program," in ibid., esp. 115–19.

[4] Engels, "Socialism: Utopian and Scientific," in ibid., 106.

(after deducting his labor for the common funds), and with this certificate he draws from the social stock of means of consumption as much as costs the same amount of labor."[5] It follows that, in the early stages of socialism, the distribution of wages would not be equal but proportional to the worker's contribution.

The "Manifesto" called for the abolition of private property in land and other instruments of production, heavy progressive taxation, abolition of rights to inheritance, centralization of credit in a national bank, the conversion of agricultural production into a type of manufacturing industry, and the widespread provision of public goods such as free private education.[6]

With these principles in mind we may now attempt to evaluate just how "Marxian socialist" (as opposed to communist) economic institutions and distribution were in the Soviet Union. The period considered here is essentially post Stalin, although the fundamental institutions of the Soviet economy in the Khrushchev-Brezhnev eras were created in the caldron of the 1930s. The New Economic Policy (NEP) of the 1920s is here viewed not as part of the transition to communism but rather as a diversion in the transition to socialism that will be discussed later in connection with today's economy.

Certain markets were abolished completely in the Soviet Union. Markets in producer goods disappeared. Markets in existing productive assets (such as factories, retail stores, and so forth) disappeared as these assets were nationalized. The stock and bond markets were abolished, too. With a few important exceptions, markets in credit and financial instruments generally were eliminated. However, as Marx implied would hold for the transition, money continued to circulate and with it a limited number of financial instruments. These credit instruments were made necessary by the continued existence of a consumer goods market, a labor market, and the need to account for inter-enterprise transactions.[7] The certificates Marx alluded to in the "Critique" as payments to workers represent, of course, a form of money—and it might as well be the ruble. As Abram Bergson pointed out in his *The Structure of Soviet Wages*, wages in the Soviet Union were indeed differentiated in accordance with individual worker contributions.[8] Once money wage payments were continued

---

[5] Marx, "Critique of the Gotha Program," 118.

[6] Marx and Engels, "Manifesto of the Communist Party," 28–9.

[7] James R. Millar, *The ABCs of Soviet Socialism.* (Urbana: University of Illinois Press, 1981), esp. chapters 3 and 4; Paul R. Gregory and Robert C. Stuart, *Soviet Economic Structure and Performance*, 4th ed. (New York: HarperCollins Publishers, Inc., 1990), esp. chapters 6 and 7.

[8] Abram Bergson, *The Structure of Soviet Wages* (Cambridge, MA: Harvard University Press, 1954).

under Soviet socialism, a central bank and its branches were necessary also. Although profits as a distributive share were abolished, enterprises were still required to keep accounts on expenses and receipts as a matter of accounting discipline. Retail outlets had to account for cash receipts and all enterprises had to calculate and account for wages and salaries. Consequently, prices continued to be charged for both consumer and enterprise purchases and sales. Transactions among enterprises included intermediate and final purchases (for investment) at set prices and were recorded in settlement accounts, unique non-cashable "certificates," paid out and received only through bank correspondent accounts. Finally, once accounting records were required for enterprises, short-term loans were necessary in order to finance time shape discrepancies between planned non-financial purchase and sale transactions. For a different reason collective farms also had access to long-term bank loans.

In general, therefore, the Soviet economy conformed to Marx's conception of a transitory socialist economic regime. Some of the most important markets for capitalism were definitely *negated*, and others were severely curtailed. This included successful efforts to provide certain public goods without charge (such as medical care and education) or at a very low cost (such as housing and public transportation). There remained, however, some critical exceptions. Several truly free private markets continued to exist despite repeated efforts to eliminate them. First there was the collective farm market (CFM) where farmers and even non-farm citizens were free to sell their own produce at market prices. In certain periods, this was a very extensive and significant market involving a considerable share of retail turnover, especially of food products. Consonant with the Marxist idea, however, purchase for resale of individually produced products was illegal, as was hiring anyone to work on one's plot or sale's outlet. The CFM and the private plots that sustained it were repeatedly squeezed but never eliminated. They were too important a source of social welfare. Other private markets also existed in the form of the sale of one's own secondhand goods and the provision of personal services such as hairdressers, minor repair activities, and so forth. These markets could not be abolished because of the persisting scarcity and/or poor quality of consumer goods and services provided by state outlets. In one sense this was a failure to conform to Marx's conception of socialism, but one could also argue that during the transition, before general plenty could be established, such discrepancies had to be accepted.

The collective farm sector represented an exception also. This was a very large sector whether measured in terms of product or employment. The kolkhozy were called cooperatives, but they were formed involuntarily and did not permit withdrawal of capital or, with some exceptions, labor. There is little question that this sector remained under coercive control of the state, which, of course, violated

Marx's conception of a socialist economic institution. During the post-Stalin years, the collective farm sector shrank as the poorer ones were converted to state farms, which conformed better to socialist standards.[9] Private illegal economic transactions that composed the underground economy grew over time from Stalin's death to the end of Gorbachev's rule as the system became more permissive, but these marketeers were prosecuted when discovered.

There are some lessons to be learned from the limits Soviet leaders encountered in attempting to create a socialist economy—at least during the transition. The transition to communism may be defined as the time it takes to get from the revolution to the beginning of plenty, where plenty refers to a situation in which there is sufficient output to satisfy all material wants without charging prices. The transition for Marx is, then, the period of socialism.

It is clear that the attempt to create socialism in the Soviet Union encountered a number of problems, many of which illustrated the limitations on implementing Marx's conception of the ultimate communist economy. First, the state had to compromise with the peasantry who refused to join true communes and demanded private plots to work on their own time, some domestic animals, and freedom to market their own products on an open market. It is true also, however, that Marx was not sanguine about the prospects for Russia to develop socialism based on the peasant institution of the *mir*. On the contrary, he argued that, "If Russia is tending to become a capitalist nation after the example of the West European countries ... she will not succeed without having first transformed a good part of her peasants into proletarians."[10] In this sense the 1917 revolution was premature.

Second, it proved impossible to eliminate money and other kinds of financial instruments in the economy, and, in fact, several types circulated. Third, as workers were paid wages, the state retail outlets, like the CFM, charged prices, and the state even paid interest to individual depositors on their savings. Third, wages were differentiated to reflect differential contributions to the economy's output. Fourth, the state set the rate of investment (including capital consumption allowances), determining thereby the goods and services remaining to satisfy current consumption. It is not clear that Marx realized that this would be an arbitrary decision of the state. In the Soviet case, the rate was set very high with the expectation of shortening the transition period, which was a policy Marx would have approved of, but which greatly curtailed the share of consumption in GDP thereby increasing the degree of scarcity

---

[9] James R. Millar, "Post-Stalin Agriculture: Performance and Prospects," in *The Soviet Economic Experiment*, ed. Suzan J. Linz (Urbana: University of Illinois Press, 1990), 90–112.

[10] Marx, "Russia's Pattern of Development" [Marx to the Editorial Board of the *Otechestvennye zapiski*. November 1877], in *Basic Writings on Politics and Philosophy*, 440.

of final goods and services. Fifth, in order to avoid having prices set willy nilly in markets, the state administration did so in all state retail outlets. Consequently, prices ordinarily did not reflect equilibrium levels with the result that some goods required queuing and others gathered dust in inventory, which invited irregularities and corruption in the distribution of consumption goods and services. The total money wage bill was set with an eye to providing gradual increases in real income and avoiding disguised inflation. Sixth, thanks to the measures listed above, the Soviet economy proved resistant to recession and inflation alike, which Marx would have looked on favorably.

Thus, Soviet socialism displayed many features essentially consistent with Marxian socialism, but it proved more difficult than Marx anticipated to move very far along the path to true communism. The fatal flaw was the irreducible character of scarcity: the fact that a society of plenty has proved a chimera even in the most advanced economies. Although Marx was correct in rejecting the doctrines of Malthus, which explained the persistence of scarcity by the inevitability of population pressure on resources, he was too optimistic about the growth of production, the absence of war expenditures and the rationality of consumers. Human wants have turned out to be unlimited, as the neoclassical economists assumed. Marx also misread what appears today as the apparently irresistible growth historically of pecuniary institutions. The advantages that money and other debt instruments offer, in the context of a complex market economy, have been too overwhelming to do without.[11]

Market Socialism as an Alternative Construct

Oskar Lange's model of market socialism was conceived after the main institutions of the Soviet socialist economy had been created. In contrast to Marxian socialism, Lange's model did not purport to eliminate most markets, money, prices, or money wages. He recognized the operational significance of both markets and pecuniary institutions. Socialism was defined by Lange as the absence of private property in the means of production. Prices were functional in consumer goods, labor, and producer goods markets. The transition from capitalism involved: 1) nationalization of all productive means; 2) conversion of all entrepreneurs to managers with no ownership rights; 3) an instruction to all managers to maximize profits just as though they were still owners; and 4) state determination of the rate of investment (arbitrarily) along with a social tax or dividend out of enterprise profits.[12]

[11] Jame R. Millar, "The Importance of Initial Conditions in Economic Transitions: An Evaluation of Economic Reform Progress in Russia," *Journal of Socio-Economics* 26, no. 4 (1997): 362.

[12] Oskar Lange, *On the Economic Theory of Socialism*, ed. Benjamin E. Lippencott (Min-

It is obvious that the Soviet economy of Stalin, Khrushchev, and Brezhnev did not correspond at all to Lange's model. However, he addressed several functional issues that Marx was silent about. Most important, Lange solved the problem of where socialist enterprise managers would come from. Capitalist entrepreneurs would simply be converted via nationalization of all enterprises into socialist managers. Moreover, he offered a solution to the problem of how managers were to manage their enterprises. They were to be instructed to follow the same procedures of profit maximization as before nationalization. This would optimize outputs and inputs and maximize social welfare. Interestingly, unlike Abram Bergson, Lange did not consider these optimization rules "capitalist."[13] What is relevant to the Soviet experience is Lange's conclusion that the greatest danger for market socialism would be the "bureaucratization of economic life." In addition, Lange declined to attempt to specify the incentive system that would be necessary to ensure that the newly christened managers of enterprises would follow profit maximization rules and not line their own pockets instead. This problem he relegated to the sociologists, as though it were of limited significance.[14] It is clear, then, that the Soviet economy in its heyday (say in the1960s) did not resemble the model of market socialism, but it did exhibit certain troublesome features illustrated by the model: 1) the bureaucratization of the economy; 2) the inevitably arbitrary nature of determination of the rate of investment; and 3) the difficulty in designing a workable managerial incentive system. The Lange model of market socialism also demonstrated the superiority of price-making markets by creating a way to simulate such markets under socialism.

Survivals of Soviet Socialism in Russia

The transition back from Soviet socialism to a standard market economy in Russia encountered a number of problems that obviously stem from the "successes" achieved in establishing Soviet socialism. The process also reflected the prevailing ideology among Western economists who advised Russian reformers, who were at best lightly trained in Western economics, that markets were the default form of economic activity and that laissez faire should govern activities of the state.[15]

There was no real problem in the conversion of markets for consumer goods

---

neapolis: The University of Minnesota Press, 1938).

[13] Bergson, *The Structure of Soviet Wages*.

[14] Lange, *On the Economic Theory of Socialism*, 109.

[15] James R. Millar, "The End of Three Ideological Eras: What is Next for Russia?" *Demokratizatsiya* 11, no. 1 (Winter 2003): 26–34.

and services into what Karl Polanyi called "price-making markets."[16] The same was true for labor markets. Although Soviet consumer goods and labor markets were restricted and constrained in a number of respects, by, for instance, central price controls, residence requirements, and the like, both of these markets became operational free markets without significant difficulties. People understood how to behave in these markets, and they adjusted readily (if not necessarily happily). The difference between the Soviet socialist markets for consumer goods, services, and labor and free markets was one of goods availability, not of kind. Consequently, there are virtually no survivals in these markets of Soviet socialism. The knowledge the population had acquired of how to live in a shortage economy, which included, for example, queuing etiquette, dealing *na levo* and out the backdoor, has lost its usefulness. Nepotism and corruption, unfortunately, have not.[17]

The situation was quite different when it came to other markets vital to a capitalist economy. Producer goods, or real investment goods, were allocated according to plan and not according to producer decisions based on a comparison of costs and expected revenue in the market. These decisions were not made at the enterprise level and enterprise managers (and owners) have found it difficult, or they have been reluctant to risk, these kinds of decisions. Moreover, the Soviet Gosbank was a central bank in many respects, but neither it nor its branches had experience in financing either public or private investments. Moreover, Stroibank, the state investment bank, was merely a conduit and supervisor for investment funds allocated in the plan. In short, there was no market in Soviet times for investment goods or for the financing of productive investment. These are markets that involve expectations of future profitability and consequently involve risks that investments in purely financial securities do not. It is not surprising that these markets have not performed adequately in Russia. The result has been relative underinvestment in domestic productive assets.

Financial markets have generally been difficult to establish in Russia mainly because they were so thoroughly eliminated in Soviet times. The early commercial banks that appeared were mainly opportunistic banks of deposit (especially of government deposits), moneychangers, money laundries, and small time lenders for non-productive purposes. The absence even today of properly functioning commercial banks is a legacy of Soviet socialism. Commercial banks are necessary in a market economy to provide short-term loans to enterprises to help them bridge the time shape gaps between receipts and disbursements on a weekly, monthly, or quarterly

[16] Karl Polanyi, *The Great Transformation* (Boston: Beacon Press, 1957), chapter 6.

[17] Millar, "The Importance of Initial Conditions in Economic Transitions."

basis. They are necessary in providing financing and advice on a long-term basis, too. They are also especially essential in the financing of small business enterprises. Customer loans for the purchase of homes and consumer durables represent another deficient area of commercial bank financing. Russian financial institutions are still not up to the standards required by a modern market economy. It takes years of experience to make wise decisions about future risks and opportunities. Without experience and workable regulation of banking and financial operations, an economy suffers from risk avoidance and a lower rate of investment and growth than would otherwise be the case, and the export of capital. In general, the number and variety of financial instruments are many fewer even today than in comparable market economies, which retards both private business investment and private residential construction and borrowing.[18]

The absence of a market in existing productive assets, such as productive enterprises, land and natural resources generally, retail outlets, and so forth contributed to the fiascos of denationalization of Soviet economic enterprises and operations. Without functioning price-making markets for final products, it is impossible to know what an enterprise is worth in a market economy. Conversely, it is impossible to determine rational prices of goods and services without privately owned enterprises that are operated for profit. The value of a productive enterprise is determined by expected sales revenue and costs of production. The inevitable confusion and chicanery surrounding the sales of state enterprises to private persons, the creation of the oligarchs for example, was a direct legacy of Soviet socialism. This is not only a very large market, it is one that has a decisive effect on the distribution of wealth and income.[19]

Soviet socialism continues to shape the expectations of Russian consumers. The emphasis upon public goods and services in Soviet times is still highly valued by Russian citizens. Free medical care (including prescriptions) and free public education remain highly prized memories of Soviet socialism. So are inexpensive housing, very low cost utilities, cheap transportation, and special benefits for pensioners and military veterans. As the Soviet Interview Project demonstrated, Soviet citizens' main criticism of the Soviet consumer's daily life was the problems posed by deficit

[18] Millar, "The Importance of Initial Conditions in Economic Transitions"; idem, "Normalization of the Russian Economy: Obstacles and Opportunities for Reform and Sustainable Growth," *NBR Analysis.* The National Bureau of Asian Research 13, no. 2 (April 2002): 5–43.

[19] James R. Millar, "From Utopian Socialism to Utopian Capitalism. The Failure of Revolution and Reform in Post-Soviet Russia," *Problems of Post-Communism,* May–June 1995, 7–14.

commodities, that is, goods and services that were under priced in state retail outlets and therefore out of stock most of the time. These markets were characterized, therefore, by the need to queue and the complementary advantages offered to those who could jump the queue. Interestingly enough, however, Soviet citizens did not recognize that the problem could be solved only by raising prices (as opposed to increasing production at a loss).[20] Russian consumers today still criticize market-clearing prices and do not seem to realize that the alternative is a return to queuing, *na levo*, and the like. There is one sense in which queuing did benefit relatively poor consumers who had more time than money. Queuing tended to equalize the distribution of final goods and services, which is why there were so many official ways to jump the queue (for example, special access stores).

Privatization: Private versus Public Ownership of the Means of Production

The story of privatization of enterprises in Russia is well known. The first phase involved the distribution of 10,000 ruble vouchers to all citizens. This was a well-meaning effort to place the ownership of the Russian share of the Soviet productive stock in the hands of the population that had created it. Unfortunately, two developments reduced the effort to a highly inequitable distribution of the enterprises offered for private ownership. First, most Russian citizens had no idea how to benefit from these ownership shares and did not realize their potential long-term value. It was easy for the few who understood their value to buy up the vouchers from the unsuspecting population for much less than the vouchers long-term value. Second, the raging inflation that followed liberalization of prices (that is, the elimination of price controls) caused many individuals to cash in their vouchers in order to eat. They either did not realize that the fixed number of vouchers that were issued would retain purchasing power in the face of the inflation or they could not afford to wait. Consequently, the distribution of ownership of what had been Soviet economic enterprises was skewed heavily in favor of former enterprise management and staff.[21]

The second major wave of privatization was the famous loans-for-shares program, which traded major resource and production companies for short-term loans in support of Yeltsin's election in 1996. Thus were created the oligarchs. If the voucher

[20] James R. Millar and Elizabeth Clayton, "Quality of Life: Subjective Measures of Relative Satisfaction," in *Politics, Work, and Daily Life in the USSR. A Survey of Former Soviet Citizens*, ed. Millar (New York: Cambridge University Press, 1987), chapter 2.

[21] Paul R. Gregory and Robert C. Stuart. *Russian & Soviet Economic Performance & Structure*, 7th ed. (New York: Addison Wesley, 2001), chapter 13.

program involved pulling the wool over the eyes of the innocents (*ochkovtiratel'stvo*), the loans-for-shares transactions were world-class scams unparalleled in the history of nationalization schemes. Whereas the voucher program was in harmony with Marxist thought in that everyone in Russia had a legitimate claim on the Soviet capital stock, the philosophical basis of the loans-for-shares transactions was pure greed. There is not a shred of evidence that efficient operation of these gigantic enterprises was a consideration in the allocation of ownership.[22]

The way in which privatization was conducted in Russia further skewed the distribution of income, the perception of which alienated the general population and, along with high inflation rates, turned the population against liberalization and the market economy. A reaction has followed against further liberalization of Russian economic institutions and in favor of retaining and expanding the role of the state in the management and operation of the economy. The reaction is seen easily, for example, in the nostalgia the population expresses today for the Brezhnev years, which were once criticized as the era of economic stagnation.[23] A new ownership model has been developing under Putin's leadership, one that draws not only on the Soviet socialist model of the post-Stalin years, but upon the preceding period of the NEP, which is associated with some of Stalin's early opponents, specifically Bukharin.

The NEP was introduced in the 1920s in reaction to the chaos that had been created by the Civil War and ideological support for War Communism, which many Bolsheviks viewed as an immediate precursor of true communism. It was thanks only to the vast authority Lenin exercised in the party that the NEP could be introduced because it violated the anti-market hopes of the most ardent revolutionists. Instead of moving directly to communism, as defined by Marx, a pause was introduced that many feared would be permanent. It called for a limited role of the state and a roll back of nationalization. The state would retain control and management of the "commanding heights" of the economy and private enterprise would be allowed to control the remainder of the economy. The commanding heights included heavy industry, natural resource extraction, banking and all financial institutions, insurance, national transportation systems, and so forth. Private ownership was retained (or returned) for agricultural producers, retail outlets, restaurants, carrying trade, and other small businesses.[24] It does not take much imagination to see in Putin's economic policies a return to something resembling the NEP. There is something nicely symmetrical

[22] Millar, "The Importance of Initial Conditions in Economic Transitions."

[23] Millar, "Normalization of the Russian Economy."

[24] Maurice Dobb, *Soviet Economic Development since 1917* (New York: International Publishers, 1948), chapter 6.

about finding that Russia's transition back to capitalism has stalled in a variant form of the NEP.

There are, of course, some significant differences. Instead of the state controlling the commanding heights alone, today the state is sharing the commanding heights with the oligarchs and other capitalists. Under Putin, the direct role of the state in the economy until recently has focused primarily upon enterprises engaging in resource extraction and industries relevant to the defense effort. The Russian government has also retained a partial interest (and say) in many enterprises that have been nominally privatized. More recently Putin has sought to substitute state-sponsored enterprise for what has been a deficiently entrepreneurial private sector, notably aircraft and automobile enterprises. The state has purchased shares, demanded places on boards of directors of private firms and persecuted recalcitrant owners. Andrei Illarionov, a former economic advisor to Putin puts it this way:

> A new model of Russia has taken shape. The state has become, essentially, a corporate enterprise that the nominal owners, Russian citizens, no longer control ...
>
> State-owned companies have become the assault weapons of this corporate state. Having mastered the main principle of state-corporatism—"privatize profit, nationalize loss"—they have turned to taking over private-sector companies, sometimes at cut-rate prices. Their victims include major industrial companies like Yuganskneftegaz, Sibneft, Silovye Mashiny, Kamov, OMZ, and Avtovaz.[25]

Western-trained economists such as Illarionov are critical of state interventions of this sort for a number of reasons. First, private enterprise is generally considered more efficient than state-controlled enterprise. This is partly because private decision makers are more likely to make economic decisions on strictly economic grounds and partly because of likely bureaucratization of economic life along the lines Lange feared. Second, when the state has a direct interest in extraction or production, it can express this interest in non-economic ways that threaten the further development of private economic initiative, especially foreign direct investment. Third, as has already been seen in the Yukos example, state intervention invites corruption and self-dealing.

The preference for central control through ownership shares or board membership reflects a carryover from Soviet practice and experience. Soviet and now post-Soviet leadership has always preferred direct control to regulation and enforcement

[25] Andrei Illarionov, "Russia Inc.," *New York Times,* February 4, 2006.

of the rule of law. The economic justification for the role of the state in today's Russia, however, has been the failure of private initiative to develop industries that are viewed at the national level as critical. The relative underdevelopment of financial and venture capital institutions in Russia is largely to blame for this situation and especially so considering the much less risky opportunities private Russian capital has to invest in secure Western securities—which has led to large-scale capital flight. If Putin's policies lead to the successful development, or redevelopment, of old Soviet industries such as aircraft and automobiles and to the successful exploitation of the extractive industries such as oil and gas, then it will have proved worth the cost in lower efficiency. The Japanese and South Korean examples illustrate the possibility that a significant role by the state in the economy can be very successful. It is not clear, however, that Russian economic and financial officials will behave as rigorously in the national interest in their interventions in the economy as have the Japanese and South Koreans. The evidence thus far indicates that private advantage tends to trump public interest. Moreover, the interest of Russian leadership in using economic leverage to achieve non-economic national goals, such as regaining Russia's status as a world power, also undermines decision making on strictly economic grounds. This probably reflects the continuation of Marxist thought: that international trade and commence is a zero-sum game and not always or even usually mutually advantageous.

As in the NEP, small business enterprise and private farms have been free to develop without state interference, but without much support either.[26] Markets are open and working normally for these businesses and individuals. Citizens are free to own their own homes and to hire others for profit. There is no indication that these activities are likely to come under the supervision or ownership by the state. The problem has been the relative neglect by the state of conditions necessary for the expansion and flourishing of small business.

Unlike the NEP, however, there is no ideological antipathy to small-scale and private individual enterprise, and the new model thus does not tend to undermine economic expectations. The population has repeatedly indicated a preference for a NEP-type arrangement. The Soviet Interview Project revealed that former Soviet citizens did not support private ownership of large-scale, national enterprises as opposed to state ownership. These former citizens did, however, prefer private business for local and small-scale enterprises.[27] Every subsequent survey to date has

---

[26] Millar, "Normalization of the Russian Economy."

[27] Millar and Clayton, "Quality of Life."

revealed the constancy of these preferences.[28] Thus, although economists like Illarionov may demur, Putin has public opinion on his side.

Conclusions

Soviet socialism continues to influence Russian economic institutions and behavior in significant ways both positively and negatively. The population still expects a high level provision of public goods, which makes it nostalgic for the heyday of Soviet socialism in Brezhnev's time. It also is opposed in principle to private ownership of large-scale enterprises and services, and the oligarchs represent the worst case of such ownership for most. The leadership under Putin may agree also in principle, but it also sees what it considers the necessity for the state to provide initiative and perhaps financing for industries that will help Russia regain status as a leading economy with the economic basis for the projection of Russian power and influence in local and in world events. Thus, it has not been possible to reduce the degree of bureaucratization of the economy inherited from Soviet days. The new corporate model that Illarionov has described is likely to be continued and even strengthened under any successor to Putin. Oddly enough, it is the presocialist Soviet economy, the NEP of the 1920s, that appears to describe the Russian economy best. It makes more sense, however, if one considers that Russia is traveling backward from Soviet socialism to some variant of capitalism. It is not surprising that historical carryover variables are significant determinants of today's institutions, beliefs, and behavior. It also reflects the failure of the attempt to substitute utopian capitalism for utopian socialism following the breakup of the Soviet Union. The reaction has produced a unique economic model that Putin is attempting to reify. Only time will tell how well the new model will work as an economic system.

[28] Millar, "Normalization of the Russian Economy."

Klychkov i Pustota

Post-Soviet Bureaucrats and the Production of Institutional Facades

Jessica Allina-Pisano

In 1996, Ken Jowitt warned of "mimic democracies" that would rise from the ashes of the Soviet empire and lead eventually to the reemergence of authoritarian politics in Russia.[1] Ten years later, Dimitri Furman described a "démocratie imitative," in which the arbiters of power in Russia produce a superficial approximation of democratic institutions.[2] In post-orange revolution Ukraine, officials and observers referring to reforms in sectors as disparate as security and secondary education have described institutional transformation as "imitation" reform.[3] In the years immediately prior to Ukraine's massive street demonstrations of 2004, such characterizations were ubiquitous, as citizens and analysts observed a broad disjuncture between de facto and de jure rules governing political and economic life.

The title of this article refers both to discourses of political and societal change and to the emptiness that sometimes lies behind those discourses. Klychkov and Pustota—respectively, characters in Dmitry Furmanov's 1923 novel *Chapaev* and Viktor Pelevin's 1999 novel *Chapaev i Pustota*—together personify the notion of institutional facades: reform without substantive transformation. In Furman's work Klychkov is the rational party commissar, friend to the revolutionary hero Chapaev. Petr Pustota, the psychiatric patient protagonist of Pelevin's novel, carries a name that is the Russian word for "emptiness." Here, Klychkov and Pustota suggest both the "men on the spot," the state officials who oversee and undermine processes of

---

The author would like to thank the participants in the "What is Soviet Now?" workshop at the University of Toronto, Eric Allina-Pisano, Dominique Arel, Timothy Colton, Paul D'Anieri, Keith Darden, Oxana Shevel, the Leibniz-Institut für Länderkunde, in Leipzig, Germany, the participants in the Kennan Institute workshop "Civil Society and Democracy in Ukraine," in Washington, D.C., May 2006, and the Chair of Ukrainian Studies at the University of Ottawa for valuable comments on earlier versions of this article. Unless otherwise noted, all translations are the author's.

[1] Ken Jowitt, "Dizzy with Democracy," *Problems of Post-Communism* 43, no.1 (January–February 1996): 3–8.

[2] Galia Ackerman, "Entretien avec Dimitri Fourman. De Gorbatchev à Poutine: Les illusions perdues," *Politique internationale* 109 (Automne 2005): 253–73.

[3] "Rishennia pro neobkhidnist'," *Dzerkalo tyzhnia* 9 (558), March 11–17, 2006. Viacheslav Epshtein, "Imitatsiia," *Dzerkalo tyzhnia* 33 (561), August 27–September 2, 2005.

social change,[4] and the void behind the facades that sometimes result.[5]

References to partial, superficial, or cosmetic change abound in the scholarly literature on political and economic transformation in post-Soviet states.[6] Likewise, scholarship on post-socialist politics in Central and Eastern Europe is full of descriptions of institutional facades: the character of institutional development in new European Union member states is "hollow,"[7] and the institutions that have emerged in those states in response to reforms emphasizing administrative capacity and policy harmonization have been described as "Potemkin institutions."[8] Like the village facades that, according to legend, were constructed to impress Catherine the Great during her travels in Crimea at the end of the eighteenth century, some post-socialist institutions exist primarily in the realm of official record. These institutions are of little de facto use to the constituencies they are meant to serve, and their function is not always governance as such. Sometimes, political actors build them to create legitimacy in the eyes of domestic constituencies and international audiences.

Some analyses of Potemkin politics not only acknowledge the existence of institutional facades, but also imagine such facades to constitute the central reality of post-Soviet politics. Andrew Wilson describes post-Soviet politics as complex stage productions conjured by the creative imaginations of political technologists.[9] In this view, politics is *dramaturgia* (dramatic art), and the action that unfolds upon the media stage in turn drives all other political life, including the activity of formal institutions of governance.

This article takes a different tack. Performances of democracy may well shape the public's experience of political life, but Potemkin institutions are not merely the

---

[4] For a discussion of bureaucratic "obfuscations and prevarications" in a colonial context, see Justin Willis, "'Men on the Spot,' Labor, and the Colonial State in British East Africa: The Mombasa Water Supply, 1911–1917," *The International Journal of African Historical Studies* 28, no. 1 (1995): 25–48.

[5] For an elaboration of literary themes in the novel(s) referenced in the title, see Angela Brintlinger, "The Hero in the Madhouse: The Post-Soviet Novel Confronts the Soviet Past," *Slavic Review* 63, no. 1 (Spring 2004): 43–65.

[6] A well-known example is Joel Hellman, "Winners Take All: The Politics of Partial Reform in Postcommunist Transitions," *World Politics* 50, no. 2 (January 1998): 203–34.

[7] Anna Grzymała-Busse, "After Enlargement: Domestic Expectations and Outcomes" (paper presented at "Post-Communist State and Society: Transnational and National Politics," Maxwell School, Syracuse University, September 30–October 1, 2005).

[8] Wade Jacoby, *The Enlargement of the European Union and NATO: Ordering from the Menu in Central Europe* (Cambridge: Cambridge University Press, 2004).

[9] Andrew Wilson. *Virtual Politics: Faking Democracy in the Post-Soviet World* (New Haven: Yale University Press, 2005).

product of political technologists' fancy. Further, although facades appear to be characteristic features of post-socialism, not all Eurasian institutions are facades. The performance of post-Soviet politics instead emerges from concrete, structural incentives in particular domains. As political actors respond to those incentives, the resulting drama may seem a post-modern dream, but the economic and social conditions that lead to the performance are real. The nature of Potemkin politics as chimerical and deceptive belies the reasons for their existence, which are tangible, concrete, and durable.

Some scholars explaining the form of post-socialist institutions draw a direct line of descent from the bureaucratic structures of the socialist past to the behavior of contemporary functionaries.[10] At first glance, Potemkin institutions would seem to follow this logic. In almost every area of life, Soviet parchment institutions were fundamentally alienated from politics and economics in practice. The Soviet constitution enshrined freedom of speech on paper, even as legislative institutions failed to protect it in fact. Firm-level incentives developed by economic planners in Moscow led managers to misrepresent production levels as well as expected input needs, leading eventually to the inscription of these distortions in the plan itself.[11] Consumers managed to circumvent official shortages through complex, informal interpersonal exchanges,[12] and on factory shop floors, *tolkachi* (fixers) managed disruptions in supply chains.[13] However, as this article shows, post-Soviet Potemkin institutions also represent a rupture with the past, as bureaucrats renovate their skills to respond to incentives that are entirely new.

This article examines the development of two institutions in post-Soviet states that are central to economic and political life and linchpins of a liberal order: property rights and elections. These are by no means the only institutions that exhibit features of Potemkin politics, but rural property rights and electoral politics—as they have been practiced in post-Soviet Russia and in Ukraine between 1999 and late 2004—provide analytical leverage on the origins of institutional facades.

---

[10] Herbert Kitschelt, Zdenka Mansfeldova, Radosław Markowski, and Gábor Tóka. *Post-Communist Party Systems: Competition, Representation and Inter-Party Cooperation* (Cambridge: Cambridge University Press, 1999).

[11] János Kornai, *The Socialist System: The Political Economy of Communism* (Princeton: Princeton University Press, 1991).

[12] Alena Ledeneva, *Russia's Economy of Favors: Blat, Networking, and Informal Exchange* (Cambridge: Cambridge University Press, 1998) and Elena Osokina, *Our Daily Bread: Socialist Distribution and the Art of Survival in Stalin's Russia, 1927–1941*, ed. Kate Transchel; trans. Kate Transchel and Greta Bucher (Armonk: M.E. Sharpe, 2001).

[13] Joseph Berliner, *Factory and Manager in the USSR* (Cambridge, MA: Harvard University Press, 1957).

Some approaches to understanding the production of institutional facades emphasize a host of domestic factors: Leninist legacies of various types, weak state capacity, and a lack of normative commitment to institutional change. Other analyses of post-Soviet politics acknowledge international factors, ascribing the failures of market or democratic development to the colonial impulses of foreign governments and international lending organizations.[14] This article emphasizes the role of structural, economic incentives at both the domestic and international level. I argue that the origins of Potemkin politics lie in the symbiotic interaction of domestic and international factors. State officials at the local level, in response to incentives generated by national economic policy and the demands of international institutions, performed multi-party elections and market reform at various points during the first post-Soviet decade. The interaction of those demands with the structural legacies of Soviet industrialization policy, and the poverty that interaction generated, provided local state officials with opportunities to reproduce their own political capital by hollowing out the market and political institutions they were responsible for creating.

"One hundred cows for one hundred peasants"

In the early 1990s, post-Soviet governments embarked on programs to decollectivize agriculture and privatize farmland. In Russia, land reform encompassed vast rural expanses of the federation that together comprised a territory as large as Australia. The plan was to reorganize collective and state farms and divide their assets among their members and employees. Those who chose to leave the reorganized collectives to establish a commercial family farm could, under law, take their share of land and non-land assets with them. Like the "forty acres and a mule" initially promised to freedmen in the post-bellum American South, or a post-Soviet version of Chapaev's "one hundred cows for one hundred peasants," land privatization policy in post-Soviet Ukraine and Russia posited a relatively equal allocation of resources among rural dwellers who had spent their labor in agriculture. That division of resources, reformers believed, would lead to more efficient use of resources and a peasant-owner bound to the soil not by the forces of tyranny but by the "incomparable joy of free labor."[15]

[14] Stephen Cohen, *Failed Crusade: America and the Tragedy of Post-Communist Russia* (New York: Norton, 2000); Peter Reddaway and Dmitri Glinski, *The Tragedy of Russia's Reforms: Market Bolshevism Against Democracy* (Washington, D.C.: United States Institute of Peace Press, 2001).

[15] "Kolkhozy: ne speshite davat' nam poslednee slovo," *Liskinskie izvestiia*, October 10, 1991, 5.

According to government statistical agencies and the records of non-governmental organizations alike, the creation of property rights to rural land was an unqualified success. In Russia, by January of 1994, 95 percent of the agricultural enterprises subject to reform had undergone reorganization.[16] Although programs to create private farms were widely judged to have failed, distribution of land shares to former members of collective and state farms appeared to have gone off without a hitch.[17]

In practice, new land ownership rights on paper provided a facade behind which local state officials, working in concert with business elites, moved commercial agricultural land out of public control and into the hands of a small number of well-positioned individuals.[18] Land distribution in post-Soviet Russia thus produced a deep chasm between property rights on paper and ownership in practice, prompting some observers to categorize land reform as illusory,[19] even as lasting changes in land tenure have taken place.[20] Importantly, formal land ownership neither improved labor incentives for individuals nor raised the production levels of enterprises. Reformers believed that land privatization would streamline production, but the agricultural enterprises that did thrive in the post-Soviet years largely have managed this through the addition of processing facilities to existing infrastructure—in other words, by expanding existing collective farms rather than shedding acreage or labor.

According to land privatization policy, individual labor incentives on reorganized collectives would come from rents and dividends paid to worker-shareholders—in this case, former kolkhozniki (collective farmers). However, most reorganized collectives were not able to compete against subsidized agriculture on world markets. Without profits sufficient even to cover operating costs, payment of dividends on land shares was a practical impossibility for most enterprises. Typically, the nominal owners of farmland, worker-shareholders, received a few sacks of feed grain, distributed annually at harvest time for the first few years after privatization. Such rents and dividends hardly exceeded the annual harvest-time distributions of grain of the late Soviet period. From the perspective of producers, private ownership

[16] *Sel'skoe khoziaistvo Rossii* (Moscow: Goskomstat, 1995), 49.

[17] Don Van Atta, ed. *The Farmer Threat: The Political Economy of Agrarian Reform in Post-Soviet Russia* (Boulder: Westview Press, 1993).

[18] Jessica Allina-Pisano, *The Post-Soviet Potemkin Village: Politics and Property Rights in the Black Earth* (Cambridge: Cambridge University Press, 2007).

[19] For example, Max Spoor, "Agrarian Transition in Former Soviet Central Asia: A Comparative Study of Kazakhstan, Kyrgyzstan and Uzbekistan," ISS Working Paper No. 298, 1999.

[20] Stephen K. Wegren, *The Moral Economy Reconsidered: Russia's Search for Agrarian Capitalism* (New York: Palgrave, 2005).

of land brought only tax liability with respect to the authorities, but no perceptible improvement over Soviet-era entitlements.

The low value of dividends did not come about solely as a consequence of an economic environment hostile to agricultural production. Managers of struggling collectives selected particular organizational forms because they paid comparatively less to worker-shareholders. The chief accountant of a collective in Voronezh oblast, for example, when asked about why the collective had chosen a particular form of organization, replied that open joint-stock company shares were too expensive. Enterprise management, therefore, decided upon an agricultural producers' cooperative—the form of private enterprise organization most like a kolkhoz.[21]

Rural and urban populations' increasing reliance upon household agricultural production further subtracted from shareholders' ownership benefits. In the absence of small-scale machinery appropriate for household production, rural people require the assistance of former collectives to plow the fields of their gardens. This and other costs are deducted from rents on land shares, leaving some shareholders in debt to former collectives at the end of the growing season. As a result, most worker-shareholders were, in Katherine Verdery's terms, utterly unable to extract value from their formal ownership of land.[22] Many were thus willing, when the time came, to part with their paper shares for a modest sum.

Administrative Resource and Elections

If Potemkin property rights came to dominate large swathes of the post-Soviet rural economic landscape, institutional facades also work in the realm of politics through hidden tools of electoral manipulation. Amidst apparently competitive multi-party elections, incumbents' favored instruments of fraud leave little trace.[23] Administrative resource has been the most widely and, it would seem, successfully used of these instruments. It refers to political actors' use of bureaucratic hierarchies and the material resources of public institutions to advance electoral gains.[24] The phenomenon has been observed and discussed in a range of Russian regions, in Eastern

[21] Allina-Pisano, *The Post-Soviet Potemkin Village*, 69.

[22] Katherine Verdery, *The Vanishing Hectare: Property and Value in Postsocialist Transylvania* (Ithaca: Cornell University Press, 2003).

[23] For a broader discussion of instruments of electoral manipulation, see Wilson, *Virtual Politics* and Alena Ledeneva, *How Russia Really Works: The Informal Practices that Shaped Post-Soviet Politics and Business* (Ithaca: Cornell University Press, 2006).

[24] Some definitions of administrative resource include the use of financial levers or media control, although those practices are not discussed here.

Europe and the Caucasus, as well as in the states of Central Asia.[25] Administrative resource, together with other tools of pre-election day vote engineering, allows for the appearance of free and competitive elections, even as the outcome of such elections may be partly a product of elite manipulation.

The use of administrative resource to produce Potemkin elections, in which a democratic facade belies manipulation behind the scenes, does not simply generate an impression of democratic rule where none exists. It also provides opportunities for defectors from democracy[26] to develop capacity unseen: elections can function not only as a tool for elites to establish legitimacy, but also as an "instrument of authoritarian control."[27] Yitzhak Brudny has written of the 1999–2000 electoral cycle in Russia that, "these two elections taught the ruling elite how it could use the electoral process to perpetuate its hold on power and destroy political opponents."[28] Finally, Potemkin elections can provide a means by which elites demonstrate to electorates that voter preferences do not drive outcomes: where electoral fraud is routinized, publics come to expect elections to yield illegitimate, but durable results. Voters' participation in such elections is ritualized but emptied of agency and meaning, save for the knowledge that their voices will go unheard by state elites.

In some forms, administrative resource works through the renegotiation of social contracts, as elites convert goods previously understood as entitlements or labor compensation into payments for compliance during elections.[29] For example, in the weeks prior to Ukraine's 2004 elections, non-partisan watchdog groups documented threats against students and workers in which employers made clear that stipends or salaries would be withheld if the incumbent prime minister, Viktor Yanukovych, did not prevail in their electoral districts. Villagers learned that they would lose access to public utilities such as gas or electricity, or that promised infrastructure development would take place only in the event of an incumbent victory. In Poltavska oblast, one village saw its bread deliveries stopped after residents refused to sign a statement

[25] A Google search on January 19, 2007, for the Russian term "administrativnyi resurs" yielded approximately 1,270,000 results.

[26] Nancy Bermeo, *Ordinary People in Extraordinary Times: The Citizenry and the Breakdown of Democracy* (Princeton: Princeton University Press, 2003).

[27] Andreas Schedler, "The Menu of Manipulation," *Journal of Democracy* 13, no. 2 (April 2002): 36.

[28] Yitzhak M. Brudny, "Continuity or Change in Russian Electoral Patterns? The December 1999–March 2000 Election Cycle," in *Contemporary Russian Politics,* ed. Archie Brown (Oxford: Oxford University Press, 2001), 178.

[29] Allina-Pisano, "Informal Politics and Electoral Competition in Post-Soviet Eurasia: The Use of Administrative Resource," (unpublished manuscript, University of Ottawa, 2007).

supporting incumbent authorities. In some cases, authorities demanded additional resources from constituencies as a precondition for delivering on earlier promises, as in the requirement that Ukrainian students pay new university "fees."[30]

Although instances of administrative resource use have been documented in private sector businesses—particularly in reorganized former collective and state farms—political elites deploy administrative resource primarily in the public sector: in state bureaucracies, social services provision, education, and state-owned or managed enterprises. Its use depends on the existence of institutional administrative hierarchies and on state budgetary allocations to those institutions. Administrative hierarchies provide the mechanism by which superiors transmit orders, and superiors ensure the compliance of their subordinates through a set of economic incentives. Financial links between state and social institutions lend credibility to the state's threat of withdrawing support. Thus, the institutions most often subject to regime capture for the purpose of altering electoral outcomes are those that rely upon national or regional budgets.[31]

The Origins of Potemkin Institutions

How is it that institutional facades have come to characterize multiple areas of post-Soviet political and economic life? What explains the disjuncture between institutions on paper and in reality? Most explorations of political development in post-socialist states focus on obstacles to liberalization rather than the production of institutional facades as such. In many accounts, weak state capacity appears foremost among such obstacles.[32] Under this rubric, Potemkin institutions would emerge as state elites expend resources sufficient to produce a thin appearance of reform, but lack the will or ability to stack bricks and mortar behind the facade. Here, even as the despotic power of the state may be preserved, its infrastructural power (in Michael Mann's terms) is too limited for genuine institutional development.[33] Other features of weak political development, such as an absence of robust party competition, likewise can obstruct successful liberalization in other domains.[34]

---

[30] Wacław Radziwinowicz, "Kampania wyborcza na ukraińskiej prowincji," *Gazeta wyborcza*, March 5, 2006.

[31] Allina-Pisano, "Informal Politics and Electoral Competition."

[32] For example, Steven Fish ascribes failures of democratic reform to weak legislature, insufficient economic liberalization, and the resource curse. Fish, *Democracy Derailed in Russia: The Failure of Open Politics* (Cambridge: Cambridge University Press, 2005).

[33] Michael Mann, "The Autonomous Power of the State: Its Origins, Mechanisms and Results," *Archives européennes de sociologie* 25 (1984): 185–213.

[34] Anna Grzymała-Busse, *Rebuilding Leviathan: Party Competition and State Exploitation in*

Alternately, scholars interpreting post-Soviet institutional stasis or entrenchment—understood often in the teleological terms of "failed reform"—sometimes focus on an absence of normative commitment to institutional change or simply the persistence of Soviet-era values. Thus, when Goskomstat (State Statistical Committee) bureaucrats are slow to adopt new accounting systems for demographic data, but rapidly accept new practices in collecting and organizing economic data, the reason is found to lie in bureaucrats' professional commitments to norms generated under an earlier modus vivendi.[35] Likewise, in the case of land privatization, regional and local bureaucrats engaged in hidden resistance to decollectivization in part because their professional norms demanded it: they understood rural development in terms of heavily capitalized, large-scale industrialized agriculture, rather than small-scale farms and family-based labor organization.[36]

Few of these approaches consider the role of international actors, international organizations, or international norms in producing institutional facades—despite wide acknowledgement of importance of such factors in explaining reform "successes."[37] Furman explains the origin of "imitative democracy" in terms reminiscent of Wilson's argument, but with an international dimension: Potemkin politics represent Vladimir Putin's deliberate effort to safeguard Russia's geopolitical status and current elites' place within it:

> At the same time, he hopes to offer a positive image of the new Russia to the West and to the whole world. To achieve that without risking losing power, there is only one thing to do: imitate democratic processes. And that's precisely what he's done. He has established an appearance of democracy ... without calling into question his own place at the head of the state.[38]

In Furman's account, the creation of institutional facades represents a conscious effort to mislead on the part of some political actors. If Furman is correct, his argument suggests one of two things: first, that the emergence of Potemkin institutions across a variety of political and economic domains is the product of extensive coor-

---

Post-Communist Democracies (Cambridge: Cambridge University Press, 2007).

35 Yoshiko Herrera, "Transforming Bureaucracy: Conditional Norms and the International Standardization of Statistics in Russia," (unpublished manuscript, University of Wisconsin, 2007).

36 Allina-Pisano, "Sub Rosa Resistance and the Politics of Economic Reform: Land Redistribution in Post-Soviet Ukraine," *World Politics* 56, no. 4 (July 2004): 554–81.

37 For example, Steven Levitsky and Lucan Way, "International Linkage and Democratization," *Journal of Democracy* 16, no. 3 (July 2005).

38 Ackerman, "Entretien avec Dimitri Fourman," 255.

dination among state elites. Arguments about weak state capacity suggest this is unlikely to be the case. Alternatively, state elites may face similar incentive structures across domains and thus make similar choices that lead to the production of facades, whether or not the construction of a false front is the initial intent of the state actors in question.

A more complete explanation for the appearance of Potemkin institutions across post-Soviet space may be found in the symbiosis of incentives produced in the economic context of post-socialism and state officials' use of renovated Leninist bureaucratic legacies.[39] The specific character of post-Soviet economic decline, including the collapse of transnational production networks and the introduction of International Monetary Fund (IMF) conditionality, created an environment that encouraged state elites to abuse electoral practices, stymie property rights development, and engage in a host of other strategies to limit further liberalization. At the same time, amidst the ebb of the coercive power of the state, these elites sought to establish legitimacy by convincing their publics and the outside world of the existence of new democratic, market-oriented institutions.

The Role of Economic Incentives

As recent research has shown, the simultaneous implementation of privatization and other components of economic liberalization can work against economic development.[40] When the four principal elements of structural adjustment programs—opening of national borders to free trade; lifting of price controls; enforcement of budgetary discipline; and privatization—occur at the same time, interaction effects among policies can undermine liberalization. In the case of post-Soviet states, the confluence of these policies, together with the collapse of supply chains that had stretched across Soviet republics, created short-term disincentives for business development and infrastructural decay. Such conditions empowered post-Soviet state elites, particularly those charged with economic oversight, to oppose political and economic liberalization at the local level, all the while producing a record of compliance with reform policy.

---

[39] Symbioses of local and transnational politics have been observed in other accounts of post-Sovet institutional development, notably Janine Wedel, *Collision and Collusion: The Strange Case of Western Aid to Eastern Europe* (New York: Palgrave, 1998) and Juliet Johnson, *A Fistful of Rubles: The Rise and Fall of the Russian Banking System* (Ithaca: Cornell University Press, 2000).

[40] Lawrence King, "Shock Privatization: The Effects of Rapid Large-Scale Privatization on Enterprise Restructuring," *Politics and Society* 31, no. 1 (March 2003): 3–30; Allina-Pisano, *The Post-Soviet Potemkin Village*.

How is it that such policies interacted to prevent business development? With the simultaneous removal of tariffs on imported goods and implementation of privatization policy, new and reorganized businesses are born into a hostile economic environment that can destroy even established, healthy enterprises.[41] In such an environment, businesses liberated from soft budget constraints must compete with their sometimes heavily subsidized counterparts in other countries. Further, with the influx of cheap foreign goods that follows the opening of national borders, and the temporary destabilization of prices for both industrial inputs and manufactured goods that occurs in response to the lifting of price controls, price scissors render production in some sectors of the economy unprofitable. The hyperinflation that frequently accompanies such changes contributes to a lack of predictability and transparency in business transactions involving multiple currencies—a likely situation in the wake of the collapse of empire and emergence of multiple new states. In such an environment, enterprises frequently are unable to pay workers on time, some companies become more reliant upon remaining state subsidies for survival, and individuals who might otherwise pursue private business are dissuaded by the prospect of low or negative profit margins.

The simultaneous implementation of multiple elements of structural adjustment affects not only businesses, but also individual citizens. IMF conditionality during the early 1990s required that states exercise budgetary discipline through reductions in spending rather than focusing on increasing in tax revenue. Budgetary decisions in post-Soviet states thus reflected not only balance of payments problems on the part of those governments, but also their choice of a specific strategy to address those problems. Without rapid development of private sector replacements for services formerly provided by the state, the negative effects of that choice are likely to be long lasting. Spending reductions required by this strategy typically target health care, education, public infrastructure, and scientific research. Reduction of budgetary expenditures thus leads to both infrastructural decline and lowered state capacity in the provision of public services.

In the case of administrative resource, the combination of economic constraints on business development and the decay of public infrastructure made informal political manipulation particularly effective. The successful use of administrative resource is possible where people are compelled, by force of circumstance or geography, to rely heavily upon public sector services, or where poverty creates a very slim margin within which it is rational to take economic risks. Where there are few affordable private sector alternatives, the redefinition of access to health

[41] King, "Shock Privatization"; David Stark, "Recombinant Property in East European Capitalism," *American Journal of Sociology* 101, no. 4 (1996): 993–1027.

clinics, educational services, and public transportation as a political quid pro quo is more likely to result in public compliance.[42] Furthermore, the decay of public infrastructure—with spotty delivery of services such as electricity, water, and heating outside the electoral cycle[43]—makes the threat of withholding services during elections credible. And where people live paycheck to paycheck, the threat of wage withholding is a particularly effective means of compelling people to support incumbent candidates.

Finally, in areas where domestic labor markets are underdeveloped (a condition that prevailed in the wake of the socialist collapse and is likely to accompany structural adjustment in most contexts, as domestic businesses find themselves at a short-term competitive disadvantage), voters may find themselves with few or no alternatives to working for their former employer. Many formerly socialist enterprises in post-Soviet states are societies unto themselves, and employees receive social entitlements in addition to or in lieu of wages: housing, healthcare, education for their children, discounted prices on food and consumer goods, and other services. Where such arrangements continue to exist, managers may easily make use of opportunities for political manipulation. In company towns, company paymasters may also oversee the local electoral precinct and there may be less de facto anonymity in the voting process. The same is true on former collective farms, where directors who disburse wages also oversee balloting procedures; in hospitals, where doctor-patient hierarchies create opportunities for electoral manipulation; in universities, where students live and vote in the same precinct; and in state offices. In the case of administrative resource, the combination of Soviet-era industrialization policy and the particular character of post-Soviet economic liberalization created opportunities for bureaucrats to undermine the development of electoral institutions.

Potemkin land rights likewise developed in the context of economically circumscribed autonomy for individuals. Increases in levels of household agricultural production during the 1990s belied those households' continuing reliance on former collective farms for inputs and social services.[44] Price scissors, the destruction of

---

[42] Allina-Pisano, "Informal Politics and Electoral Competition."

[43] For example, Stephen J. Collier and Lucan Way, "Beyond the Deficit Model: Social Welfare in Post-Soviet Georgia," *Post-Soviet Affairs* 20, no. 3 (2004): 258–84.

[44] Allina-Pisano, "Reorganization and its Discontents: A Case Study in Voronezh oblast'," in *Rural Reform in Post-Soviet Russia*, ed. David O'Brien and Stephen Wegren (Washington, D.C. and Baltimore: Woodrow Wilson Center Press and Johns Hopkins University Press, 2002), 298–324; Gavin Kitching, "The Revenge of the Peasant? The Collapse of Large-Scale Russian Agriculture and the Role of the Peasant 'Private Plot' in that Collapse, 1991–97," *Journal of Peasant Studies* 26, no.1 (1998): 43–81.

savings through hyperinflation and currency devaluation, lack of availability of machinery appropriate for small-scale cultivation, underdeveloped rural transportation and storage infrastructure, and a variety of other problems suppressed demand for land.[45] Suppressed demand allowed local bureaucrats to claim they had offered rural people ownership rights to land, but that those people had refused. Meanwhile, local state actors faced other incentives to preserve former collectives in their entirety, avoiding at all costs the prospect of governing a countryside populated primarily by the unemployed.[46]

The Role of Bureaucratic Resistance

If the economic policies of the early post-Soviet period generated incentives that contributed to the production of institutional facades, Potemkin politics also required the participation of state actors as agents of that process. The bureaucrats who are the proximate causal links in the chain that explains the emergence of Potemkin institutions used old tools to address new problems, mustering skills from their former socialist lives to address challenges linked to capitalism and democracy.[47] Political actors who complied with orders to produce particular electoral outcomes in the context of apparently competitive balloting, as well as local bureaucrats who privileged Soviet forms of agricultural production but reported the creation of private ownership rights, drew upon Soviet-era administrative practices in response to the incentives created in a new economic environment.

Some accounts that privilege the role of state actors attribute the nature of institutional change in Eastern Europe to direct bureaucratic legacies of the communist past.[48] However, it is important to note that it is not possible to draw a straight line from Soviet practice to the present for either of the cases considered here. Verdery observes that, "what might look like legacies are better seen as responses to quite contemporary processes."[49] Bureaucrats did not have immediate use for certain skills cultivated during the Soviet period; for both land privatization and multi-party elections, the first years of liberalization were relatively successful. Potemkin institutions developed only later, partly in response to difficult economic conditions. Only

---

[45] Allina-Pisano, *The Post-Soviet Potemkin Village.*

[46] Allina-Pisano, "Sub Rosa Resistance."

[47] Anna Grzymała-Busse, *Redeeming the Communist Past: The Regeneration of Communist Parties in East Central Europe* (Cambridge: Cambridge University Press, 2002).

[48] Kitschelt, Mansfeldova, Markowski, and Tóka, *Post-Communist Party Systems.*

[49] Verdery, *The Vanishing Hectare*, 11.

then did practical opportunities for making use of new property rights dissipate and political elites begin to resort to authoritarian tactics in conducting elections.

For example, after the fall of the Soviet Union in 1991, the largest wave of private farmers leaving collectives to start their own businesses occurred in Ukraine and in Russia within the next three years. After that brief period, it became more difficult for those who wished to leave collectives to do so—both because of greater resistance on the part of local elites and the disappearance of material support for private farms (credit at reasonable rates, subsidies for purchase of farm machinery, and so forth). Joel Hellman provides an explanation for the initial gains of economic liberalization and subsequent stagnation: early winners usurp the gains of the first rounds of reform and then stall subsequent reform.[50] However, in the case of land privatization, those who benefited during initial rounds of privatization were vocal advocates of further distribution of land.

Likewise, the first electoral cycles in some post-Soviet states included genuinely competitive, multi-party balloting. In Ukraine, where the use of administrative resource has been most widely documented, this tool of authoritarian consolidation did not emerge as a decisive instrument of electoral manipulation for close to a decade.[51] In other words, independent Ukraine experienced six years of relatively free political contestation before the Kuchma regime was able to render elections and referenda largely predictable affairs.[52] Similarly, centralization of political power and consolidation of national parties in Russia did not occur until the late 1990s.

---

[50] Hellman, "Winners Take All."

[51] See, among others, Mikhail Myagkov, Peter C. Ordeshook, and Dimitry Shakin, "Fraud or Fairytales: Russia and Ukraine's Electoral Experience," *Post-Soviet Affairs* 21, no. 2 (April–June 2005): 91–131, and Myagkov and Ordeshook, "The Trail of Votes in Ukraine's 1998, 1999, and 2002 Elections," *Post-Soviet Affairs* 21, no.1 (January 2005): 56–71.

[52] Some would say the outcome of the 2004 elections was genuinely uncertain. It was clear to many observers, however, that Viktor Yanukovych would prevail in the second round of elections through the use of administrative resource. Only Andrew Wilson predicted the massive street demonstrations that followed. Discussions at workshop "Understanding the Transformation of Ukraine: Assessing What Has Been Learned, Devising a Research Agenda," University of Ottawa, October 2004.

Potemkin Institutions and the Social Sciences

> "Fedka, why waste paper?" Andreev would say. "Why bother writing down every bit of nonsense? What does it matter who did what, who said what—can you possibly capture everything? But if you're going to write, you've got to write it *all* down, understand? It makes no sense to write down only a part, it'll even do damage, because you'll be misleading people."[53]

The failure adequately to integrate local incentives generated by economic policy choices into causal accounts for limited liberalization or the genesis of Potemkin institutions—even as international factors are so readily identified as crucial determinants of policy successes—may indicate an epistemological, as well as an analytical, problem. Critical analysis of economic reform is nearly a cottage industry in post-Soviet politics. However, such critiques center primarily on the political shortcomings of economic policy implementation from above rather than on the political consequences of those policies' short-term economic effects.[54] Here, the epistemological problem lies in the confusion of outcomes that bear a phenotypical resemblance to Soviet-era practices with a genealogical linkage to those practices: similarities between past and present do not necessarily indicate an unbroken line of continuity with the past.

An example from rural political economy illustrates this confusion. Economists have documented cases of deindustrialization and "de-development" across post-Soviet space.[55] However, some observers consistently have interpreted the existence of that poverty as an indication of cultural or political deficiency, whether that deficiency is manifest in corrupt leadership, societal resistance to capitalism, or in a recapitulation of late nineteenth-century colonial tropes, a population congenitally resistant to work.

Thus, a visitor to the Ukrainian countryside at the turn of the millennium would have been likely, in late autumn or early spring, to observe young men, long straps over their shoulders, pulling wooden ploughs through cleared fields. Such a landscape, in which agricultural machinery, irrigation systems, and other accoutrements of twentieth-century rural life are absent, could suggest deeply entrenched poverty and a "backward" population.

Only a decade earlier, however, the same fields had been worked by tractors

---

[53] Dmitry Furmanov, *Chapaev* (Moscow: Molodaia gvardiia, 1957), 34.

[54] Reddaway and Glinski, *The Tragedy of Russia's Reforms*.

[55] Mieke Meurs and Rasika Ranasinghe, "De-Development in Post-Socialism: Conceptual and Measurement Issues," *Politics and Society* 31, no. 1 (March 2003) 31–53.

and combines and watered by rolling sprinklers. The introduction of national policies of economic liberalization wreaked havoc upon agricultural production in the countryside, producing a prolonged scissors crisis in which the market prices of agricultural commodities rarely exceeded the cost of their production.[56] The elimination of price controls on industrial goods, just as post-Soviet governments threw open the doors to international trade, created an environment in which even previously healthy enterprises were unable to compete.[57] In the space of a few years, tractors and combines were used until they were beyond repair, and enterprising villagers, in the words of their bemused and irritated neighbors, "privatized" the metal that carried water to the fields and sold it for scrap.[58]

Understood in the context of the recent past, in which most post-Soviet policymakers temporarily rejected Marxist-Leninist approaches in favor of the libertarian economic theory promulgated by international lending organizations, the story of retrograde bureaucrats and backward peasants erecting obstacles to progress no longer holds. Instead, the policy choices of the years between the Soviet collapse and authoritarian retrenchment contain a key to the puzzle of post-Soviet economic outcomes. In the case of rural poverty, infrastructural decay and an economic environment hostile to business, rather than political, economic, or cultural stasis, explain the replacement of machinery by human labor. In this light, the young men tilling Ukrainian fields are not members of a timeless peasantry opposed to forces of modernization. Rather, like Benjamin's angel of history, they are accidental witnesses to progress, their wings beaten back against the wind.[59]

Such confusion may in part be a product of social scientific methods of research. Much of political science, including work in political economy, accepts as given official narratives of democratization and property rights creation, including the existence of competitive elections and "ownership societies."[60] In the case of

---

[56] There is general agreement about the effects of economic liberalization in rural Russia. See, for example, Steven K. Wegren, *Agriculture and the State in Soviet and Post-Soviet Russia* (Pittsburgh: University of Pittsburgh Press, 1998), 88.

[57] David Stark and László Bruszt, *Postsocialist Pathways: Transforming Politics and Property in East Central Europe* (Cambridge: Cambridge University Press, 1998); King, "Shock Privatization."

[58] Allina-Pisano, *The Post-Soviet Potemkin Village*; Gerald Creed, "The Politics of Agriculture: Identity and Socialist Sentiment in Bulgaria," *Slavic Review* 54, no. 4 (Winter 1995): 860; Verdery, *The Vanishing Hectare*, 293.

[59] Walter Benjamin, *Illuminations: Essays and Reflections* (New York: Schocken Books, 1968), 257–8.

[60] Hough notes that Russian reformers repeatedly referred to state weakness in order to deflect blame for policy failures. Such claims then entered the literature as neutral observation

land privatization, many political and economic analyses of property rights development rely upon the measures and laws produced by governments and organizations involved in reform. The informal mechanisms that prevent rural people from using nominal property rights do not appear in these empirical records, nor can they be discerned in the structure of parchment institutions. In the case of elections—particularly the *perevybory* (re-elections) of entrenched national executives—informal techniques of voting manipulation may not be evident on the world stage until years after their institutionalization. In the case of Ukraine, administrative resource was in use in elections by 1999, but widespread international recognition of that fact followed only upon the mass mobilization campaigns in that country of 2004.

Acceptance of formal narratives of policy outcomes, and the trail of data that they leave, can occlude our vision of the processes by which poverty and political domination are reproduced. To the extent that tools of social science research and policy assessment do not allow policymakers to discern the existence of Potemkin institutions in good time, and to the extent that local elites may have reason to trumpet their own accomplishments, early indications of superficial success may mislead.

In recent years, dominant narratives of political development in post-Soviet Russia and other post-Soviet states thus indicate a "surprising" reemergence of authoritarian rule and executive consolidation—reemergence that has subsequently been imputed in the popular Western imagination to an historical predilection for tyranny in Eurasian societies. Potemkin institutions provide shelter for such changes in their early stages of development; when a new political phenomenon finally emerges, it may be taken for something that has been there all along. Instead, however, such change may be the result of more immanent processes. Here, the language of literary accounts may best capture the phenomenon, as the local arbiters of institutional transformation are less assured, politically astute Klychkovs of Furmanov's post-revolutionary heroic landscape than surprised Petr Pustotas of Pelevin's Moscow psychiatric ward, awoken into the confusion of post-Soviet politics and compelled to make decisions in response to a strange new world.[61]

rather than as an artifact of political positioning. See Jerry F. Hough, *The Logic of Economic Reform in Russia* (Washington, D.C.: Brookings, 2001), 19.

[61] Viktor Pelevin, *Chapaev i Pustota* (Moscow: Vagrius, 1999).

Informal Networks in Postcommunist Economies

A "Topographical Map"

Alena V. Ledeneva

The postcommunist transition in Central and Eastern Europe is often associated with the Soviet legacy, informal economy, and a "captured" state—a state in which particular group interests dominate the policy-making process, when these interests in an illicit way shape the rules of the game. The state can be captured by oligarchs and predatory elites; formal institutions can be penetrated by informal networks. Assessing the role of informal, or social, networks is perhaps most difficult.

In order to answer the questions of whether the impact of social networks in postcommunist economies is diminishing, whether they are conducive to state capture, and whether the postcommunist reforms change the nature of social networks, it is essential to "locate" social networks on a "topographical map" of approaches to the study of networks, analyze the ambiguous nature of networks, define the key features of networks that are associated with the informal workings of Russian society, and assess the prospects of the instrumental use of social networks in postcommunist contexts.

Most postcommunist network studies in the 1990s have been relatively unrelated to the general field. Once the initial "one size fits all" prescriptions of Western specialists and international financial institutions failed to deliver equally positive results throughout the region,[1] some alternatives had to be found. In a way, focus on informality appeared to be a response to the difficulties of the theories of transition. In the search to find reasons why the Western model had not proven directly applicable to all the transition economies, it became apparent that Western prescriptions had not taken into account the fact that the command economy had relied heavily on complex social networks to compensate for its economic defects. My own research into *blat*, the use of personal networks for obtaining goods and services in short supply and for getting things done in Soviet Russia, has given some explanatory power.[2] In fact, it could be argued that success of transformation is in a reverse proportion to

---

This paper has appeared in *Transit Spaces: Frankfurt/Oder-Poznan, Warsaw, Brest, Minsk, Smolensk, Moscow*, ed. Regina Bittner (Berlin: Jovis, 2006). The author is grateful to the editor and Edition Bauhaus for permission to reprint the text.

[1] Joseph E. Stiglitz, *Globalization and its Discontents* (New York: W.W. Norton, 2002).

[2] Alena V. Ledeneva, *Russia's Economy of Favours: Blat, Networking and Informal Exchange* (Cambridge: Cambridge University Press, 1998).

the degree of integration with the Soviet economy. Countries and former Soviet republics that have been exposed to the Soviet regime for longer periods and in a more integrated way have been struggling through the 1990s and subject to state capture much more than those in which land was never collectivized (Poland) or where the private sector sustained itself throughout the Soviet rule (Hungary and Czechoslovakia), arguably due to a more substantial role that those informal networks and practices assumed in order to compensate for the deficiency of the planning systems. These networks had not only survived the transition, but in some cases—most notably the privatization process in Russia—had provided channels to capture the state, to substitute for the market mechanisms, and to provide for the informal economy, thereby hindering both economic and political reforms.

In turning their attention to social networks, students of postcommunist transition stepped on the ground that had already been developed in Western studies but in different contexts.[3] This created a certain gap between those in possession of the method of studying networks and those in need of understanding the ways in which networks work in the postcommunist world and their implications for the emerging markets. While scholars dealing with Western countries have developed the study of networks to the point where it is subject to fairly rigorous methodological standards—including the use of dedicated computer software—studies of networks in emerging market economies are far less structured and are predominantly based on qualitative methods. Furthermore, because studies of networks in postcommunist societies evolved spontaneously as a response to the importance of networks to almost every aspect of transition, they cover a broader spectrum of topics—from technological networks and firm networks to networks that serve large-scale corruption and those used for survival. In this article, I will consider social networks that are

[3] Studies of networks are a wide-ranging and multidisciplinary field. Its mainstream dimension, social network analysis, is grounded in a specific technique used to analyze network data. It is focused on concepts of centrality, cohesion, cores, prestige, roles, personal and occupational ties in the allocation of resources, etc. See, for example, Barry Wellman and Stephen D. Berkowitz, *Social Structures: A Network Approach* (Cambridge: Cambridge University Press, 1988). Network analysis is concerned with how to locate people in various kinds of networks, how to estimate who and what they know, the resources to which they have access, and the social constraints affecting their behavior. Network analysis uses graph theory and models such as p1 and its relatives. Software packages have been developed to analyze network data, such as UCINET and Krackplot. The field has been booming in the United States and the United Kingdom, and has achieved a high degree of formalization. See, for example, Stanley Wasserman and Katherine Faust, *Social Network Analysis: Methods and Applications* (Cambridge: Cambridge University Press, 1994). Social network analysis is also widely used in business studies and management. See, for example, Albert-Laszlo Barabasi, *Linked: The New Science of Networks* (Cambridge, MA: Perseus, 2002).

based on human interaction and penetrate every society. I will argue, however, that although the range of functions of social networks overall is fairly universal, the specific configuration of functions that networks perform in transition economies, the nature of social networks and their embeddedness in the Soviet system, can undermine the potential comparability of social networks.

The attempts to bridge the gap and to build a base for comparisons, say by introducing categories such as social capital to the research into emerging markets and democracies, have produced mixed results for reasons that will be analyzed in detail below. For example, on the basis of their data, Endre Sik and Barry Wellman argue that people in the communist countries of Central and Eastern Europe used to rely on network capital—the use of networks—more than people in developed capitalist countries, and that they do so even more in the postcommunist era.[4] The scope and role of network capital varies among societies; it is a simultaneous function of a society's culture, its past and present social organization, and the changing socioeconomic situation.[5] The *volume* of an economic actor's[6] network capital is equal to the size and number of the networks that it can mobilize in case of need. The *value* of an actor's network capital is a function of the number and availability of network members, and the resources and amount of network capital that these members themselves possess. Sik and Wellman emphasize two ways in which network capital can operate in relation to the market and the state: as a substitute or as an addition. When network capital is a substitute, it is used as an institution independent from the dominant institutions—as when people exchange among themselves the goods and services needed for survival. In every society from ancient to modern times, various forms of network capital have persisted through altruism, barter, and reciprocity.[7] Sik and Wellman describe several ways in which network capital was used as a substitute in communist countries: the reciprocal exchange of labor among workers to deal with routine problems, emergencies, and the special case of house-building, and managers' reciprocal transactions in aid of their organizations. According to them, under communism and postcommunism, network capital was and is more commonly

---

[4] Endre Sik and Barry Wellman, "Network Capital in Capitalist, Communist and Post-communist Countries," in *Networks in the Global Village*, edited by Barry Wellman (Boulder: Westview Press, 1999), 225–55.

[5] Mark Granovetter, "The Strength of Weak Ties," *American Journal of Sociology* 78 (1973): 1360–80; idem, "Economic Action and Social Structure: The Problem of Embeddedness," *American Journal of Sociology* 91, no. 3 (1985): 481–510.

[6] An economic actor could be a person, household, organization, state, etc.

[7] Karl Polanyi, *The Great Transformation* (New York: Rinehart, 1944).

an addition, operating within the framework of the state and the market.[8]

The metaphor of "capital" is useful for assessing the impact of networks at the macro level, but can be misleading at other levels of analysis. Apart from being an "addition" or "substitute," networks play a generically ambiguous role, that is, they can be associated with both positive and negative implications of social capital. To make this point clearer let us create a "topographical map" of existing perspectives on networks. Having analyzed many studies of networks, I have found a way of accommodating the existing perspectives by dissecting the basic assumptions that are implicitly or explicitly made about networks by the authors:

1) Networks are viewed as *personal*, that is, organized as a system of nodes and ties centered around a particular node (or around several nodes, as in the 1996 study of St. Petersburg teachers' personal networks for example[9]) or *impersonal*, that is, based on a de-centered organizational principle (a chain of restaurants, firms, etc.).

2) Networks are viewed *internally*, as interesting in themselves, in which case micro data on networks are collected, or *externally*, when the implications of networks for the wider context become the focus of study, in which case networks are seen as an instrument or a factor at the macro level.

The intersection of choices made about the focus of the analysis of networks provides us with four principal perspectives on networks, illustrated in the scheme in Table 1. Because social networks can be viewed from all four perspectives and because the boundaries between these perspectives are construed by the analytical focus of a given researcher, it is crucial to see both the strengths and limitations of every perspective on the "map" and the linkages between different perspectives. Let us illustrate these linkages and an ambiguous and context-bound nature of networks in the context of the (post)communist order.

[8] Sik and Wellman, "Network Capital in Capitalist, Communist and Post-communist Countries."

[9] Markku Lonkila, *Social Networks in Post-Soviet Russia: Continuity and Change in the Everyday Life of St. Petersburg Teachers* (Helsinki: Kikimora Publications, 1999). Alapuro Risto, "Categories, Networks and Civil Society: Teachers' Social Ties in St. Petersburg," *Civil Society in the European North: Concept and Context* (St. Petersburg: Center for Independent Social Research, 1996), 109–16.

Table 1. Type of Network

Focus on	*Personal (centered or multi-centered)*	*Impersonal (decentered)*
Internal constitution (Micro)	Sociability	Enabling structure
External influence (Macro)	Access to resources	Social capital

From "Sociability" to "Access to Resources"

In conventional sociological discourse, the term "network" is used to designate social ties between people and to cover "sociability" (micro, personal), that is, relationships with friends, leisure associates, and colleagues; networking can be defined as connecting nodes and building up networks. Under certain conditions, however, as used to be the case in the Soviet economy of shortage, friendship and the use of friendship become blurred. Friends (and acquaintances) were expected to provide each other with access to goods and services in short supply and help out in other ways, too. Networking acquires a connotation of the pragmatic use of networks, and the term "network," therefore, ceases to be just a basis for sociability. Along with sociability, personal networks also provide unauthorized access to institutional resources, and thereby form certain patterns of mediation between state and society, the public and the private. There is no Soviet word to denote "network" or "networking" (the technical term *seti* is now being used in academic circles in Russia), but the most related idioms—such as *blat*, "people of the circle" (*svoi liudi*), "one of us" (*svoi*), and "circles of mutual dependency" (*krugovaia poruka*)—connote the exclusive (closed) nature of networks and their calculated use. This prompts one to look into the micro dimensions of networks—the nature of ties constituting networks, their openness/closeness, norms and ideas channeled by those networks—in addition to the analysis of their functional or dysfunctional implications for the economy. In fact, it appears to be the case that the role social networks play in a wider economy has a close correlation with the nature of ties, norms, and ideas within a network.[10]

[10] For example, Li Bennich-Bjorkman illustrated the variation in state capture in the Baltic states by showing that "old" networks (anti-communist, student movements) in Estonia

The more dependent the formal economy is on personalized networks, the more instrumental the ties within social networks are and the less developed the impersonal systems of trust are.[11] In such economies the fact of belonging almost automatically provides a member of a social network with access to a whole variety of institutional resources available "for people of the circle only," while a wider social fabric is rather unwelcoming and even hostile. Needless to say, the legacy of such personal networks impedes the emergence of impersonal systems of trust and the development of a fully-fledged market economy in the post-Soviet period. This is not helped by the fact that the market economy does not work as it should for a variety of structural and macro-economic reasons, which makes the preservation of personal networks a perfectly rational economic response to a high-risk environment.

Once the sociability aspect of networks moves to the background, the instrumental use of networks comes to the fore. Wellman argues in the introduction to *Networks in the Global Village* that the use of social networks is one of the five basic means by which people and institutions acquire necessary resources—along with market exchanges, state distributions, and, to a lesser extent, self-provisioning and coercive appropriations.[12] "Just as people use their financial capital to purchase things on markets and their human capital to gain better access to markets and state distributions, they also use *network capital*, their connections with people and organizations. Such network capital can assume many forms, such as altruistic, long lasting and multipurpose relations; short-term instrumental relations; asymmetric patron-client relations; corrupt, exploitative unequal exchanges."[13] Despite the "antisocial" nature of many of these forms, Sik and Wellman's argument is that networks are an important form of social capital.

From "Access to Resources" to "Social Capital"

The analogy between networks and financial capital is taken further by those using the concept of social capital (macro, impersonal) in order to measure the effect of

---

have contributed toward the development of party politics and transparency of the economy, whereas "new" networks in Latvia have become a cause for exclusivity and corruption. See Bennich-Bjorkman, "Explaining State Capture in Estonia and Latvia: Identity, International Role Models and Political Formation," *The Baltics: Culture, Society, Politics* (forthcoming).

[11] The instrumental use of networks is usually "misrecognized" by the members. The aspect of misrecognition is not considered in this paper. For details see Ledeneva, *Russia's Economy of Favours*.

[12] Wellman, *Networks in the Global Village*, 4–12.

[13] Sik and Wellman, "Network Capital in Capitalist, Communist and Post-communist Countries."

networks on economic performance or political participation. The best known definitions of social capital are associated with the following authors:

- Bourdieu (1986): Social capital is "the aggregate of the actual or potential resources which are linked to possession of a durable network of more or less institutionalized relationships of mutual acquaintance and recognition—or in other words, to membership in a group—which provides each of its members with the backing of the collectivity-owned capital, a 'credential' which entitles them to credit, in the various senses of the word."[14]

- Coleman (1988): "Social capital is productive, making possible the achievement of certain ends that in its absence would not be possible."[15] Informal social relations can be critical in creating the potential for and conditioning the nature of social and economic activity. Coleman proposes to think of these relations as "social" capital. Social relations may have important effects on trust that may be critical to efficient exchange, important to the flow of information, and basic to the development of norms and effective social sanctioning.

- Putnam (1993): Putnam sees social capital as those "features of social organization, such as trust, norms, and networks that can improve the efficiency of society by facilitating co-ordinate actions."[16] He defined social capital as "features of social life—networks, norms, and trust—that enable participants to act together more effectively to pursue shared objectives."[17]

For Bourdieu, social capital is one of three forms of capital (economic, cultural, and social), which taken together "explain the structure and dynamics of differentiated societies."[18] Fundamental structures that produce and reproduce access

[14] Pierre Bourdieu, "The Forms of Capital," in *Handbook of Theory and Research for the Sociology of Education*, ed. John G. Richardson (New York: Greenwood Press, 1986), 248–9.

[15] James S. Coleman, "Social Capital in the Creation of Human Capital," *American Journal of Sociology* 94 (1988): S98.

[16] Robert D. Putnam, Robert Leonardi, and Raffaella Y. Nanetti, *Making Democracy Work: Civic Traditions in Modern Italy* (Princeton: Princeton University Press, 1993), 167.

[17] Robert D. Putnam, "Tuning In, Tuning Out: The Strange Disappearance of Social Capital in America," *PS* 28, no. 4 (1995): 664–5.

[18] Pierre Bourdieu and Loïc Wacquant, *An Introduction to Reflexive Sociology* (Chicago:

to social capital are *networks* of connections, which themselves are "the product of an endless effort at institution." If the ways of producing and reproducing of social capital in Bourdieu's account may appear vague, his understanding of how to measure social capital is clearer than that found in Coleman and Putnam. For Bourdieu, "the volume of the social capital possessed by a given agent ... depends on the size of the network of connections he can effectively mobilize and on the volume of the capital (economic, cultural or social) possessed in his own right by each of those to whom he is connected."[19]

Bourdieu and Coleman's conceptions of social capital emphasize the analogy with financial capital, seeing it as *instrumental* in the flow of goods and services to individuals and groups. Putnam, in contrast, has popularized a notion of social capital tied up with the production of collective goods such as "civic engagement" or a spirit of cooperation at a community or national level. For Putnam, associations, particularly those featuring face-to-face, horizontal relations among individuals, generate trust, norms of reciprocity, and a capacity for civic engagement, which are essential to the functioning of a modern democracy.[20]

Coleman's definition of social capital is somewhat problematic because social capital is defined in terms of its outcome and implies that social capital normally leads to "productive" outcomes.[21] However, Coleman himself does leave room for unproductive social capital. Regarding the productivity of social capital, he notes that a given form of social capital that is valuable in facilitating certain actions may be useless or even harmful for others.[22]

Another important difference in Coleman's and Putnam's approach towards social capital is that Coleman uses the concept of social capital as part of the theory of human action and applies it primarily at a micro level, while Putnam deploys social capital as a concept to study institutional and economic performance at regional level. Thus, the use of the concept of social capital ranges from the membership in networks and/or collectives (Bourdieu) to the macro- and regional economic

University of Chicago Press, 1992), 119.

[19] Bourdieu, "The Forms of Capital," 249.

[20] See Putnam et al., *Making Democracy Work* and Robert D. Putnam, "Bowling Alone: America's Declining Social Capital," *Journal of Democracy* 6, no. 1 (January 1995): 65–78.

[21] Anthony Bebbington and Thomas Perreault, "Social Capital, Development and Access to Resources in Highland Ecuador," *Economic Geography* 75, no. 4 (1999): 395–418; Alejandro Portes and Julia Sensenbrenner, "Embeddedness and Immigration: Notes on the Social Determinants of Economic Action," *American Journal of Sociology* 98, no. 6 (1993): 1320–50.

[22] Coleman, "Social Capital in the Creation of Human Capital," 98, 105.

approach concentrating on the relationship between economic growth, democracy, and social capital (Putnam). In the former case, relations themselves are treated as resources. In the latter case, the network location affects an individual's access to assets that are not in themselves characteristics of networks.[23] The multiple use of the concept and its context-bound nature makes the existing empirical studies of social capital incompatible in a comparative (capitalism vs. communism) or dynamic (communism vs. postcommunism) perspective. To complete the description of our range of perspectives, let us move on to consider networks as "enabling structures."

From "Social Capital" to "Enabling Structure"

Shifting our focus onto the membership in networks, we arrive at the fourth (micro, impersonal) perspective, which refers to a large number of people, groups, institutions, etc., that have a connection with each other and work together as a system.[24] It is used in relation to anything from a public telephone or television network to the supportive network of the extended family and global production networks.[25] Technically speaking, it is a system of nodes and ties representing a "web" principle of organization. Thus, Manuel Castells promotes the idea of a network society[26] based on the new technologies and communicational networks characteristic of the information age, while Dirk Messner in *The Network Society*[27] focuses on social networks and excludes electronic networks, media networks, intra-firm networks, or even production networks.[28] As emphasized by many authors, perpetuating role of networks as "enabling structures" has been particularly essential in the context of postcommunist transformation. The enabling structure of networks has not only served the purposes of interpersonal or inter-enterprise survival/success, but also buffered the

[23] Ronald S. Burt, "The Social Structure of Competition," in *Networks and Organizations, Structure, Form and Action*, ed. Nitin Nohria and Robert G. Eccles (Boston: Harvard Business School Press, 1992); Ronald S. Burt, "The Contingent Value of Social Capital," *Administrative Science Quarterly* 42 (1997): 339–65.

[24] *Collins Cobuild English Language Dictionary* (London; Glasgow: Collins, 1987), 966. See also Wellman and Berkowitz, *Social Structures: A Network Approach*.

[25] David Held, Anthony McGrew, David Goldblatt, and Jonathan Perraton, *Global Transformations: Politics, Economics and Culture* (Cambridge: Polity Press, 1999), 259–82.

[26] Manuel Castells, *The Rise of Network Society* (Oxford: Blackwell, 1996), 165.

[27] Dirk Messner, *The Network Society: Economic Development and International Competitiveness as Problems of Social Governance* (London: Frank Cass in association with the German Development Institute, Berlin, 1997).

[28] Markus Perkmann, "The Two Network Societies," *Economy and Society* 28, no. 4 (1999): 620.

uncertainty of the postcommunist transformation. As David Stark and Balazs Vedrez put it, network ties are a "resource both for navigating the uncertainties of postsocialism and for managing the new uncertainties of internationalization of the economy."[29] In their original sequence analysis of network formation, they provide substantial evidence that foreign investment and network evolution in Hungary are intertwined processes. In their capacity as "enabling structures," networks represent a third dimension to the existing dichotomy of the vertical (hierarchies) and the horizontal (markets) ones. Networks are neither vertical nor horizontal; their enabling quality resides in their ambiguity and their "navigational" (between vertical and horizontal) capacity. Their logic is both to compensate for the defects of vertical and horizontal structures, and to turn these defects into advantage of network members.

To reiterate the points in Table 1:

- Because networks stretch across all dimensions indicated in the table—networks serve both access and sociability, provide both a structure and its outcome (capital)—with insufficiently identifiable boundaries between these functions, they are inherently ambiguous in their impact on both micro and macro structures;

- Networks constitute a social form that cuts across conventional micro-macro divisions and personal-impersonal dimensions;

- The generic functions of networks coincide with all four perspectives on networks, "sociability," "access," "enabling structure," and "social capital," each of which can have both positive and negative implications.

Let us formulate the positive implications of the functioning of networks:

1. *Safety net (sociability).* Social networks are conducive to human cooperation and mutual help, providing sociability, emotional support, and assistance for routine domestic needs and health care.

2. *Survival kit at the micro-level (access).* Social networks constitute a basis for survival strategies. Cooperation is a way to cope when facing hardships. It is

[29] David Stark and Balazs Vedrez, "The Social Times of Networks Spaces: Sequence Analysis of Network Formation and Foreign Investment" (paper presented at the workshop on "Networks and Markets," Santa Fe Institute, May 2003), 4.

less costly, more effective, and more easily accessible than any other alternative, such as market purchases or acquiring state redistributions.[30]

3. *Beating the system (enabling structure)*. Networks can be used as a means to avoid competition or to increase one's chances in it. Investing into and maintaining networks of partners represent a routine business strategy. For example, there are personal networks between buyers and sellers in local markets,[31] and business executives often make personal deals to avoid the rigidities of contracts.[32]

4. *Compensatory effect (social capital)*. Social networks compensate for the defects in formal systems, say in a high-risk environment or where impersonal systems of trust are not working as they should. By providing what formal systems cannot, networks not only enable their members to operate, but also contribute to their own reproduction.

In practice, social networks are operational both in the "access" mode (thus channeling the network/social capital to the macro-level in order to maintain existing formal institutions) and in the "sociability" mode (by servicing the social relationships at the micro-level that constitute networks); social networks are both a structure and its outcome. The ambiguous nature of networks, however, results in the fact that the "positive" implications of networks associated with access—flexibility, psychological support, reduced risks and transaction costs—may at the same time have "negative" implications for the economy, for the networks themselves, and for the individual members.[33] Woolcock finds that "high levels of social capital can

---

[30] Karl Polanyi, "The Economy as Instituted Process," in *Trade and Market in the Early Empires: Economies in History and Theory*, ed. Polanyi, Conrad M. Arensberg, and Harry W. Pearson (Glencoe: Free Press 1957), 243–70; Barry Wellman and Scot Wortley, "Different Strokes from Different Folks: Community Ties and Social Support," *American Journal of Sociology* 96 (1990): 558–88.

[31] See Stuart Plattner, "Economic Behaviour in Markets," in *Economic Anthropology*, ed. idem (Stanford: Stanford University Press, 1989), 210–21; Harrison White, *Identity and Control* (Princeton: Princeton University Press, 1992).

[32] See Stewart Macaulay, "Non-Contractual Relations in Business: A Preliminary Study," in *The Sociology of Economic Life*, ed. Mark Granovetta and Richard Swedberg (Boulder: Westview Press, 1992), 265–83; Ronald S. Burt, *Structural Holes: The Social Structure of Competition* (Chicago: University of Chicago Press, 1992).

[33] The "positive" and "negative" implications are referred to in quotation marks because their evaluation depends on whether the interests of networks are consistent with the interests

be … "negative" in that it also places high particularistic demands on group members, thereby restricting individual expression and advancement, permits free riding on community resources; and negates, in those groups with a long history of marginalization through coercive non-market mechanisms the belief in the possibility of advancement through individual effort."[34] At the macro level, the predominance of networks does not necessarily improve or inhibit economic growth, as the contrast between recent developments in China and Russia illustrates. The impact of networks depends on their inner structure and its projection onto the economy.[35]

Similar ambivalence is characteristic of the role of informal networks in the Soviet system. Many scholars ranging from Merle Fainsod to J. Arch Getty viewed the significance of informal networks in the Soviet economy primarily as a hindrance to efficient governance.[36] Others, building on the work of T. H. Rigby and Graeme Gill, viewed personal networks as central to the workings of the system.[37] It seems essential to reveal both the functional and subversive roles of informal networks in the formal economy. On the one hand, personal networks became embedded in the institutional order to such an extent that agents stopped reflecting upon them, which in turn made them an integral part in the functioning of the economy. On the other hand, they also subverted the economy, especially its ideological and moral founda-

---

of the economy and on the concrete perspective from which the assessment is made. For example, limits that the group or community put on individuality cannot be seen as outright negative. Studies of stress levels indicate that stress is much higher in so-called "atomized" societies than in network-based societies where individuals might be subject to certain restrictions imposed by networks.

[34] Michael Woolcock, "Social Capital and Economic Development: Toward a Theoretical Synthesis and Policy Framework," *Theory and Society* 27 (1998): 165.

[35] The genesis and the functions of networks are somewhat reflected in the nature of the structure (nodes, ties, and the "maintenance cost" of the network) that should be explicated. For example, whether one inherits or invests into a self-made network will define the nature of the ties and nodes and the functions of this network. Whether business is the result of an existing network or a network is the outcome of business is not perhaps the most important question. It's much more crucial to see the dynamic process in which social relationships facilitate or impede the development of market institutions.

[36] Merle Fainsod, *How Russia is Ruled* (Cambridge, MA: Harvard University Press, 1963); J. Arch Getty, *Origins of the Great Purge: The Soviet Communist Party Reconsidered, 1933–1938* (New York: Cambridge University Press, 1986).

[37] T.H. Rigby, "Early Provincial Cliques and the Rise of Stalin," *Soviet Studies* 33, no. 1 (January 1981); idem, "Was Stalin a Disloyal Patron?" *Soviet Studies* 38, no. 3 (July 1986); Graeme Gill, *The Origins of the Stalinist Political System* (New York: Cambridge University Press, 1990); Gerald M. Easter, *Reconstructing the State: Personal Networks and Elite Identity in Soviet Russia* (Cambridge: Cambridge University Press, 1999).

tions. In other words, there is no linearity in the relationship between networks and functioning of the economy: any universal formula like "the more networks, the better" is unlikely to work. The reason for this is the ambiguous nature of networks, as there seems to be a reverse side to each of their "positive" implications. Let us now consider the "negative" implications of networks in more detail:

1. *High cost of implicit contract (the reverse side of sociability).* Even if one "inherits" a network, rather than builds one's own, the network does require maintenance and investment. Maintaining social ties (satisfying reciprocal demands and thus reproducing trust) generates cost. In other words, belonging to the network creates obligations towards the other members of the network, or implicit contract. Therefore, whatever advantages one receives from being embedded in a network (incurring fewer transaction costs) is counterbalanced by the obligations of the implicit contract.[38] These obligations, imposed by the relationships of trust and reciprocity, may force one to over-exploitation of one's resources (or access to resources) by other members of his network, which in turn can lead to a *free-riding problem.*

2. *Limits to individual action (the reverse side of access).* Membership in a closed social network (with consequent sanctions to enforce the implicit contract) can subject members to restrictive social regulations and limit their individual action. All kind of leveling pressures keep members in the same situation as their peers[39] and strong collective norms in communities may restrict the scope of individuals.[40] Noncompliance with the demands of membership can also result in a loss of reputation as a reliable member of the network.

3. *Lock-in effects (the reverse side of enabling structure).* It should be noted that a negative impact is strongly enhanced within closed networks. It is the belonging to the closed networks, rather than networks in general, that reduces adaptive capacity and carries the dangers of lock-in effects. These lock-in effects

[38] In Bourdieu's terms, such implicit contract consists of "institutional rites" and gift giving that transform "contingent relations, such as those of neighborhood, the workplace, or even kinship, into relationships that are at once necessary and elective, implying durable obligations subjectively felt." Bourdieu, "The Forms of Capital," 249–50; emphasis added.

[39] See Alena Ledeneva, "The Genealogy of *Krugovaya Poruka*: Forced Trust as a Feature of Russian Political Culture," in *Trust and Democratic Transition in Post-Communist Europe*, ed. Ivana Markova (Oxford University Press, 2004), 85–108.

[40] Portes and Sensenbrenner, "Embeddedness and Immigration."

may be strengthened by processes of cognitive dissonance in tight groups.[41] Individuals who make up a dense network tend to develop a commitment to one another and to their group. Information that disturbs the consensus of the group's perception of reality is likely to be rejected. Belonging to a network seems to yield positive results up to a certain threshold. Hence, the positive effects of being a member of a network are the same mechanisms that cause negative effects. The same processes of lock-in are found at the level of sectors, localities, and regions. Part of the especial problem encountered by de-industrialized regions is that they are locked-in to institutional structures that were relevant to an earlier phase of successful economic development, but which now constitute a barrier to moving onto a new path of development.[42]

4. *The reverse side of social capital.* The adaptive ability seemingly intrinsic in network structures can be, however, reduced as a result of path-dependency effects.[43] Portes and Landolt suggest that the assumption that social capital is only positive is wrong and that there are also negative sides to social capital.[44] Portes and Sensenbrenner further argue that "it is important not to lose sight of the fact that the same social mechanisms that give rise to appropriable resources for individual use can also constrain action or even derail it from its original goals."[45] In other words, networks not only organize and facilitate, they also divert and misappropriate the structures organizing the economy's dominant functions and processes. For example, networks that have been used as a resource, say, in starting up businesses (studies of social capital emphasize

[41] Eva M. Meyerson, "Human Capital, Social Capital and Compensation: The Relative Contribution of Social Contacts to Managers' Incomes," *Acta Sociologica* 37, no. 4 (1994): 383–99.

[42] In a study on the banking sector, Uzzi found that firms were more likely to get loans and receive lower interest rates on loans if their network of bank ties had a mix of embedded ties and arm's-length ties. Brian Uzzi, "Embeddedness in the Making of Financial Capital: How Social Relations and Networks Benefit Firms Seeking Financing," *American Sociological Review* 64, no. 4 (1999): 481–505.

[43] David Stark and Laszlo Bruszt, *Postsocialist Pathways: Transforming Politics and Property in East Central Europe* (Cambridge: Cambridge University Press, 1998), 7–8, 82–3; idem, "One Way or Multiple Paths?: For a Comparative Sociology of European Capitalism," *American Journal of Sociology* 106, no. 4 (January 2001).

[44] Alejandro Portes and Patricia Landolt, "The Downside of Social Capital," *The American Prospect*, issue 26, May 1996, 18–21.

[45] Portes and Sensenbrenner, "Embeddedness and Immigration," 1338.

> this aspect of networks) can later become a serious obstacle for the further development of the business environment (skills of maintaining networks might not fit the context of competition, transparency, and market values). Finally, negative externalities from intense group membership result from the effects described by Olson.[46] When groups become too large and powerful, rent-seeking behavior and lobbying costs influence economic development negatively. However, Knack and Keefer do not find empirical proof for this postulated negative relationship of Olson. [47] It might be the case that both "too little" and "too much" social capital can impede economic performance, which suggests that social capital should be optimized and not maximized, and a careful analysis of the nature of social networks and their functions should be made.

In other words, because networks can work both for and against state and market institutions, the volume of network capital is not necessarily an "addition" to the economy, especially when networks are conducive to corruption.

Let us take the example of social networks that are associated with the informal workings of the economy. By serving the "economy of favors," social networks have a considerable bearing on the nature of both personal relations and institutions. Personal relationships become "colonized" and used for matters going far beyond sociability, while formal institutions get "informalized," which results in "privatizing" the Soviet state, as Vladimir Shlapentokh put it,[48] or in the post-Soviet "state capture," using the terminology of the World Bank. There is literature on the sociology of organizations that looks into the impact of personal networks on organizations. What is less explored is the impact of the instrumentality of social networks on their nature and on the ideas and values channeled through them.

The exploitative use of social networks as well as the exploitative use of state or institutional resources is the basis of the economy of favors. Certain specific features by which such networks can be identified are as follows.

They are quite literally "in-formal," that is they operate on the basis of personal relationships but intertwine with the formal institutions (say, if a friend is also a colleague, a boss, or a functionary in charge of distribution of a resource). In framing these networks, I follow the logic of Endre Sik and Pal Peter Toth's concept of

[46] Mancur Olson, *The Rise and Decline of Nations* (New Haven: Yale University Press, 1982).

[47] Stephen Knack and Philip Keefer, "Does Social Capital Have an Economic Pay-off? A Cross Country Investigation," *Quarterly Journal of Economics* 112, no. 4 (1997): 1251–88.

[48] Vladimir Shlapentokh, *Public and Private Life of the Soviet People. Changing Values in Post-Stalin Russia* (New York: Oxford University Press, 1989).

the "hidden economy" and *Eurostat* classifications, which do not take account of housework, do-it-yourself activities, social work, the exchange of produce between households, crime or activities that count as productive but are not legal (for example, the production of drugs and the trade in them). Under the category of "hidden," Sik and Toth list the unreported activities of registered enterprises and the activities of enterprises that, although not registered, conduct otherwise legal activities.[49] Following this logic, networks that serve the economy of favors are constituted by channels either penetrating or residing within formal structures. I thus exclude personal networks that serve domestic and do-it-yourself exchanges, and focus on favors that are given at the expense of institutional resources. These are so-called "favors of access" that serve to channel institutional resources into private pockets, thus constituting a parallel currency in an economy where money previously played only a limited role. Values and ideas channeled through these networks are associated with mutual help, beating the system, cooperation on a micro level to compensate for the unfairness or harshness of the macro order, or notions of entitlement. In a Soviet context, all these features are rooted in mutual parasitism between the state and the population: parasitism towards state resources on the part of the population and traditionally exploitative attitudes of the state towards its population. In the post-Soviet "piratization"[50] of Russia, informal networks served the constituencies of grand corruption at the top involved in insider dealings for the benefit of cliques, clans, or oligarchic groups.

The change of context during the postcommunist reforms in Eastern Europe, Russia, or post-Mao China and the subsequent change of role that informal networks play in an economy can be referred to as the "dynamic puzzle,"[51] that is, the question of whether certain forms of social capital can be thought of as universally desirable regardless of historical context (For example, does the evolution from industrial to

[49] Endre Sik and Istvan Janos Toth, "Some Elements of the Hidden Economy in Hungary Today," in *Social Report 1998*, ed. Tamas Kolosi, Istvan Gyorgy Toth, and Gyorgy Vukovich (Budapest: Tarki, 1999), 100. See also Endre Sik, "Network Capital in Capitalist, Communist and Post-Communist Societies," *International Contributions to Labor Studies*, 1994, no. 4: 73–93.

[50] Marshall I. Goldman, *The Piratization of Russia: Russian Reform Goes Awry* (New York: Routledge, 2003).

[51] Fedderke and colleagues address three puzzles associated with the concept of social capital. First, they pose the question whether more social capital is always better for purposes of economic growth (non-linearity issue), whether over time economic development may bring the need for different forms of social capital (dynamic puzzle), and whether any society at a given point in time is likely to be characterized by rival, competing forms of social capital, and that it matters which comes to predominate (local optima puzzle). Johannes Fedderke, Raphael De Kadt, and John Luiz, "Economic Growth and Social Capital: A Critical Reflection," *Theory and Society* 28, issue 5 (1999): 709–45.

post-industrial economic activity lead to a change in the form of social capital?). The literature on postcommunist transition seems to indicate also that the value of networks is not universal: in one political and economic framework they might play one role, but once that framework changes, networks adapt and may function in different ways. One of the most conspicuous outcomes of the postcommunist transformation in Russia is the spread of corruption that to some extent grew out of and was enhanced by the "monetarization" or instrumental use of those network channels that already existed. In the economy where money did not play a role, informal exchanges were largely non-monetary, involved humanizing relationship, and were more available to poor people. Once the informal exchanges within networks serving the economy of favors became monetarized, the following tendencies were noticed:

- Humanizing relationship gave place to calculation of time and cost (*sociability*);
- Networks used for obtaining items of personal consumption became used for "making money" (*access*);
- Networks became less available to the poor and appropriated by the rich and powerful (As people say, the society in which one was connected at the bottom and lonely at the top has changed into the one in which one is lonely at the bottom and connected at the top. In Bourdieu's terms, *social capital* has become less accessible, but its volume has increased dramatically.);
- Networks became more "closed," turning into clubs and circles[52] (*enabling structures*).

The latter point is important. In fact, it can be argued that although there might not be any linear correlation between types of social capital and economic and political development, the implications of networks do depend on their inner structure (open or closed), on the ideas and values they channel, and on the practices they organize. Below I illustrate this point by outlining the generic features of networks that serve the economy of favors, relying on my own research,[53] in contrast to the features of

[52] Clubs and circles may in turn transform into ambitious cliques thus creating "parallel power systems." Janine R. Wedel, *Collision and Collusion: The Strange Case of Western Aid to Eastern Europe 1989–1998* (New York: St. Martin's Press, 1998).

[53] My research was prompted by the question "What kind of networks existed under the Soviet regime and do they continue to exist?" See Ledeneva, *Russia's Economy of Favours*.

networks characteristic in the network society, as suggested by Manuel Castells.[54] These are the ideal types that can be used for assessing the role of networks in Soviet times, their transformation in the post-Soviet Russia, and prospects for change.

It follows from the evidence provided by Castells and Kiselyova that some features of the network society model are already visible in Russia.[55] My own views on the possibilities of a smooth transition in Russia to a network society are rather pessimistic. There is evidence that even emerging networks of a "network society" type still have the features of Soviet informal networks.[56] For a fully-fledged market and democracy to emerge, networks will have to cease being exploitative of friendships and of institutional resources—features that have been described as somewhat inherent to the Russian character.[57] So far this has not been the case. Social networks have become linkages between Soviet and post-Soviet society, and have been held responsible not only for their "safety net," "survival kit," "enabling," and "compensatory" functions, but also for their aggressive and instrumental use in barter and the shadow economy, arrears and tax games, corrupt exchanges, and criminalized contexts. These have had important implications for the state, market, and civil society during the "formative" period. To sum up:

- Networks have been conducive to state capture and corruption. The organized groups that breached the state monopoly of legitimate violence and took over the function of conflict-*resolution* and law and contract enforcement in the private sector of the economy used a ramified network of informal control and forced sanctions (gangs, private protection firms, etc).[58] They also offered, among other things, services of "solving problems" through informal channels in local and regional authorities, tax inspection offices, and the state coercive institutions.

---

[54] Manuel Castells, *The Rise of Network Society* (Oxford: Blackwell, 1996).

[55] Manuel Castells and Emma Kizelyova, "Russia and the Network Society: An Analytical Exploration" (paper prepared for the conference on "Russia at the End of the 20th Century," School of Humanities and Sciences, Stanford University, November 5–7, 1998), available at http://www.stanford.edu/group/Russia20/volumepdf/castells.pdf (accessed September 27, 2007).

[56] See Li Bennich-Bjorkman's research of the networks of political elite in Latvia in "Explaining State Capture in Estonia and Latvia."

[57] Kseniya Kasianova, *O Russkom natsional'nom kharaktere* (Moscow: Institut Natsional'nykh Modelei Ekonomiki, 1994).

[58] See Vadim Volkov, *Violent Entrepreneurship* (Ithaca: Cornell University Press, 2002).

Table 2

Networks in the Economy of Favors	Networks in the Network Society
Existing structures grounded in the past	Emerging structures permeating all societies
Networks account for anti-modern nature of institutions	Networks are the institutions of the information age, enabling and innovative
Socio-political basis: statism	Socio-political basis: global capitalism
Networks are exploitative of the state, parasitic on state property	Networks transcend all states
Networks are personalized, based on a priori existing social contacts	Networks (both technological and social) are of an impersonal nature
Networks of "*svoi liudi*" bound by mutual obligations and closed to outsiders	Networks imply openness, dynamism and flexibility for individuals, firms and countries
Discipline imposed by ethics, etiquette, and unwritten rules	Discipline imposed by global financial markets, military technology, control of knowledge
Unwritten rules are followed more than laws	The only rule is that there are no rules—laws are enforced with difficulty by global and national institutions
Ambivalent relationship between networks and the socio-economic order: networks are both functional and subversive	Networks generate a new order (assumes decline of the state)
Fragmentation of the state, with state institutions being "colonized" by antagonistic networks	The new state will be a decentralized network state (devolution of power and resources to regions, local governments and NGOs, initiated by the state)
Indicators of economy of favors: diversion in workings of formal institutions (ineffectiveness of the rule of law, oversized informal economy, spread of corruption and customary practices)	Indicators of network society: number of communication devices (telephone lines, TV, PCs, Internet hosts, etc.)

- Networks have undermined the free-market principles of profitability and open competition. The "favors of access" given to "people of the circle" are likely to account for the super-profits made on the Russian market, for the 1995 loans-for-shares auctions, GKO-pyramids, and the notorious role of "authorized" banks in covering state budget deficits before the 1998, as well as for large-scale corruption.[59] The anti-bankruptcy alliances between industrial firms and local authorities, the spread of financial scheming, complex ownership schemes and so-called "authorized" business structures, among others, all indicate the crucial role of informal networks in the Russian "market."[60]

- Networks of mutual help and informal exchange—developed under the Soviet regime outside the state and the market domain—did not contribute, as some would perhaps expect, towards the constitution of civil society because of the exploitative nature of informal associations and the parasitic use of state and non-state resources.[61]

These tendencies illustrate the closed nature of networks in Russia in the 1990s as well as all four types of negative implications that networks can have. Moreover, Sik and Wellman argue that the need to use networks to compensate for the permeability, fluidity, and uncertainty of postcommunism have fostered even greater reliance on networks. The implications of closed networks in postcommunist contexts need to be explored further and related to the findings of network studies elsewhere.

To sum up the discussion of the closed networks serving the economy of favors, the following hypotheses can be formulated for further consideration:

---

[59] See Heiko Pleines, "Large-Scale Corruption in the Russian Banking Sector" and other articles in *Economic Crime in Russia*, ed. Alena Ledeneva and Marina Kurkchiyan (The Hague: Kluwer Law International, 2000).

[60] Woolcock uses the term amoral familism to describe the presence of social integration within a group but no linkages outside this group. In his view, amoral familism undermines the efficiency of all forms of economic exchange by increasing transaction costs. On the other hand there is amoral individualism. In this case there is no familial or generalized trust at all and only narrow self-interested individuals exist. Individuals are not embedded in a cohesive social network. See his "Social Capital and Economic Development." The term first used in Edward Banfield, *Moral Basis of a Backward Society* (Chicago: The Free Press, 1958).

[61] See Alena Ledeneva, "Informal Networks and Civil Society in Post-Soviet Society," special issue on civil society, *Pro et Contra*, Fall 1997.

- As follows from Table 2, "closed" networks are essentially different from the networks characteristic for the "network society";

- "Closed" networks have proved sustainable in a postcommunist context, and the World Bank survey on state capture indicates that only a limited constituency for "opening up" exists in Russia;[62]

- There are vested interests in sustaining the influence of personalized and closed networks in Russia and consequently the resistance towards Russia's integration into the international community. In Russia's political climate, the closed nature of networks impedes internationalization and substantial change. Rather, by reproducing themselves (and their links to the state system that originally empowered them) these networks adapt, reinvent, and reinforce the forms of their integration into the political and economic system. It is these forms that are essential to grasp in order to understand, for example, how *guanxi* and *blat* networks, which, on the surface of things, were similarly integrated into the state centralized systems in China and Russia, now generate *guanxi* capitalism and use the networks' capacity to back up the state-driven reform in one case and undermine state capacity in the other.

[62] See the types of firms in the survey by Joel Hellman, Geraint Jones, Daniel Kaufmann, and Mark Shankerman, *Measuring Governance, Corruption, and State Capture*, The World Bank Policy Research Working Paper, April 2000.

Administrative Styles in Soviet History
The Development of Patrimonial Rationality

Peter H. Solomon, Jr.

Students of post-Soviet legal transition are increasingly aware that the development of legal order in countries like Russia requires more than better laws and legal institutions. A *rechtsstaat*, not to speak of rule of law, calls for fundamental changes as well in the role of laws and law in governance itself. For one thing, Russia needs to allocate prerogatives to different levels of government and agencies within them, rather than merely assigning functions in a loose way, if only to supply a basis for accountability. For another, law must come to play a fundamental role in public administration, such that officials come by and large to serve the public interest through the application of impersonal legal rules, rather than private interests through decisions based upon network relations. The leadership of Russia in 2007 is still facing these challenges, and partial responses to both are on the political agenda. But arguably, these are problems that require more than legislation on intergovernmental relations and civil service reform can accomplish.

In other places I have explored variations in Soviet-style bureaucracy within the socialist world and the extent to which public administration in post-Soviet Russia has met the standards of a law-based state.[1] In this chapter I explore the evolution of styles of public administration through the course of Soviet history, in order to establish the legacy of Soviet bureaucracy for the creation of post-Soviet variant(s). I will start by considering different approaches to understanding public administration, in search of useful concepts and insights into administrative change.

Styles of Administration

Observers of Russia in the new millennium see a lot of corruption, and may well conclude that for various reasons (weakness of the state, the recent privatization process) government in Russia today is more corrupt than it was under Brezhnev.[2] This

---

[1] Peter H. Solomon, Jr., "Socialist Bureaucracy and the Law-Based State," in *Forging a Common Legal Destiny: Liber Amicorum Honour of William E. Butler*, ed. Alex Kolodkin (London: Wilde, Simmonds and Hill, 2005), 347–54; Solomon, "Law in Public Administration: How Russia Differs?" *Journal of Communist Studies and Transition Politics* (forthcoming in 2008).

[2] Leslie Holmes, *Rotten States: Corruption, Post-communism and Neoliberalism* (Durham: Duke University Press, 2006).

observation may well be true, but it relies on discourse that often proves counterproductive. In stigmatizing conduct of officials as "corrupt," the observer is applying a standard of law or analysis (usually the Weberian ideal type) that is not shared by the people who are being studied. Ethnocentrism aside, the struggle against corruption focuses attention on law enforcement and manipulation of incentives on a small scale, and fails to bring to light the deeper, systemic nature of the behavior.[3]

There is an alternative way of understanding the conduct of officials who favor friends, acquaintances, and benefactors, and that is to see this conduct as the reflection of patterns of social relations of longer standing in the history of mankind than modern bureaucracy, namely clientelist relations or, in the context of government, a patrimonial form of administration. Patrimonialism is the term used by Max Weber to describe an ideal type of administration to be counterposed to the legal rationality of the modern state. Patrimonialism is characterized by a set of relationships based upon personal ties and loyalties, especially between patrons and clients, and the patrimonial state as a household with no clear separation of the public and the private.

The real worlds of bureaucracy in twentieth-century states usually embraced characteristics of both legal rationality and (neo)patrimonialism, and in many different blends, but only recently have scholars begun adding to the conceptual repertoire by postulating a spectral typology. An insightful instance comes in a recent essay by Vadim Volkov, in which the author proposes as a middle construct that he calls "patrimonial rationality." This particular blend seems to emerge when the bureaucratic rationalist ideal is imposed (from above, and even from the outside) onto a preexisting patrimonial structure. The result is that traditional administrative practices are redefined as "corrupt," but they continue to exist, even predominant, along with elements of the new ideal. Or, as Volkov writes, "if bureaucratic rationality consists in the conversion of any concrete action … into an impersonal rule-governed operation, a place should be reserved for the reserve procedure. Patrimonial rationality … is the subjection of formal rules to personal discretion." In other words, the conflict between traditional practices and an alternative normative framework can be

[3] See for example, *No Longer Business as Usual: Fighting Bribery and Corruption* (Paris: OECD, 2000); *Monitoring the EU Accession Process: Corruption and Anti-corruption Policy*_(Budapest: Open Society Institute, 2002); Rasma Karklins, "Typology of Post-Communist Corruption," *Problems of Post-Communism*, July–August 2002, 22–32; Karklins, *The System Made Me Do It: Corruption in Post-Communist Societies* (Armonk: M.E. Sharpe, 2005); and for a good sampling of the debate in Russia the four issues of the journal *Chistye ruki*, 1999–2000. For sophisticated dissection of corruption in contemporary Russia see Fond INDEM, *Diagnostika Rossiiskoi korruptsii: Sotsiologicheskii analiz* (Moscow, 2002), and Igor' Kliamkin and Lev Timofeev, *Tenevaia Rossiia: ekonomiko-sotsiologicheskoe issledovanie* (Moscow: RGGU, 2000).

resolved in more than one way.[4] A Ukrainian sociologist Aleksander Fisun contends that underlying the formal institutions of contemporary government constructed in post-Soviet states lies a patrimonial system dominated by patron-client relations. He proposes distinguishing among types of neopatrimonial systems—sultanistic, oligarchic, and bureaucratic—depending upon who holds power.[5]

The idea of mixed, or hybrid, systems of administration strikes me as useful for the analysis of Russian history, especially in its Soviet phase. I will take as my starting point the proposition that the Soviet Union at all times had a hybrid system, and one that often resembled of "patrimonial rationality," but that the balance of its ingredients (and its bias) changed over the course of Soviet history. Ironically, while the Stalin revolution may have produced an increase in centralization and elements of formal rationality such as hierarchy, it also led to an increasing reliance upon networks and patron-client relations. And the post-Stalin years tipped the balance further in favour of patrimonial elements, at least in some sectors of administration.

To begin, some cautionary notes. First, my pursuit of these arguments should be taken as conjecture, or a set of hypotheses that, if promising, may suggest questions for research. Secondly, in speculating about these matters, I draw on the existing stock of scholarly knowledge, which privileges the top and the bottom of the administrative hierarchy and largely omits the crucial middle layers. Finally, I have decided to focus upon two variables—the prevalence and importance of personal ties for officials, and their relationship to laws and other legal rules. These might even be seen as two sides of the same coin, but they represent the crucial behavioral variables that define modern bureaucracy. In my understanding, the Weberian ideal has a number of attributes: hierarchy, rational division of labor, systems of discipline, merit based recruitment, and stable career paths—some of which are easy to develop (because they do not threaten the interests of rulers or elites), others of which, such as merit based recruitment and stable career paths, are more problematic and came about in Western history only in peculiar circumstances.[6] These attributes

[4] Vadim Volkov, "Patrimonialism versus Rational Bureaucracy: On the Historical Relativity of Corruption," in *Bribery and Blat in Russia: Negotiating Reciprocity from the Middle Ages to the 1990s*, ed. Stephen Lovell et al. (London: Macmillan, 2000), 35–47. On clientelism in general see S.N. Eisenstadt and L. Roniger, *Patrons, Clients and Friends: Interpersonal Relations and the Structure of Trust in Society* (Cambridge: Cambridge University Press, 1984).

[5] Aleksandr Fisun, "Politiko-rezhimnaia transformatsiia Ukrainy: Dilemmy neopatrimonalnogo razvitiia," in *Politichnii rozvitok Ukraini na suchasnomu etapi* (Kyiv: Stilos, 2002), 4–14.

[6] Bernard S. Silberman, *Cages of Reason: The Rise of the Rational State in France, Japan, the United States, and Great Britain* (Chicago: University of Chicago Press, 1993).

are supposed to lead to the conduct of officials that lies at the core of the Weberian ideal—efficiency, an ethos of service to society, and, most difficult of all, the application of impersonal rules deriving from law (and not simply from the ruler or the bureaucracy itself). But the connection of the attributes to the desired conduct is by no means automatic or direct.

Clientelism and Law in Russian and Soviet Administration

On the eve of the First World War, government in Tsarist Russia had a decidedly mixed character. The ministries in St. Petersburg were staffed by officials making careers (from middle and upper class backgrounds) and with defined specializations, though usually lacking security, since offending the Tsar could lead to termination. While some ministries (like Finance) had become rule governed, others (like Internal Affairs) remained politicized and their officials exercised inordinate discretion, especially in the localities where rules from the center mattered little.[7] Most central ministries were struggling to extend their influence into the towns and villages. To Yaney, the period 1906–30 was marked by the campaign by central officials to penetrate and tame rural administration, which was still operating to a considerable extent "as a family." Of course, the importance of laws was also limited by the priority given to the Tsar's decrees. In fact, both the decrees of the Tsar and the instructions of powerful ministries like Internal Affairs and Finance often took precedence over laws, rendering Russia at best "*reglamentstaat*" rather than a *rechtsstaat*.[8]

During the 1920s, the Bolsheviks intensified the struggle to subordinate regional and local government operations to central direction, but their commitment to staffing government with members of the toiling classes ("our people") led to massive patronage operations in provincial and district centers, focused upon the party apparatus. For the more important positions in government (line posts, as well as positions in the party apparatus), they developed the system of nomenklatura, above all to ensure that key posts were held by persons approved at higher levels in the political structure.[9] But the nomenklatura operations proved insufficient to impede the

---

[7] Dominic Lieven, *Russia's Rulers under the Old Regime* (New Haven: Yale University Press, 1989), chapter 9; Daniel Orlovsky, "Recent Studies on the Russian Bureaucracy," *Russian Review* 35, no. 4 (October 1976): 448–67; Geoffrey Hosking, "Patronage and the Russian State," *Slavonic and East European Review* 78, no. 2 (April 2000): 301–20.

[8] George Yaney, *The Systematization of Russian Government: Social Evolution in the Domestic Administration of Imperial Russia, 1711–1905* (Chicago: University of Illinois Press, 1973); Marc Raeff, "The Bureaucratic Phenomena of Imperial Russia, 1700–1905," *The American Historical Review* 84, no. 2 (April 1979): 399–411.

[9] T.H. Rigby, *Communist Party Membership in the USSR, 1917–1967* (Princeton: Princeton

spread of networks of politicians and officials at the provincial and local levels that took advantage of opportunities for enrichment (as the Smolensk scandal of 1928 demonstrated). And the system of nomenklatura itself encouraged vertically based clans, with serious career advancement often aided by ties to a political patron.[10] Needless to say, Soviet history in the Stalin years would provide more than the usual opportunities for both horizontal and vertical personal networks to influence staffing of government and bureaucratic careers. The huge expansion in governmental positions in the early 1930s, followed by the effects of purge and war, resulted in high levels of mobility and assured that personal networks mattered in the formation of the Soviet state.[11]

During the New Economic Policy (NEP), laws and legal enactments of the Sovnarkom (Council of People's Commissariats) were produced in large quantity, changed regularly, and usually published. Many of the commissariats in Moscow also published their regulations (for example the People's Commissariat of Internal Affairs, or Narkomvnudel RSFSR). This says nothing about the degree of implementation of laws and directives from the center, and the surveys of Rabkrin (People's Commissariat of Worker's and Peasant's Inspection) suggest that it was uneven. But at least there was an attempt to keep laws current and most regulations consistent with the laws. All of this would change when NEP ended.

The staticization of the economy that accompanied the industrialization and collectivization drives produced a huge expansion in the public sphere, a growth in the number of government officials, and a production bias within government itself. Along with this, the Stalin revolution took public administration in the USSR further away from the legal-rational ideal. Personal networks assumed greater significance than they did under NEP and the role of law and observance of laws within government and by state officials declined.

At least three changes made patron-client relations more important. First was the extension of the nomenklatura system to economic officials (including factory and enterprise directors, all of whom were now state employees. From 1930 to 1988

University Press, 1967); Bohdan Harasymiw, "Nomenklatura: The Soviet Communist Party's Leadership Recruitment System," *Canadian Journal of Political Science* 2, no. 3 (1969): 493–512.

[10] Daniel Brower, "The Smolensk Scandal and the End of NEP," *Slavic Review* 45, no. 4 (Winter 1986): 689–706; Gerald Easter, *Reconstructing the State: Personal Networks and Elite Identity in Soviet Russia* (Cambridge: Cambridge University Press, 2000); James Harris, *The Great Urals: Regionalism and the Evolution of the Soviet State* (Ithaca: Cornell University Press, 1999).

[11] Easter, *Reconstructing the State*.

the persons who ran the economy at the operational level owed their positions and well-being to their patrons and protectors; and this connection would assume greater import just before and after Stalin's death.[12] Secondly, for all employees of the state the ties between office and access to goods increased, to the point where the perks and benefits associated with a post or given at the discretion of a patron were more substantial than what was available for money. Thirdly, for many officials, especially responsible ones like enterprise directors, the good will of patrons was needed to protect them from being held personally responsible for accidents, substandard production, or evasion of rules in the use of state funds. In administering the state-owned economy, Stalin's team discovered the utility of the criminal sanction to encourage and discipline its managers (for example through charges of "criminal negligence" [*khalatnost'*]), but often their patrons (either party bosses or higher ministerial officials) could intervene and limit the damage.[13] As we shall see, this became especially relevant when managers were exposed for mismanaging state funds and cooking their accounts, acts that became necessary parts of fulfilling their responsibilities.

The Stalin revolution also brought about a lasting decline in the role of law in Soviet public life. Collectivization and industrialization of the early 1930s were based on directives rather than laws, many of which were not made public. Even after the pressure of the campaigns had concluded, and Stalin endorsed the "stability of laws" as a consequence of the completion of socialism, the rule of "instructions" continued, and many legal norms, especially those related to the economy, remained hidden, if not also secret. From 1930 on, the execution of laws depended upon how they were interpreted in bureaucratic directives (ranging from party edicts and Sovnarkom resolutions to instructions of individual agencies), and the latter assumed such importance that legal hierarchy itself was threatened.[14]

Not only did the role of law decline within the administration of the Soviet state, many of its employees were encouraged to engage in illegal conduct of one kind or another. The political priority from 1930 to 1988 became the fulfilment of the annual operational plan, for enterprises and higher units like trusts and chief

[12] Gorlizki and Khlevniuk depict Stalin in his last years as a "neo-patrimonial leader," who allows his charges to run their ministries and intervenes at his discretion but only occasionally. Yoram Gorlizki and Oleg Khlevniuk, *Cold Peace: Stalin and the Soviet Ruling Circle, 1945–1953* (Oxford: Oxford University Press, 2004), esp. 58–65.

[13] Peter H. Solomon, Jr., *Soviet Criminal Justice under Stalin* (Cambridge: Cambridge University Press, 1996), chapter 4.

[14] Eugene Huskey, "Government Rulemaking as a Brake on Perestroika," *Law and Social Inquiry* 3 (1990): 419–32. See also D.A. Loeber, "Legal Rules 'For Internal use Only,'" *International and Comparative Law Quarterly*, January 1970, 70–98.

administrations. The combination of high production targets and plans that left no margin for error assured that the fulfilment of production plans by individual enterprises would require both violations of law and the cultivation of new personal connections. Using data from the Harvard interview project, Joseph Berliner gave the classic portrait of the manager who relies on a *tolkach* (fixer) to encourage suppliers and relevant transport officials to deliver the necessary inputs (where encouragement implies side-payments) and hides the payment of the *tolkach* and the money he spends from his accounts. But it is clear from other sources (even the journal of the Procuracy *Sotsialisticheskaia zakonnost'*) that the institution of the *tolkach* was already commonplace in the early 1930s.[15] Likewise, the networks of trust developed by the *tolkachi* became so important to an enterprise's well being that in the event of failed deliveries managers often preferred not to sue their supplier in state *arbitrazh*[16] for fear of spoiling the relationship. In short, right away the new system of planning generated coping mechanisms that allowed it to function. But those mechanisms involved a whole series of violations of law, which had to be overlooked by a variety of higher officials and control agents, and usually they were.

By the 1960s and 1970s informal norms had emerged governing the range of discretion that enterprise managers were allowed in creative accounting. We know from Stephen Shenfield's study within the Soviet Interview Project that faking statistical accounts, or the sin of "*pripiski*" (exceeding acceptable norms of statistical manipulation), was tolerated by *revizory* (inspectors), as long as they did not exceed 15 percent of the overall budget of the firm. It was assumed that directors needed this much flexibility to fulfil the plan and therefore "serve the cause," and that in so doing they were not making excessive personal gains. Cooking the books beyond this limit suggested some kind of operation that was not "*dlia pol'zy dela*" (for the good of the cause) at least the *delo* (affairs) of the state.[17]

---

[15] Joseph Berliner, *Factory and Manager in the Soviet Union* (Cambridge, MA: Harvard University Press, 1957); David Granick, *Management of the Industrial Firm in the USSR: A Study in Economic Planning*_(New York: Columbia University Press, 1959); Eugenia Belova, "Economic Crime and Punishment," in *Behind the Façade of Stalin's Command Economy: Evidence from Soviet State and Party Archives*, ed. Paul Gregory (Stanford: Hoover Institution, 2001), 131–58.

[16] State *arbitrazh* is a set of tribunals established in 1930 within the executive branch to resolve disputes among stated owned firms belonging to different ministries or governments with the USSR.

[17] Stephen Shenfield, "The Functioning of the Soviet State Statistical System: Findings from Interviews with Former Soviet Statistical Personnel," CREES Special Report SR 86-1 (Birmingham, 1986). See also his "The Struggle for Control of Statistics," in *Cracks in the Monolith*, ed. James R. Millar (Armonk: M.E. Sharpe, 1992), 89–102; and "*Pripiski*: False Statistical Reporting in Soviet-type Economies," in *Corruption: Causes, Consequences and*

Of course, the directors of enterprises and their supervisors represent only a portion of Soviet officialdom. The question is how many other officials were drawn into illegal activity (apart from the desire for personal gain)? Officials in the trade sector administered changing laws and regulations, and the work of Osokina and Hessler suggests that they sometimes tolerated (if not also participated in) activities that were at the time illegal.[18] In an economy of shortages, shopkeepers and other purveyors of goods occupied privileged positions, for they could allocate the best goods to customers who treated them well or whose good will might prove helpful. And outside the economic realm? Local government officials in the 1920s and 1930s alike, and with them the police and other agents, were regularly accused of *shtrafomania*, that is, creating ordinances or simply extracting fines in ways that exceeded their legal authority, whether against individuals or shops, restaurants, or small businesses.[19] Underfunded local governments needed the revenue, and their officials also were able to benefit personally from the discretion to impose or not impose a particular extraction. No doubt there were other sectors of public administration as well where officials faced incentives to bend legal rules.

In the post-Stalin period, as controls relaxed under Khrushchev and the Brezhnevian policy of "trust in cadres" allowed officials to develop stable networks of trust, the nature and degree of illegal activities conducted by government officials underwent further change. Whereas under Stalin most of violations of law by enterprise managers focused upon plan fulfilment, in the post-Stalin period many enterprises came to undertake production activities on the side and outside of the plan, much of which was illegal and unreported. The "second economy," which by the late 1970s involved some 40 percent of economic activity, was inextricably connected to the official or first economy, for most of the goods that were sold in the underground markets were produced at state-owned factories. Production for the second economy involved a new set of violations of law and often required an even larger number of supervisory and higher officials to turn a blind eye. Often the latter had every incentive to so do because they were themselves beneficiaries of the very illegal production and sales that they might otherwise have considering exposing. In some

Control, ed. Michael Clarke (London: Frances Pinter, 1983), 239–58.

[18] See Elena Osokina, *Our Daily Bread: Socialist Distribution and the Art of Survival in Stalin's Russia, 1927–1941* (Armonk: M.E. Sharpe, 2001); Julie Hessler, "A Postwar Perestroika? Toward a History of Private Enterprise in the USSR," *Slavic Review* 57, no. 3 (Fall 1998): 516–42; Hessler, *A Social History of Soviet Trade: Trade Policy, Retail Practices, and Consumption, 1917–1953* (Princeton: Princeton University Press, 2004).

[19] Peter H. Solomon, Jr., "Criminalization and Decriminalization in Soviet Criminal Policy, 1917–1941," *Law and Society Review* 16, no. 1 (1981): 9–43.

instances, complicity reached the highest levels of political authority.[20]

The addition of illegal production and sales to the already existing illegal operations to guarantee supply of inputs made reliance on networks of trusted acquaintances all the more important. Increasingly, members of these networks were themselves beneficiaries of the illegal activities, which amounted to private business that fed off of state resources. Obviously, these activities exposed managers to attempts at extortion, but it appears that until the perestroika period illegal business functioned largely with protection from within government and party circles and that criminal racquets were not well developed. Extortion and racquets became a major operation only when the businesses of the second economy were legalized under perestroika.

The growth of a second economy under Brezhnev produced a de facto revival of private business and the considerable involvement of government officials in that business. Arguably, it was two or three decades of such experience that prepared Soviet officials for the opportunities provided by the economic reforms of the Gorbachev era, reforms that legalized some of the earlier underground business and provided legal means for converting public property into private enterprise.

Patrimonial Rationality as a Legacy of Socialism

Public administration in the USSR in the years right before perestroika demonstrated increased activity by officials outside or contravening law and even greater reliance on personal networks of trust and protection than was previously the case. If anything, the real order of things was more patrimonial that it had been under Stalin or before. Yet, according to informed observers, during the late Soviet years norms of administrative morality still operated as a restraining factor and prevented the wholesale pursuit of private interests by government officials. This process went into full gear only with the breakdown of Soviet government in 1989 and was reflected in the "spontaneous privatization" of 1990.[21]

---

[20] Gregory Grossman, "The Second Economy in the USSR," *Problems of Communism* 26, no. 5 (1977): 25–40; Konstantin Simis, *USSR: The Corrupt Society The Secret World of Soviet Capitalism* (New York: Simon and Shuster, 1982); Arkady Vaksberg, *The Soviet Mafia* (London: Weidenfeld and Nicholson, 1991).

[21] A.B. Obolonskii, *Biurokratiia dlia XXI veka? Modeli gosudarstvennoi sluzhby. Rossiia, SShA, Angliia, Avstraliia* (Moscow: Delo, 2002), chapter 5; Eugene Huskey, "The Politics of Civil Service Reform in Russia" (paper prepared for the workshop on "Civil Service Reform in Russia and Ukraine," University of Toronto, September 30, 2002). See also Simon Johnson and Heidi Kroll, "Managerial Strategies for Spontaneous Privatization," *Soviet Economy* 7, no. 4 (1991): 281–316.

The post-Soviet Russian bureaucracy is still in formation, but thus far it has continued from the Soviet period patrimonial features and incentives for officials to act outside the law. The best research on Russian bureaucracy indicates that it is better than its reputation would have it, both in competency and degree of corruption, whose prevalence increases dramatically as one moves down the administrative hierarchy from the center through the region to the municipality. The presidential administration seems committed to introducing reform of the civil service that would inter alia create many of the attributes of the Weberian model, such as merit based recruitment and stable career paths.[22] The administration is also struggling to create a hierarchy of laws and normative acts in the Russian Federation, and the courts are deeply involved in this process. But these changes alone are unlikely to remove from Russian bureaucracy the strong elements of patrimonialism and change its members' relationship to law.[23]

One crucial step would be a full and proper separation of business from government, but thus far too many persons inside and outside of government benefit from the peculiar and overlapping relationship, with both legal and illegal dimensions. Another necessary condition is the strengthening of the state and the revival of its capacity to perform functions that properly belong to it, like protection. (Under Putin protection was typically offered by police but on a commercial basis.[24]) More broadly, there must develop a demand for a public service that operates impersonally and according to legal rules among politicians, the public, or relevant elites. Even so, it would remain to restructure public administration and develop a new administrative ethos to support it, and to accomplish these things not only in the central government but also in regional and local ones.

But my purpose here is not to sort out the challenges for Russian bureaucracy in the twenty-first century, but rather to raise questions about its nature under Soviet socialism. "Real socialist government" in the last decades was itself partially privatized, as particular domains became captured by networks of officials and used to serve private or commercial purposes.[25] This characteristic of government was

---

[22] On administrative and civil service reform in Russia see T.V. Zaitseva, *Reforma gosudarstvennoi sluzhby Rossii: istoriia popytok reformirovaniia s 1992 po 2000 god* (Moscow: Ves mir, 2003); Natalia Kostenko, "Tupiki i perspektivy administrativnoi reformy," *Nezavisimaia gazeta*, April 7, 2006.

[23] See Solomon, "Law in Public Administration: How Russia Differs?"

[24] Peter H. Solomon, Jr., "The Reform of Policing in the Russian Federation," *Australian and New Zealand Journal of Criminology* 38, no. 2 (2005): 30–40.

[25] Vladimir Shlapentokh, *Public and Private Life of the Soviet People: Changing Values in Post-Stalin Russia* (Oxford: Oxford University Press, 1989).

consistent with the evolution of Soviet society, whose members themselves participated in an ever expanding set of informal, semi-legal, and illegal activities, as a distinguished ethnographic literature makes clear.[26] By the Gorbachev era, Soviet specialists in the study of bureaucracy were able to recognize the role of groups, formal and informal, in public administration in the USSR, including their criminal dimension.[27]

At the same time, I am convinced, parts of that government operated satisfactorily and without undue distortions. After all, the Brezhnev era witnessed a renewed emphasis among the ideologists of administration on "scientific management," a term that at that time embodied a desire among some leaders for a professional style of administration that valued expertise.[28] Experts and expertise played an increasing role in the policy-making process.[29] There was a marked interest in academic circles in the rationalization of management, including modes of accountability, and in developing the role of law and legal norms in public administration, which, according to one expert, was "underestimated by some officials."[30] A joint resolution of the Central Committee and the Council of Ministers of June 1975 called for enhanced supervision of legality in public administration to promote economic development. At least one sociological survey was mounted among high level ministerial officials to explore violations of law and legality in their agencies. The study found that only 6 percent of known violations of law involved ministerial regulations that contradicted laws, whereas 41 percent of violations involve individual actions in violation of laws. Occasionally (12 percent of the time), they resulted from ignorance of the law, but more often reflected either "a higher purpose" (*tselosoobraznost'*), careerist concerns (24 percent), or unclarity in the laws (17 percent).[31]

---

[26] Alena Ledeneva, *Russia's Economy of Favours: Blat, Networking and Informal Exchange* (Cambridge: Cambridge University Press, 1998); Caroline Humphrey, *The Unmaking of Soviet Life: Everyday Economies after Socialism* (Ithaca: Cornell University Press, 2002).

[27] A.B. Obolonskii, *Chelovek i gosudarstvennoe upravlenie* (Moscow: Nauka, 1987), 136–58.

[28] Peter H. Solomon, Jr., "A New Soviet Administrative Ethos" (paper presented to the Ninth Congress of the International Political Science Association, Montreal, Quebec, July 1973); V.G. Afanas'ev, *Nauchnoe upravlenie obshchestvom* (Moscow: Politizdat, 1968); Afanas'ev, *Sotsialnaia infomatsiia i upravlenie obshchestvom* (Moscow: Politizdat, 1975).

[29] Peter H. Solomon, Jr., *Soviet Criminologists and Criminal Policy: Specialists in Policy-Making* (New York: Columbia University Press; London: Macmillan, 1978).

[30] See, for example, Iurii Tikhomirnov, ed., *Sluzhashchii sovetskogo gosudarstvennogo apparata* (Moscow: Iuridicheskaia literatura, 1970), quotation at 14.

[31] V.I. Remnev, *Sotsialisticheskaia zakonnost' v gosudarstvennom upravlenii* (Moscow: Nauka, 1979), 126–30.

Moreover, in the late 1960s and 1970s politicians endorsed experiments in the rationalization of administration in particular places (for example, industrial ministries in Estonia, the Shchekino chemical combine in Ukraine), and a variety of sociological studies of aspects of public administration (for example, personnel management in Leningrad).[32] Still, overall we know far too little about the actual performance of public administration in the USSR in the 1970s and early 1980s and the mindsets of its officials, many of whom were well educated and increasingly aware of the standards of the outside world.[33]

Although I have emphasized the persistence and deepening of patrimonial features in Soviet administration, I have no doubt that it remained a hybrid that exemplifies "patrimonial rationality," an administration in which elements of rational legal bureaucracy coexisted with patrimonialism. I encourage colleagues to undertake sociological study of world of late Soviet officialdom as part of a reassessment of "real socialism."

---

[32] Ibid., 271–6; B.I. Levin, "O nekotorykh aspektakh izucheniia raboty sluzhashchikh promyshlennykh ministerstv (po materialakh Estonskoi SSR)," in *Organizatsiia raboty ministerstv v usloviiakh ekonomicheskoi reformy*, ed. A.E. Lunev (Moscow: Nauka, 1972), 156–62; B.D. Lebin and M.N. Perfil'ev, *Kadry apparata upravleniia v SSSR: Sotsiologicheskie problemy podbora i rasstanovki* (Leningrad: Nauka, 1970).

[33] On the penetration of a pragmatic and rational approach to administration into the Central Committee apparatus, see Georgyi Arbatov, *The System: An Insider's Life in Soviet Politics* (New York: Time Books, 1992).

II. History Inside Out

"By A Different Yardstick"

Boris Mironov's *A Social History of Imperial Russia, 1700-1917*, and its Reception in Russia

Ben Eklof

Умом Россию не понять,
Аршином общим не измерить:
У ней особенная стать—
В Россию можно только верить.

Russia cannot be understood with the mind alone,
No ordinary yardstick can span her greatness:
She stands alone, unique—
In Russia, one can only believe.

Fedor Tiutchev

Tiutchev's famous lines, "Russia cannot be understood with the mind alone / No ordinary yardstick can span her greatness," like Churchill's oft-cited "riddle wrapped inside an enigma, inside a mystery," are by now hackneyed tropes of an imaginary Russia. Yet they provide a useful entry for my topic, the different receptions which Petersburg historian Boris Mironov's two-volume magnum opus, *A Social History of Imperial Russia, 1700-1917*, first published in Russian in 1999, encountered in the West and at home.[1] I examine these differentiated responses to illustrate the largely

Earlier versions of this paper were presented as "The World of the Post-Soviet Russian Historian" at the University of Georgia Conference on Russian and Soviet History (December, 2003); "By a Different Yardstick: The Reception of Boris Mironov's *Social History of Imperial Russia* and the Russian Historical Profession Today," at the Midwest Russian Historians' Biannual Conference (University of Illinois, Champaign-Urbana, April 2004).

[1] B.N. Mironov, *Sotsial'naia istoriia Rossii perioda imperii (xviii–nachala xx v.): Genesiz lichnosti, demokraticheskoi sem'i, grazhdanskogo obshchestva i pravovogo gosudarstva*, 2 vols (St. Petersburg: Dmitrii Bulanin, 1999). In the text I have used an abbreviated version of the English title, but the reader should be aware that the texts of the English and Russian versions differ somewhat (the English language version is, in full: Boris Mironov with Ben Eklof, *A Social History of Imperial Russia, 1700–1917*, 2 vols. (Boulder: Westview Press, 2000). The first Russian edition is actually a later, revised version of the English language translation. The Russian language version has since subsequently gone through two editions. The most recent, 2003, includes critical essays by Peter Gatrell, David Macey, and Gregory Freeze, as well as a lengthy response by Mironov to his reviewers, and a rich bibliographic appendix listing sources on civil society in Russia. Mironov's response to his critics, which I

unexamined relationship between knowledge and power, which continues to dominate western (but especially American) scholarship on Russia, as well as the unchallenged assumption that, in relationship to Russian history, western historians presume to occupy an Archimedean point allowing them to render impartial judgments upon their peers in Russia, with little critical self-examination. This is a surprising conclusion in the age of post-modernism, when all such claims are suspect. But it also helps explain the huge outpouring of critical, largely admiring, commentary offered Mironov's volumes in Russia.

Two anecdotes from my own past explain the musings which led to this essay. In the early 1970s, I worked in Moscow as a translator for Progress Publishers. There, among the motley assortment of foreigners, who for one reason or another had ended up stranded in Brezhnev's Soviet Union, was a sizeable group of highly educated Russians, working as editorial staff. Among the few of the latter who had been promoted from the dreary task of checking every Marxist-Leninist citation in manuscripts destined for English-language audiences, to editorial positions slightly less demeaning was one Alexander Markov. A typical Muscovite *intelligent*, Markov had a fierce devotion to learning, but also the caution in his eyes foreigners of my generation often encountered. On occasion, out of sight of others, when pleased at the fruits of our collaborative translating and editing, he would whisper to me, "You know ... we are all part of a *republic of letters*."

This claim to a trans-national community, though slightly unorthodox in that environment, was not likely to get the bearer in serious trouble during the period of stagnation. But it did represent a mental pilgrimage, in the way that Benedict Anderson deploys the term to describe how invisible pathways (first religious, then administrative, and finally, in colonial settings, educational) create collective identities. The notion of *pathways*, as well as the frequently encountered term of the late Brezhnev and early perestroika eras, that what middle class professionals yearned for was a normal life, or *normal'naia zhizn'*, will form the leitmotifs of the text below.[2]

My second anecdote concerns a minor revelation I had in the mid-1980s. I was visiting the home of my mentor, the accomplished scholar of the Great Reforms, Larissa Zakharova of Moscow State University. At that time, the wall unit, containing handsome sets of the complete volumes of major Russian writers, was a neces-

have in manuscript only, is referred to below as "Predislovie" (foreword); the pages numbers refer to the manuscript version.

[2] For a recent discussion of American scholars' personal experiences doing research in Russia, see *Adventures in Russian Historical Research: Reminiscences of American Scholars from the Cold War to the Present*, ed. Samuel H. Baron and Cathy A. Frierson (Armonk: M.E. Sharpe, 2003).

sary appurtenance of the middle-class Moscovite apartment. Professional historians would have their apartments crammed with complete sets of Kliuchevsky, Soloviev, and the scholarly monographs of *Akademkniga*. Larissa Georgievna also had a living room filled with books on Russian history, but entire rows were in English, largely the gifts of her British and American colleagues. She often held her seminars in this room, and her graduate students greedily pored over these books.

I was proud of my own contribution to that collection (*Russian Peasant Schools*, 1986). But in retrospect, I am also struck by the incongruity of the situation: why was it that erudite, distinguished scholars in the Soviet Union were encouraging their best students to look at western monographs to learn about Russian history?[3] Why, indeed, were English language works privileged? After all, what role do American scholars play in English historical scholarship on England, in French scholarship on France, in German scholarship on Germany? Given the indisputable global preponderance of American research universities, a significant role, no doubt, but also a secondary, subordinate role, and this is how it should be.[4] Below, however, I argue that the situation in late Soviet historical scholarship was an anomalous one; that American scholarship exerted a hegemonic role, and that this situation has been perpetuated in the post-Soviet era, as grant competitions have fostered an asymmetrical environment best described not as a republic of letters, but in terms of James C. Scott's public and hidden transcripts.[5]

[3] As many western scholars have since pointed out, this was only part of a much larger phenomenon; by the late Brezhnev era the reputations of Soviet scholars in their own communities in virtually all fields were validated largely by the attention they received in western scholarly periodicals and their contacts with western scholars and institutions.

[4] The history of other nations, countries, regions, plays a greater role in American historical scholarship than it does in Germany, France, Russia, and elsewhere; thus, the greater number of monographs originating in the United States could contribute to the attention given to American monographs abroad. But there is, for example, a venerable Russian School of European history, whose roots trace back to the last quarter of the nineteenth century. However, a search of the American Historical Review produced no record of a book review of any Russian-language monographs on European history, and none as well on American history (except those involving Russo-American relations). For the Russian School of Europeanists, see G.P. Miagkov, *Nauchnoe soobshchestvo v istoricheskoi nauke: opyt russkoi istoricheskoi shkoly* (Kazan, 2000) and a review by V.P. Zolotarev in *Otechestvennye zapiski*, 2005, no. 6: 219–21.

[5] James C. Scott, *Domination and the Arts of Resistance* (New Haven: Yale University Press, 1991). I deploy Scott and Anderson in this article fully realizing that the analogies I make can only be done with considerable stretching of original authorial intent. Yet I feel that the analogy with colonialism is appropriate and best describes the unspoken assumptions of cultural superiority embedded in East-West academic transactions as well as the unexamined connection between knowledge and power I assert below.

The extraordinary response given to the recent publication of Mironov's *A Social History* can best be understood as part of this hegemonic discourse. Comparing early discussions of *A Social History* organized respectively by the journals *Otechestvennaia Istoriia*[6] and *Slavic Review*, David Ransel concluded "A Single Research Community? Not Yet."[7] But Ransel's valid assertion needs to be taken a step further. In fact, while western reception has been polite, if tepid, the extraordinary attention given in Russia to *A Social History* is unprecedented, and may represent a turning point in the Russian historical profession, especially in its relations with the West. As Europeanist A.B. Kamensky wrote on the pages of the prestigious journal *Odysseus (Odissei: Chelovek v istorii)*:

> It is clear ... that this book is not just ... a "significant event" in the historical profession, but something grander; both the work itself and the discussions of it are, on the one hand, evidence of the existing state of contemporary Russian historical studies [*istoricheskaia rusistika*], and for that reason everything published on this occasion of this work's appearance merits its own study ... at the same time *A Social History of Imperial Russia* is a landmark in its own right.[8]

Below I will elaborate upon these assertions. I begin with an outline of the contents and arguments of *A Social History*. I then turn to its reception in the United States and in Russia. Along the way I include some observations about the historical profession, public interest in history, and the ideological constellation of history texts and instruction in schools and universities in Russia. My comments about the Russian context in which *A Social History* was introduced are anecdotal, not based upon survey research. Nor do they take into consideration the small but talented and resourceful cohort of Russian trans-national scholars, brought up in the former Soviet and educated both there and abroad, and now making a striking contribution to Russian historical scholarship (largely, but not only, in the West). Substantive discussion of the rich fabric of this work at the *middle level of generalization* will be deferred, although I personally feel that it is at this level, rather than that of the global generalization or overarching framework, that Mironov is at his best, indeed

---

[6] See "Rossiiskii staryi poriadok: opyt istoricheskogo sinteza," *Otechestvennaia istoriia*, no. 6, November–December 2000, 43–93.

[7] *Slavic Review* 60, no. 3 (Fall 2001): 550–7. Ransel's essay was part of a forum based upon a panel devoted to Mironov's *A Social History* at the 2000 National Convention of the AAASS. Contributors to the forum included (besides Ransel) William G. Wagner, Willard Sunderland, Steven L. Hoch; on these pages Mironov also replies separately to each of his commentators. The entire forum can be found on pp. 550–99.

[8] A.B. Kamenskii, "Uroki, kotorye mozhno bylo izvlech'," *Odissei: Chelovek v istorii*, 2004, 408–21.

unmatched as an historian.

Since the author of these pages was personally involved in the editing and translation of the English language version of *A Social History*, I have sought to avoid all evaluation of its worth, both positive and negative. Instead I focus on the response to *A Social History* by two different communities, and what it tells us about both. Thus, we are dealing strictly with reception and not with truth value.

Summary and Outline of *A Social History*

For those who have not perused *A Social History* the following is a brief summary, written by the late Reginald Zelnik in the *American Historical Review*:

> The thread that runs through the story … looks something like this: Russia was, at least potentially a "normal" European country, but a European country that was not lacking in important peculiarities, including what is sometimes described as the relative backwardness of its economic, social, and political development. To use Mironov's language, Russia experienced all the important developments in these areas, but they were "asynchronic" in the way they evolved. Russia's peculiarities, most of which are familiar to specialists, are not presented as virtues (in Slavophile style) but as obstacles or impediments to a broad and balanced "social modernization," an outcome whose positive value Mironov has no wish to deny. But these were obstacles that could be mastered with time, and Mironov goes to great pains to help us follow the sometimes tortuous but nonetheless rapid processes that suggest that the obstacles were being genuinely if (on the eve of world war and revolution) incompletely overcome. At the same time, he is too honest a historian to ignore the contradictory, more depressing, "pessimistic" evidence of incomplete modernization and continued, even growing social tension and political crisis, so much so that one can read whole paragraphs—his discussion of the civilizing of the Russian village versus the partial "peasantization" of the Russian city is a good case in point—that seem to take opposite positions, or at least to produce conflicting moods and expectations in the reader as one moves from page to page. In the still contested (if by now somewhat hoary) debate over the degree of influence of close peasant background on the social and political volatility of industrial workers, Mironov judiciously explains the case for each side but ends with something resembling a neo-Menshevik position; that peasant disrespect for private, individual wealth, and peasant attachment to collectivist institutions and habits help explain the rapid rise of working class radicalism and indifference to market-based liberalism in the early twentieth century.[9]

[9] Reginald Zelnik, *American Historical Review* 106, no. 5 (December 2001): 1904.

Volume 1 is organized as follows: 1) territorial expansion, 2) social structure and social mobility, 3) demographic processes and problems, 4) the family, 5) town and country, 6) serfdom, and 7) the main societal organizations of the peasantry, nobility and urban estates, and the genesis of individualism and individual identity (*lichnost'*); volume 2, 1) law and the courts, 2) the evolution of the Russian state, and the establishment of a law-governed state, 3) state, society and public opinion, and the establishment of civil society, and 4) the societal development of Russia in the imperial period, and Soviet modernization.[10] Treatment of the pre-Petrine era is cursory. Likewise, except for in his concluding remarks, the Soviet period does not come into view.

Reception: The West

Anglo-Western reception of *A Social History* has been mixed. To be sure, publication of the two-volume history prompted a special session at the 2000 National Convention of the American Association for the Advancement of Slavic Studies (AAASS), and a follow-up forum on the pages of the *Slavic Review*, as well as individual reviews by leading scholars in all of the major journals. But the *Slavic Review* panel, attended by Mironov himself, was, in the words of Reginald Zelnik and Louise McReynolds, excessively critical, at times even condescending. David Ransel, Willard Sunderland, and William Wagner all provided measured but substantive critiques of Mironov's views on empire, law, social structure, modernization, and for neglect of religion, gender, private life—in short, "many topics at the center of Russian studies in the west today." But Steven Hoch caustically sought to demolish the very foundations of *A Social History* by attacking his quantitative approach as wrong-headed and fundamentally incompetent.[11]

Individual reviews suggested that Mironov is "out of step with Western methods and conceptualizations," that (Okenfuss) Mironov's "strident anti-Marxism" and "Soviet-bashing intentions" as well as "prickly nationalism" shape his arguments,

---

[10] Boris Mironov has recently created a website (http://bmironov.spb.ru), which includes, among other items, a detailed, chapter by chapter abstract, or *referat*, of the two volumes which serves as a useful guide to the book's themes, arguments, and organization. It bears note that this *referat* clearly expresses an authorial voice with qualitative judgements as well as textual summaries. This summary, along with Mironov's autobiographical sketch included in the English version of *A Social History* (vol. 1, xviii–xxxviii), a genre clearly unfamiliar and awkward to the author, could serve as markers of the different cultural traditions (Russian and American scholarship) continuing to shape the format and style of historical documents.

[11] For these views, see note 7; the quotations are from Ransel, "A Single Research Community," 555, 556, and 557.

and that "many of his questions are terribly old-fashioned, tilting as he must at collapsed conceptual windmills, and still dueling with silenced foes."[12] According to John Alexander, "Mironov understands social history primarily in a sociological sense, depicting the development of large population groups and institutions, with a major focus on statistical measures in tabular form (but not) topics such as recreational pursuits or medical or sexual mores." Alexander, while noting that Mironov "draws on several historiographic traditions," adds that the text "lacks drama, wit, and humor," and "omits personalities and events that give color and texture to more conventional or narrative history."[13]

Most readers looking for personalities and events would not turn to social history, especially one that relies heavily upon numbers and seeks to identify and elucidate the deeper currents flowing beneath the froth of events. In short, this is a criticism not of Mironov, but of social history as such. As for "drama, wit and humor," it is true, Mironov's mission, and hence his voice, do not lend themselves to the light touches of humor or irony; as Madhavan Palat perceptively notes:

> Boris Mironov has deliberately assumed one of the traditional burdens of the modern historian, that of building the nation … He sees the Russian nation as sorely in need of construction after the searing experience of the Soviet Union. He accuses Soviet historians of having derided Russian traditions on a scale that other nations could contemplate … Russians have been purveyed a vision of their past so tawdry and gloomy that they could not identify with it. They were compelled to regard their history as a hideous blot on the face of humanity … [the past] has nurtured in them a profound sense of inadequacy; and it has caused a wound that must be healed. The physician at hand is none other than the historian himself; and he shall administer a dose of *cliotherapy* to the patient. It would reveal to the Russian that his society is a *normal* one, with as many successes and failures as any other, which is to say, European. This vast opus … is just such a redemptive dose of physic and revelation.[14]

[12] Max Okenfuss, *Jahrbücher für Geschichte Osteuropas* 49, no. 1 (2000): 96–99. Comparing *A Social History* with Janet Hartley's *A Social History of the Russian Empire, 1650–1825* (London: Longman, 1999), Okenfuss praises the latter for its rich treatment of "complex religiosity," intellectual currents (especially Masonry), and "lifestyle and belief" in general.

[13] John T. Alexander, *History: Reviews of New Books* 28, issue 2 (Winter 2000): 78. Alexander's review, as a whole, is by no means censorial or dismissive, and he acknowledges that "this type of work tends to be dense and difficult to digest." He adds, "there is no other book in English that treats the same topics over such a long period."

[14] Madhavan K. Palat, "The Mironov Thesis of Russia as a Normal Society" (2001), unpublished paper, an abridged version of which was published in Russian translation as M.K. Palat, "Tezis o Rossii kak 'normal'nom obshchestve'" (Razmyshleniia po povodu knigi B.N. Mironova "Sotsial'naia istoriia Rossii perioda imperii")," *Rossiia i sovremennyi mir*, 2001,

Given the mission of psychic redemption and national healing that Mironov has set himself (he, of course, is more modest in his phrasing), the tone of earnestness and sobriety that pervades the text, as jarring as it may be to a western scholarly community prizing irony and mordant wit, is entirely natural and appropriate.

In fairness, not all commentary has been nugatory. In his contribution to the *Slavic Review* forum, Ransel concludes that *A Social History* is "the most ambitious and challenging personal synthesis produced in Russia since the collapse of communism."[15] In his review, Norman Saul concludes that Mironov should be "stormily applauded."[16] Zelnik goes further; he claims that the work is "a tour de force ... perhaps the most impressive overview of this subject written by anyone, anywhere."[17] Zelnik does point out self-contradictory and problematic aspects of Mironov's grand theory.[18] Yet he concludes that "this is a book that cannot be bypassed by serious historians of Russia ... We are all in the author's debt for years of first-class research ... and for the limpidity and discretion of his nevertheless passionate writing."[19]

McReynolds calls the work "one of the most useful histories of the imperial period to appear in any language." Palat, who is very critical of Mironov's defense of the autocracy as largely "law-governed" and progressive, and his finger-pointing at the Russian intelligence for its failure to work harmoniously with the state (a view quite popular in Russian educated circles today),[20] nevertheless calls the work a "landmark."

---

4 (33): 144–59. Ransel also describes Mironov's project as one of Clio-therapy, as does I.M. Supinitsiaia, on the pages of *Odysseus,* "Sotsial'naia istoriia Rossii i problema modernizatsii: o knige B.N. Mironova," *Odissei: Chelovek v istorii,* 2003, 378–89.

[15] Ransel, "A Single Research Community," 557.

[16] Norman E. Saul, *History: Reviews of New Books* 28, issue 3 (Spring 2000).

[17] Zelnik, *American Historical Review*, 1904.

[18] For example, he writes that "Mironov's admittedly forceful case for Russia's evolution toward a 'normal' European form of social and political life is undermined by an equally forceful if at times reluctant recognition of significant evidence to the contrary. If, as he concludes, the October Revolution was in some respects an 'anti-modernist' rebellion, then popular resistances to the Europeanizing processes that he values weaken the case for the approaching advent of 'normality.'" Ibid. Zelnik's brief criticisms of Mironov's framework are replicated and forcefully elaborated in Palat, "The Mironov Thesis."

[19] Zelnik, *American Historical Review*, 1903; Louise McReynolds, *The Historian* 64, issue 2 (Winter 2002): 457.

[20] "He repudiates anything that belongs to the revolutionary tradition in Russia, whether socialist or liberal; and he endorses whatever springs from the statist modernizing traditions of Imperial Russia" (Palat, "The Mironov Thesis"). In Palat's view, Mironov is a statist liberal in the vein of nineteenth-century reformers such as Kavelin and Chicherin.

Still, only a handful of western reviewers have fully appreciated the scope and depth of Mironov's research. He may be criticized for eschewing post-modernist approaches, for leaving out ideology and "cross-cultural interaction" (McReynolds), or his fundamental perspectives and arguments challenged, but those such as Max Okenfuss and others who argue that the 750 western sources (not including those in footnotes) are "spotty, often oddly selected, and fragmentary"[21] do not appreciate the singularity of his mastery of pre-revolutionary, Soviet-era, and western historiography, including, as Zelnik points out, western writings on non-Russian (primarily European) history.[22] If this truly were a republic rather than an empire of letters, it would seem preposterous to criticize Mironov for "spotty" application of western sources cited, on Europe, no less. Imagine a book review in the *American Historical Review* criticizing an American scholar writing on American history for incomplete knowledge of Russian *Amerikanistika*.[23] Or, more precisely, an American writing on American history, criticized for incomplete knowledge of Russian writing on German history! There is a built-in hierarchy of knowledge and power, a remarkable conceit in such presumptions. At the very least, as McReynolds argues, "Mironov ... deserves far more acclaim for what he accomplished than [criticism] for what he left aside."[24]

---

[21] Okenfuss, *Jahrbücher*, 97. Okenfuss' review is mixed, not entirely negative; in particular he praises Mironov's research in "often obscure Russian and Soviet publications," his summary of "several long-standing historiographic debates," his "especially lucid and insightful" use of Dal's collection of folk wisdom and proverbs, his (earlier) research on the impact of the agrarian price revolution after 1750 in Russia, and his examination of the "participatory ethos" of nobles, peasants and urban estates, which challenge traditional notions of autocracy and help explain how an undergoverned country could be successfully ruled by the Romanovs for two centuries.

[22] Elise Kimmerling Wirtschafter, in a nuanced and detailed review, writes that "the author has assimilated a large body of foreign scholarship—primarily 'new social history' produced by Anglo-American authors, along with a sprinkling of European economic and demographic history ... which is effectively incorporated into his own very deep empirical knowledge." *Kritika: Explorations in Russian and Eurasian History* 2, no. 1 (Winter 2001): 1–7.

[23] In fact, a cursory search of reviews in this journal for the past 20 years produced no reviews of Russian scholarly books on American history. Nor is there any knowledge among American historians of the venerable Russian School of European history, which has its roots back in the scholarly world of pre-revolutionary Russia. And Russian Orientalism, which dates back to the middle of the nineteenth century, would find no reflection among American historians. The argument that few Americans know Russian simply reinforces the link between knowledge (and language) and power.

[24] For Mironov's own comments on American Russianists, and on the linguistic turn, see M.V. Rabzhaev, "Interv'iu s professorom B. N. Mironovym," *Zhurnal sotsiologii i sotsial'noi antropologii* 3, no. 2 (10) (2001): 183; Boris Mironov, "Has Postmodernism Come to Russia?

The Russian Historical Profession: Is There a Community?[25]

Andrei Sakharov, Director of the Institute of History of the Academy of Sciences, writes, in an overview of the Russian historical profession, "Today, Russian historical science is vibrant, dynamic and discursive. It is closely linked with global historiography; the research of historians is based upon an ever expanding incorporation of both world and national historiographical legacies, on the utilization of more and more archival resources. It is growing in conditions of freedom and ... has a solid future."[26] On the pages of *Kritika*, a number of informative articles have recently been published mapping the changing ideological constellation of Russian historical writing, and seem to confirm Sakharov's claims.[27] And Mironov himself, summarizing the response to the publication of *A Social History*, argues that "this vibrant discussion demonstrates that...the gap is being eliminated between the level of historical research carried out in the capital cities and the provinces; the wall between Western and Russian historiography is collapsing ... and a community of Russianists is emerging."[28]

But let us look briefly at the demographics and the communication pathways of this profession. Benedict Anderson wrote eloquently of the school "pilgrimages," that is, the educational pathways pursued by "natives" and "creoles" in colonial settings which helped give birth to and sustain the notion of a nation in sites such as "*Indochine*" and "Indonesia."[29] It is a stretch to argue that Russia, in its diminished glory, has become a colony of the West, and I am certainly not arguing that there is no "Russia" outside these pathways, but Mironov's assertion of a progressively more integrated community seems optimistic, given the collapsing budgets of universities,

Comments on the Anthology 'American Russian Studies'," *Kritika: Explorations in Russian and Eurasian History* 4, no. 1 (Winter 2003): 201–5.

[25] To sample current Russian historiography, see the special issue of *Otechestvennye zapiski*, 2004, no. 5.

[26] A.N. Sakharov, "Obshchie problemy istoricheskoi nauki. O novykh podkhodakh v rossiiskoi istoricheskoi nauke 1990-e gody," *Istoriia i istoriki*, 2002, no. 1: 3–28. Inexplicably, for my purposes, Sakharov makes no mention of Mironov's *A Social History*, in this broad survey of trends in Russian historical scholarship.

[27] See, for example, "The State of the Field: Russian History Ten Years after the Fall," special issue, *Kritika: Explorations in Russian and Eurasian History* 2, no. 2 (Spring 2001); Aleksandr I. Filiushkin, "Post-Modernism and the Study of the Russian Middle Ages," *Kritika: Explorations in Russian and Eurasian History* 3, no. 1 (Winter 2002): 89–110.

[28] Mironov, "Predislovie."

[29] Benedict Anderson, *Imagined Communities: Reflections on the Origin and Spread of Nationalism* (London: Verso, 1983).

rising costs of travel, limited access to books and to the Internet characteristic of life outside Moscow and St. Petersburg. Let us turn briefly to this situation.

First of all, the demographics. We are all familiar with some basic developments in the Russian knowledge industry.[30] In the post-Soviet era the venerable networks comprising the Academy of Sciences and its branches have been drained of resources and in many areas survive only as shells. Many in the Academy have been forced to flee to the universities and post-secondary (VUZ) institutes, where they take on multiple teaching loads in order to survive—85.5 percent of all *VUZ* teachers in 2000 had multiple appointments.[31] In most (57.3 percent) cases, this involved supplementary teaching at another institution.[32] One reviewer of Mironov's book lamented that it was truly an academic book in that nobody in the teaching world could possibly have found the time to write it! Anecdotal evidence suggests that academic institutes in many fields of research are staffed primarily by scientists of retirement age, and that few young people find a professional career in academics an alluring possibility.[33] In fact the ageing of the scholarly community has been well established, with most scientists today in Russia being in their mid-fifties.[34] The number of scientists/scholars who have left to work abroad has been variously estimated at between

[30] For a survey of conditions in higher education institutions, see Organization for Economic Co-operation and Development, *Reviews of National Policies for Education*: *Tertiary Education and Research in the Russian Federation* (OECD Publishing, 1999), esp. chapter 6, "Research in Higher Education" and chapter 7, "Students and Teachers." However, this volume was based upon on-site visits conducted in 1997–1998. More recent perspectives can be found in regular articles in the *Chronicle of Higher Education* by Byron MacWilliams, which, however, are basically anecdotal. Anna Smolentseva, a sociologist at Moscow State University, has recently completed extensive survey research on the Russian professoriate, which will be available in a series of forthcoming publications.

[31] Frants Sherigi, *Sotsiologiia obrazovaniia: prikladnye issledovaniia* (Moscow: Akademiia, 2001), 406. The average monthly salary of teachers in higher education institutions in 2000 was 2033 rubles, or $75 (404). It has risen considerably since then, but still lags behind wages and salaries in most sectors. Russia currently spends less than 4 percent of GDP on education, and the Ministry of Education estimates that only 10 to 20 percent of institutions of higher education maintain Soviet-level standards.

[32] Sherigi, *Sotsiologiia obrazovaniia,* 408.

[33] Conversation with Dr. Maria Loskoutova of the European University in St. Petersburg, September 2002.

[34] To be sure, according to Frants Sherigi, the average age of teaching faculty at vuzy has slightly declined recently, to 44.6 years in 2000, because of an "inundation" of younger teachers. Thus, between 1994 and 2000 the percentage of faculty 31 and under rose from 9.9 to 18.8 percent; those over 50 years old declined from 36.1 to 30.6 percent. The percentage of males has slightly increased, to 53.6 percent, but women dominate in the youngest cohort. See Sherigi, *Sotsiologiia obrazovaniia*, 400–1.

80,000 and 200,000.[35] Of course, the new freedom to pursue research in controversial or formerly forbidden subjects has been heady and has produced a wealth of new research, but has it compensated for the precipitous decline in status and relative standard of living in the academic profession as a whole? Do most academics have greater access to books and articles than in earlier times? In point of fact, subsidies for the publication of academic books have virtually disappeared: the price of books has skyrocketed as the number of titles has declined and the print runs have shrunk. Scholarly listings in bookstores are almost insignificant [36]

More important, for my purposes, is the question of communications networks and hierarchy. In the Soviet era, research and critical commentary were overwhelmingly embedded in print culture as well as research travel. At some point during the perestroika era, the average Muscovite subscribed to over thirty journals and periodicals.[37] Today, by all accounts, fewer and fewer people read national newspapers, subscriptions to journals have declined by more than 50 percent (that is, for those journals which have survived), and libraries are unable to purchase books, especially outside a handful of cities. As for international connections, even in St. Petersburg the purchase of foreign books and periodicals by central libraries has virtually ended. Outside the capital cities, few libraries buy books or subscribe to journals in foreign languages.[38] In pedagogical institutes, always the poor stepdaughter in academics, the situation is even drearier; libraries in such institutions do not even have copies of the new generation of textbooks future teachers will be expected to use.[39] As for books,

---

[35] The weekly *Poisk* is a good source of current information on higher education and scientific research in Russia.

[36] For articles on "the abject state of scholars" and the "degradation of higher education," including crumbling infrastructure, unreplenished libraries, and pervasive corruption see Bryon MacWilliams "For Russia's Universities, A Decade of More Freedom and Less Money" and "Corruption, Conflict, and Budget Cuts Afflict Academe in Former Soviet Republics," *The Chronicle of Higher Education* 48, issue 16 (December 14, 2001): A42 and A43.

[37] See my *Soviet Briefing: Gorbachev and the Reform Era* (Boulder: Westview Press, 1989), esp. 42–65.

[38] These observations are based upon conversations with several librarians who attended the Fischer Forum, Seminar on the History of the Book at the University of Illinois, Champaign-Urbana in June 2006, and upon extensive conversation between the author and former director of the Herzen State Library, Dr. Viacheslav Pozdeev, as well as Mikhail D. Afanasev, Director of the Historical Library in Moscow. Although Kirov is a small city, with half a million residents, the Herzen Library is a venerable institution. On the situation in St. Petersburg, my comment is based upon queries addressed to Boris Mironov.

[39] For a recent study of the professoriate in Russia, based upon systematic survey research, see Sherigi, *Sotsiologiia obrazovaniia*, chapter six on conditions of research and chapter seven on a composite profile of faculty.

the price of them has increased dramatically in the post-Soviet era compared to average household income, and the print runs of scholarly books have declined sharply.

According to Catherine Merridale, western grants and collaborative projects have played a major role in sustaining academic research and dialogue by resort to the Internet.[40] One example that comes to mind is *auditorium.ru*; another is the Open Society's funding of new generations of textbooks for schools and universities. Yet studies show that only 2 to 8 percent of the population has access to the Internet, and that this is heavily clustered in a few locations, especially Moscow (where the figure is 27 percent). Moreover, access is often limited, episodic, and expensive. Outside the major cities, by some accounts, "fewer historians today read foreign languages."[41]

Who then would be aware of the outpouring of commentary on Mironov's *A Social History,* which filled the pages of journals, both prominent and obscure?[42] There are individual reviews, but also round-tables, discussions, interviews, including translations into Russian of contributions by American, British, German scholars. But who, outside Moscow and St. Petersburg, at least, would have easy access to this conversation? Across Russia, most students are limited by family budgets to attending local universities; few can afford the cost of living away from home. Likewise, few graduate students or scholars can afford to visit the large cities to attend forums or conduct research. Thus, with the breakdown of the distribution network and market for books and journals, contact is at best episodic, unsystematic, and limited. To be sure, many of the participants in the round-tables devoted to *A Social History* themselves came from universities outside Moscow and St. Petersburg. And most of us working in Russian history have the pleasure of rather regular contact with scholars scattered across the former Soviet Union.[43] Still, such contacts engage only a tiny fraction of Russian scholars. For most it is indisputable that Russia's academic contact with the West is tenuous and concentrated in a few sites, perhaps even more

---

[40] Catherine Merridale, "Redesigning History in Contemporary Russia," *Journal of Contemporary History* 38, no. 1 (2003): 17.

[41] Merridale, "Redesigning History," 22.

[42] According to Mironov's count (see his "Foreword" to the third edition), there were 19 reviews and four round-tables (*Otechestvennaia istoriia*, *Slavic Review*, one sponsored by the School of Economics of St. Petersburg State University, and another by the House of Scholars [*Dom uchenykh*] in St. Petersburg). All in all, Mironov counted 61 participants in the various responses to his work.

[43] I am grateful to Charles Halperin for his comments about his own widespread contacts with Russian medievalists, as well as the observation about the geographic origins of participants in the round-tables, as a corrective to my own categorical assertions about scholarly isolation.

so than in Soviet times. For most too, the contacts so essential to the professional practice of history, and once conducted through patronage networks as well as subsidies for academic publishing and research travel, are now fragmented, disjointed, and only episodically maintained.

Public History and School Textbooks[44]

Another topic of real importance is how history is taught in schools and universities. Is it conceivable that *A Social History* could have a ripple effect, its approaches and arguments spread to the lay community through secondary school and university textbooks, and affect public memory in some way? Catherine Merridale sees a significant generational decline in interest in the past (especially for those born after 1980) and a widening gap between lay and scholarly interests. At the same time she argues that a discursive field does persist, one in which distinctively Russian tropes continue to dominate, such as "a tendency to seek undivided truth ... a fascination with charismatic authority, and especially with the personalities of leaders; an equal fascination with the irrational, and especially with the idea of miraculous deliverance; the hoped-for but elusive 'special path,' and a taste for making extreme judgments about events.[45] As for schools and textbooks, as is well known, there was a huge spike of interest in history in the perestroika era, but then a sharp decline after 1991, as people everywhere found themselves preoccupied with the struggle to survive and the social woes accompanying drastic impoverishment.[46] In 2001, public interest in how history is taught was rekindled, however, by then Prime Minister Mikhail Kasianov's

[44] Space does not allow me to include a discussion over the recent furor surrounding the decision by the then Ministry of Education to "recall" the controversial school textbooks by I. Dolutsky. Western commentators saw this as yet another sign that Putin is restricting freedoms in Russia. The truth is that discontent with the text led the Expert Commission of the Ministry to remove it from the "recommended" to the "permitted" category, *not* to prohibit its use, as was often reported in the West. For discussion of history textbooks in the post-Soviet era see several essays in *Educational Reform in Post-Soviet Russia: Legacies and Prospects*, ed. Ben Eklof, Larry Holmes, and Vera Kaplan (London: Frank Cass, 2005).

[45] Merridale, "Redesigning History," 22. This article is strong on public ceremonies and discourse, but, despite claims to the contrary, weak and outdated on school syllabi and textbooks.

[46] The best available studies of the human costs of the "transition" in the former Soviet Union, Eastern, and Central Europe are by the Innocenti Center of UNICEF. See especially *A Decade of Transition*, Regional Monitoring Report #8; CEE/CIS/Baltic States (Florence, 2001) and the more recent *Social Monitor 2003* (Florence, 2003). These publications can be downloaded at http://www.unicef.icd.org. For a brilliant survey of the collision between liberal and democratic ideals and the impoverishment of schools, see I.D. Frumin, *Vvedenie v teoriiu i praktiku demokraticheskogo obrazovaniia* (Krasnoiarsk, 1998).

notorious public temper tantrum about the quality of Russian history textbooks, and the government announced a "competition" to find the "top three" new textbooks to be used in the schools (the winners were announced in July 2002).[47] In addition, the new standardized school leaving/university admission exams have forced a reexamination of the school curriculum in history and other subjects. All of this has generated interest in the press and among parents about how history is to be taught, part of renewed attention given in the periodical press to education in general.

The first generation of post-Soviet high school textbooks (up to about 1998) has been carefully analyzed by scholars.[48] But since 2001 a plethora of new textbooks have appeared; one multi-media curriculum package that has gained popularity and been used in schools in many areas pursues learning objectives for the high school that would prompt the admiration of most American *university* teachers, in terms both of the sophistication of analysis called for and density of factual grounding, but also of the search for a usable past, combining the quest for truth, empathetic understanding, and pride in one's country.[49] It indeed makes use of *A Social History*. But only a systematic investigation of new textbooks, teachers' guides, and syllabi, as well as of the selection, production, marketing and distributing networks, all of which have substantially changed since 2000, will tell us much about new, or persisting ideological constellations, as well as about the relationship between academic and public history.

As for university instruction, it is futile to look for *A Social History* as a classroom textbook, at least according to one report by a foreign observer:

> Under-funding is particularly harmful in the area of textbooks. Russian higher education institutions, like those in France and some other countries, attempt to provide students with textbooks free of charge. They do this from the woefully inadequate budgets of their tiny university libraries. Present funding levels do not allow Russian universities to purchase anywhere near enough

[47] On this, see Elena Kostiuk, "Pervaia Polosa. Istoriia s Istoriiei,"*Vremia MN*, August 31, 2002, no. 155: 1; Natal'ia Savitskaia, "Otkrytyi uchebnik," *Nezavisimaia gazeta*, September 27, 2002, no. 205: 8.

[48] See especially Elena Lisovskaya and Vyacheslav Karpov, "New Ideologies in Postcommunist Russian Textbooks," *Comparative Education Review* 43, no. 4 (November 1999): 522–43, and the articles by Vera Kaplan, "History Teaching in Post-Soviet Russia: Historical Legacy and the Challenge of Change" and Aleksandr Shevyrev, "Rewriting the National Past: New Images of Russia in History Textbooks of the 1990's," in *Educational Reform in Post-Soviet Russia*.

[49] I reviewed these (anonymous) multi-media textbook proposals with extensive developed individual modules, for a funded competition administered by a St. Petersburg education developmental program in 2006.

> textbooks for all students … *The result is that many professors and students rely exclusively on pre-Gutenberg technology: lectures delivered extremely slowly so that students can take verbatim notes*. Lack of textbooks also means that universities must require many more hours of faculty contact with students than western universities do, because professors are practically the only source of information for many students in many classes.[50]

There could be a silver lining here: several participants in roundtables devoted to *A Social History* observed that Mironov's concepts and arguments had transformed their *lectures* … thus leapfrogging over Gutenberg. Working in the city of Kirov in 2006, I found a smattering of citations in works of local history to Mironov's *A Social History,* but few graduate students or faculty at the universities were even aware of the work, and none knew of the debate it had provoked. That is to say, the book might gradually make its way into the canon of scholarship cited by provincial historians in their own work, but there is no evidence that an all-Russian, never mind international, dialogue is emerging on the basis of the printed word.

A Social History: Grand Theory, Middle-Level Argumentation, and Russian Reception[51]

On the pages of the *Slavic Review*, David Ransel summarized the praise lavished by Russian historians on Mironov's *magnum opus*:

> Russian commentators are struck, first of all, by the genre of Mironov's study: a personally crafted interpretation of a broad sweep of history, so different

[50] Donald K. Jarvis and Marat Tukhfatullin, "Faculty Development in Russian Higher Education" (paper presented at the National Convention of the American Association for the Advancement of Slavic Studies, Toronto, Ontario, November 20–23, 2003; with permission of the author). Emphasis added.

[51] A caveat is in order here: below I treat domestic reception to Mironov's volumes as overwhelmingly positive, and all the reviews in my file confirm this. But in one interview conducted with Mironov, the interlocutor mentions that at several venues, including the Russian National Library, the House of Scholars (*Dom uchenykh*) and even his own work team, the reception was frosty, even hostile. In this same interview Mironov concedes that after giving two talks at the St. Petersburg branch of the Institute of History of the Academy of Sciences, based on chapters in the book, "from the reaction of colleagues" he determined it would be pointless of continue such presentations. He adds that *A Social History* did not bear the imprint of the seal of the Institute (Rabzhaev, "Interv'iu s professorom B. N. Mironovym," 180–5). Finally, in the foreword to the third edition, Mironov comments that in general, western historians were more favorably disposed to his work than were his compatriots. In Mironov's calculations, the domestic reception had a generational component: the younger the reviewer, the more enthusiastic the response to *A Social History*.

> from the collectively written general histories produced in the Soviet period … With regard to Mironov's general framework, Russian commentators accept uncritically his use of … modernization theory and Ferdinand Tonnies's much earlier notions of Gemeinschaft and Gesellschaft. They do not question Mironov's construction of a static "traditional" society giving way to a "modern society" as measured by standard indexes of commercial growth, urbanization, industrialization, and legal and political reform. Like Mironov himself, they also accept analytical categories such as national and eth[n]ic identity, gender, and culture as given and unproblematic.[52]

This is a judicious summary. At the same time, when Ransel wrote these lines, he could not yet be fully aware of the scale of the Russian response to *A Social History*, for it was just getting underway. And these lines, of course, contain an embedded implicit stance of superiority: Russian commentators accept uncritically … They do not question … they accept … categories … as given … and unproblematic. This is, of course, part of the academic give-and-take we all trade in. But it fails to situate this response in what can almost be described as a post-colonial setting. To describe intellectual relations between Russia in the West as post-colonial of course leaves out the Soviet Union's history as a superpower and "adjacent" empire, but it accurately describes the cultural and academic transition from Soviet to post-Soviet eras.

My argument that this is so is based on a seeming paradox: Mironov's scholarship, while hostile to Marxist-Leninism, and barely tolerated in the Soviet era, and while informed by western (especially Annales school) scholarship[53] is now being hailed as a heroic deed (*podvig*),[54] accomplished by a deeply patriotic, home-grown scholar, as an unparalleled accomplishment—the first serious grand synthesis of Russian history of the post-Soviet era. It also offers a synthesis that can contribute to finding "a usable past," and provides a "professional" alternative to the "numerous 'historiosophies' proliferating in our time and literally taking over the book stalls on

---

[52] Ransel, "A Single Research Community," 554–5.

[53] One Russian reviewer pointed out that of the 3,500 sources listed in the bibliography, "more than 750 were works of foreign scholarship!" Contributors to the forum included (besides Ransel) William G. Wagner, Willard Sunderland, Steven L. Hoch; on these pages Mironov also replies separately to each of his commentators. See note 7.

[54] I use this term deliberately, in the discursive context described by Nancy Ries in *Russian Talk: Culture and Conversation During Perestroika* (Ithaca: Cornell University Press, 1997), but in the same sense that it was used in the pre-revolutionary era in numerous obituaries of self-sacrificing intellectuals who had taken on self-sacrificial tasks in the service of people and country, at great personal cost to themselves, and in the face of incomprehension or hostility by officialdom.

the street with their homegrown 'theories of Russian history'." That is, it is a first step in combating the growing gap between public and scholarly history.[55]

Moreover, Mironov has argued forcefully for both the distinctiveness and the normalcy of Russian history, for reviewers have both harked back to Tiutchev's famous dictum,[56] and hailed Mironov's situating of Russia in a European continuum.[57] By a dazzling application of the techniques (especially quantitative) of the new "new social history," Mironov has both demonstrated a mastery of "western tools" and reasserted a continuity (or at least comfort zone) in Russian scholarship that includes the Soviet era. This continuity has been much harder to establish by deploying the techniques of the post-structuralist linguistic turn in the West, for post-modernism, and specifically cultural history, is treated in Russia as an exotic fruit, or worse, a hegemonic imposition from the outside.[58]

The laudatory tone of the overall response to *A Social History* is reflected in the flyer for the awards ceremony sponsored by the Russian Academy of Natural Sciences bestowing its Distinguished Medal upon Mironov in 2005. In its announcement the Academy noted that "his work had been met with broad acclaim, both in Russia where today he is among the most widely cited historians, and abroad ... Mironov's foundational two-volume work *A Social History of Imperial Russia*, has met especial resonance, both throughout Russia and internationally."[59] And *A Social* History has caught the attention of sociologists and economists, as well as historians. One notable example is former Premier Egor Gaidar, Yeltsin's first "economic tsar," who cites Mironov heavily in his recent work on the history of Russian economic relations with the West.[60] Many shared the sentiments expressed by S.S. Sekirinsky:

[55] Kamenskii, "Uroki, kotorye mozhno bylo by izvlech'." For an insightful study of the Soviet public's pursuit of authentic historical truth and facticity, see Denis Kozlov, "The Historical Turn in Late Soviet Culture: Retrospectivism, Factography, Doubt, 1953–1991," *Kritika: Explorations in Russian and Eurasian History* 2, no. 3 (Summer 2001): 577–600.

[56] M.D. Karpachev, "Umom Rossiiu ponimaia," *Novyi mir*, 2000, no. 6: 218–25.

[57] The phrase belongs to Elise Kimmerling Wirtschafter.

[58] This is not the impression of Catherine Merridale. See "Redesigning History." I do not mean to indicate that cultural history has no roots in Russia (Lotman, Ginzburg, Bakhtin); see Laura Engelstein, "Culture, Culture, Everywhere: Interpretations of Modern Russia, across the 1991 Divide," *Kritika: Explorations in Russian and Eurasian History* 2, no. 2 (Spring 2001): 363–93. For a sampling of recent Russian work, see "New Cultural History in Russia," special issue, *Russian Studies in History* 35, no. 4 (Spring 1997).

[59] This quotation is from the flyer announcing the roundtable sponsored by *Odysseus*. The flyer was sent to the author of this article by Boris Mironov.

[60] Egor Gaidar, *Dolgoe vremia. Rossiia v mire: Ocherki ekonomicheskoi istorii* (Moscow: Delo, 2005).

A Social History provides a "matrix" the modification and expansion of the core concepts of which will be the agenda of future historians."[61]

At the same time, Russian historians were not hesitant to criticize the volumes. One historian found a profound contradiction between the first volume (on society) which was "pessimistic," and the second (on the state), which was "optimistic" in its conclusions. A heated discussion took place on Mironov's interpretation of the impact of geography on Russian history, and even more so on issues of colonization and empire. Some objected vociferously to Mironov's rejection of Russian "exceptionalism." Some labeled him a monarchist or a "right-wing Kadet," or even worse, a Eurocentrist. Critics were incensed by his reductionist treatment of bondage (especially its seemingly undifferentiated application to both noble and serf), his uncritical use of Chaianov's labor theory, his positive treatment of the economics of serfdom, his treatment of population migration as a "safety valve." Others disagreed with his criticism of the purported irresponsibility of the Russian intelligentsia; or the argument that the Russian state was essentially law-abiding and its policies in advance of the country; or that Russia after 1905 was evolving into a parliamentary framework, with a nascent civil society; or that in some ways the Bolsheviks turned the clock of history back and in collectivization imposed a "second serfdom." Some pointed to imprecision or inaccuracy in terminology and concepts.

While generating a lot of characteristically Russian argumentation about grand theory, seemingly ungrounded in the building blocks of empirical research,[62] *A Social History* has also stimulated a lot of discussion in Russia of what the socialist Robert Merton called "middle level generalization," something that has been missing in the Russian scholarly tradition. In my view, this is noteworthy because it is precisely here, at the middle level generalization,[63] that the work excels, and

[61] See Mironov, "Predislovie," 5–6.

[62] For example: was Russia a "typical" European Empire and did ethnic Russians benefit from empire; who is to blame, autocracy or intelligentsia, for the October Revolution; was Russia evolving successfully and organically into modernity; was an anti-capitalist mindset prevalent in Russian culture; did a patriarchal culture predominate into the twentieth century; did individual personalities play a major role in historical change?

[63] Robert Merton, "On Sociological Theories of the Middle Range," *Social Theory and Social Structure: Towards the Codification of Theory and Research* (New York, 1949; revised edition, 1967), 39–72. Merton defines middle range theory as that "which lies between the minor but necessary working hypotheses that evolve in abundance during day-to-day research, and the all-inclusive systematic efforts to develop unified theory that will explain … social change." He continues, "Middle-range theory is used to guide empirical inquiry. (It) involves abstractions, of course, but (is) close enough to observed data to be incorporated in propositions that permit empirical testing. Middle-range theories deal with deliminated aspects of social phenomena" (39–40).

consistently rewards close reading. In particular, attention has been focused on his analysis of the Russian family (both size and intrafamilial relations); on demographics and the reproductive cycle; on infanticide; on the productivity of serf labor and viability of serfdom itself; on the growing impact of law upon the autocracy; on the relationship between territorial expansion and economic practices; on town and country relations (and the peasantization of the cities in the late nineteenth century); on the formation of estates, the distribution of wealth, and social mobility; and on standard of living (measured by height of military recruits). It is especially here that the breadth of Mironov's grounding in several historiographies and remarkable training in methods is brought to bear. Unfortunately, an exploration of these themes would take us far afield here.

In his foreword to the third edition, Mironov addresses his critics and acknowledges the merit of many of the criticisms leveled against his volumes. Most of the shortcomings of his work he attributes to the primitive state of research in certain areas, In his opinion, the dearth of studies of marginal social groups, of mentalité, of internal family relations, of daily life in general, of crime and criminality, even of colonization and borders ("forbidden topics in the Soviet era"), and of civil society, made it difficult to address these topics with a sure hand. He concludes that when he sits down to rewrite his social history of Russia—and this cannot be done until a new monographic literature provides the base for such a rewrite—he will do three things: expand the framework to include marginal populations, voluntary associations, etc; supplement his analysis of the "formal legal" side of law, crime, and statecraft to breathe life into the reality of these spheres (move from the de jure to the de facto through empirical studies of lived experience and legal practices); and, finally, refine the methodological and conceptual base by more rigorous use of sociological conceptions, and "by taking into consideration post-modernist conceptions, and especially the 'linguistic turn.'"[64] He cknowledges that work in regional archives in the future will surely modify his "centrist" (in the sense of national rather than regional) approach to Russian history

Yet what a laundry list of points at issue ignores is the tone of respect, almost awe of Mironov's scholarship that suffuse most commentaries, the frequent assertions that post-Soviet scholarship on Russia had come of age. But perhaps the most resounding praise can be found on the pages of the prestigious journal *Odysseus*, founded by renowned historian of medieval Europe, A.Ia. Gurevich, in 1989. At a round-table organized in 2004 by Gurevich,[65] Europeanist A.B. Kamensky joins

[64] Mironov, "Predislovie," xv–xl.

[65] *See Odissei: Chelovek v istorii*, 2004, 390–421, with contributions by L.M. Batkin, A.Ia. Gurevich, A.B. Kamensky, M.Iu. Paramonova, and I.M. Suponitskaia.

virtually all other reviewers in agreeing that "since Kliuchevsky there has been no work of this scope founded on precisely defined scholarly conceptions" and in praise of the "extraordinary grounding in sources and historiography." Kamensky also finds significance in Mironov's ability to "carry out a distinct synthesis of Russian (*otechestvennye*) and foreign scholarship; the work being an attempt to overcome the distance (between two traditions) and establish a common space for scholarship."[66]

Others made the same point. As noted above, in acknowledging deficiencies in his work, Mironov pointed to "the general condition of (Russian) historiography,"[67] as a partial explanation. In response, N.I. Tsimbaev of Moscow University (while commending Mironov for the exhaustive use of not only home-grown, but also foreign scholarship") called Mironov's criticism of Soviet historical scholarship "harsh," and "unproven." Yet his elaboration is most interesting here: "This is a very unexpected comment from an historian whose book, after all, is a summation of the work of several generations of historians as well as an adaptation of the achievements of Russian historical scholarship to the concepts and terms of (in Mironov's words) 'the dynamically evolving social science of the West.'"[68]

Take note: "a summation of the work of several generations" and "an adaptation of the achievements of Russian historical scholarship" to western concepts and terms. In a nutshell, I think this comment explains the resonance of *A Social History* among Russian historians as a whole and the respectful, even admiring tone of reviews, even those most critical. Tsimbaev and many other reviewers of the volume describe a bold work of synthesis which, while controversial and perhaps flawed, clearly measures up to the rigorous methodological standards of "foreign" scholarship ("after all, his work has been translated into seven languages").[69] Moreover, as social history, it does not displace, or reject, Russian (*otechestvennaia* is the term Tsimbaev uses repeatedly) historical traditions; instead it builds upon and adapts the work of generations of scholars, without whose labor Mironov's work could never have been "built."

Mironov's *A Social History* normalizes Russian history but also the Russian historical profession. One western reviewer noted that Mironov's conceptual framework restores continuity to Russian historical development; it also restores continuity to the country's historical profession. The fact that, as Ransel points out, Russian commentators "do not hesitate" to challenge Mironov on a broad front of

---

[66] Kamenskii, "Uroki, kotorye mozhno bylo izvlech'."

[67] B.N. Mironov, "K istine vedet mnogo putei," *Otechestvennaia istoriia*, 2001, no. 2: 107–8.

[68] I.I. Tsimbaev, *Otechestvennaia istoriia*, 2002, no. 2: 201–2.

[69] A Chinese edition is in press.

issues, including many others not mentioned above, does not alter this picture. The commentary is normalized, organic, and self-confident, based upon a common and continuous historiography, in a comfortable relationship with western scholarship, because an affinity is claimed, and felt, between the social history which is the foundation of this work and the Russian historical tradition. In this collective response, the boundaries between pre-revolutionary, Soviet, and post-Soviet are elided and Russian historiography emerges as both integrated with and distinctive from western scholarship—its peer, and rightfully so.

Conclusion

In conclusion, a comment on normalcy (*normal'nost'*[70]) and the "Enlightenment project" of modernization.[71] My perspective is that the binary opposition of traditional and modern embodied in modernization theory is of course simplistic and misleading, as is the linear trajectory embedded in it, for reasons that are too familiar to rehearse here.[72] Yet this may be entirely beside the point. Since 1991, Russian historians, both academic and textbook, have struggled to find a suitable framework for Russian history ... which after all "begins" in Kyiv. In the West today, it is a truism among historians that "Russia was a state before it was a nation"[73]; but then, if the "juridical (statist) school" is no longer suitable, what will the master narrative be? Textbook authors have turned, with some success, to the civilizational approach, but it does not easily transfer to the realm of specialized scholarship.[74]

[70] There is an entire cottage industry of scholarship around the use of this term in the late Soviet period by the middle class to describe their aspirations, drawn largely from their notion of an "imaginary West." See, for example, Ries, *Russian Talk*, Eklof et al., *Educational Reform in Post-Soviet Russia*, Alexei Yurchak, *Everything Was Forever, Until it Was No More* (Princeton: Princeton University Press, 2005), and Mary Buckley, *Redefining Russian Society and Polity* (Boulder: Westview Press, 1993).

[71] See the conference report on "Protsessy modernizatsii v Rossii i Evrope: Sotsiokul'turnye, politicheskie i dukhovnye aspekty," the second international congress held in Voronezh, June 27–29, 2002 (*Otechestvennaia istoriia*, 2003, no. 2: 204–6). Interestingly, one of the authors of this report, M.D. Minakov, is the author of the volumes which won the recent Ministry of Education competition for the "best textbook" to be used in 9th and 11th grade history classes.

[72] Many of Mironov's Russian critics criticized his treatment of the transition from the Muscovite to the Imperial era, and the author accepted the validity of this criticisms. For an English language evaluation, see Maureen Perrie, "The Muscovite Monarchy in the Sixteenth Century: 'national,' 'popular,' or 'democratic'?" *Cahiers du Monde Russe* 46, nos. 1–2 (2005): 234–5 and 241. For Mironov's comments, see the forward to the third edition (2003).

[73] See, for example, Geoffrey Hosking, *Russia: People and Empire 1552–1917* (London: Fontana Press, 1997).

[74] On the "civilizational" approach see several essays in *Educational Reform in Post-Soviet*

The post-modern approach, fundamentally deconstructive, offers no recognizable heuristic framework by which to write a textbook-level historical synthesis of world, empire, or nation. In Mironov's words, "the post-modern view of the world (depicts reality) as chaotic, lacking links between cause and consequence, without important landmarks—decentralized, disordered, fragmented ... to accept post-modernism means to lose an ideal and any hope of achieving it."[75] For Russians, who have lived through two decades of chaos and plummeting standards of living, concisely summarized by Perry Anderson as "liberation, depression, expropriation, attrition, demotion [of status in the world]"[76] such epistemologies offer little comfort, and certainly provide few guidelines for a usable past. As Mironov puts it, "(post-modernism) does not jibe well with Russia's current attitudes, and ... it distracts from the resolution of issues that are important to Russian society." [77] Moreover, in many places it is regarded as alien, imposed, connected with western agendas, disconnected from Russian traditions. At the very least, the potential for injured national pride is obvious. I heard forceful confirmation of this at the 2003 AAASS national convention in Toronto. At a session on gender and history in post-Soviet historical scholarship, a speaker, Elena Gapova, spoke of her own efforts to bring gender studies to a Siberian university.[78] Initially enthusiastic, she had come to the realization that this approach tended to privilege an existing elite with strong western ties in grant competitions. By contrast, it often met with disinterest or even hostility outside the university community, or even in university circles outside Moscow. Thus, she had come to view gender studies in this context as inadvertently perpetuating hegemony rather than fostering emancipation and intellectual growth. We should ponder the fact that the term *gendernye* is not only awkward and imported to the Russian language, but undecipherable to those who know no foreign language; it has

Russia, and N.A. Proskuriakova, "Konseptsiia tsivilizatsii i modernizatsii v otechestvennoi istorii," *Voprosy istorii*, 2005, no. 7: 153–65.

[75] Mironov, "Has Postmodernism Come to Russia?" 220.

[76] "Russia's Managed Democracy," *London Review of Books* 29, no. 2 (January 25, 2007). Anderson's portrayal of the cultural world in Russia today is similar to my depiction of scholarly fragmentation and demoralization.

[77] Mironov, "Has Postmodernism Come to Russia?" 220.

[78] Elena Gapova, "On Writing Women's/Gender History in Countries in Transition," (paper presented at the "Post-1991 Dynamics of Russian and East European Women's History" panel at the National Convention of the AAASS, Toronto, November 21, 2003). However, according to Bryon MacWilliams, gender and women's studies have made some headway under the term *feminologiia.* See "Scholarship on Women Starts to Take off in Russia," *The Chronicle of Higher Education* 46, issue 7 (October 8, 1999): A59.

no recognizable word root.[79] Likewise, much of post-Soviet Russian scholarship has been formulated with an eye to western grant organizations, and a sensitivity to what would "fly" with western academic reviewers. Although in some happy circumstances, Russian scholarly aspirations and western reviewers' preferences coincide, this "adult supervision"[80] and need to "talk the talk" in order to win funding inevitably evokes "hidden and public transcripts" in which private and public agendas and feelings don't often match one another.

Mironov explicitly describes his own approach as modified (through the lens of cultural anthropology) modernization theory, which, he acknowledges, "is out of fashion in the West, but just now being fruitfully employed in Russia."[81] Mironov provides a clear trajectory for future research, even a challenge, in the assertion that "the substance of societal modernization in Imperial Russia, as elsewhere, consisted in the genesis of personal identity (*lichnost'*), of the nuclear, democratic family, of civil society, and of the law-governed state."

The search for a "usable past," if not a viable intellectual project in the minds of some, is "an important quality of Mironov's work, and underscores his "moral or cathartic purpose."[82] As the Europeanists commented at the round-table published in *Odysseus* also noted, finding a "usable past" is also a vital political task today, essential to the stability and very survival of Russia, and to combat nativistic currents which have emerged in response to Russia's diminished place in the world since the collapse of the Soviet Union. Even more, the Russian Europeanists argue, if Russia

[79] Of course I am not commenting on the intrinsic value of gender studies, but on its "imposition" and "reception" in Russia. Using the "modernization" framework, Mironov pays much attention to patriarchy, and reproduction. He does not, however, deploy "masculinity" or gender concepts in his approach.

[80] The term is used by Perry Anderson in a slightly different context, to describe the tutelage exerted by American advisors and the IMF over the Russian economy under Yeltsin, and the widespread resentment of this tutelage by many Russian middle-level policy makers, especially among the *siloviki* (personnel of the power ministries such as defense and the interior). See Anderson, "Russia's Managed Democracy."

[81] Mironov, "Predislovie," 38; also idem, "Has Postmodernism Come to Russia?" 216. See also Mironov's robust defense of "the topicality in contemporary social science," especially sociology of "revamped" modernization theory in the West, in "Has Postmodernism Come to Russia?" 217–18.

[82] Ransel, "A Single Research Community?" 556. Indeed, Mironov describes his approach as "Cliotherapeutic"; by normalizing Russian history to a broad audience he explicitly wants to help configure a usable past so that Russians can look at their country, in its early years, as an "at-risk child" … normal, but evolving in difficult circumstances and with slightly arrested development.

is to become part of the European Union, if Europeans are to think of Russia as part of their realm, Russians must themselves believe this to be true. The modernization framework, with all its deficiencies, is amply broad, inclusive and open-ended to allow Mironov, despite all the contradictions of his interpretation pointed out alike by Russian and western scholars, to present a *passionate and patriotic* (but not nativistic) vision of Russian history acceptable to both scholarly and lay audiences. [83]

At the individual level too, there are strong presentist elements to Mironov's read of Russian history, especially in his depiction of the emergence of civil society, of individualism, and of personal autonomy as measures of progress. These presentist elements can be traced to his own personal biography, to his early years as a

---

[83] Madhavan Palat has noted the trap Mironov falls into here. His comments have not been fully published, hence merit space here: The problem with such analysis is that it can discover only inadequacy, never accomplishment. Thus Mironov can offer to his countrymen only the consolation prize that Russia has been modernizing effectively, but without reaching the same plane as Europe. Three centuries of Russian development reveal only failure, not success, although he has claimed it as success. This logic denies the Russian the capacity to measure himself against abstraction and to abstract from his historical achievement. Thus the utterly incomplete social modernization of Britain, with its retention of antimodernist estate privileges and a hereditary monarchy, and the anti-secularism of an Established Church, have all been theorized into a constitutional ideal or even idyll, worthy of emulation worldwide. The ceaseless chaos of French politics has been projected as the paradigm case of the democratic republic and nation-state, both deriving their legitimacy from the fountainhead of modernity, the French Revolution. American politics, premised on the genocide of American Indians, chattel slavery, and extreme levels of racism, has been held up as a model of democratic politics, and of equality and liberty. The astonishingly archaic German Imperial constitution was the perfect *Rechtstaat* to three generations of Russians, among others. But Russians were never capable of emulating these achievements at theorizing; they could not raise their politics to theory; they were doomed to present it as shoddy practice against the model conduct of Europeans. This has been Mironov's fate as he depicts the *normalcy* of Russian society: its *normalcy* lies its being, not a model in itself, only an approximation to Europe, in its perennially fleeing from Russia but failing to reach Europe. Mironov's predicament seems to suggest, as has often been said, that Russia can not resolve her problems at universal and theoretical levels, that she may attempt to do so only in practice. From Mironov's account it would appear that Russia can not be Europe, that it dare not be Russia, that it may merely try to be Europe and end up becoming its shoddy imitation, the despised *narod-podrazhatel'*... A *normal* society eventuates in an *anormal* one, the Soviet Union, which in its turn dissolves into a *normal* one again, the Russian Federation. The Soviet Union interrupted a *normal* development; and normalcy lay and lies in imitating the West energetically on the premise that Russia is not *quite* western. Russia is however doomed to remain perpetually backward to the West despite the effort as the historical record shows. Normalcy, by Mironov's account, amounts to westernization as a Sisyphean labour, not the consummation of that process. His strivings reflect the inverse of Balaam's performance in the Book of Numbers: his two-volume benediction has brought forth an eternal curse.

scholar whose freedoms were unduly restricted even once he had gained western recognition, and to his generation as a whole, a middle class chafing at the humiliating limits imposed by the state, who had little voice in public affairs and who yearned for a normal life, even if this notion was based upon an "imaginary West."[84] From this perspective it is easier to understand the feeling behind the argument that "On the whole, during the Imperial era, Russia successfully underwent societial modernization: first of all, people gained autonomy from the collective, whether it be familiar, communal, corporative, or other ... and individuals gained an intrinsic worth."[85]

At the same time, it is amply broad, inclusive, and open-ended, allowing him to bring into perspective and analyze, at the middle level of generalization, a rich harvest of developments, themes and issues, to pursue the notion of evolutionary change in the family, in society, and in state building. Mironov fully acknowledges the "schematic" and sometimes reductionist qualities of his relentless effort to fit the evolution of so many dimension of economy, polity and society into the straitjacket of modernization theory, and he notes that asynchonicities (what another school would call "uneven development") were at the root of many of the formidable social tensions wracking the Russian Empire in the early twentieth century. Mironov argues that a positivist approach still has much to offer us in understanding Russian history; at the same time, he argues that he has inserted insights from cultural anthropology throughout the text, not only in his descriptions of lived experience, but also in his conceptualization of the relationship between state and society.

In short, modernization theory is arguably a very decent heuristic framework that, with all its shortcomings, still has considerable explanatory power. For many in

[84] The reference to "imaginary West" is frequently encountered in postcolonial studies and is the title of a chapter in Alexei Yurchak's recent work, *Everything Was Forever, Until it Was No More*. This stimulating book is a history largely of the Soviet cohort born under after Khrushchev, and argues the paradox that nobody expected the Soviet Union to collapse, but also that nobody was surprised when it did. I agree strongly with his first point, but, given his sample, the second point is accurate only in regard to a small segment of that generation. For my comments on Mironov's own life, see his autobiographical sketch in the English-language version. Also relevant here is the article by Irina Paperno in *Kritika* describing Alexander Herzen's autobiographical account *My Past and Thoughts* as the master narrative of the Soviet intelligentsia (a persecuted minority confronting a repressive state and indifferent, if exploited population). See, Paperno, "Personal Accounts of the Soviet Experience," *Kritika: Explorations in Russian and Eurasian History* 3, no. 4 (Fall 2002): 577–610.

[85] Ironically, in his gracious response to critics both Russian and western, Mironov acknowledges that his "positivist and empiricist" inclination dictates a certain approach to his subject, namely that "history happens to people," which in turn underplays "agency." For an interesting analysis of the lingering legacy of pre-revolutionary positivism on late Soviet historical writing, see Kozlov, "The Historical Turn in Late Soviet Culture," 577–600, esp. 599.

Russia, even those critics who reject Mironov's efforts to make Russian history a part of European history, this framework allowed the author to deploy an array of methodological tools, and connect them with a native historiographical tradition, and in so doing restore luster to their on past as historians. As Russian Europeanist L.M. Batkin put it in his contribution to *Odysseus*, "Mironov has given us back our past."[86]

[86] L.M. Batkin, "K sporam ob istoricheskikh putiakh sotsial'nogo razvitiia Rossii: o monografii B.N. Mironova, *Odissei. Chelovek v istorii*, 2004.

From a "Prominent Biologist" to a "Red Frankenstein"

Ilya Ivanov in Soviet and Post-Soviet Biographies

Nikolai Krementsov

Answering the question "What is Soviet now?" requires first answering the question "What was Soviet then?" Even leaving aside the historiographic debates on when exactly the Soviet period began and when exactly it ended, answering the second question is a difficult task given the simple fact that the "then" covers some seventy years of history. During those years the very notion of "Soviet" in various domains was continuously reshaped and dramatically transformed on more than one occasion. As this comparison of two biographies of the Russian biologist Ilya Ivanov (1870-1932)—one published in 1964, another in 2003—demonstrates, numerous Soviet templates are available to post-Soviet writers and their audiences. What remains highly questionable, however, is how "Soviet" those templates actually are and whether modern writers of Soviet history actually employ them.

The Genre of "Scientific" Biography

In 1964, the leading Soviet academic publisher Nauka issued fifteen volumes as part of its recently established, but already highly reputed biographical series.[1] Along with the life stories of such renowned scientists and inventors as Claude Bernard, Johann Wolfgang Goethe, August Kekule, George Stephenson, and Thomas Edison, which appeared that year, the publisher released the biography of Ilya Ivanov (1870–1932), a biologist and animal breeder, hailed as the creator of the first practicable

---

Research for this article was supported by the Canadian Social Sciences and Humanities Research Council (through a Standard Research Grant) and by the U.S. National Institutes of Health (through the National Library of Medicine's publication grant no. 5 G13 LM008632-02).

[1] The history of the series has been thoroughly documented in several publications, see Z.K. Sokolovskaia, *200 nauchnykh biografii: bibliograficheskii spravochnik* (Moscow: Nauka, 1975); idem, *300 biografii uchenykh: o knigakh serii "Nauchno-biograficheskaia literatura," 1959–1980: biobibliograficheskii spravochnik* (Moscow: Nauka, 1982); idem, *400 biografii uchenykh: o serii "Nauchno-biograficheskaia literatura," 1959–1986: biobibliograficheskii spravochnik* (Moscow: Nauka, 1988); Z.K. Sokolovskaia and V.I. Sokolovskii, *550 knig ob uchenykh, inzhenerakh i izobretateliakh: spravochnik-putevoditel' po serii RAN "Nauchno-biograficheskaia literatura," 1959–1997* (Moscow: Nauka, 1999).

technique of artificial insemination in mammals.[2] Entitled *The Prominent Biologist Ilya Ivanovich Ivanov*, the one-hundred-plus pages volume followed all the canons of the genre of "scientific" biography promoted by the publisher.

Unlike such popular series of the time as "The Life of Notables" ("ZhZL"—*Zhizn' zamechatel'nykh liudei*) issued by the Young Guard press, which specialized in literary, often fictionalized, biographies, the goal of the academic series was the production of "strictly scientific biographies" written by "specialists": professional scientists and historians of science.[3] The Institute for the History of Science and Technology of the USSR Academy of Sciences had initiated the series and the Institute's staff supplied the majority of both its authors and its editors. "Scientific" biography aimed at informing the readership of "the life and work of prominent representatives of science and technology in a popular way." From its inception in 1959, the series editors emphasized the need for writing biographies on a "strictly documentary foundation" and for a detailed analysis of the protagonist's scientific ideas, research, and accomplishments.

Written by Petr Skatkin, Ivanov's former student and collaborator, who had recently retired from his own scientific work and joined the staff of the Institute for the History of Science and Technology, the book was based on extensive exploration of state and personal archives, the careful analysis of the protagonist's published works and relevant secondary literature, as well as the author's personal recollections. It was supplemented by a complete bibliography of Ivanov's publications and works written about him. The book focused on Ivanov's scientific ideas and methods, tracing their origins and developments, outlining their reception at home and abroad, and emphasizing their practical and theoretical importance, as well as Ivanov's general "contribution to the development of science."

The opening chapter, "The Life Path"—occupying almost one third of the entire volume—provided a broad chronological outline of Ivanov's biography from his birth in August 1870 to his death in March 1932. The remaining five chapters presented detailed analyses of Ivanov's scientific predecessors (chapter 2), his research on the biology of reproduction in domesticated animals (chapter 3), his development of a practicable technique for artificial insemination in mammals (chapter 4), his "scientific-practical activities" (chapter 5), and his studies of interspecies hybridization (chapter 6).

Along with conforming to the newest standards of "scientific" biography,

---

[2] P.N. Skatkin, *Il'ia Ivanovich Ivanov—Vydaiushchiisia biolog* (Moscow: Nauka, 1964).

[3] Sokolovskaia, *400 biografii uchenykh*, 24, passim. The following quotations are from this source.

Skatkin's book also bore marks of an older Soviet tradition—the biography of a "founding father."[4] The image of a "founding father" emerged amidst militant ideological attacks on "bourgeois scientists" of the early to mid-1930s and embodied all the characteristics of a "true Soviet scientist." It quickly evolved into a rigid formulaic rhetoric used to demonstrate ideological loyalty and devotion to the current party line and provided a simple, effective hagiographic template for numerous biographies of both prominent scientists such as Dmitri Mendeleev, Nikolai Lobachevsky, Ilya Mechnikov, and Ivan Pavlov, and Soviet "scientists," including Ivan Michurin and Vasily Vil'iams.

Closely adhering to this template, Skatkin's account emphasized Ivanov's "difficulties" under the Tsarist regime, which derived from his involvement in the "revolutionary movement" as well as his "progressive, materialistic" worldview. It underscored Ivanov's "immediate acceptance" of the Bolshevik revolution and "his active participation in the construction of new life," as well as the recognition and support accorded to Ivanov by the Soviet state. It stressed the "practicality" of Ivanov's research and its importance to the "people's economy." It underlined Ivanov's contribution to the "development of Darwinism"—Soviet biologists' codeword for Marxism in their own field. It also highlighted Ivanov's "patriotism" and "struggle for the priority of Russian science," as well as his close connections with other "founding fathers" of Russian and Soviet science, including Aleksander Kovalevsky, Ilya Mechnikov, and Ivan Pavlov.

Ivanov himself clearly qualified as a founding father and probably would have been granted the high title in the mid-1930s, if it were not for a small "glitch" in his otherwise exemplar biography. In December 1930—on the heels of the campaign against "bourgeois specialists" inaugurated by the infamous Shakhty trial, which is not even mentioned in the book,—Ivanov was arrested, as Skatkin put it, under "a false accusation." After spending six months in prison, he was exiled to—again Skatkin does not use this word, noting instead that Ivanov simply "moved to"—Kazakhstan's capital, Alma-Ata. There he continued his teaching and research at a local veterinary institute and even managed to establish a special laboratory of "reproductive biology" under the auspices of the recently created All-Union Academy of Agricultural Sciences. It was in Alma-Ata that Ivanov suffered a stroke and died in the spring of 1932.

Although Ivanov died in "disgrace" and thus could not attain the "founding father" status in the 1930s, a decade later, during the campaign for the "priority of Russian science" ignited by the early Cold War, he was acclaimed as the "founder

[4] For a general discussion of the phenomenon of "founding fathers" in Soviet science, see Nikolai Krementsov, *Stalinist Science* (Princeton: Princeton University Press, 1997).

of artificial insemination." A series of articles published in 1948–50 in newspapers and journals hailed his work on artificial insemination in domesticated animals as the achievement of Soviet science.[5] With the dawning of Khrushchev's anti-Stalinist campaign, Ivanov was officially "rehabilitated"—all charges against him were dismissed in 1959. During the late 1950s and early 1960s, a number of publications about Ivanov appeared in various encyclopedias and periodicals. Skatkin's biography was a culmination of the rehabilitation campaign waged by Ivanov's family and his former students, although, of course, the author does not even mention it.

Skatkin's book betrays its "Sovietness" not only by what was highlighted on, but also by what was omitted from, its pages—not merely details of the arrest, exile, and the subsequent rehabilitation, but most notably the entire personal life of its protagonist. Although the biographer thanked Ivanov's daughter and son for granting access to the family archive, aside from a reference to Ivanov junior as his father's companion during an expedition to West Africa in 1926–27, there is no mention of Ivanov's marriage, family life, or the birth of his children. His wife does not even appear in the text and the reader could only learn her name (but nothing else) from a facsimile of Ivan Pavlov's letter of condolence, which was reproduced in the text as an illustration of Pavlov's high regard for the deceased. Although the author studied under and worked with Ivanov for a number of years, there is no mention of personal friends, personal tastes (in music, literature, food, arts, etc.), personal beliefs, or indeed anything outside the confines of Ivanov's scientific exploits.

Post-Soviet, Anti-Soviet, or Soviet Still?

Following a short-lived decline induced by the general economic chaos of the early 1990s, the Russian public enjoyed a dramatic increase in the production of biographies by both "old" Soviet-era publishers (like Young Guard and Nauka) and new "commercial" presses. The publishers' approach in this biographical boom was two-pronged. On one hand, they aimed at filling gaps in the past biographical series by bringing to the readership the life stories of individuals considered for various reasons "undesirable" under the Soviet regime. This subset of biographies ranged from Russian royalty and nobility to Western celebrities, and from prominent foreign leaders to famous courtesans of bygone eras. On the other hand, publishers sought to "correct" the misrepresentations and misinterpretations in the previously published

[5] See, for instance, B.I. Zbarskii, "O prioritete sovetskikh uchenykh v razrabotke metoda iskusstvennogo osemeneniia zhivotnykh kak zootekhnicheskogo meropriiatiia," *Sotsialisticheskoe zemledelie*, February 19, 1948, 2–3; N.P. Shergin, "Professor Il'ia Ivanovich Ivanov—osnovopolozhnik metoda iskusstvennogo osemeneniia sel'sko-khoziastvennykh zhivotnykh," *Vestnik zhivotnovodstva*, 1948, no. 4: 9–20; G.V. Parshutin, "50 let iskusstvennogo osemeneniia loshadei," *Konevodstvo*, 1950, 27–31.

biographies, by issuing the "true" life stories of prominent Soviet leaders and cultural figures, ranging from Vladimir Lenin and Joseph Stalin to Valery Chkalov and Yuri Gagarin, and from Dmitri Shostakovich and Mikhail Sholokhov to Ivan Pavlov and Andrei Sakharov. A new version of Ivanov's life story that appeared in September 2003 clearly falls into this second category of "corrected" biographies.[6]

The book was released by a recently (in 2002) established "leftist" publishing house Ultraculture, whose claim to fame (or at least publicity) was laid by issuing scandalous books written by the leader of "national-bolshevism" Eduard Limonov.[7] The new biography of Ivanov was penned by Oleg Shishkin, a young professional writer, who had already distinguished himself in the genre with two bestsellers: *The Struggle for the Himalayas* (1999), loosely based on the biography of the prominent painter and mystic Nikolai Rerikh, and *To Kill Rasputin* (2000), an account of Grigori Rasputin's murder. The title of Shishkin's new book, *The Red Frankenstein: The Kremlin's Secret Experiments*, clearly indicates that it was intended as an exposé of both Ivanov (the Frankenstein) and the Soviet state (the Kremlin). Indeed, if Shishkin's book had appeared (either in *samizdat* or in *tamizdat*) during the Soviet era, it would have certainly been considered "anti-Soviet." But as we will see shortly, it also exhibits certain apparently "Soviet" features.

In many ways Shishkin's book provides a striking contrast to the earlier depiction of Ivanov's life story. Although it is almost twice as long as the previous account, the sixteen-chapter book could hardly qualify as a comprehensive biography of its protagonist. The nearly fifty years of Ivanov's life and research prior to the Bolshevik revolution amount to only four out of three-hundred-plus pages in Shishkin's book, while Ivanov's work on his technique of artificial insemination and its implementation and uses in animal breeding during the Soviet period (which occupied nearly one third of Skatkin's account) is barely mentioned at all. Indeed, the entire volume revolves around one particular episode in Ivanov's life and work: his expedition to French West Africa in 1926–27, which aimed to produce hybrids between apes and humans by means of artificial insemination.

Contrary to the book's sensationalist claims about their "secret" character, Ivanov's experiments on ape-human hybrids had at the time been covered extensively by the media and were described in considerable detail in the earlier biography.[8] In fact, Skatkin devoted eight out of fifty-two pages in his first chapter to

[6] Oleg Shishkin, *Krasnyi Frankenshtein. Sekretnye eksperimenty Kremlia* (Moscow: Ul'tra Kul'tura, 2003).

[7] See the publisher's website http://www.ultraculture.ru.

[8] In fact, they attracted considerable attention from the post-Soviet press as well. See, for instance, Irina Alekseeva, "V Sukhumskom pitomnike uchenye skreshchivali liudei i obez'ian,"

outlining the goals and outcomes of Ivanov's expedition and experiments.[9] However, if for Skatkin the expedition was indeed just an episode in his protagonist's life and work, for Shishkin, it represents the essence of not only (and not even primarily) Ivanov's life-long scientific exploits, but also (and most importantly) of the Soviet leadership's—"the Kremlin's"—relationship to these exploits.

Like his predecessor, Shishkin builds his account on a "strictly documentary foundation," but, reflecting the differences in the focus of the two books, that foundation differs considerably from Skatkin's. Skatkin's biography was largely based on Ivanov's personal archive, supplemented by a few sources from both imperial and Soviet periods, mostly from the archive of the Academy of Sciences. Shishkin's account is based almost exclusively on the examination of the "secret" archives of the Bolshevik party and Soviet state agencies, ranging from the Politburo and the Council of People's Commissars to the secret police and the Red Army. He did not even mention (or perhaps did not even know) that Ivanov's personal papers had been deposited to and are readily available for scrutiny in one of Moscow's archives.

There is a certain similarity between the earlier and the later renderings of Ivanov's life story in that both accounts thoroughly ignore Ivanov the individual. Although Shishkin's biography gives many more details about Ivanov junior's role in his father's expedition to West Africa, aside from this, there is no description of Ivanov's marriage, family, personal likes and dislikes, friendships—in short, there is nothing to make the portrait appear even remotely human.

The most obvious difference between Skatkin's and Shishkin's biographies lays in their approach to Ivanov's science. Following the cannons of "scientific" biography, Skatkin strove to place Ivanov's ideas and research in their *intellectual* context through careful comparison with similar ideas and research pursued by Ivanov's predecessors and contemporaries. In contrast, Shishkin attempts to situate Ivanov's ideas and research within the *social, political, and ideological* contexts of 1920s Bolshevik Russia, and ignores their intellectual contexts. And, in doing so, Shishkin follows a distinctly "Soviet" template.

Indeed, it was a Soviet physicist-turned-historian, Boris Hessen, who pioneered the examination of science through the lens of its social, economic, political, and ideological contexts.[10] In his oft-cited essay, "The Social and Economic Roots of

Vechernii Cheliabinsk, March 22, 2001, 2–3.

[9] Skatkin, *Il'ia Ivanovich Ivanov*, 46–54.

[10] On Hessen and his essay, see Loren R. Graham, "The Socio-political Roots of Boris Hessen: Soviet Marxism and the History of Science," *Social Studies of Science* 15 (1985): 705–22.

Newton's *Principia*," presented to the Second International Congress on the History of Science in London in 1931, Hessen elaborated a Marxist analysis of the origins and contents of Isaak Newton's physics as reflections of social, economic, and political developments in sixteenth- and seventeenth-century England. Hessen's essay inspired such leading Western historians of science as Joseph Needham, Robert Merton, and Alexander Koyre, and laid a foundation for the now widely practiced *externalist* and *social* histories of science.

Back in the Soviet Union, the social analysis of science, though loudly proclaimed "the true Marxist" direction in the history of science, suffered a somewhat different fate.[11] Its originator, Boris Hessen, perished in the Great Terror, and his approach to the history of science quickly devolved into two distinct trends. One, purporting to illuminate "social influences" in Soviet science, deteriorated into formulaic statements about the "leading role of the party" and its leaders personally (be it Lenin, Stalin, Khrushchev, or Brezhnev) in "the development of science in the USSR," supplemented by claims that "true" science was possible only "under socialism." Another trend, aiming to uncover "social influences" in foreign science, degenerated into similarly formulaic statements about science and scientists being "lackeys and servants of capitalism," supplemented by claims that foreign science was in fact "pseudo-science." Both trends advanced (explicitly in the latter and implicitly in the former) a simplistic view of science and scientists as mere instruments of the ruling class (either doomed capitalists or victorious proletarians), ignoring other factors and dynamics of scientific development. Both trends flourished throughout the Soviet period, serving as important propagandistic tools in the Cold War confrontation between East and West, and becoming the domains of party ideologues and scientific demagogues.

It was to distance themselves from such party hacks and to avoid "political engagement" that professional historians of science concentrated much more on "internalist" than "externalist" studies when the history of science became an established academic discipline in the Soviet Union after the Second World War.[12] This is also why the academic series so actively promoted the "scientific" biography that dealt

---

[11] For details, see "Soviet Attitudes toward the Social and Historical Study of Science," in Loren R. Graham, *Science in Russia and the Soviet Union: A Short History* (Cambridge: Cambridge University Press, 1993), chapter 7.

[12] For a detailed analysis of the development of the Soviet history of science in the post-war period see Slava Gerovitch, "Writing History in the Present Tense: Cold War-Era Discursive Strategies of Soviet Historians of Science and Technology," in *Universities and Empire: Money and Politics in the Social Sciences During the Cold War*, ed. Christopher Simpson (New York: The New Press, 1998), 189–228.

almost exclusively with the actual research and scientific ideas, reducing a social analysis of the protagonist's work to a few rhetorical clichés. Not until the late 1980s and early 1990s—the heydays of perestroika—was a social approach "reintroduced" into the works of professional historians of science in Russia.[13]

This reintroduction took two distinct paths. One was the "legalization" of a genre that had briefly appeared during Khrushchev's Thaw and had since been flourishing in both *samizdat* and *tamizdat* publications—the "oppressed science."[14] This genre represented a simple inversion of the older "social analysis" of Soviet science, substituting "the oppression by" for "the leading role of" the Communist party and its leaders.[15] The works of this genre drew a sharp and fast divide between "science" and "the state," reducing the multitude of interactions between science and society to "oppression" and "resistance." The entire history of Soviet science was portrayed in simple black-and-white dichotomies of "executioners" and "victims," "triumphs" and "tragedies," "heroes" and "villains," loaded with explicit moral judgments of historical events and actors.[16] Yet undergirding these dichotomies was an unshakable belief in the ultimate "goodness" of science, which the Bolsheviks and their sidekicks had somehow "perverted" or "manipulated."[17]

The second path was the application to Soviet scientific developments of the sophisticated social analysis pioneered by Boris Hessen and since then well advanced in many Western histories of science, but almost entirely absent in the Soviet ones.

[13] On the general trends in the history of science in Russia during perestroika, see Slava Gerovitch, "Perestroika of the History of Technology and Science in the USSR: Changes in the Discourse," *Technology and Culture* 37, no. 1 (1996): 102–34.

[14] The best examples of this genre are works by Zhores Medvedev and Mark Popovsky on the history of Soviet genetics, which had first circulated in samizdat, later appeared in tamizdat, and finally published in Russia during the perestroika, see Zhores Medvedev, *The Rise and Fall of Lysenko* (New York: Columbia University Press, 1969); and Mark Popovsky, *The Vavilov Affair* (Humden: Archon Books, 1984).

[15] Characteristically, one of the leaders of this genre during perestroika, the chief-editor of a two-volume series of collected works entitled "Oppressed Science," Mikhail Iaroshevsky, had distinguished himself in the older genre as an active "critic" of "bourgeois cybernetics." See Mikhail G. Iaroshevskii, ed., *Repressirovannaia nauka*, vol. 1–2 (Leningrad, St. Petersburg, 1990, 1994).

[16] See for instance, V.A. Soyfer, *Vlast' i nauka. Istoriia razgroma genetiki v SSSR* (Ann Arbor: Hermitage, 1989); idem, *T.D. Lysenko and the Tragedy of Soviet Science* (New Brunswick, N.J.: Rutgers University Press, 1994); Simon Shnol', *Geroi i zlodei rossiiskoi nauki* (Moscow: Kron-Press, 1997).

[17] See, for instance, Mark Popovsky, *Manipulated Science: The Crisis of Science and Scientists in the Soviet Union Today* (New York: Doubleday, 1979); Vadim Birstein, *The Perversion of Knowledge: The True Story of Soviet Science* (Boulder: Westview Press, 2001).

The followers of this path rejected the simplistic dichotomies and called for careful examination of the multiple ways in which science and scientists interacted with the Soviet state and society.[18] They supplemented the descriptions of "oppression" and "resistance" with analyses of negotiations, borrowings, adaptations, overlapping interests, cooptation, symbiotic interrelations, appropriations, cooperation, shared rituals and rhetoric, mutual influences, competition, recruitments, patron-client relations, symbolic exchanges, and numerous other forms of interactions.[19] As one might have expected, Ivanov's life story and, more specifically, his research on ape-human hybrids, became the subject of such complex analysis, which, so far had been published only in the English language.[20]

Shishkin follows neither of these newest paths in the social history of Soviet science. Rather, he apparently uses an older Soviet template developed within the "social analysis" of "capitalist" science. Indeed, his rendering of Ivanov's biography most resembles such infamous examples of the genre as "Fly-lovers, man-haters" by Trofim Lysenko's disciple A.N. Studitsky[21] or B.E. Bykhovsky's "Cybernetics—American pseudoscience" and "The Science of Modern Slaveholders,"[22] which appeared at the height of the Cold War in the late 1940s and early 1950s.[23]

[18] See D.A. Aleksandrov, and N.L. Krementsov. "Opyt putevoditelia po neizvedannoi zemle: predvaritel'nyy ocherk sotsial'noi istorii sovetskoi nauki (1917–1950-e gody)," *Voprosy istorii estestvoznaniia i tekhniki*, 1989, no. 4: 67–87; idem, "Sotsio-kul'turnye aspekty razvitiia sovetskoi nauki v 1920–1930-e gg.," ibid, 1990, no. 1: 166–8.

[19] For examples of such works see Krementsov, *Stalinist Science*; idem, *The Cure: Story of Cancer and Politics from the Annals of the Cold War* (Chicago: University of Chicago Press, 2002); idem, *International Science between the World Wars: The Case of Genetics* (London: Routledge, 2005); Slava Gerovitch, *From Newspeak to Cyberspeak: A History of Soviet Cybernetics* (Cambridge, MA: MIT Press, 2002); a special issue on "New History of Soviet Science" of *Science in Context* 15, no. 2 (2002), and many others.

[20] See Kirill Rossiianov, "Beyond Species: Il'ya Ivanov and His Experiments on Cross-Breeding Humans with Anthropoid Apes," *Science in Context* 15, no. 2 (2002): 277–316. Since this article has been written, a Russian version of Rossianov's article finally appeared, see K.O. Rossiianov, "Opasnye sviazi: I.I. Ivanov i opyty skreshchivaniia cheloveka s chelovekoobraznymi obez'ianami," *Voprosy estestvoznaniia i tekhniki*, 2006, no. 1: 3–51.

[21] For an English translation of this article, see A.N. Studitsky, "Fly-lovers and Man-haters," *Journal of Heredity* 40, no. 11 (1949): 307–14.

[22] See B.E. Bykhovskii, "Kibernetika—amerikanskaia lzhenauka," *Priroda*, 1952, no. 7: 125–7; idem, "Nauka sovremennykh rabovladel'tsev," *Nauka i zhizn'*, 1953, no. 6: 42–4.

[23] On the campaign against cybernetics see Slava Gerovitch, "'Mathematical Machines' of the Cold War: Soviet Computing, American Cybernetics and Ideological Disputes in the Early 1950s," *Social Studies of Science* 31 (2001): 253–87; idem, "'Russian Scandals': Soviet Readings of American Cybernetics in the Early Years of the Cold War," *Russian Review*, 60 (2001): 545–68.

Shishkin not only portrays Ivanov's Bolshevik patrons as "slaveholders" and "man-haters," but the very research they patronized is depicted as "racist," "inhuman," and "immoral"—the favorite epithets of the earlier Soviet propagandists in their diatribes against both genetics and cybernetics. Like his Cold War predecessors, Shishkin "unmasks" Soviet scientists as willing accomplices and instigators of the Kremlin's diabolical experiments. Although Ivanov might seem a good candidate for a story about an "oppressed" and "victimized" scientist, Shishkin presents his arrest and exile as "deserved punishment" for his collaboration with the regime.

Shishkin's account obviously struck a chord with its audiences. A year after the book's release, a "documentary" with the same title was produced and aired on Rossiia, one of the leading national TV stations.

So What? Questions and Reflections

The above comparison of the two biographies suggests that there is a variety of Soviet templates, formulas, and clichés available to both post-Soviet writers and their audiences. What remains questionable however is how *Soviet* these templates and clichés actually are.

I suspect that many of the formulas that at first glance look distinctly "Soviet" might prove not to be such. The apparently Soviet hagiography of the "founding fathers" in fact has much older and more "universal" origins in the disciplinary struggles and was successfully employed by scientists in numerous countries, as Paul Forman and many others after him have convincingly demonstrated.[24] The ostensibly Soviet denigrating portrayal of Western science during the Cold War as "bourgeois, capitalist, fascist pseudo-science" had its clear parallels in concurrent depictions of "proletarian, communist, Marxist pseudoscience," for instance, in the Western response to "Michurinist" biology.[25] The seemingly Soviet standards of "scientific" biography are in fact nothing more than atavism—a return to an old respected tradition of "the great men of science," which had been highly popular in the late nineteenth and early twentieth centuries and which some historians still practice almost everywhere. All these examples are given not to say that there was

[24] See Paul Forman, "The Discovery of the Diffraction of X-rays by Crystals: A Critique of Myths," *Archive for the History of Exact Sciences* 5 (1969): 38–71; Jan Sapp, "The Nine Lives of Gregor Mendel," in *Experimental Inquiries,* ed. H. E. Le Grand (Dordrecht: Kluwer Academic Publishers, 1990), 137–66.

[25] See for instance, Nikolai Krementsov, "Lysenkoism in Europe: Export-Import of the Soviet Model," in *Academia in Upheaval: Origins, Transfers, and Transformations of the Communist Academic Regime in Russia and East Central Europe*, ed. Michael David-Fox and György Péteri (New York: Garland Publishing Group, 2000), 179–202.

no such thing as "Soviet," but rather to point to what Jonathan Harwood has forcefully demonstrated in his *Styles of Scientific Thought*, namely that the claims about the "specificity," "particularity," and "localness" of certain practices and styles—in this particular case, the "Sovietness"—could only be substantiated through careful comparative analysis of practices and styles in different locales.[26]

But even if we have successfully identified certain practices and styles as distinctly Soviet, what could be accomplished by asking and answering the (deliberately?) vague question posed in the name of our conference: "What is Soviet now?" Certainly, the question has a clear historiographic import in prodding us to be aware that our present understanding of Soviet history has changed as compared to that of fifteen years ago. But historiography aside, are we trying to better understand the present through the lens of the past? Or, are we hoping to gain a better understanding of the past by examining its current reincarnations and permutations? As a historian, I see both approaches as equally flawed, methodologically suspect, and ultimately unproductive.

The past is ever present. Post-Soviet Russia bears and will for a very long time continue to bear the "birthmarks and remnants of the damned communist past"—to paraphrase a popular cliché of the Stalin era. It would be highly unusual (and historically extremely interesting) if it did not. The thorough knowledge of those "birthmarks" is, of course, an obligatory prerequisite for a fruitful examination of modern-day Russia. But by training our gaze on the "remnants" we risk overlooking the most interesting and important questions about "now": how it differs from the past, what new features it exhibits, and where these novelties came from.

Furthermore, even identifying something in the present as "remnants of the past" does not automatically make it such. I suspect that my uncovering of apparently Soviet templates and formulas in Shishkin's book would come as a complete surprise to both its author and its publisher. I doubt that the "Soviet" elements of Shishkin's book resulted from either deliberate borrowing or even unconscious imitating of certain Soviet models. Most likely, their origin is totally different. What Shishkin's book shares with its Soviet Cold War predecessors is its ultimate goal—propaganda. The purpose of the newest rendering of Ivanov's biography is not to actually analyze, and thus understand, the Bolshevik state, science, Ivanov, and the multitude of interrelations and interactions among the major protagonists of the story. Rather, using the favorite verbs of the Soviet era, its aim is to "unmask," "disclose," "expose," "reveal," and "debunk" the "Kremlin tyrants" and their "accomplices." It is this common propagandistic zealotry that leads to the similarities in arguments,

[26] See Jonathan Harwood, *Styles of Scientific Thought* (Chicago: University of Chicago Press, 1993).

styles, and language between the Cold War attacks on genetics and cybernetics in Soviet Russia, on the one hand, and Shishkin's expose of Ivanov in post-Soviet Russia, on the other.

Moreover, the most characteristic feature of the latest retelling of Ivanov's life and work, in my opinion, has nothing to do with whatever remnants of past Soviet practices and styles one can uncover on its pages. Its main motif is explicit, militant anti-scientism. In Shishkin's book, gone is the belief in science's ultimate "goodness" so prominent in both Soviet and anti-Soviet writings of the earlier period. Instead, science is presented as a dangerous, irresponsible, immoral activity epitomized in the popular image of Frankenstein placed prominently in the title of Shishkin's book. And clearly, Shishkin's point of reference is not Mary Shelly's *Modern Prometheus*, but rather Hollywood's celluloid myth of scientific ambitions that create monsters and lead to human destruction.

Ironically, in the end, this anti-scientism even forces Shishkin to partially negate his own main theses—that Ivanov's research was quintessentially Soviet and that it was the Bolshevik government that was solely responsible for these "inhuman" experiments. He accusingly refers to support accorded to Ivanov by a number of prominent foreign scientists and the Pasteur Institute as a whole—after all, Ivanov's actual experiments on the artificial insemination of female chimpanzees with human sperm had been carried out at the Institute's experimental station in French Guinea. Obviously, the roots of this anti-scientism lay not so much in the Soviet past as in the present worldwide concerns about the frightening powers of science and about the role of scientists, governments, and the public in defining acceptable limits of scientific research—concerns that had been reawakened by the rapid advances of modern science, particularly biology (production of genetically modified foods, cloning, xenografting, etc.).

Which brings us to the second side of the coin—"presentism." Attempts to explain the past through the lens of the present have long been criticized as "presentist," teleological, and "whiggish." And this is exactly what Shishkin's account does, particularly as regards the "morality" of Ivanov's research and its support by the Bolsheviks, as well as by other scientists. Instead of placing his actors and their actions into their concurrent moral universe (which, by the way, included neither informed consent nor many qualms about human experimentation), Shishkin projects modern bioethical concerns into the past and, of course, finds that past abhorrent, which, in turn, serves as additional "proof" for characterizing Ivanov, his experiments, his patrons, and his supporters as quintessentially "inhuman."

As historians, we are (or at least are supposed to be) acutely aware of our personal "embeddedness" in our own social, political, ideological, institutional, familial, and other contexts. In our research we try desperately to shed our present contexts and immerse ourselves in the past. We ridicule "presentist" histories and despise the ones produced by "vested interests." Yet, all too often, even the best of histories are still written not to better understand the past but to stroke certain present sensibilities.[27]

[27] For instance, Kirill Rossiianov's otherwise exemplary analysis of Ivanov's work exhibits certain whiggish features, by looking at Ivanov's ape-human hybridization experiments through the present-day "bioethical lens" and, of course, finding them "obviously immoral" (see Rossiianov, "Beyond Species," 302, 310).

Who's Afraid of Joseph Stalin?

Tracy McDonald

What follows is an exploration of the narratives that have entwined themselves through and around a rebellion of February 1930 against the forced collectivization of the peasantry in the Pitelino district of Riazan province.[1] The narrative begin with the almost daily state security (OGPU) reports on the uprisings in Pitelino and the reasons security agents understand and record as being behind the violence in the region. The second layer of narrative, almost concurrent with the events, is the interpretation of the violence by district party members. The fanciful 1957 recorded memories of a "party worker" at the scene, A.N. Ianin, who saw all manner of enemies, real and imagined behind the uprising, provides the material for the third layer.[2] The fourth layer of interpretation is found in the novel *Muzhiki i baby* (Peasant Men and Women) by Boris Mozhaev, written between 1976 and 1980. The village-prose writer Mozhaev was born in Pitelino and was seven years old when the uprising occurred. His father was arrested in connection with collectivization in the area. Lastly, the fifth layer comes from the oral testimony, collected in 2004 and 2005, of three women who witnessed the Pitelino uprising.

What is striking about the various layers of narrative is the difficulty of reconstructing some basic aspects of the events. How many people were killed? Who was killed? *How* were those who perished killed and by whom? Lenin's formula of "who gets whom" (*kto kogo*) is one of the most difficult questions to answer. What is easier to ascertain from these layers of narrative is, who was afraid of whom, how, and when. What emerges is a sense of how history is created and recorded, of interpretation and spin, of myth and memory.

According to what can be pieced together from the archival record, at the end of February 1930, peasants from at least twenty villages in the northeastern Pitelino district engaged in a rebellion against collectivization. The rebellion raged openly for six days, simmered for months, and involved thousands of the district's villagers. The collectivization brigade working in the district was especially zealous. Brigade members already had a reputation for shooting off their weapons in the middle of the night in order to frighten the villagers of the area. And on January 27, a woman had

[1] Pitelino is one the of province's most western districts. Riazan province itself is located in central Russia and borders Moscow province to the southeast.

[2] The first three layers are explored in detail in Tracy McDonald, "A Peasant Rebellion in Stalin's Russia," *Journal of Social History* 35, issue 1 (Fall 2001): 125–46. They are summarized here for context.

been raped in the village of Malye Mochily. Toward the end of February, the collectivization brigade went door to door seizing all grain. The collectivizers fined middle peasants heavily and pulled village girls who protested around by their braids.

On February 22, the villagers of Veriaevo and Gridino decided that they could tolerate the brigade no more and chased the collectivizers out of the villages. The crowd took back confiscated grain and property that had been stripped from peasants who had been labeled as kulaks, and returned it to its owners. Village schoolchildren tore up posters of the Soviet leaders, suggesting they were not yet afraid of Joseph Stalin. The disturbance lasted until five or six in the evening. Throughout the night, small groups of local peasants patrolled Veriaevo. In fact, for days, the peasants of Veriaevo staffed checkpoints and barricades, and refused to allow officials into the village until they had agreed to address the issues of the violations, excesses, and scandalous behavior (*bezobrazie*) of the brigade and rural soviet members. Whenever officials approached the village, the church bells in Veriaevo rang out and the peasants of Gridino came running.[3]

The morning of February 23 was a Sunday. An armed detachment from the nearby town of Sasovo arrived in Veraievo. When three members of the detachment decided to go and search for something to eat, a group of women blocked their path. The men responded by firing warning shots into the air. In response to the sound of shooting, the church bells rang out and a crowd of peasants gathered. In Gridino, the bells summoned a crowd, which then attempted to detain the retreating officials, stopping their horses and throwing sticks at them. The detachment then withdrew to the district center of Pitelino. In response to the bells of the villages of Veriaevo and Gridino, a crowd of several thousand peasants converged in Veriaevo from at least ten surrounding villages. The documents do not detail how this enormous crowd was dispersed, although more troops were dispatched and stationed in Pitelino and the OGPU dispatched 150 specially trained officers to the area.[4]

That Sunday night, at 11 p.m., villagers called a general meeting in Gridino, which was attended by more than three hundred people, mainly women. At the meeting, the women demanded that the chairman of the district soviet executive committee Subbotin, and his assistants, Ol'khin and Kosyrev, be put on trial in the next forty-

---

[3] Gosudarstvennyi arkhiv Riazanskoi oblasti (hereafter GARO), f. 5, op. 2, d. 5, ll. 404, 406.

[4] Rossiiskii gosudarstvennyi voennyi arkhiv (hereafter RGVA), f. 33987, op. 3, d. 332, l. 81. (Report of the commander of the Moscow okrug military forces to K.E. Voroshilov, March 2, 1930) published in *Tragediia sovetskoi derevni*, vol. 2 (Moscow: Rosspen, 2000), 279.

eight hours.[5] The women threatened to hang these officials on meat hooks if they fell into their hands. They also demanded the return of their recently socialized grain reserves, noting that the grain was simply rotting in its current storage conditions. At the end of the meeting, the villagers resolved to elect a new rural soviet immediately and to launch an investigation into the excesses of the collectivization drive.[6] It is worth drawing attention to the fact that that the villagers themselves recognized the pivotal role of the rural soviet and sought reelections in order to promote and protect their interests. Across the district, peasant women took back collectivized livestock and seized grain, and demanded that all villagers regain their voting rights.

According to the archival record, the loss of life occurred in the village of Potap'evo. OGPU troops fired into a gathered crowd wounding two men and killing a woman.[7] It took until March to bring the area under control and over three hundred arrests were made in connection with the uprising. In a report of February 20, Pitelino district was said to be 100 percent collectivized.[8] Yet by April, that percentage had dropped to six.[9] Based on OGPU reports and telegrams sent from the troubled district, a portrait emerges of a peasant rebellion that spread like a fire from village to village. The reports suggest that the rebellion was caused by the "tactless behavior" of those responsible for collectivizing agriculture in the district and that the rebellion was supported and engaged in by almost all of the region's peasants. Support crossed class lines and was rooted in the desire, on the part of the local peasantry, to address the "excesses" of the collectivizers and to protect its political and economic interests.

A slightly different story, one that appeared nowhere in the OGPU reports, surfaced at a late February meeting of Riazan district party secretaries. The secretary of the Pitelino district party committee blamed the agitation in Veriaevo on a former deputy to the tsarist state duma who had a "two-story house" and who, the secretary claimed, was such a large landholder that he was practically the equivalent of a noble landowner (*pomeshchik*). This former deputy supposedly conducted agitation among the peasants after being dekulakized. By retelling the story in this way, the district party secretary downplayed the events in Pitelino, blaming them all on acceptable,

[5] Ol'khin was head of the RAIZO (district land department), and Kosyrev was chairman of the local collective farm.

[6] GARO, f. 5, op. 2, d. 5, l. 426.

[7] The report added that she was the wife of a church elder, perhaps as an attempt to make the murder easier to stomach.

[8] GARO, f. 5, op. 2, d, 5, l. 290.

[9] GARO, f. 2, op. 1, d. 66, l. 124.

traditional enemies—the "*pomeshchik*" and the "kulak"—when in fact the uprising involved almost all of the inhabitants of the unruly villages. History was being rewritten practically as it happened. In fact, by the time the report on the Pitelino uprising reached the center, kulaks were blamed entirely for the unrest.[10]

Another account of the riot was written in 1957—twenty-seven years after the uprising—by A.N. Ianin, a former party worker who witnessed the events in the district. The account was part of an official history of the origins of regional party organizations and collective farms in the Pitelino district and the riot was presented as an example of dangerous kulak opposition to the collective farms. While Ianin wrote of a rebellion which he claimed occurred in early March, his recollection was likely a kind of stylized montage of the February events. His account, an interesting and problematic variant, is significant precisely because it captures the essence of the official Stalinist depiction of peasants and peasant rebellion.

In Ianin's version, the trouble began when the secretary of the Pitelino district party committee was replaced by one Fediaev "who was considered a talentless worker even in the district." According to Ianin's recollection, the new chairman of the district soviet executive committee was a "mediocre" member of the local police, one Subbotin, who had been transferred to Pitelino from Shatsk—in other words, both incompetent and an outsider. And the district worker Ol'kin, "a man little acquainted with agriculture," was named the chief of the district land department (RAIZO).[11] This "troika"

> began to throw its weight around [*khoziainichat'*] in Pitelino district. Without any preparatory work among the population [the troika] began to lead wholesale collectivization there, where they did not permit a common meeting ground, embittered the population, and provoked an open uprising against Soviet power.[12]

Ianin maintained that the dissatisfaction which the troika produced in the population was further exploited by a group of "conspirators" consisting of the "kulak" Os'kin, "who was a former member of the tsarist state duma"[13]; the "kulaks"

[10] Federal'naia sluzhba bezopasnosti, f. 2, op. 8, d. 40, l. 87. Documents shown to me by Lynne Viola collected for the project *Tragediia sovetskoi derevni*.

[11] Ianin, "Vtoroe kulatskoe vosstanie i ego likvidatsiia, *Minuvshee* 4 (1987): 298.

[12] Ibid., 299.

[13] An editorial note in *Minuvshee* claimed that there was no such Duma member in the first Duma, although there was a Nikita Grigor'evich Osichkin from Tambov in the second Duma. Ianin, "Vtoroe kulatskoe vosstanie," 299, note 2. In Pitelino in August 1929 an I.M. Os'kin was recorded in an OGPU report as someone who complained about the *zaem* (state bond), about the better treatment of workers over peasants and about the war with China. See GARO,

Papkin and Miagkov; the local priest from Veriaevo; a white guard officer and former "emissary of Antonov" who was hiding to avoid prosecution; and "some kind of 'woman-kulak' (*zhenshchina-kulachka*) with a criminal past."[14] This list of the guilty implicated in the events at Pitelino district offered a virtual catalogue of recognizable and acceptable enemies of the Soviet state. Ianin left no stone unturned as he unmasked those behind the extraordinary events: political-economic enemies (the kulaks); political-historic enemies (white guards and emissaries of Antonov all rolled into a unique hybrid); former tsarist officials (members of the tsarist duma); religious enemies (the local priest); wayward women; recidivist criminals; and even gypsies (Ianin made a point of mentioning that one of the villages was a "gypsy village").[15] Further, demonstrating a literary flair with just a hint of the supernatural, Ianin added a host of more traditional characters to the mix including wanderers (*stranniki*), soothsayers (*predskazateli*), all spreading "wild rumors" that women and children would be socialized.[16] According to Ianin, February was marked by "rabid" agitation among the population against the collective farm and against collectivization in general. The procession and the riotous demonstrators were led by a "woman-kulak." There is certainly a mocking tone in Ianin's prose as he recalls the masculine role of this "Alena-bogatyr"[17] of Pitelino. The mutineers, Ianin claimed, intended to surround Pitelino and take it by storm. They were confronted by a detachment of three hundred Red Army soldiers from Sasovo led by the chairman of the okrug-level[18] soviet executive committee Shtrodakh, and the secretary of the okrug party committee Gilinskii. According to Ianin, Shtrodakh "rudely" asked the crowd, with his revolver in hand:

> "Why are you rioting (*buntuete*)? You don't like the collective farms?" To which members of the crowd responded with, "And you come here with your gun to terrify us and drag us into the collective? ... (sic) We won't go! ... (sic) Down with the collective farm! Down with the kommuna!"

---

f. R-4, op.3, d. 11, l. 20.

[14] Ianin, "Vtoroe kulatskoe vosstanie," 298.

[15] Ibid., 299. For a similar example of blaming outside, traditional enemies for peasant rebellion, see E.J. Hobsbawn and Georges Rude, *Captain Swing* (London: Lawrence and Wishart, 1969), 239–50.

[16] Ianin, "Vtoroe kulatskoe vosstanie," 299.

[17] A bogatyr was a *male* knight of Russian medieval lore, known for his extraordinary strength.

[18] Okrug was a newly created, and temporary, administrative division. Riazan became an okrug or region within the larger Moscow oblast (large territorial division).

In Ianin's account, the Alena-bogatyr then began to taunt Shtrodakh and eventually raised her skirt at him. Strodakh shot and killed her and the crowd reacted with extreme rage.[19] Only repeated volleys from the detachment finally dispersed the crowd, which then turned its attention to the collective farm, taking back grain and cattle and destroying account books. "Three collective farm chairmen and several collective farm members, communists, and komsomol members were killed."[20] If Shtrodakh did indeed shoot and kill a peasant woman engaged in a traditionally effective, peaceful, harmless, and age-old tactic of protest, the "moral" violation of the peasant community by outsiders was even further reinforced by his actions.

Ianin's account, written almost thirty years after the Pitelino events, continued the reconstruction of the Pitelino rebellion already initiated at the February meeting of the district party secretaries. He depicted a backward, ignorant peasant mass easily led astray by outside agitators and the archetypal enemies of Soviet power: backward and untamed peasant women; over-zealous and corrupt local officials, the scapegoats of dizzy with success; kulaks; and tsarist remnants.

A fourth layer of narrative is provided by one of Riazan's greatest native sons, the village-prose writer, Boris Andreevich Mozhaev. His two-volume novel, *Muzhiki i baby* was written as an "historical chronicle" of the events of 1929–1930 in Pitelino.[21] Mozhaev was born in Pitelino on June 1, 1923, and witnessed the events of

[19] Ianin, "Vtoroe kulatskoe vosstanie," 299

[20] Ibid., 301.

[21] The representative "fictional" villages of the novel are Tikhanovo, Gordeevo, and Veret'e. I suspect the proximity to Gridino and Veraievo is not accidental. Gordeevo may be a reference to the martyr Gordyi, who is celebrated on January 3. A reading associated with Gordyi is Matthew 10: 16–22, eerily appropriate verses for the rebellion itself and perhaps Mozhaev's own faith:

> I am sending you out like sheep among wolves. Therefore be as shrewd as snakes and as innocent as doves. Be on your guard against men; they will hand you over to the local councils and flog you in their synagogues. On my account you will be brought before governors and kings as witnesses to them and to the Gentiles. But when they arrest you, do not worry about what to say or how to say it. At that time you will be given what to say, for it will not be you speaking, but the Spirit of your Father speaking through you. Brother will betray brother to death, and a father his child; children will rebel against their parents and have them put to death. All men will hate you because of me, but he who stands firm to the end will be saved.

Gordyi or Gordias was born at the end of the III Century. A centurion, he stood up against the prefect of his city for persecuting Christians. He was tortured and beheaded for his troubles.

collectivization, like all of the witnesses below, through the frightened eyes of a child. His father, Andrei, was arrested in connection with his opposition to collectivization and appears in *Muzhiki i baby* as Andrei Borodin, a member of the rural soviet who takes a moderate position on collectivization.[22] Mozhaev grew up in Pitelino, attended school in neighboring Potap'evo, and worked as district school teacher until his military service in the Far East. In 1943, he was sent to a higher military engineering school in Leningrad and later evacuated to Iaroslavl. In the 1960s, he returned to Riazan where he lived across the street from one of Russia's native sons, Alexander Solzenitsyn, who had settled in Riazan after his time in Vladimir to teach mathematics. The two writers toured the province together by car in 1969 and Mozhaev apparently told Solzhenityn of his plan to write about the Pitelino rebellion.[23] Mozhaev's first Riazan story was *Zhivoi* (*Alive*), better known as *Iz zhizni Feodora Kuz'kina* (From the Life of Fedor Kuzkin) published in 1966. Fedor Kuzkin, like Andrei Borodin, is an intelligent, honest, hard-working peasant who is arrested for his incomprehension and questioning of the decisions surrounding collectivization in his village.

Throughout his career as a village prose writer, Mozhaev faced criticism and censure. He began writing *Muzhiki i baby* in 1976. By this time, Mozhaev was free of the mythical enemies that parade through Ianin's narrative, but not of some of the conventions that characterized socialist realism. There are no women mutineers or bogatyrs, only rioting peasant women and one distressed young communist, Mariia, who battles for decency and order and loses her love in the violence. There is no overt "naturalism" in Mozhaev, although he does restore an off-color sense of humour to the peasantry. But like his fellow village prose writers, Mozhaev boldly embraces local peasant dialect, thereby rejecting the classic Soviet language that was supposed to be part of socialist realist literature.[24] Village prose was a testament to the fact

---

Gordeevo may also be a reference to the word for pride (*gordost'*). And while a Veret'e can be a dry place in a swamp, it may also be an allusion, on Mozhaev's part to the word for faith (*vera*). See Vladimir Dal', *Tolkovyi slovar' zhivogo velikorusskogo iazyka,* vol. 1 (repr., St. Petersburg: Diamant, 1996).

[22] Volume one was finished in 1976 and published in 1980. Volume two was finished in 1980 but not published until 1987. L. Vil'chek, "Vot moia derevnia…," in B. Mozhaev, *Izbrannye proizvedeniia,* vol. 1 (Moscow: Sovremennik, 1982), 3, and David C. Gillespie, "History, Politics, and the Russian Peasant: Boris Mozhaev and the Collectivization of Agriculture," *Slavonic and East European Review* 67, no. 2 (April 1989): 184, 192–3.

[23] "Mozhaev Boris Andreevich (1923–1996)," http://hronos.km.ru/biograf/mozhaev.html (accessed January 21, 2007.) For more on Solzhenitsyn in Riazan see Vladimir Krylov, *Riazan' pomnit Solzhenitsyna* (Riazan: Poverennyi, 2004).

[24] For an excellent exploration of the creation of a classic Soviet language, see Michael

that the 1960s and 1970s were not an era of stagnation, but rather a clear transitional period from the fears of Stalinism to the hopes and dreams of glasnost. Village prose was about addressing the wounds inflicted on the countryside by collectivization and its concurrent dehumanization of the peasant. Village prose writers tried to give the villagers back, to some degree, their voices free from the judgements inherent in the Bolshevik civilizing process in a desperate search for the world they had lost. For example, Mozhaev writes a beautiful dialogue that represents both the bawdy side of peasant speech and the local flavour of the Riazan accent. The following exchange is between the forest patroller, Sen'ka Knut, a solitary old man (*bobyl*), and two young women to whom he gives a ride in his tarantass:

> — Кнут, а ты когда-нибудь влюблялся?
> — Чаво?
> — Почему не женишься?
> — Устарел я, девки.
> — Кнут, а ето правда, будто у мужиков, которые боятся баб, отсыхает?
> — Чаво?
> — Поливалка ...
> — У меня, девки, ишо хватит на семейку.
> — Воды, что ли?
> — Ах вы забубенные! ...[25]
>
> — Knut, have you ever been in love?
> — What?
> — How come you never married?
> — I got old, girls.
> — Knut, is it true, that men who are afraid of women, dry up?
> — What?
> — The watering can ...
> — Girls, I still have enough for the sowing.
> — Water?
> — Ah, you wild things!

Knut's "chavo" is indicative of a strong akanie in Riazan speech.

Gorham, *Speaking in Soviet Tongues: Lanuage Culture and the Politics of Voice in Revolutionary Russia* (DeKalb: Northern Illinois, 2003)

[25] Boris Mozhaev, *Muzhiki i baby* (Moscow: Sovremennik, 1988), 106.

Another indicative moment of such "local color," occurs at a meeting of the Tikhanovo village *aktiv*. Senechka Zenin, the secretary of the local party cell, gives a long speech, in a series of long speeches, about events in China and the importance of purchasing the third industrial bond. One peasant woman, Tarakanikha, falls asleep and snores loudly, causing much hilarity among the gathered peasants. When the group is chastised, one asks:

> — Что ж, выходит, у Тараканихи классовое лицо, ежели над ней смеятся нельзя?
> — А какая у нее задница?[26]
>
> — So it turns out that Tarakanikha [from the Russian for cockroach (*tarakan*)] has a class face, so it is forbidden to laugh at her?
> — And what kind of ass does she have?

The collective-farm organizers were not amused.

Still, many of Mozhaev's characters would indeed be at home in a socialist realist novel. Ozimov, for example, is a police chief who is in misery at the role he is forced to play during collectivization. He is killed by the crowd and buried in a red satin coffin in his uniform. He is a communist martyr who is sacrificed because of the excesses of a few. In some ways Mozhaev is not free of parts of the official line either. The excesses in Pitelino are the fault of a few over-zealous, local activists like Senechka Zenin. Zenin criticizes the local collective farm for not turning over its surplus to the state but instead wasting money on "women's apparel." The collective farm had bought cloth to make uniforms for the collective farmers—red dresses for women, black pants for men.[27] Mariia, the kind-hearted communist girl, tells Zenin, when he is pushing forced grain requisitioning, that he is worse than the village thief Vanka Zhadov because at least Vanka had the decency to rob people at night, not in the daytime, and to stab people openly with a knife.[28] Mozhaev works within many of the strictures of socialist realism; there are good communists who would have made socialism work, perhaps, if not for fools like Zenin. There is a good, caring, loving communist woman, other women are background.

Yet some of the subtleties that can be gleaned from the archival record, and which are missing from Ianin's account, are found in the depth and richness of

[26] Ibid., 395.

[27] Ibid.

[28] Ibid.

Muzhiki i baby. Mozhaev lived in these villages and when one visits them, one sees how accurate his descriptions are. Mozhaev writes that the pre-revolutionary merchant, Kamanin, who had a large house, practically gave it to the local state authority (the raion / district executive committee). Kamanin had wanted to build a new house across from his old one, but the local authority said no because the square had to be kept for demonstrations. Kamanin gathered his family and moved to Kasimov, a district within Riazan province just north of Pitelino.[29] The reader of Mozhaev's novel finds colorful and varied markets; the role of the village churches; rural soviet meetings that resist the decisions of the November plenum and drink to Soviet power; the overlapping of the rural soviet and the gathering; distress over the loss of voting rights; local police officers; short-staffed criminal investigation units; popular justice (*samosud*); moonshine (*samogon*); horse theft and retribution; the horse thief who is aided by the forest warden; threats of arson; taxation; arguments over the buying of state bonds; the central role of women in resistance to collectivization; and the unenviable position of being a decent rural soviet chair. Evdokim Akimov, chairman of the Gordeevo soviet, for example, refuses to search from household to household for "excess" grain. When he is asked to account for his failure to act, he says: "I am the chairman of the rural soviet…If you do not believe in me, then replace me with the village librarian or someone else who will grope around in stoves and beds."[30] When the violence of February is in full swing, Andrei Borodin looks to the chair of the Tikhanovo soviet, Pavel Krechev, as "*vlast'*" (power) in the village. Borodin argues that the soviet is the *real* power locally, not the members of the communist party. But the chairman, cowed by the collectivization brigade, just looks at the floor.[31]

Mozhaev's descriptions of the Pitelino uprising echoes the village songs still remembered in the region and the telegrams and documents of the archives. In Mozhaev's narrative, the peasants of Gordeevo run to Veret'e and tell their neighbors that they are being dragged into the collective farm by force. The younger men hide in the forest. Old men and women run to the holding pen that had been built for the collectivized livestock and smash it to pieces, throwing the broken boards into the street. The peasants take back their grain, some recognizing their own bags. The collectivization brigade leader arms himself and calls in the police. The chief of police sees men on the edge of the forest with axes and pitchforks, and hears the sound of the church bell. Villagers call for new elections of local power through the gathering (*skhod*). and in another moment ask to elect a rural soviet based on the rules

[29] Ibid., 207.

[30] Ibid., 226.

[31] Ibid., 65–6.

of 1925, with no voters denied their voting rights. The actual days of the uprising in Mozhaev's narrative become more literary and more symbolic than the archival documents and the memories of the women below. The chief of police, Ozimov, a relatively sympathetic character in the novel, is shot by a frightened villager. Women capture the leading local collectivizer, Zenin, and flog him, such that he lies on his stomach in the nearby hospital cursing. The crowd invades the hospital, looking for him. The crowds use the church bells to call the villagers to gather and thus the bell-ringer, Ivan Kukurai—who is introduced in book one as a kind of holy fool, half-blind and deaf and constantly surrounded by small, taunting children—is naturally a target for the troops' attempts to control the situation. Dmitry Uspensky, the village schoolteacher and level-headed intellectual, is shot protecting Ivan. Ozimov and Uspensky are buried on the same day. Still, Mozhaev points the finger at the OGPU. Zenin writes the okrug-level administrative department a telegram, complaining of terror acts in the district including: the theft of apples from the former noble estate; the shooting out of a window during a komsomol play; and the beating of collective farm agitators. When the local police investigate, however, the apples, it turns out, where taken by young people organizing a social gathering and were returned; the window was broken by a stone and not a gun, and by "drunken hooligans" and not kulak enemies; and the beating was only one punch in the nose, pretty mild as far as village brawling went. Implicitly, the arrival of the OGPU is the reason for bloodshed in Mozhaev's version. The telegram is what brings the OPGU to the villages, and their presence leads in turn to the escalation of violence and the loss of life.

Throughout the novel, Uspensky represents Mozhaev's point of view. He shares not a few characteristics with his creator. Uspensky loves history and philosophy, and he is the village schoolteacher. It is through this character that Mozhaev's own position, confused and in tension, is revealed. Uspensky had fought on the Bolshevik side in the civil war. He was the son of a priest who responds, when his class origins are held against him, by pointing out that Chernyshevsky and Dobrioliubov were also sons of priests.[32] The chairman of the raion party committee, Vozvyshaev, tells Krechev to confiscate Uspensky's house and use it as a base from which to organize the collective farm. Krechev, however, hesitates. He sees Uspensky as a good man who signed up for the state bond (*zaem*) which everyone else had run away from like a "demon from incense." On the one hand, then, Uspensky represents hope for socialism of a certain kind. On the other hand, he is martyred trying to save a holy fool and after coming to the conclusion—"I am neither red nor white, Mama. I am too Russian."[33]

[32] Ibid., 76.

[33] Ibid., 650.

Mozhaev, like many village prose writers, was Orthodox with strong traces of Russian nationalism running through his work. The tension for Mozhaev in *Muzhiki i baby* is between faith in a better Leninist line and the rejection of Bolshevism altogether as something foreign. The explicit line in the novel is that the party's "left-wing" was responsible for the policy at the top that led to the excesses of the first collectivization drive. Together with over-zealous local officials, who bring in the OGPU, they create the violence at the bottom. In discussing *Muzhiki i baby* in 1988, Victor Danilov argued that Mozhaev's novel represented a dangerous fantasy:

> Very characteristic—and dangerous—is the fantasy of B. Mozhaev's novel *Muzhiki i baby*, where the responsibility for the violence that peasants were subjected to in the course of collectivization in the winter of 1929-30 is transferred from the real perpetrators (Stalin and his closest associates, in first place Molotov and Kaganovich) to Trotsky, Zinoviev, Kamenev, Iakovlev, and Kaminsky, of which the first three by 1927 already had no relationship to the political decisions made, and Trotsky was deported already from the Soviet Union in February 1929. All of these fantasies were not born in perestroika. Perestroika and glasnost only made them visible.[34]

Some of the danger here may be anti-Semitism; Trotsky, Zinoviev, Kamenev, Iakovlev, were all Jewish.[35] Uspensky's claim that he is "too Russian" lends more credence to such a charge. Yet, could Mozhaev have blamed Stalin in 1976 or even 1980 for the path collectivization took? Was he bound by fear, by the residue of socialist realism, by convention, by the limits of his historical training, by his own prejudices? His official analysis of collectivization followed the accepted line. If anyone at the top was mistaken, it was the Left Opposition and mistakes were made by over-zealous communist officials at the lower levels. Still, Mozhaev was brave in implicating the OGPU to the extent that he does in *Muzhiki i baby*. In his epilogue, Mozhaev concludes his "historical chronicle" with what would become the official line of early glasnost; collectivization involved excesses which were a violation of the Leninist line. Lenin had advocated gradual transformation without coercion. If Lenin's line had been followed the violence could have been avoided and agriculture peacefully collectivized. The novel concludes by pointing out that despite the excesses, the collective farms were constructed more slowly, and successfully, in the years that followed the violence of the first drive.

---

[34] "Kruglyi stol: istoricheskaia nauka v usoliviakh perestroiki," *Voprosy istorii*, 1988, no.3: 22.

[35] See works by David Gillespie and the dissertation by David Michael Holihan, "Collectivization and the Utopian Ideal in the Works of Boris Andreevich Mozhaev" (University of Bath, 1994), esp. 210, who both note traces of anti-semitism in Mozhaev's work.

Yet, if one pushes Mozhaev's critique of the "left," one sees a Russian nationalist critique that rejects Bolshevism as fundamentally anti-Russian. Uspensky laments:

> Everything connected with the people, its way of life, its faith and religion, all of this is alien to our left-wingers. Not only do they not accept the faith of the people, but they are also hostile to the most sublime manifestations of the people's national spirit. To them Tolstoy is a religious fool, Dostoevsky an obscurantist, even Pushkin expresses the culture of the nobility. And this is without even mentioning their hatred of all Russian philosophers, from Khomiakov to Bulgakov. For them the Russian historical experience is merely foul soil which has to be cleared away, and that's where their historical intolerance, lack of moderation, and desire to create a social miracle comes from. So where do little kids and old men and women come in? We'll just create history as fast as possible according to our own plan. At the moment people believe in it, and if anyone doesn't we'll make them … Just a little bit more and we'll be in paradise. We only need to force everyone into a collective farm. Give us a miracle. A little bit more and we'll be there. That's where the rot is. That's the whole point.[36]

In his excellent analysis of Mozhaev's position on collectivization as expressed in *Muzhiki i baby*, David Gillespie concludes,

> There are some, though, who would see Mozhaev's defense of Lenin as incompatible with his attack on utopian and socialist thought as developed under Stalin, for Mozhaev stresses the continuity of Russian historical development and the relevance of the national experience for an understanding of the problems of today. The underlying idea of Mozhaev's novel is that ideology is responsible for Russia's suffering in the recent past, but the future can only be built on a sense of historical integration and national self-awareness, in which politics plays little or no part. It thus seems entirely possible that on the philosophical level, as well as on the level of historical accuracy and interpretation, Mozhaev's novel could test the limits of *glasnost'*.[37]

When Boris Mozhaev wrote *Muzhiki i baby* between 1976 and 1980, there was still much that could not be said about collectivization and about the unrest in Pitelino as well. Mozhaev's novel and the nuances that it introduced to the understandings of the villages of the 1920s and the collectivization drive of 1929–1930

[36] Mozhaev, *Muzhiki i baby*, 646–7. Translation is David Gillespie's from "History, Politics, and the Russian Peasant," 202.

[37] Gillespie, "History, Politics, and the Russian Peasant," 206–7.

were prophetic of the historiographical developments that were to come. Initially, during glasnost Lenin was sacred. It was only when Lenin, and Leninism, came under attack that openness and restructuring took on a life of its own that could not be controlled from above.[38] Perhaps Boris Mozhaev was still afraid of Joseph Stalin.

That was Pitelino, Soviet then. What follows is Soviet now, Pitelino today. In the summers of 2004 and 2005, I went with a small group of documentary filmmakers[39] to the narrow streets of the villages of Pitelino district to look for anyone who remembered the events of 1930. The journey began in the village of Pet, where the ruins of the starch factory are still visible from the grounds behind the shell of

Pet

Nesterevo

a still majestic church. The remnants of the church of Nesterevo were equally, distressingly, beautiful.

When we asked a local inhabitant where the rural soviet was located, the response was a very suspicious, "Who are you and why are you looking for it?" No further information was forthcoming. It was in Pet in July 2004, that we met Anna Petrovna. She had recently moved to Pet from Gridino. She spoke of her relatives

[38] See R.W. Davies, *Soviet History and the Gorbachev Revolution* (Bloomington: Indiana University Press, 1989) for an excellent exploration of this process.

[39] *The Uprising* (Chemodan Films, 2006) was the result. See http://www.chemodanfilms.com for more on the expedition and resulting film.

who had found the stones themselves to build a house with a partition and a storage barn with its own cellar:

> He made a home with a partition inside, a storage barn. Under the storage barn he made a cellar, all by their own strength and then they dekulakized him. Dragged him off to Siberia, they threw his children out of the house. They all left to Moscow, to live there. Now we have beds, feather pillows, and blankets there. But before you slept in your homespun coats and slept in some straw, nothing under your head, in your homespun coat. They lived very poorly then. And everything was stolen [she trips over the word and changes it to] everything destroyed. What kind of kulaks did they find? Who were kulaks then? I can't believe it now, how stupid I was then. What for? Throw people out of their homes, send them off to Siberia, there, dekulakized. To create this life, they dragged us to the collective farm by force … I remember, in 1934, I was ten years old, we went to the collective farm. And they took everyone's horse and cow. They dragged away horses and cows. Whoever did not want to go to the collective farm, they took away all their livestock. That's what they did.

Anna Petrovna came out against the concept of kulak, the process of dekulakization, the cruelty in the face of local poverty, the injustice, exile to Siberia; but when we asked her about the Pitelino rebellion, she assured us that no relative of hers participated. We asked her if she remembered the rebellion. She said,

> Oi. No, I don't remember, only through the stories. A woman came to us, and my mother said, 'Oi what's happening in the village?' And with pitchforks, and sticks, and axes. And our peasants, my grandfather did not go, nor papa. They were not at the uprising. They were afraid. What can you do with sticks? Idiots. Many people ended up there, at that rebellion. But ours, I remember, my parents, they did not go … They were not at the uprising. No one was there, none of my relatives. They all lived right next to me, my grandfather had four brothers. They all lived together, and no one went to the uprising, never, no one. They were obedient people. They were so obedient, they went nowhere. Never against the authorities. If they were told to be somewhere, they were there. If you are told do something, you do it. Submissively, they went to the authorities. Even though all of the strips of land had been sown, and the peas, and sheep and winter crops, and spring crops, everything. All of it, all was handed over, and the horses, and our things, everything. They gave it to the collective farm. And then they went to work there, grandpa, mama, and dad.

We continued talking to Anna Petrovna about when the roofs of the village were no longer built from thatch but metal, when electricity came to the village, when mechanized farm equipment was more common. Some years after the war, was the answer. She spoke of the war years when women did all of the farm work by hand with scythes and continued to do so long after the war. We asked her if there had been hungry years after the war. She said, no, "we had potatoes and some people had radishes." Then she suddenly returned to the collectivization of the district:

> In the thirties there was hunger, after they came through with the red broom. They went from household to household. I remember. They ferreted everything out, flour, they turned the woodpile over in our courtyard. I remember, everything we hid, they found. Although we were hungry. I was five years old and I said to one of those men, 'Uncle please leave some for us or we will die without bread. Uncle, don't take everything from us, leave us some. We are dying.' Still they took everything and whatever they found they put in a bag.

We asked her if the collectivizers were local. She said, yes, they were "ours. One of them was an old, old woman, a hunchback, she participated."[40] We asked Anna Petrovna if there had been good times in her life. She instantly replied that there were good times and bad times but that life itself, "Life was wonderful. You just have to know how to live it." Anna Petrovna is not beaten. She finished talking with us with an impassioned argument with one of our team about the impossibility of reviving the farms without capital and technology.

We returned to Pitelino in the summer of 2005. In Gridino, we meet Niura Marfina, who was five years old at the time of the uprising. Niura Marfina imbeds her recollections of the events in another traumatic memory, Stalingrad 1943:

> They came to the school and killed a police officer. And then the rich ones. Well, "rich"; they had a mill. They shot those millers too. And you know what happened? In 1943, in the war, in Stalingrad, they herded us there to a construction site ... I was only nineteen. And we came there to work and build, and some Petukhov, I remember his last name, he said. "Where are you from?" We say, "From Pitelino raion." "And from what village?" We said, "From Gridino." "And do you know Veriaevo?" And I say. "We know it. It's not far from us, half a kilometer." "You remember, maybe you remember?" I say, "A little, I remember." I said, I was eight or nine. We, I say, our parents did not let us out of the house ... They are here with pitchforks and stakes.

We asked Niura if her parents or relatives participated in the uprising. Her denial extended to all of her fellow villagers as well. "Our parents did not go anywhere. Only those from Veraievo ... ours, no, no, no. Ours, from Gridino, they did not go

[40] It is significant that in the memory of a five-year-old, the enemy was basically the local witch—a marginal woman in the village, demonized in the elastic and impressionable mind of a young girl.

anywhere. Ours from Gridino. They had a mill, there, by the river.[41] But our people, from Gridino, no one went." Her mind jumps back to Stalingrad and to Petukhov who had wanted to talk about the uprising with her in 1943.

> Only those that they shot, right there, where the old post office was, there they shot them. That's it. And that Petukhov, that Petukhov, about that Petukhov, they started to say. And you he says, you strikers, you are far from us, from Veriaevo? I say, "not far." We, I say, are not like that, I say. And my parents are not any kind of strikers, no way. And you know what interested him. And they say there is this, the last name is familiar. They were exiled. Maybe he was at that age … What more can I tell you. I can't. Some went, others didn't go. My parents went to the collective farm, my father, he was a carpenter, his whole life a stockman. And my sister, and brother, all my relatives went to the collective farm. No one forced us. We all went. No one did anything.

We asked Niura why there had been an uprising at all. And she repeated that it was not our people but "those Veriaevo people." When we asked why the villagers of Veraievo had risen up, Niura gave up on remembering, "And that I don't know, my dear one. My granddaughter, dear one, I don't know. No, remember, I am eighty years old."

From Gridino we went on to Veraievo. We stopped to ask a group of women directions and ask them about the uprising. They advise us to see the chief administrator of the district, she will have something to say on the matter. The only one left who remembers, they tell us, is Tania Kozlova. In the village of Veriaevo, Tania Kozlova agrees to tell us her recollections of the uprising because, "I am ninety years old and I can tell you." Because Tania Kozlova was the only one who was no longer

[41] Millers have a special place in the village across cultures and were especially persecuted during collectivization. As Carlo Ginsburg points out in *The Cheese and the Worms: The Cosmos of a Sixteenth-Century Miller*, trans. John and Anne Tedeschi (Baltimore: Johns Hopkins University Press, 1980), 119–20, the mill was a place where peasants gathered and talked. The miller was often a middle-man between the more privileged and the mass of the peasantry. Millers made a living; they had a captive market if you wanted to get your grain ground. Moreover they seemed vaguely magical and not in a good way, a lot of grain went in and only a small amount of flour came out. Ginsburg writes: "The age-old hostility between peasants and millers had solidified an image of the miller-shrewd, thieving, cheating, destined by definition for the fires of hell" (119). For more on millers as targets during collectivization, see Lynne Viola, "The Second Coming: Class Enemies in the Soviet Countryside, 1927–1935," in *Stalinist Terror: New Perspectives*, ed. J. Arch Getty and Roberta Manning (New York: Cambridge University Press, 1993), 73; *Peasant Rebels under Stalin: Collectivization and the Culture of Resistance* (New York: Oxford University Press, 1996), 41, and Sheila Fitzpatrick *Stalin's Peasants: Resistance and Survival in the Russian Village after Collectivization* (New York: Oxford University Press, 1994), 56, 158–9, 161.

afraid of Joseph Stalin. The story is vivid, the narrative builds in the present tense, and the very corporeal nature of the memories is captured:

> When the collective farms were formed, they found the kulaks and dekulakized them. And horses, cows, they took them. They fenced them in. Whoever had a bigger home, they took everything for the collective farmers. They took everything. And then, the next morning, the men and women gathered, with sticks, around the village. And they were here, how do you call them, the ones that agitated for the collective farms. One peasant hit one with a stick. He kind of killed him. He never came back. They put him in prison. He was in prison somewhere. Here, the next morning, it was a holiday, Sunday, I went to midday service. The police came from Pitelino. On horses, sleighs, everything was frozen. It was so cold. The sleighs are approaching, drawn by horses, the police, they are coming, coming … They arrived at the church. They came to the church. There was a little lodge there, there we gathered, warmed ourselves, had baptisms. There they began to try to persuade us … And then they began to ring the bells, not the police, but the peasants, to gather the people. So that the people gather for the uprising … They began to urge us: don't do this … But it was too late, everyone turned up with sticks, the women and the men … And ours killed a police officer … there happened to be this pole there, and they killed him. Yes, yes, with a big stick, they killed him. And then they were all fighting, mass confusion. They left, and then they gathered again. And the police left. We gathered to go to Gridino, to have an uprising there … And there was confusions again. And the next day, the police came back and began to pick people out, they took a lot of people away. Arrested them. Some were able to return and some vanished. That was all they could do. The collective farm was created anyway after all this. That was the kind of uprising. I remember, I was not so little, I was big. I went to morning services. Back then, everyone went to morning service. They came, the police on horseback and began to tell us not to ring the bells. And everyone left the service and ran here and there. They asked us, why are you doing this? Don't do it. They told us to try and calm us. Like I said, they killed one of them. They had no need for the collective farm, they wanted to push that power aside, they wanted their own. They came from Gridino here … Now, when we had that uprising they came from Gridino. Our people gathered and went to Gridino. We were afraid. They came … To beat us … They came the next day to pick out those who had been denounced. They had this leader who agitated for the collective farm, from the administration, and on these sleighs, they wrapped him in a sheepskin coat and took him away to bury him.

She told us how the old women had destroyed the holding pens created to hold the collectivized livestock, just as Mozhaev had described it. In fact, it could have been one of the wooden boards thrown into the street that killed the police officer in Tania Kozlova's version of events. When we told Tania Kozlova that the people in Gridino denied participating, she laughed and said that there was even a song about the event, that proved they participated because it ended with the line, "We helped the people from Gridino, and broke our bare feet."

Gridino

Women in their eighties, and there were only women left who were old enough to remember the rebellion, were still afraid of Joseph Stalin. I use this line as a shorthand for the constraints on historical memory imposed on or accepted by the major actors here, ranging from the district party secretaries, to Ianin, to Mozhaev, to Anna Petrovna and Niura Marfina. They were/are still invested in the Soviet system or its post-Soviet incarnation. They are still bound not to draw criticism to themselves, their families, or their communities. Tania Kozlova, at ninety, was free of these bonds. She ended her exchange with us with the words, "I've had enough of this life."

The explicit position of the officials, Ianin, Mozhaev, and even Anna Petrovna was that the unrest reflected pointless, elemental, peasant revolt. But both *Muzhiki i baby* and the archival record cannot help but capture local politics, organization, sophistication, and complexity. I would go further and argue that the record captures a strong commitment on the part of peasants to organized politics and due process. The people that helped us find and interview Anna Petrovna, Niura Marfina, and Tatiana Kozlova, were the young school teacher from the village of Malyi Studenets, Natasha Zhuravleva; her cousin, Viacheslav Egorkin; and her mother, the chair of the rural soviet, Raisa Egorkina. It is worth noting that they represent a kinship network of sorts. They also continue the tradition of village intellectuals and of local rural inhabitants committed to the functioning of their village, largely on their own and against significant odds. And once again, all of them are women. Viacheslav lives in the city. Despite the fact that women were at the forefront of the rebellion in Pitelino, no one remembers the story as a tale of women's protest, except perhaps Ianin, and even then, his heroine was a most peculiar mix of mythical, shemale bogatyr and shameless flasher. In Mozhaev, the women can talk dirty and they can flog Zenin, but they cannot wax philosophical on the past and future of Russia. The eyewitnesses (the OGPU and Ianin) report that a woman was shot and killed, but in Mozhaev's version the victims are men. Women preserve the memory of the rebellion, but always as a tale of "muzhiki i baby," of men and women.

The Pitelino uprising is a kind of looking glass for the historian. The historian looks in and sees the challenges of the discipline such as the profound difficulty of capturing any historical event with sufficient accuracy. I cannot state with certainty how many people were killed during the uprising, where they were killed, who killed them, and who they were. Yet the historian can fall through the looking glass of Pitelino into the retellings of the events and discover rich insights into the development of historiographical debates and the creation and (re)writing of history, of historical memory and gender, of what was Soviet then and what is Soviet now.

Whither Anti-Stalinism?

Kathleen E. Smith

> If we agree that the symbols of the preceding epochs, including the Soviet epoch, must not be used at all, we will have to admit then that our mothers' and fathers' lives were useless and meaningless, that their lives were lived in vain. Neither in my head nor in my heart can I agree with this.
>
> *Vladimir Putin, 2000*

> I share the anger and indignation of all Soviet people about the mass repressions which occurred in the thirties and forties and for which the party-state leadership of the time is to blame. But common sense resolutely protests against the monochrome depiction of contradictory events which has become prevalent in some press organs.
>
> *Defender of the communist past, Nina Andreeva, 1988*[1]

Have the views of Nina Andreeva, as expressed in her famous anti-glasnost epistle, now become more popular than ever? In justifying his support for preserving the music of the old Soviet anthem, President Putin similarly called for a generous approach to remembering the communist era. Indeed, Nina Andreeva's preference for a national history in which unfortunate events remain in the shadows, while feats of labor, military valor, and artistic accomplishment take center stage seems little different from Putin's ideal portrayal of Russia's past. Yet, it would be intemperate to dub Putin a neo-Stalinist or to place him in the camp of socialist diehards. What Putin shares with perestroika-era conservatives, I would argue, is disaffection with anti-Stalinism rather than an admiration for Stalinism. This essay traces the development of official attitudes toward anti-Stalinism in the post-perestroika period and analyzes them in light of broader approaches to national history.

Nina Andreeva enjoyed a brief moment of fame in 1988 when publication in a

---

An earlier version of this paper appeared in *Ab Imperio*, 2004, no. 4. The author is grateful to the editors for permission to reprint portions of that text and to Cornell University Press for permission to use excerpts from Kathleen E. Smith, *Mythmaking in the New Russia: Politics and Memory during the Yeltsin Era*, copyright (c) 2002 by Cornell University.

[1] Quotations are from Patrick E. Tyler, "Soviet Hymn is Back, Creating Much Discord," *New York Times*, December 6, 2000, 1, and Nina Andreeva, "Ne mogu postupat'sia printsipami," *Sovetskaia Rossiia*, March 13, 1988.

major newspaper of her impassioned protest against sensationalist stories of Stalinist crimes seemed to signal a halt to glasnost. Rereading Andreeva's letter in 2006, one is struck by the artful fashion in which she posed her argument in favor of a positive version of national history. Nina Andreeva introduced herself to readers as a teacher concerned about the patriotic upbringing of young people. She framed her fears about anti-Stalinism with the example of students questioning a decorated veteran of the Second World War about repressions in the army. Nina Andreeva cited some listeners' disappointment and disbelief when the colonel told them that he had not encountered any. "Now that it has become topical," she warned, "the subject of repressions has been blown out of all proportion in some young people's imagination and overshadows any objective interpretation of the past." She went on to observe that criticism of the past had ballooned to the extent that, "Industrialization, collectivization, and cultural revolution, which brought our country into the ranks of great world powers, are being forcibly squeezed into the formula 'cult of personality.'" The purges, she argued, should not color perceptions of a whole complex era.

In her carefully crafted letter, Nina Andreeva placed herself in the same camp as the experienced old veteran. She contrasted his real memories (and her family's experiences) with the media-generated false impressions held by naïve youths. In this morality tale, the teacher and the colonel stood for patriotism and wisdom. In trying times, they were defending the achievements of socialism and continuing the Party tradition of service by mentoring the new generation. As an experienced moral guide (*vospitatel'nitsa*), Nina Andreeva was warning Mikhail Gorbachev that the young generation was alienated from reform and that obsession with repressions was producing nihilistic attitudes. By directly connecting interest in past crimes and current pessimism, Nina Andreeva explicitly challenged Gorbachev's rationale for permitting discussion of socialism's mistakes.

During the years of perestroika, Gorbachev consistently took a very pragmatic stance toward Soviet history. Soviet people needed, in his view, to be cognizant of shortcomings of past Soviet leaders and policies. Complacency could not mobilize the "human factor." Therefore, Party leaders had to take the initiative in pointing out problems and their historical roots. Anti-Stalinism became the popular litmus test for commitment to liberal change in the late 1980s. But, even as chapters of the anti-Stalinist Memorial society sprang up across the Soviet Union and as intellectuals began to identify the roots of Stalinism in Leninism, Gorbachev continued to approach criticism of the past as a tool for motivating reformers, not as an inherently good thing. Though his own evaluation of Stalin was clearly negative, Gorbachev was not deaf to conservatives' pleas for restraint. He shared their fear that reform might gather too much momentum and sweep away the foundations of socialism.

Gorbachev was right to worry. Anti-Stalinism often did lead to anti-Sovietism. The facts about the purges soured some people on socialism. For many others, disappointment with Gorbachev's cautious approach to coming to terms with past repressions served as a catalyst for radicalization. Party officials' hindrance of measures to commemorate the victims of Stalinism, their reluctance to countenance a reevaluation of collectivization, combined with ever more revelations in the press about the horrors of the Soviet past, bred disillusionment about the Soviet system's capacity for change. Continued dissembling about the extent of past repressions inspired in some liberals an increasingly fierce commitment to total democratization.[2]

By the time of the first Congress of People's Deputies in March 1990, Soviet citizens were attuned to debates about the past and the future. At the Congress, the nation was bombarded with harsh truths from the podium and it seemed as if a turning point had been reached. Even a conservative crackdown would not be able to erase new understandings about the consequences of the socialist experiment in Russia. Defenders of Stalin and Stalinism had been pushed to the margins. With a sense of success, activists who had begun by organizing around the issue of commemorating Stalin's victims shifted their attention to more contemporary political topics.[3]

Ironically, however, the emotional catharsis achieved by glasnost and its tidal wave of truth-telling about Russia's painful past had started to dissipate by the time of the actual downfall of the Soviet system. By 1991, even faithful readers of liberal editions seemed weary of history, inured to tragic tales, and understandably preoccupied with their own survival in a precarious economy. Capitalist woes may have fostered nostalgia for Brezhnev era prices and stability, but economics cannot explain growing distaste with anti-Stalinism.[4] After the fall of communism, battles over how to interpret the past continued, but with a twist. Politicians, not citizens or journalists, took over the leading role in propagating revised versions of the Soviet experience and they had their own reasons for downplaying or recasting Stalinism.

---

[2] For a fascinating analysis of individual motivations for pro-democracy sentiments, see Alexander Lukin, *The Political Culture of the Russian "Democrats"* (Oxford: Oxford University Press, 2000).

[3] On the decline of the Memorial Society, see Kathleen E. Smith, *Remembering Stalin's Victims: Popular Memory and the End of the USSR* (Ithaca: Cornell University Press, 1996).

[4] For an accounting of the subsequent vagaries of private and official remembrances (and omissions of remembrance) about the Stalinist terror, see Nanci Adler, "The Future of the Soviet Past Remains Unpredictable: The Resurrection of Stalinist Symbols Amidst the Exhumation of Mass Graves," *Europe-Asia Studies* 57, no. 8 (December 2005): 1093–120.

The Yeltsin Years: Reluctant Combat over the Past

Communism's collapse inspired its would-be heirs to study history. Those who wanted to resurrect socialist ideals desperately needed to revise the Soviet historical narrative. They needed scapegoats for the collapse of the USSR and the CPSU and some relevant modern heroes. While Gennady Ziuganov and other communists concentrated on actively revising the Party line on its own past, liberal intellectuals and politicians had their eyes on the present. Yeltsin and his administration had no choice but to deal with pressing issues of governance—such as dismantling the planned economy and working out relations with the former constituent republics of the USSR. The focus on destroying old institutions and building new ones, however, was not accompanied by attention to creating new national myths to legitimize and differentiate the new Russian state. Yet the future would demand attention to the past.

In *Mythmaking in the New Russia*, I contended that the Yeltsin administration squandered the opportunity to institutionalize a revised version of Soviet history in the process of creating a new state.[5] Puny official commemorations of the defeat of the August Coup, the belated trial of the Communist Party, and the feeble celebration of Russia's new national day in the 1990s plainly showed liberal politicians' laissez-faire attitudes toward crafting legitimating myths for the new Russian state. Lack of anti-Stalinist initiative was most evident in the genesis of the so-called "trial of the CPSU"—which stemmed not from democrats' interest in evaluating the past, but from Communists' desire to save their old party organization. In the first years in power, the Yeltsin government eschewed pompous parades and displays of state symbolism, but did not create new, different national celebrations. Liberals mocked communists' love of public demonstrations and banners, but did not mobilize their own supporters in any way.

I see two primary reasons for the failure by Russian democrats to propagate a new national narrative in the 1990s. First, Yeltsin and his advisors thought that an anti-Soviet (including anti-Stalinist) consensus had been firmly consolidated by 1991. Second, they considered propaganda (including promotion of a national identity) to be one of the ignoble aspects of totalitarian regimes. Democrats believed that they neither needed to nor ought to use state resources in promoting a politicized version of the past.

In the early years of the new Russian state, few liberal politicians were disturbed by polemics defending Stalin and Lenin. It was easy to dismiss rants by

[5] The section of this paper on the Yeltsin years draws heavily on my book *Mythmaking in the New Russia: Politics and Memory during the Yeltsin Era* (Ithaca: Cornell University Press, 2002).

Viktor Anpilov, Ziuganov, and others as the last gasp of a dying ideology. Even the strong showing in the 1993 parliamentary election by the Communist Party of Russia (KPRF) evoked mostly ridicule in the form of references to a communist electorate of brainwashed pensioners. One of the few people to react strongly to the resurgence of the Communist Party was Aleksander Iakovlev, the most liberal of Gorbachev's former advisors. In 1988, Iakovlev had written the authoritative response to Nina Andreeva's missive. In that unsigned *Pravda* editorial, Iakovlev had defended anti-Stalinism and attacked the notion of patriotism based on the search for internal enemies. He wanted to see a new patriotism grounded in constructive deeds for the good of the country and a new morality based on respect for the truth. Liberals, he had argued, did not disdain the contributions of millions of ordinary citizens during the Stalin era, but—unlike Nina Andreeva—neither did they interpret honest labor and loyal service as indications of popular support for Stalinist illegality.[6]

By 1993, Iakovlev was clearly worried that nostalgia for the past might lead to a whitewashing of the many crimes committed under Soviet communism. In the aftermath of the disappointing parliamentary election results, he pushed Yeltsin to take the step of publicly rehabilitating the participants in the Kronstadt uprising of 1921. Speaking for the President, Iakovlev emphasized that the decree was intended to confirm the view that repressions, executions, and deportations of civilians began already under Lenin. He sought to force the Communists to "look at the bloody trail you left and to draw a lesson."[7] A deeper expose of communism, however, attracted little popular attention and did nothing to address the need for a new, nuanced patriotism such as Iakovlev himself had touted back in 1988.

Meanwhile, the KPRF and other nationalists were winning acclaim for their defense of Russia's past achievements and for their attacks on western cultural colonization. The "reformed" Communist Party gained support with the template demonstrated by Nina Andreeva; it kept positive slogans such as "for our Soviet motherland," while declaring that it was not "the party of Trotsky and Beria, Vlasov and Iakovlev, Gorbachev and Yeltsin." In the new Russia, unpleasant truth telling seemed to be losing out to facile scapegoating. Most importantly, conservative nationalists and reformed communists had captured the patriotic high ground with their rhetoric about the Great Patriotic War. The public did not want to hear about negative aspects of the war—Stalin's disregard for human costs on the battlefield, the use of punishment battalions, and so forth. Whereas liberals took a more sober view of victory as

[6] "Printsipy perestroiki: revoliutsionnost' myshleniia i deistvii," *Pravda*, April 5, 1988.

[7] Cited by Serge Schmemann, "Yeltsin Extols 1921 Rebellion," *New York Times*, January 11, 1994, 3.

an achievement by the people in spite of the regime, communists simply honored all veterans as loyal patriots.

Only the prospect of the fiftieth anniversary in 1995 of victory in the Second World War seemed to finally push the Yeltsin government toward recognizing the need for some state patriotism to compete with the Communists' claims to represent national pride. After 1991, Russian officials had tried to dispel any nostalgia for the old Soviet-style celebrations by recalling the pompous nature of official events and war memorials under the old regime. Instead, they endorsed the notion that Victory Day should be marked in low key celebrations by former soldiers and their families. Such celebrations were intended to appeal to veterans' pride in their own actions and to reinforce the democrats' version of victory as having come in spite of the Stalinist state. But, the competition between democrats and Communists over patriotic credentials led democrats to reconsider their experimentation with untraditional forms of marking Victory Day.

Hence, in 1995, the Yeltsin administration invested considerable financial and diplomatic resources in marking the jubilee anniversary of Victory Day with showy military parades. The use of Red Square and the presence of foreign dignitaries added to the authority of the ceremonies. Besides reviving the form of celebrating through a display of military might, the Russian government also "rehabilitated" Soviet symbols perceived to be close to hearts of veterans. In 1995, they allowed the red victory banner with its five-pointed star to be hung alongside the Russian tricolor. In 1996, the military parade featured the actual Soviet flag that flew over the Reichstag in 1945. Moreover, in his 1996 address Yeltsin declared that, "All the country now clearly sees the continuity of times contained in our symbols, the proud spirit of the motherland in the unity of generations, in each of us."[8]

Despite Yeltsin's proclamation of patriotic continuity with the Soviet period and his revival of old political rituals and symbols, he and other liberals retained their untraditional perspective that the Soviet Union had won the war in spite of, not because of, Stalin. Though liberals had toned down reminders of the horrors of war and had begun to avoid explicit critiques of wartime policies, they continued to recall the USSR's losses, as well as its victories, on the battlefields of the Second World War. And they traced the roots of Russia's present woes back to the totalitarian system, which they argued had begun in 1917 and which had been inadvertently strengthened by the USSR's victory in the war.[9] The new patriotic mix did not always

---

[8] Cited in Lee Hockstader, "Politics in the Aftermyth of War," *Washington Post*, May 10, 1996, A32.

[9] For liberal mythologizing about the war, see Evgenii Aleksandrov, "Nastoiashchii prazdnik ne otmenit nikto. 9 maia–Den' pobedy," *Nezavisimaia gazeta*, May 7, 1994, 1; Otto Latsis,

ring true. A newspaper correspondent complained of the contradictory messages sent by the 1995 ceremonies:

> the synthesis of great power status (*derzhavnichestvo*) and democracy clearly did not succeed. The ritual of the first parade of the "democratic epoch": the leader on the mausoleum, the minister of defense inspecting the columns of soldiers from an open car to a loud "hurrah"—was totally in accord with the scenarios of Soviet times. The Red banners with hammers and sickles supplanted the tricolor, and Soviet marches and songs sounded out more often than the Russian hymn.[10]

The ceremonies were now too Soviet and yet still did not accomplish their goal of uniting all Russian citizens. Political opponents of the Yeltsin regime, although pleased for veterans' sakes with the return of the red flag, ridiculed democrats for hanging garlands over Lenin's name on the mausoleum. "Recycling" Soviet symbols had evident pitfalls for those who had scorned them so vigorously in the recent past.

Nevertheless, Yeltsin soon found himself again turning to the past as a resource in his 1996 election campaign. Initially, he followed the advice of those in his inner circle who advocated against an anti-Communist strategy. In his early speeches, Yeltsin told voters that, "We have ceased to see the world in terms of red and white. Before our eyes it became multicolored, vivid, and bright."[11] But, with his main opponent, KPRF leader Gennady Ziuganov, running on a platform that combined nostalgia for the Soviet past and Russian nationalism, Yeltsin could not avoid taking a stance on national history. In this case, however, he was able to mobilize divisive collective memories to his advantage.

Yeltsin's most powerful election advertisements used striking black and white images, group portraits of young people taken in the 1940s and 1950s and more recent photos of veterans. The smiling faces of today's grandparents were accompanied by the simple handwritten text: "I believe, I love, I hope" and Yeltsin's signature. Television clips from the same series featured old family snapshots and voice-overs recalling the good and bad of the past, followed by a contemporary shot of the speaker explaining why, despite the difficulties of the present, he or she would vote for Yeltsin. Carefully choosing excerpts that focused on the hardships of the past and hopes for the future, the ads' designers skimmed over the problems of the

---

"My ne zabudem, kto bral Berlin, dazhe esli komu-to ne khochetsia ob etom vspominat'," *Izvestiia*, May 7, 1994, 1.

[10] Evgenii Krasnikov, "Oppozitsiia," *Nezavisimaia gazeta*, May 11, 1995, 1.

[11] Speech of April 9, 1996 reproduced in *Obshcherossiiskoe dvizhenie obshchestvennoi poderzhki B.N. El'tsina na vyborakh Prezidenta Rossiiskoi Federatsii* (Moscow: Pressa, 1996), 5–20, quotation at 6.

present day, problems that might easily be ascribed to Yeltsin's administration. The unadorned personal histories collected by the Yeltsin campaign contrasted sharply with official, faceless version of the past long propagated by Soviet history textbooks. Although the short clips did not provide complex narratives of the past, they did directly challenge the nostalgia promoted by the KPRF.

Yeltsin's campaign also featured a series of posters calculated to draw on differences between life before and after the end of the Soviet system. The "Vote or Lose" signs juxtaposed a denim jacket and a prisoner's striped coat, a globe and a coil of barbed wire, and a person's feet shod in sneakers and the bronze legs of a statue. Designers placed once unobtainable western consumer goods next to objects evoking the most disliked aspects of Soviet life, the GULAG and the cult of the leader. These posters also reminded young people of the sorts of freedom—to travel, to speak out, to enjoy foreign cultures—that their parents had not had. Without actually using political symbols, the ads drew a sharp contrast between the ideological monopoly of the past and the freedom of the present, and hence contributed to the Yeltsin team's emerging theme that this election constituted a choice between polar opposite political systems, not just between personalities or policies.

Toward the end of the campaign, the Yeltsin team foreswore gentle reminders of stagnation. Instead, they tried to frighten viewers by painting the prospect of a second communist revolution, complete with bloodshed, turmoil, even civil war. Yeltsin won with this creation of a stark choice between the past and the present. Yet just a few weeks after his victory, President Yeltsin announced that Russia needed a national idea. He asserted that, unlike every other period of modern Russian history, the new democratic era had no ideology. Hence, he called upon his supporters to "think about what national idea, what national ideology is the most important for Russia."[12] His administration quickly assembled a commission to head the search. Meanwhile, the government newspaper *Rossiiskaia gazeta* initiated a year-long contest for readers to identify or compose a set of principles capable of inspiring Russian citizens to unite as a nation.

What motivated the members of the Yeltsin administration to admit that they had failed to unite citizens around democratic or other values at a point when they might have rested on their laurels? I would argue that the political establishment feared that the anti-Stalinist and anti-Communist rhetoric employed so frequently in the 1996 presidential campaign would not mobilize voters in the future. Yeltsin's advertising designers succeeded in using individual life stories to persuade voters to stick with the President in 1996, but these ads reflected democrats' inability to distill

---

[12] "El'tsin o 'nasional'noi idee," *Nezavisimaia gazeta*, July 13, 1996, 1.

personal stories into unambiguous symbols or clear historical analogies. In contrast to the Communists, neither the Yeltsin administration nor liberal political parties had been able to discover or "manufacture" some potent, meaningful shorthand to communicate their principles to the public.[13]

When Yeltsin stepped down from the presidency three years later, he had not found a new "idea for Russia" and the contest initiated by his advisors had been quietly discontinued without a winner. The broad, abstract nature of the enterprise allowed for extreme diversity and encouraged high-minded rhetoric. Readers' suggested values ranging from "communication" to "repentance" to "empire."[14] To a certain extent, the contest entries simply mirrored Russian society's diverse concerns about economic development, Russia's status in the world, federalism, the environment, and so forth. Yet, unlike the Communists' invocation of specific heroes and concrete collective memories, the liberals' discussion of cultural traditions did not excite any patriotic fervor. Lists of virtues or sets of priorities neither provided blueprints for action nor sparked strong emotional reactions. Stereotypes about national character could be positive and forward looking, but they made a poor substitute for dramatic, memorable narratives about statehood.

Despite the fact that the "idea for Russia" contest produced no winner, it did offer several revelations about the potential grounds for "democratic patriotism." Not surprisingly, the Soviet period was conspicuously absent as a source of positive role models or moral lessons. On the anniversary of the October Revolution in 1996, Yeltsin spoke of a "Year of Reconciliation." But his recasting of the anniversary of the Bolshevik revolution as an occasion for forgiveness and mutual tolerance appealed to neither Communists nor anti-Stalinists. A second interesting feature of the "idea for Russia" contest was its revelation of a strong disdain on the part of many "liberal" patriots for the dissident tradition. The contest's opening announcement quoted Andrei Sakharov and Aleksandr Solzhenitsyn, yet, several commentators actually denigrated the role of dissidents in the history of democratization.

[13] Regarding awareness of the need to translate ideas into "a language of images, metaphors," see Aleksandr Rubtsov, "V ozhidanii idei," *Nezavisimaia gazeta*, November 4, 1997, 5; see also Michael Urban's discussion of "'technologies of discourse' which shape the social world by establishing the ensemble of words, expressions and symbols that can be meaningfully communicated about it." Urban, "Remythologising the Russian State," *Europe-Asia Studies* 50, no. 6 (1998): 969.

[14] Iurii Grechishkin, "Akh muzhik, davai poobshchaemsia!" *Rossiiskaia gazeta*, September 10, 1996, 3; Valentin Miloserdov, "Vsiu zhizn' ia byl kulach'em nedobitym," ibid., December 19, 1996, 3; Aleksei Firsanov, "Ne putaite imperiiu chuvstv, bankov ili sala s velikoi derzhava," ibid., December 5, 1996, 5; Vladimir, Mordashev, "My, konechno, ne Amerikantsy. No ne glupee zhe ikh," ibid., September 17, 1996, 5.

Most notably, Aleksei Kiva—a political scientist and member of Yeltsin's Commission on Human Rights—contended that the former dissidents had no place in modern Russia. The time had come for constructive work, but dissidents were too accustomed to fighting authority and to mistrusting officials. Kiva even alleged that, "For a long time, if not forever, they will feel closer to the person on the defendant's bench than to the person who guards him." Hence, former dissidents made unsuitable candidates for government service. The whole dissident tradition came under fire from supporters of the Yeltsin regime for being overly judgmental. The dissidents' highly developed consciences had led them to hold all governments to strict standards. Such attitudes, Kiva believed, led former dissidents like Sergei Kovalev to exacerbate Russian relations with the breakaway republic of Chechnya by siding with the underdogs, rather than supporting the guardians of law and order. Kiva felt that human rights activists were oriented toward the West and scornful of their own heritage to the point of ridiculing love for state and army. The dissidents, along with radical democrats, had added to Russians' inferiority complex.[15]

In sum, a variety of commentators in the late 1990s expressed the view that previous liberal attitudes toward the national past had been too critical. Outspoken anti-Soviet stances no longer garnered praise. Though new patriots did not rush to praise the Soviet period, they wanted all Russian citizens to be able to take satisfaction in their long shared history. Even Yeltsin seemed to show a change of heart toward dealing with the past with his call for reconciliation on the 1996 anniversary of the Bolshevik revolution. The President, who had campaigned with harsh anti-Communist rhetoric, now wanted more harmony, even if it meant tolerating some distasteful symbols.

The Putin Years: A New Patriotic Mix

From the very first, Vladimir Putin eschewed Yeltsin's relatively laissez-faire style of mythmaking. In one of his initial appearances as Prime Minister in 1999, Putin warned Moscow State University students that "sausage and freedom" would not do as an idea for Russia.[16] Russians needed history for a specific reason—to instill pride in the nation. Neither a market zealot nor a western style liberal, Putin's view on history probably comes closer to that of Gorbachev's conservative critic, Yegor

[15] Aleksei Kiva, "Blesk i nishcheta," *Rossiiskaia gazeta*, February 20, 1997, 5, and February 21, 1997, 4, 5. For another typical attack on the role of dissidents in contemporary Russia, see Viktoria Sharinova, "Pravozashchitniki i sovremennaia Rossiia," *Segodnia*, August 17, 1996, 10.

[16] "Vladimir Putin: Lozung 'kolbasa i svoboda!' ne mozhet byt' natsional'noi idei," *Izvestiia*, September 2, 1999, 1.

Ligachev, than to that of Aleksander Iakovlev. Looking back after the end of the USSR, Ligachev argued that,

> At first this striving to restore historical justice was salutary: it emancipated people's minds, liberated them from a feeling of fear, and generated initiative… But later, the stress shifted and some writers started talking about past lawlessness caustically, gloatingly; with castigation rather than healing...In so doing, they were leading the readers to a single conclusion: the social system was guilty of everything, and therefore had to be changed.[17]

Putin has benefited from the new political system; his political success has come solely under the new democratic rules of the game. But, as an ardent patriot, he is suspicious of anyone who dwells on his nation's misfortunes. He probably shares the mistaken view that anti-Stalinists gloat over every new tragic revelation about the past. (It seems to me that anti-Stalinists' sometimes exultant tone over new discoveries of Stalinist atrocities, such as mass graves, really largely reflects bitter triumph at having overcome substantial bureaucratic obstacles to rescue another piece of long hidden information.[18])

Putin's general attitude toward Soviet history quickly became clear during his first term in the debate over the Russian anthem. In 2000, Putin pushed for, and won, adoption of the music of the old Soviet anthem with new patriotic lyrics by one of its original lyricists. Liberal politicians and intellectuals accused Putin of pandering to public opinion and of honoring a repressive regime with the restoration of the popular tune of Soviet anthem. Even Yeltsin criticized his heir: "The president of a country should not blindly follow the mood of the people. On the contrary, it is up to him to actively influence it."[19] But Putin defended the compromise that finally brought Russia a full set of state symbols. In terms reminiscent of Ziuganov's campaign speeches, the President reminded opponents of the anthem that the Soviet period had consisted of more than "Stalin's prisons and repression." He cited Soviet achievements in space and culture, while noting that the tsarist regime "had repressed peoples and dissidents of its own."[20]

---

[17] Yegor Ligachev, *Inside Gorbachev's Kremlin*, trans. Catherine A. Fitzpatrick, Michele A. Berdy, and Dorochna Dyrcz-Freeman (New York: Pantheon, 1993), 285.

[18] On tension with officials in the St. Petersburg region over the search for mass graves, see Steven Lee Myers, "As Its Past Is Exhumed, Russia Turns Away," *New York Times*, October 20, 2002, 6.

[19] Cited in Patrick Lannin, "Yeltsin Derides Anthem Proposal as Vote Looms," *Moscow Times*, December 8, 2000, 4.

[20] Ibid.

Yeltsin had been willing to appease veterans by producing the red banner on Victory Day. But it was one thing to recognize a historic relic as such, and another thing to adopt an old symbol as fitting for the present. Liberals never endorsed forgetting that Russian sacrifices and ultimate victory in the Second World War had come under the communist flag. But they had come to power seeking to replace the Soviet regime with a democratic one and, even though that promise had not been fully realized, they saw the old system as the opposite of what they wanted to create. Hence Yeltsin and his allies could not really reconcile with the Soviet era.

Putin, by contrast, has taken a more tolerant stance toward the Soviet past. Not one to indulge in the soul-searching favored by liberals, Putin has expressed no regrets or qualms about his own career in the KGB. He apparently sees no contradictions between his past work and his more recent service in ostensibly democratic administrations—first under Sobchak in St. Petersburg and then under Yeltsin. In all of his positions, he served the needs of the state for security, prosperity, and stability. As befits his own history, Putin could easily endorse an amalgam of Soviet and Russian symbols for the state. In this, he clearly showed that he did not share earlier democratic leaders' self-consciousness about borrowing from the Soviet political repertoire.

Nor does Putin share the liberals' discomfort with patriotic pomp. One need only look at the celebration of the sixtieth anniversary of Victory Day in 2005 to see an extravagant display of the nation's military power and martial glory. In front of a huge number of foreign dignitaries—including the presidents of many former Soviet republics, some of whom attended under duress—Putin orchestrated a showy celebration that far outstripped all previous anniversaries. Such was the extent of official celebrations (and security) that ordinary Muscovites were advised to spend the holiday outside of the city!

It should be noted, however, that Putin's show could not overcome all political divisions. Whereas Putin's supporters describe May 9 as "an official state holiday," liberals and communists prefer to call it "a popular holiday" (*narodnyi prazdnik*).[21] Statists praised the holiday pomp—"I felt a sincere feeling of patriotism and pride for the nation. I am happy that the holiday was organized not just as a Moscow or even Russian or post-Soviet event, but as a world event. I think that respect and understanding of Russia have been strengthened." By contrast, a bitter nationalist argued, "It turned out to be a holiday not for the people, but for the authorities. There was the sense that an attraction had been built not even for Putin, but in honor of Bush, Schroeder, Chirac, and Berlusconi."[22]

---

[21] "Mnenie. 9 maia—eto…" *Moskovskaia pravda*, May 8, 2004.

[22] Quotations from Konstantin Kosachev, head of Duma Committee for Foreign Affairs, and

Putin's attention to patriotic holidays has not been restricted to Victory Day. Fondness for martial history can be further seen in addition of a whole list of dates of "military glory" to the state commemorative calendar. Whereas the Soviet regime had marked only the ends of the First and Second World Wars and five battle dates from the Second World War, as of 2003, the Russian calendar included nine victorious events spanning the period from 1242 to 1853. One of these dates—Minin and Pozharsky's rout of Poles from Moscow—was even raised to a non-working holiday in 2005. Due to its rough proximity to anniversary of Bolshevik revolution, it has now been elevated and substituted for the November 7 vacation—not without raising the ire of thousands of communists.[23] Indeed, the angry response to this rare case of Putin demoting a Soviet symbol may well cause the administration to rethink its approach. Perhaps the November holiday period will expand to cover both dates.[24]

The Putin administration has even transformed the relatively unknown and unpopular "Day of Russia" into a national, patriotic holiday. This holiday celebrates the anniversary of the day Russia declared sovereignty, June 12, 1990. Under Yeltsin, Communists marked it as a day of national mourning for lost empire. But most ordinary people could not recall the day's meaning or genesis. Now Putin has turned June 12 into another occasion to celebrate Russia's renewed might and its unity. Starting in 2003, the Putin administration began to mark the date with a showy parade and concert in Red Square, as well as a fly by of military jets over the Kremlin. Of late, the parade has featured riders in military dress of different historical periods and representatives of Russia's 89 regions in folk costumes—here diversity is stripped of its threatening characteristics.[25] As one commentator noted, June 12 has begun to take on a different meaning; it is no longer a day to think about the break up of the old union but rather to take pride in the Russia's acquisition of statehood. Comparing Russia to a phoenix rising from the ashes, he touted the day's "enormous political and educational (*vospitatel'nogo*) potential." Indeed, on the local level,

from Alexander Prokhanov, editor of the nationalist paper *Zavtra*, cited in "Vopros dnia. Kak vam prazdnovanie?" *Komsomol'skaia pravda*, May 11, 2005.

[23] Andrei Kamakin, "Za pobedu u Sinopa! Iz bole chem 80 prazdnikov Rossiia vyberte odin—natsionaly'nyi. Im budet 9 maia," *Itogi*, June 19, 2001, 20–2; "Daty. Novye prazdniki v pamiat' istoricheskikh pobed russkogo voinstva," *Moskovskaia pravda*, November 26, 2003.

[24] "10,000 Scold Putin Over 'Sacred Day'," *The Moscow Times*, November 8, 2005, 1. New Year holidays have been expanded to encompass orthodox Christmas and May holidays span both May Day and Victory Day.

[25] Mikhail Mishin, "Strana otmetila svoi natsional'nyi prazdnik," *Rossiiskie vesti*, June 18, 2003, and "Russia Day Pomp on Red Square," *The Moscow Times*, June 15, 2004.

officials now use the day to teach children about Russian state symbols.[26]

Putin's preference for positive historical memories goes hand in hand with a reluctance to spend much time on negative issues. This trend is evident not only in revisions to commemorative calendar, but also in dealing with problematic aspects of the national past.[27] For instance, commemoration of the end of the Second World War raised some difficult questions about how to evaluate Stalin and his leadership, especially how to interpret the Molotov-Ribbentrop pact and the Soviet occupation of the Baltics. In interviews with German media on the eve of Victory Day in 2005, Putin set forth his views. First, he refused to apologize to citizens of the Baltics for occupation—they were citizens of a different state, the USSR, and the USSR Supreme Soviet had condemned the Molotov-Ribbentrop pact back in 1989.[28] Second, commemoration of the war was not about Stalin. Only when pushed did Putin define his relation with Stalin:

> Stalin and his epoch—this is an inseparable part of the complex, at times contradictory history of my country. This history must be known and its lessons remembered. One of these is evident: dictatorship, crushing of freedoms—this is a dead end for state and for society.

He went on to cite political repressions and the deportations of whole ethnic groups as examples of crimes of the Stalin era.[29] Third, Putin rejected any equation of Stalin and Hitler. "Yes, Stalin was undoubtedly a tyrant, many call him a criminal. But he was no Nazi! And it wasn't Soviet troops that crossed the German border on June 22, 1941, but quite the opposite."

In sum, Putin does not deny the negative aspects of Soviet history, as Nina Andreeva and some conservative communists have done, but he does not really care to

---

[26] "Pervaia Polosa. Den' Rossii." *Rossiiskie vesti*, June 15, 2005. For an example of a rich educational program for Russia Day, see "Priglasitel'nyi bilet. Den' Rossii, kotoryi otmechaetsia 12 iiunia, v Zapadnom okruge planiruetsia otmetit' mnozhestvom kul'turnykh meropriiatii," *Moskovskaia pravda*, June 2, 2005.

[27] Putin has not gotten rid of National Flag Day, the official title of the day marking the failure of the August 1991 coup, but he has not marked it either. Similarly, he does not participate in commemoration of victims of political persecution on October 30.

[28] "Interv'iu germanskim telekanalam ARD i TsDF," May 5, 2005, http://president.kremlin.ru/text/appears/2005/05/87570.shtml (accessed September 30, 2007).

[29] Interestingly, in the same interview German Prime Minister Gerhard Schroeder noted that his generation continues to carry an obligation "for all periods of our history." "Sovmestnoe interv'iu s Federal'nym kantslerom FRG Gerkhardom Shrederom gazete 'Bil'd," May 7, 2005, http://president.kremlin.ru/text/appears/2005/05/87603.shtml (accessed September 30, 2007).

invoke "inverse legitimacy," that is, to hold up the old regime as a negative example. His reluctance to express anti-Stalinism, however, should not be ascribed solely to a more tolerant attitude toward Communism. It also reflects the priority that the new president has given to strengthening state power. Yeltsin was driven by the tasks of transition to underscore breaks with the past; Putin promotes consolidation by avoiding divisive memories.[30] In theory, transition and consolidation could involve taking positive lessons from the past, but Russian liberals could never find some "golden age" from which to draw inspiration. Some intellectuals preferred critical approaches to the past to simple patriotic myths, but humility regarding the nation's common history seemed weak, even shameful, to state builders. Putin wants Russia to reclaim the good from its whole history—including the Soviet period.

A fine example of combining positive referents from diverse epochs of Russian history can be seen in Putin's visit to Sarov, the Russian city once better known as Arzamas-16. The city's two names capture the most salient features of its past; it is both the former home of St. Serafim of Sarov, a monk and hermit canonized at the urging of Nicholas II, and "the homeland of the first Soviet atomic bomb."[31] In 2003, Putin visited the town, which has remained a closed city, to mark the hundredth anniversary of St. Serafim's sainthood. He followed in the steps of the last tsar who traveled there in 1903 for the canonization itself. Putin brought a four-ton bell as a gift; he visited the newly rebuilt church on the heels of a special mass celebrated by the Patriarch; and he gave a short speech in which he congratulated the orthodox on this holiday made possible by new freedom of religion in a multiconfessional Russian state. Though Putin carefully tempered his participation in a purely religious event with recognition of other religions, he both displayed his own faith (crossing himself) and honored the restoration of orthodox churches and traditions.[32] His appearance side by side with the Patriarch and a crowd of pilgrims clearly conveyed a message of warm relations with the church, if not a total return to the special "harmony" enjoyed by church and state in pre-revolutionary Russia.

---

[30] J. Samuel Valenzuela, "Democratic Consolidation in Post-Transitional Settings: Notion, Process, and Facilitating Conditions," in *Issues in Democratic Consolidation*, ed. Scott Mainwaring, Guillermo O'Donnell, and J. Samuel Valenzuela (Notre Dame: University of Notre Dame Press, 1992), 78–80.

[31] Maria Nikiforova, "Putin poshel po stopam Nikolaia Vtorogo. Godovshchinu kanonizatsii Serafima Sarovskogo prezident sovmestil s poseshcheniem iadernogo tsentra," *Nezavisimaia gazeta*, August 1, 2003, 3.

[32] As with Church of Christ the Savior in Moscow, the church built in Sarov was putatively funded by donations from ordinary people, businesses, institutions, and so forth. In fact the great bulk of the money—some ten million dollars—came from state coffers. Aleksandr Soldatov, "Grazhdanin. Serafim-16," *Moskovskie novosti*, August 5, 2003, 16

The trip to Sarov offered an additional opportunity for mythmaking and Putin seized upon that as well with a visit to the atomic center where nuclear weapons are still designed. Putin listened to the requests of scientists and assured them that their city would keep its special status. He praised their zeal in creating new weapons for Russia, but offered them a statesmanlike reminder that testing was constrained under international accords. The visit to the birthplace of the Soviet atomic bomb was calculated to showcase, if only in vague detail, the talents of Russia's scientists and the strength of its defense systems. Perhaps not surprisingly, Putin did not mention the service of Russia's most famous dissident, Andrei Sakharov, to the realization of the Russian atomic project in Sarov.[33]

Does Putin's statist approach to mythmaking mean the inevitable rehabilitation of Stalin? Not necessarily. Putin has not echoed Ziuganov's praise for Stalin as a great military leader, sincere nationalist, or nurturer of Russian culture. Nor has he endorsed the logic behind positive reinterpretations of Stalin's leadership. He clearly does not want to turn the clock back.[34] But the statist motivation does require remembering industrialization and the conduct of the Second World War at the very least as unmitigated successes. While liberals and historians still ask to what extent Stalinist policies facilitated or undermined these processes, these questions are to be absent from state commemorations of the past. Without such analysis, in my opinion, one gets a dumbed-down, overly simplistic, and hence fragile patriotism. National myths that do not allow for complexity cannot hold up well in the in real world in which politicians use the past to compete for attention.[35] Moreover, an insistence on honoring the positive opens the door for Communists to promote a creeping rehabilitation of Stalin, Dzerzhinsky, and other historical figures who have some record of state service amidst their myriad of disservice to individuals.

Is the dearth of anti-Stalinism a danger to Russian democracy? Recent poll data showing young Russian's ambivalence toward Stalin has been interpreted by some western analysts with great alarm. In January 2006, Sarah E. Mendelson and Theodore P. Gerber warned that,

[33] Schroeder cited anti-Nazi resisters as heroes of the Second World War. I have not found a case of Putin describing anti-Soviet dissidents in similar terms.

[34] In explaining his reference to the break up of the USSR as a tragedy, Putin has noted "We say: those who don't regret the dissolution of the Soviet Union have no heart, but those who want to put it back the way it was have no head." "Interv'iu germanskim telekanalam."

[35] Given that Putin barely campaigned in 2000 or in 2004, we lack evidence as to what he would have said in a direct clash with politicians from other camps.

> Nostalgia for Stalin in Russia is not simply a relic that will die out with the older generation. And as long as young Russians remain ignorant about or have positive feelings toward a murderous dictator who institutionalized terror throughout their country, they are unlikely to mobilize behind calls for greater justice, human rights, or transparency—factors critical to Russia's transformation into a modern democratic society.[36]

While I have argued that collective memories are important material in the hands of politicians and opinion makers in their efforts to win support for current policies, interpretations of the past are only one factor in individual decision making on matters such as whether to protest to protect one's rights. Putin's salvaging of some aspects of Soviet history need not mean tolerating violations of human rights in the past or the present. Indeed, I would remind that views of Stalin are not the same as views of Stalinism. As disheartening as it may be to hear ambivalent evaluations of Stalin, such opinions should be analyzed carefully—if Stalin gets some credit for victory in the Second World War that is a different matter than denying the purges.

Putin's attempt to have the best of both worlds, as with the national anthem—keeping the form while changing the content—is unlikely to have the effect he desired, that is, to resolve the controversy over state symbols. Putin's pragmatic approach to overcoming the deadlock on state symbols by granting concessions to the Soviet part of the Russian people could not end the battle over what to take from the past. The subsequent furor simply reaffirmed the extent of the divisions. Perhaps what really matters for the future is that debate about the past continues. As long as Russians are fighting about their history, there is a chance that critical approaches to the Stalinist past may come back into fashion. For the present, anti-Stalinists can console themselves with the knowledge that all the historical revelations of the past two decades cannot be stuffed back into Pandora's box.

---

[36] Sarah E. Mendelson and Theodore P. Gerber, "Failing the Stalin Test: Russians and their Dictator," *Foreign Affairs*, January–February 2006, 3.

III. Dispensing Welfare and Punishment

"Untraditional Sex" and the "Simple Russian"

Nostalgia for Soviet Innocence in the Polemics of Dilia Enikeeva

Dan Healey

In 2001, Elena Baraban proposed that after Russia's decriminalization of male homosexuality in 1993, state-directed antigay policies had been replaced by "everyday homophobia." In the Soviet era, homophobia had been "a fundamental constituent of norms of social behavior"; despite the wide gap between attitudes expressed by the state and by society on a range of questions, in their homophobia, "the Party and people were one." With decriminalization in the Yeltsin reform era, a new social question arose: how was this marginal group, the so-called "sexual minority," to be regarded by society? Baraban's grim conclusion, based on a reading of popular fiction, was that homophobia had now been eagerly interiorized in mass consciousness.[1]

Baraban's readings of homophobic characters and scenarios in pulp crime and battle-action literature (*detektivy* and *boeviki*) are insightful, but her article does not explore the origins of Russia's "everyday homophobia." Her thesis, that "everyday homophobia" became embedded in popular attitudes during the 1990s as official homophobia receded, is problematic. If we accept that until the 1990s "Party and people were one" in their hostility to same-sex love, then it follows that "everyday homophobia" had Soviet roots and might well have been expected to evolve, unless a seismic shift in sexual culture dislodged it. Reform-era liberalization certainly did bring more open discussion of sexuality in media and academe. Liberally minded sexology acquired some influence in the shaping of education, family planning, and anti-HIV/AIDS programs, as exemplified in the work of Academician Igor Kon.[2] Yet if an undeniable "sexual revolution" took place during the 1990s, it was not accompanied by a sustained national conversation between heterosexuals and homosexuals. Everyday homophobia evolved rapidly, and well beyond the pages of pulp fiction. The first generation of post-Soviet lesbian, gay, bisexual, and transgender (LGBT) activists burnt out during Yeltsin's second term, unable to establish stable

[1] Elena Baraban, "Obyknovennaia gomofobiia," *Neprikovsnovennyi zapas*, 2001, no. 19: 85–93.

[2] Igor' S. Kon, *Seksual'naia kul'tura v Rossii: Klubnichka na berezke* (Moscow: OGI, 1997; 2nd ed. Moscow: Airis Press, 2005); on the rise of Russian sexuality studies, see Dan Healey, "Sexual Cultures in Russia," in *The Blackwell Encyclopedia of Sociology*, ed. George Ritzer (Oxford: Blackwell, 2007).

non-governmental organizations (NGOs) and publications. They encountered a society basically unwilling to register their existence or tolerate their voices.[3]

In fact it is not necessary to read detective novels to demonstrate the widespread and popular nature of homophobia in the decade after decriminalization. Viktor Gulshinsky's prodigious catalogue of antigay attitudes, a dossier of media reports from 1993 to 2001 reflecting Russian homophobia, can be consulted in Toronto's and Amsterdam's queer archives. In his introduction to the dossier, Gulshinsky argues that official homophobia persists because equality guarantees in the Constitution are not extended to those who suffer discrimination on the grounds of sexual orientation; that local authorities stifle gay and lesbian voices by refusing NGO registration; that police, prisons, and army persist in inflicting extortion and beatings, rape, and murder on gay citizens; and that Russia's media disseminate homophobic material and ignore alternative opinion.[4] Society's discomfort with feminism and its challenges to conventional gender roles, often read as a threat to nationhood itself, also underpin popular homophobia.[5]

The Gulshinsky dossier ends as Vladimir Putin's presidency was beginning. Since that time political developments have transformed life significantly for the worse for Russia's citizens who wish to speak openly about their homosexuality. NGO activity has been sporadic and largely unofficial, and of course subject to the increased state scrutiny that all civil society now endures. Official attitudes toward public displays and declarations of same-sex affinity are hardening. A second, Putin-era generation of LGBT activists has until recently retreated to two privileged spaces: the world wide web, and commercial operations (gay bars, clubs, and shops). One glossy magazine aimed at affluent Moscow gay men, *Kvir* (Queer), appears to

[3] This generation is captured in the rich observations of a San Francisco journalist: David Tuller, *Cracks in the Iron Closet: Travels in Gay & Lesbian Russia* (Boston: Faber & Faber, 1996); see also, Laurie Essig, *Queer in Russia: A Story of Sex, Self and the Other* (Durham: Duke University Press, 1999). For a critique of Tuller and Essig, see Brian James Baer, "Russian Gays/Western Gaze: Mapping (Homo)Sexual Desire in Post-Soviet Russia," *GLQ: A Journal of Lesbian and Gay Studies* 8, no. 4 (2002): 499–520.

[4] Viktor Gul'shinskii, "Gomofobiia v sovremennoi Rossii: Vse ottenki chernogo," in *Gomofobiia v sovremennoi Rossi 1993–2001 g.g. Dokumenty, fakty,* ed. idem (Moscow: The author, 2001). On deposit in Homodok, International Resource Centre for Gay and Lesbian Studies, Amsterdam; and in Canadian Lesbian and Gay Archives, Toronto.

[5] On sexism and Russian nationality, see Baer, "Russian Gays/Western Gaze," 513–16; Michele Rivkin-Fish, "From 'Demographic Crisis' to 'Dying Nation': The Politics of Language and Reproduction in Russia," in *Gender and National Identity in Twentieth-Century Russian Culture*, ed. Helena Goscilo and Andrea Lanoux (DeKalb: Northern Illinois University Press, 2006).

survive as a marketing extension of the commercial realm.[6]

More significant perhaps than the containment of queer voices themselves has been the rise of a new, nationalist, and conservative antigay rhetoric that has been adopted and refined by political opinion makers of the Putin era. I argue that the new politics of homophobia is qualitatively different from the spontaneous, uncoordinated, and often wretchedly unsophisticated outbursts from politicians and commentators of the 1990s. Increasingly, converging political voices have elaborated a discourse of outward respect for the private life of queer citizens while zealously rebuffing any attempt by them to escape the containment zones of internet and commerce. The last blast of the old homophobia came in early 2002, when, during a debate about a bill to raise the age of consent, Duma deputy Gennady Raikov proposed the re-criminalization of sodomy. Copycat proposals to ban lesbian sex, and masturbation, contributed to a carnivalesque atmosphere in parliament. Deputies across the political spectrum denounced Raikov's initiative, and obliquely more sober voices spoke about the need to honor Russia's Council of Europe commitments, which included the decriminalization of gay relations. Forces for "traditional moral and spiritual values" quickly regrouped, and launched their own cross-party lobby group in the Duma after the 2003 elections. Their chief success has not perhaps been in terms of concrete legislation but in shifting the terms of debate about sexual politics. Dilia Derdovna Enikeeva's 400-page tract, *Gays and Lesbians*, published in early 2003, has arguably supplied a blueprint for the new rhetoric.[7]

Enikeeva is a sexologist, a "co-chair" of the Association of Russian Sexologists, an organization of medically trained specialists in sexual dysfunction, counseling, and therapy. The association's membership includes practitioners from a diverse range of disciplines: its president, Irina Leonidovna Botneva, trained as an obstetrician-gynecologist; another "vice-president," Evgeny Aleksandrovich Galchuk, is a

---

[6] One of the oldest principal organisations is "Together," a youth group registered with the Moscow City authorities (albeit, not as an openly "gay" organisation); it operates the website www.gay.ru. Its leader, Ed Mishin, publishes *Kvir*; gay shops named Indigo operate in Moscow and St. Petersburg. The organizers of www.gayrussia.com, led by Nikolai Alekseev, attempted to hold a Gay Pride Parade in Moscow on May 27, 2006; the initiative was opposed by LGBT groups and societies in Moscow, St. Petersburg, and elsewhere but the action stimulated them to greater public activism. I will describe the gay pride parade conflict of 2006 in a forthcoming article.

[7] Dilia Enikeeva, *Gei i lesbiianki* (Moscow: Astrel'/AST, 2003). I have described the Duma debates of 2002 in "'Let them move to France': Homosexuality, Nationality and Masculine Anxiety," in *Without a Script: Performing Homosexuality in Post-Soviet Russia*, ed. Serguei Oushakine and Brian Baer (forthcoming).

psychiatrist; its secretary, Lev Moiseevich Shcheglov, is a psychoanalyst. The association participates in expositions and conferences promoting scientific discussion of sexual problems, from a decidedly heteronormative and conventional standpoint.[8] Enikeeva trained as a psychiatrist and sexopathologist (*seksopatalog*) during the Soviet era; she has transformed herself into a sex counselor with a formidable media presence, authoring 145 books including over 50 self-help titles (*Love: A War of the Sexes?*; *An Encyclopedia of Love and Sex for the Whole Family*; *How to Re-Educate Your Husband*) concentrated on sex and love problems. She participated in the 2002 debate on the age of consent as an expert witness to the Duma's Legislation Committee, commenting on the dangers of teenage sexual activity.[9] While her media persona can appear lightweight, her Duma intervention and her links to an association claiming to speak for post-Soviet sexology as a medical enterprise suggest that her views deserve scrutiny.

Indeed, Enikeeva's analysis of the problem of homosexuality in *Gays and Lesbians* is interesting for its elements of continuity with the past. The book resonates with ideas that have been prevalent in Russia about homosexuality since the late tsarist period; it also reflects discourses from the Stalin era and the late Soviet years. It can be difficult sometimes to reconcile these often incommensurate discourses, however, it is worth recalling that the conflicting nature of "modern" ideas of homosexuality is a poor substrate to begin with. We are trying to make sense of a Russian reworking of concepts that do not necessarily hang together in the "modern" medical and cultural originals. To give one example made famous by queer theorist Eve K. Sedgwick, "minoritizing" views of homosexuality (as the practice of a "sexual minority"—to introduce a term used in Russian) conflict and coexist with "universalizing" notions of homosexuality, as a form of sexual activity or expression anyone might engage in, perhaps via "mental infection" (a favorite trope of Soviet thinking).[10]

With thirty-one breezy chapters, the sexologist-turned-polemicist's book is intended for a popular Russian audience. She wrote it in two weeks ("I usually write

[8] For the association's participation in an exposition-conference 'Eros-Moskva', see http://www.eros-expo.ru/news.php?id=320&category=1 (accessed December 21, 2006). Officers of the association: Kul'gavchuk, http://doctorsexolog.ru/; Botneva, http://www.woman.ipd.ru/club/health/seks.shtml; Shcheglov, http://az.gay.ru/authors/contemporary/sheglov.html (all accessed December 21, 2006).

[9] Healey, "'Let them move to France'"; on Enikeeva's publications see her website, http://www.enikeeva.ru/index1.htm (accessed December 21, 2006).

[10] Eve K. Sedgwick, *Epistemology of the Closet* (Berkeley: University of California Press, 1990).

quickly and easily," her website gushes) following the Duma sex debates of 2002.[11] Peppered with jokes and slogans distinguished in bold typography, Enikeeva's prose is conversational and chatty; the anecdotes range from the salty and puerile to the downright homophobic. Enikeeva evidently intends to illustrate popular Russian attitudes towards the "sexual minority" with these witticisms. When she wishes to lay down a serious precept about gays and lesbians, it appears in italics in a box; she avoids citations but uses footnotes to explain sexological terminology. Her target readers are the father or mother seeking to prevent their son or daughter turning homosexual and the young woman seeking to avoid hearing the words "Darling, I'm gay" from her husband. The book presents a potted history of homosexuality, descriptions of how straight teenagers are recruited by confirmed homosexuals into gay sexuality, the tragedies of women married to gay men, "gay censorship" in the media and entertainment, and stories about gay pedophilia, prostitution, rape, and murder. It concludes with a series of chapters about how Russia's "sexual majority" should respond to its sexual minority, and in particular how "propaganda" for same-sex love should be repressed to protect young people and the nation as a whole.

My reading of Enikeeva's diatribe against gays and lesbians is organized around three themes: the myth of Russia's sexual innocence; the notion of a "traditional," unproblematic sexuality; and her antiliberal responses to the problems posed by homosexuality. By examining how these three broad themes are expressed in her work, it should be possible to see how Enikeeva condenses and focuses what Baraban identified as Russia's "everyday homophobia" into something more politically powerful, drawing on reserves of nostalgia for lost innocence and invented traditions of Soviet sexual life.

Russia's Heritage of Sexual Innocence

The idea of a Russia free of sexual depravity has a long pedigree. Russia's chattering classes of the nineteenth and early twentieth centuries understood depravity, whether imagined as innovation, excess, inappropriateness of object, or amorality, as problems of civilization. The product of urban life and commercialized lifestyles, sexual depravities were therefore not significant Russian problems. Since the requisite conditions scarcely existed, an overwhelmingly peasant *narod* (people) was held not to display such vices. This bucolic sexual simplicity was part of a wider romanticization of the peasantry, and after 1905 Russia's professionals and experts slowly began to abandon such views, including the notion of peasant sexual innocence. Liberal and increasingly medicalized discourses of sexuality flourished and proliferated in

[11] http://www.enikeeva.ru/index1.htm (accessed December 31, 2006).

Russia between 1905 and 1930.[12] The political direction of the revolutionary era dictated who the new moral exemplars would be.

If sexual disorder existed in the countryside, nevertheless it was "primitive"; as social democrat G.S. Novopolin explained in 1909, Russia's characteristic sexual vices were "coarse and simpleminded" by comparison to the sophisticated debaucheries practiced in Paris or Berlin.[13] Taking education, economic development, and medical advances to the Russian or Soviet countryside would eventually overcome sexual ignorance there.[14] Meanwhile, especially during the 1920s, worker sexuality was an arena of struggle. On the one hand, proletarian sexual behavior was held to be natural, free of petty-bourgeois philistinism, and inherently virtuous when contrasted with bourgeois sexuality. On the other hand, workers displayed confusion as a result of the Revolution and Civil War, and the political compromise of the New Economic Policy—a confusion that expressed itself in outrages like the 1926 Chubarov Alley gang rape. Worker sexuality needed tutelage and time: Party and expert training in sexual enlightenment programs, political consciousness-raising to appreciate women's emancipation, improved knowledge of hygiene, but also time for socialist economic development to create the conditions favorable to the natural expression of workers' innately virtuous sexuality.[15] In effect, because of an historic great leap forward into socialism, the Revolution offered to experts the possibility that the sexual depravity of a Paris or Berlin might be side-stepped and never become embedded in Russian soil. Bourgeois commercialization of sexuality would not accompany a socialist industrial take-off, and the sexual amorality, excess, and misdirection apparent in Soviet urban life would wither away like other forms of the "old way of life."

---

[12] Laura Engelstein, *The Keys to Happiness: Sex and the Search for Modernity in Fin-de-Siècle Russia* (Ithaca: Cornell University Press, 1992); for the evolution of the sexual innocence model in the 1920s, Susan Gross Solomon, "Innocence and Sexuality in Soviet Medical Discourse," in *Women in Russia and Ukraine*, ed. Rosalind Marsh (Cambridge: Cambridge University Press, 1996).

[13] G.S. Novopolin, *Pornograficheskii element v russkoi literature* (St. Petersburg, 1909), 169; see Dan Healey, *Homosexual Desire in Revolutionary Russia: The Regulation of Sexual and Gender Dissent* (Chicago: University of Chicago Press, 2001), 253.

[14] See, for example, Stephen P. Frank, "Ask the Doctor! Peasants and Medical-Sexual Advice in Riazan Province, 1925–1928," in *The Human Tradition in Modern Russia*, ed. William B. Husband (Wilmington: Scholarly Resources, 2000).

[15] Eric Naiman, *Sex in Public: The Incarnation of Early Soviet Ideology* (Princeton: Princeton University Press, 1997); Frances Bernstein, *The Dictatorship of Sex: Lifestyle Advice for the Soviet Masses* (DeKalb: Northern Illinois University Press, 2007); Gregory Carleton, *Sexual Revolution in Bolshevik Russia* (Pittsburgh: University of Pittsburgh Press, 2005).

Russian radicals and experts subjected homosexuality to these lenses, too. Hence same-sex love was held to be infrequent among Russia's peasantry, and if liberal medicalization after 1905 found more evidence of homosexuality as a biological or psychiatric anomaly, it was still believed to be a rare and urban phenomenon. Sympathetic and antipathetic voices spoke of same-sex love. Sympathy came in both literary and scientific discourse. Yet according to Evgeny Bershtein, the medical language of homosexuality as anomaly was transformed into a politicized discourse pitting an allegedly undefiled left versus a degenerate right in late Imperial Russia.[16] Early Bolshevik policies on homosexuality expressed this ambiguity. Sodomy was decriminalized and humane views about the homosexual individual as citizen could be axiomatic among intelligentsia and medical leaders. The international left hailed such sympathies as a tenet of the Soviet sexual revolution, and yet in Moscow sexological science approached the subject with caution. Although Soviet psychiatrists commenting on homosexuality seldom mentioned class, they tended to present it as primarily a bourgeois or aristocratic anomaly; implicitly, it was thus likely to disappear as these classes died off.[17]

All of these "minoritizing" ideas applied to European Russians or Soviet citizens: in the "primitive" south and east of the country, Russians simultaneously viewed homosexuality as a "universal" affliction typical of societies where the seclusion of women and other benighted customs were widespread.[18] Thus in the Russian imagination, homosexuality was displaced eastward and westward: a *vice* of Eastern, primitive peoples who would one day be raised to European levels of civilization and thereby leave such practices behind, and an *illness* of Western civilization that Soviet socialism would eventually avoid as it constructed its new scientific, rational and socialist civilization. Soviet Russia was virtually without an indigenous homosexual minority in this view (and indeed, even during the era of early Soviet medical sympathy for the homosexual individual, doctors found the discussion of homosexuals as a collectivity troubling). Stalinist and post-Stalin policy rendered homosexuals "invisible" with prison sentences of five years for voluntary sodomy,

---

[16] Evgenii Bershtein, "'Psychopathia sexualis' v Rossii nachala veka: politika i zhanr," in *Eros i pornografiia v russkoi kul'ture*, ed. M. Levitt and A. Toporkov (Moscow: Ladomir, 1999).

[17] Healey, *Homosexual Desire in Revolutionary Russia*, 126–51.

[18] See, for example, the two distinct articles on "homosexuality" (one treating it as a medical phenomenon in "modern" societies and the other treating it as a social one among "primitive" peoples), which appear under that heading in the first edition of the *Great Soviet Encyclopedia*: Mark Sereiskii, "Gomoseksualizm," *Bol'shaia sovetskaia entsiklopediia*, 1st ed., vol. 17 (1930), 593–6; see Healey, *Homosexual Desire in Revolutionary Russia*, 170–1.

between 1934 and 1993; and the silencing of all sexology under Stalin made the idea of medical sympathy for a biologically determined sexual minority impossible to articulate. Even after 1953, the cautious revived discipline of sexual pathology (*seksopatologiia*) often conducted itself as a form of police psychiatry. In ideological terms late Soviet Russia was a place without homosexuality. In the ideal conditions of "mature socialism," perversions were rare biological dysfunctions. Otherwise, "natural" sexual desire—a carefully crafted Soviet heterosexuality, whose history remains to be written—was meant to flow with *zhizneradost'* (*joie de vivre*) through the socialist channels erected by the Party's planners. Homosexuality—if ever mentioned at all—was elsewhere, most notably in the decadent capitalist West, where social conditions generated the illness.

Dilia Enikeeva's fantastic presentation of the history of Russian treatment of homosexuality in the twentieth century and her critique of current trends in society offer a nostalgic resurrection of the innocent Russia myth. For her Russia is relatively innocent of homosexuality and innocent of homophobia as well. Enikeeva frequently compares Russia to the United States of America, or to a generic "West," where in her view homosexuality was handled more brutally. To be sure, "in totalitarian society" (i.e., Stalin's Soviet Russia of the mid-twentieth century) homosexuality was made illegal and society responded with the unmasking of gays and persecution; but Enikeeva argues that Stalin's law against sodomy was used "very rarely, only when there was nothing else to send someone to prison for." In Enikeeva's view, the Stalinist antihomosexual episode was nothing extraordinary, just a part of what an entire society experienced at the hands of irrational leadership. Her contention that Soviet sexual pathologists dealt with homosexuality humanely is harder to credit. She claims that in contrast to the United States, where force (electroshock, lobotomy, castration) was used in cures of homosexuality in the 1950s, "in our country homosexuals were never subjected to forced therapy ... In our country homosexuals were only given therapy voluntarily when they themselves requested assistance, or as part of the treatment of another mental illness. Neither I nor any of my colleagues know of even a single case of forced curing of homosexuals."[19]

Enikeeva's contemporary Russia does differ from historical constructions in that it consists of a "sexual majority" (*seksbol'shinstvo*) of "millions of simple Rus-

[19] Enikeeva, *Gei i lesbiianki*, 56–7. For a discussion of late-Soviet attempts to cure homosexuality, including the use of drugs, "persuasion," and electroshock therapies, see Healey, *Homosexual Desire in Revolutionary Russia*, 237–44. For U.S. experience in compulsory and voluntary cures during this era, see Jennifer Terry, *An American Obsession: Science, Medicine, and Homosexuality in Modern Society* (Chicago: University of Chicago Press, 1999).

sians" (*milliony prostykh rossiian*), and a "sexual minority" (*seksmen'shestvo*) of gays and lesbians. Gays and lesbians have become an undeniable presence in Russian society. One of Enikeeva's wittier jokes refers to the colors of the Russian flag: they demonstrate that democratic Russia is an inclusive place with room for—"the Reds, the Whites, and the ... Well, in general, for everybody!"[20] (Light blue—*goluboi*—is the third color of Russia's flag and *goluboi* is slang for "gay" in Russian.) This is one of the few moments in her book in which Enikeeva associates gay Russians with citizenship—and in highly ambiguous fashion. Elsewhere, references to the nation refer insistently to the "sexual majority" and the national interest is entirely imagined as heterosexual.

The sexopathologist develops a construction of the innocence of Russia's sexual majority with frequent references to positive social traits. The heterosexual majority are "simple Russians who wrack their brains trying to make ends meet so that they can feed their children and find a normal job" (236). "[A]ny Russian" who cares about their country's future—the patriotic majority—will read her book to learn about the insidious spread of "gay censorship" and influence among the structures of power (9). Such Russians show strength of character, appropriately masculine or feminine resolve in the face of the creeping "homosexualization of the entire country" (32). In Enikeeva's view it is simply axiomatic that no heterosexual Russian man ("unless he is a homophile"—a dangerously deluded straight) would knowingly vote for a homosexual politician, and no ordinary Russian woman would cast her ballot that way because gay lawmakers have no understanding of the challenges of parenting (237). The Russian majority is also tolerant, and gifted with a rough-and-ready sense of humor that, "if things had proceeded naturally" would have resulted in a "correct if not exactly warmly loving" attitude towards the homosexual minority (248). She writes,

> The overwhelming majority of Russians are neither homophobes nor homophiles, and they express their attitudes towards devotees of same-sex sex by laughing at them, by thinking up insulting nicknames, by mimicry of their habits.
>
> [Joke] One soldier, grumbling to another: "There's a queer among the new recruits." "How do you know?" "Somebody stole my compact!" (22)

The problem for the nation is that the while these kind-hearted, humorous, and simple Russians struggle to make a living and raise children, the sexual minority has

[20] Enikeeva, *Gei i lesbiianki*, 58; all further page references from this book are given in the text.

consolidated its grip on money and power. By Enikeeva's reckoning (extrapolating from American surveys) the homosexual population of Russian can be no more than 5 percent of the total, "yet the question of homosexualism is constantly being whipped up. How can such an *insignificant* part of the Russians draw so much *loud public* attention to itself? Not even the problems of the disabled are spoken about as much as those of the devotees of non-traditional sex" (251–52, emphasis in the original).

The innocence of the simple majority contrasts starkly with the insidious character of this shrill and insignificant gay minority. The minority has a fatal flaw: "Devotees of same-sex relations are too concerned with their homosexuality" (258); they "spend too much time and energy proving that they 'are no worse than anyone else'" (239); the homosexual is "extraordinarily concerned about his homosexuality all his life ... is consumed by love and the search for an ideal beloved" (236). Such self-absorption and selfishness reminds Enikeeva the sexologist of a cartoon character: "a little dragon ... who cries 'Everything for me, me, me!'" (252). While they may have the outward appearance of a man, homosexuals "resemble women in many ways, they are emotionally immature" (252).

The homosexual minority is also dangerously close to the levers of power and wealth in post-socialist Russia—a trait that also puts it at odds with the millions of simple, hardworking Russians. They go into politics "to resolve their own problems"; far from being "altruists ... who care for the welfare of Russians, night and day, dealing with our problems" gay and lesbian politicians are in power to pass laws guaranteeing gay marriage and gay adoption rights (239). Homosexual lawmakers and politicians "lobby [only] for the interests of homosexuals" (239) Enikeeva, apparently quoting herself, declares—"Let homosexuals demonstrate their talents in the opera and ballet, on the stage, in the fashion business, in the creative professions, but not in politics" (247). They form clusters of "*golubizna*" (gayness) in the media—she claims a critical mass of gays dominated NTV until its ownership and personnel changes and that these then decamped to TV-6 and later TVS (261). They dominate journalism (and she recounts many bitter stories of how they conspire to keep her work out of print) (263–66 and passim). "Telephone justice" supplements the corrupting power of money in the media and entertainment business to protect gays and crush straight journalists and commentators (242). The *golubizna* has captured the Union of Rightist Forces party, in which the boyish Sergei Kirienko serves as a honeytrap for the gay male vote, while Irina Khakamada inspires an outburst that "She's the personification of feminism! Women power! And among the feminists there are not a few lesbians" (240). They even get married and have children to mask their lesbianism.[21]

There is much here that resonates with tsarist and Soviet anti-Semitism: the conspiratorial groups huddled behind closed doors, exploiting money-grubbing business and politics over the heads of a simple-minded, toiling and far too generous majority of Orthodox (or good Soviet) Russians.[22] Like anti-Semitism, it is a viewpoint that yearns for a nation purified of undesirables. Despite her claims that gays and lesbians would get along fine with ordinary Russians if they left the political and media arenas and confined themselves to occupational ghettos and private spaces, Enikeeva's understanding of authentic Russianness excludes "devotees of same-sex sexuality." Real manhood and womanhood, real work for honestly acquired pay, familial love, emotional continence, and maturity: these are not characteristics Enikeeva sees in Russia's gays and lesbians. They are the preserve of the majority, who cling to the practice of "traditional sex."

Inventing "Traditional Sex"

In Russia, it appears that so-called "traditional" sex is an invented tradition. I am not aware of any instances of the use of the "traditional" label for a particular sexuality or kind of sexual behavior prior to the post-Soviet era. Indeed, if we think of the late Soviet years as at time when there was no explicitly sexual discourse (*U nas seksa net*—"We have no sex," in the oft-repeated saw), it is hard to know precisely what commentators who use the term "traditional sex" actually mean.

I would like to propose a slightly mischievous model of "traditional sex"—one that draws on the conventions of Stalinist and Soviet discourse about gender and (when it turns up) sex, and suggest that Enikeeva's notions of normal sexuality owe a lot to this nostalgic amalgam, even if she departs from it in one respect. The three characteristics of "traditional sex" are: discursive silence about sexuality, *beskonfliktnost'* ("conflictlessness") in gender relations and *zhizneradost'* in the physiological arena. The product of these three elements was and is a sexual orthodoxy that naturalized heterosexual relations within a framework of Soviet values and social engineering, themselves based on aspects of pre-revolutionary ideas.

Discursive silence about normal, non-pathologized sexuality is well described

[21] Enikeeva published her "diagnosis" of Russia's politicians in book form: Dilia Enikeeva, *Diagnoz: Politik. Rossiiskaia politicheskaia elita glazami psikhiatra-seksopatologa* (Moscow: AST, 2004).

[22] The tsarist dimensions of anti-Semitism in relation to sexuality are discussed in Engelstein, *Keys to Happiness*, especially in her chapter on the anti-rational and homophilic Vasily Rozanov.

in the historical and sociological literature about Soviet life.[23] It was felt that it was not necessary to educate youngsters about normal sexuality, nor was it necessary to discuss everyday, unproblematic sexual matters; indeed, to do this was unduly prurient and likely to stimulate sexual desire artificially.[24] Such desire threatened to erupt in "disorderly" ways. Better to let nature take its course within the channels laid down by Party dogma about education, training, and family life. If there was any energy left over for sexuality outside those channels—sublimation was the social engineer's chief response.

Beskonfliktnost' marked relations between the sexes in this worldview: this was particularly the case after the Great Patriotic War as gender relations, unsettled by the privations of the 1930s and the terrible losses of the 1940s, remained a problem that the Party answered with renewed calls for maternal devotion and responsible family life. The "absence of conflict" in the socialist realist fiction of the late Stalin era was a characteristic of cultural stasis, but in its gender dimension it was also, arguably, a patriarchal healing strategy to restore exhausted and crippled male pride after the war. Men wanted to come home to be soothed by traditional wives, and women—if they were going to win a husband in the new circumstances of a deficit of men—needed to contend with these expectations.[25] Naturally, the roots of patriarchal *beskonfliktnost'* were not only Soviet, but pre-war Stalinism had reinscribed hierarchies of gender in Soviet culture. An excellent example of the idealized "absence of conflict" in gender relations can be seen in the 1949 musical film *Kubanskie kazaki* (The Kuban Cossacks) in which two rival collective farm chairmen, Cossack Gordei Voronin (a "better" than average manager) and the businesslike but cheerfully feminine Galina Peresvetova (an example of the "best" of farm managers) find love together. The Cossack's male pride and masculine inability to emote prevents him from making a declaration. Peresvetova—and a name signifying "renewed light" is significant here—respects his pride even as she competes with him in a horse-drawn sulky race. Peresvetova lets Voronin's trotter win, and he then finds the courage to make an avowal. The lovers are united and the socialist-realist tension between "better" and "best" that has been the motor of this film's plot is dissolved.

[23] Bernstein, *The Dictatorship of Sex*, discusses the origins of the discursive silence; for the fully worked out ideology of silence, see e.g., D. Gorfin, "Polovaia zhizn'," in *Bol'shaia sovetskaia entsiklopediia*, vol. 46 (Moscow: OGIZ RSFSR, 1940), 163–9.

[24] Kon, *Seksual'naia kul'tura v Rossii*, 224–41.

[25] A vivid example of this imperative in post-war gender relations is the anxiety, frequently repeated by Soviet women combatants of the Great Patriotic War, that their battle experience would nullify their chances on the peacetime marriage market; see Svetlana Alexiyevich, *War's Unwomanly Face*, trans. K. Hammond, L. Lezhneva (Moscow: Progress, 1988).

The story of the Kuban Cossacks explains the mechanisms of *zhizneradost'* as well. The film of course does not depict the natural resolution of the loving pair's desire by showing its physical consummation—that would have violated canonical norms of discursive silence! However it shows a substitute: the finale depicts the two kolkhoz director-lovers striding through wheat fields as ranks of tractors and harvesting machines, attended by joyful collective farmers, scythe and bind a harvest for the motherland. The sun is shining, the earth is bountiful, and mankind has mastered nature's bounty for the benefit of a grateful nation. Sexual desire and the urge to toil for produce are subtly linked in a purposive, cheerful, and vibrant amalgam that is illustrative of an unspoken Soviet sexual norm—*zhizneradost'*. According to this norm, within the economic, political, and social channels erected by the Party, nature's bountiful energies were best able to flow towards productive ends. The repopulation of the depleted Soviet nation would happen spontaneously as normal life resumed because heterosexual energy was of a piece with the sun in the sky, the fertility of the earth, and the ever-returning ears of corn. Reproductive sexuality was natural and only needed the right channels to be mastered by Communist man.

Enikeeva's understanding of "traditional" sex relies heavily on biomedical concepts of what is "normal" and therefore "natural." In a chapter entitled "Is same-sex love normal?" she argues that since the number of individuals preferring homosexual contacts in Russian society is no greater than 5 percent of the population, these individuals are "special, unusual persons"—a minority—"and the norm is always taken to be that which is in the majority." Just as society would not refuse someone with only one ear, or six fingers, their rights, "society has adjusted to the existence of homosexuals, but it does not consider same-sex love to be natural" (208). With the authority of medicine, Enikeeva confirms the opinion of the "majority ... that to love a person of one's own sex is against nature" (209). It is axiomatic that "homosexuality is a consequence of a dysfunction of psychosexual development and therefore is a deviation from the norm." Homosexuality may occasionally be a psychopathological inborn condition (citing the leading 1920s Soviet psychiatrist P.B. Gannushkin), but Freud teaches that sexuality is a pivotal constituent of the human character and "only sexually adequate people are psychologically and socially adequate" (209). An adequate man is a "real man" capable of potent performance in the presence of an alluring woman; an adequate woman is a "mature" (*zrelaia*) woman "who wants to have a family, children, and a loving husband" and who eschews the tragic future of the frigid old maid (210).

Gender prescriptions for Enikeeva become the key pathway back to lost natural heterosexuality. Medicine has a role to play in enforcing gender conformity.[26] The

[26] Baer noticed the insistent linkage of sexual postures with gender roles in a 2002 guide to

genuine, medically trained, sexologist[27] "is an unwearying mentor to his patients, he helps the troubled young lad to become a real man, and the erotically unawakened entity—a real woman" (378-79). Sexually confused, immature adolescent males need the calm ministrations of qualified sexological experts to learn correct sexual behavior and techniques (379, 118). In this, medicine is simply following common wisdom expressed by the majority in society: "A man should be a man" (357). "With one voice, all of my clients tell me that they are nauseated by the effeminate mannerisms of gays" (355).

Conversely, to be a real woman, a fully realized, sexually adequate woman, is to be or become heterosexual. Submission to the elemental force of masculine sexuality, embracing the *beskonfliktnost'* model of relations between the sexes, is crucial to the psychosexual fulfillment of woman. Enikeeva presents the case of Tamara, a lesbian who makes an unexplained transition to heterosexuality. In her new husband she finds "a friend and a lover"; she has "brilliant sex" (*uletnyi seks*) with him:

> The most important thing is to choose a worthy cadre. My husband was like a sexual hurricane, I lost control of myself in a way that never happened with women. Now he's calmed down, but the memory remains. He is an excellent husband, I love him and I respect him ... Write about me in your new book, let other women make the right decision. (133–4)

Her "cadre" having unleashed the hurricane of passion that naturally erupts between healthy Russians, Tamara has found an authentic life partner in a representative of the opposite sex. She has discovered how gender *beskonfliktnost'* leads to sexual *zhizneradost'*.

It is nevertheless striking that Enikeeva's traditional sexuality is no longer one that dare not speak its name, as it was under Soviet rule. Tamara tells the sexopathologist to write about her transition from same-sex to different-sex love, to give it discursivity. And that is the key difference, I propose, between the "traditional sex" of the Soviet mid-twentieth century and today. In a time when homosexuality refuses to shut up, but instead propagandizes its virtues, and allegedly deploys "gay censorship" over the Russian mass media, it is necessary for the sexual majority to fight discourse with discourse. The old Stalinist strategy of discursive silence, of a public blank spot marking "sex" while the social engineer (whether sexopathologist, pedagogue, or psychiatrist) furtively scurried about backstage dealing with failed

sex penned by the indefatigable Enikeeva; "Russian Gays/Western Gaze," 513.

[27] Enikeeva contrasts medically trained *seksopatalogi* such as herself to the allegedly "self-styled" "pseudo-sexologist," Igor Kon, in a vicious ad hominem attack, *Gei i lesbiianki,* 7, 56, 379–87.

exemplars of "traditional sexuality," is over. Now the expert has come out of her closet and her formula for heterosexuality is voiced. Heterosexuality may be natural, but in the current climate, the *naturaly* (straights) need help: normal sex, ordinary sex, non-alternative sex, "*buterbrodnyi seks*" (bread-and-butter sex) needs its advocates.

Antiliberal Sexology and Russia's Gay Question

Russians may have recognized the existence of a gay and lesbian "sexual minority" living in their midst, but that does not mean they have to do more than be absolutely correct in their dealings with these internal aliens. Certainly, no national conversation between sexual "minority" and sexual "majority" should be opened. Such is the conclusion Enikeeva develops as she lays out a range of anti-liberal suggestions for coping with the gay problem in Russia today. Some of these ideas have the backing of a neoconservative, nationalist lobby group in the Duma (led by Aleksandr Chuev), and an authoritarian "sovereign democracy" could well find some version of the anti-liberal agenda a useful political tool in the PR arsenal. One senses that some of these ideas are being trailed for later use if some political conjuncture requires it.

A key axiom in Enikeeva's sexology (as in most traditional Soviet sexology) is that teenagers have little or no natural sexual desire. In old-style Soviet "traditional sex" embryonic young desire waited in the discursive vacuum, only to spring fully formed from a youth's breast when invoked by the right girl who became a loving wife. However in the reform era since 1991, the mass media has been handed to the market and money dictates that sexual themes are inescapable, necessary to sell just about anything. Turning on the TV, the "troubled young lad" yearning "to become a real man" encounters a barrage of sexual messages, including something new—"propaganda for homosexualism." This is extremely dangerous, since the plastic adolescent psyche seeks out heroes to idolize and obnoxious behavioral codes to contradict his or her parents (374-75). The image of the cool gay or the fashionable lesbian is poisonously seductive to innocent teenagers propped in front of the TV. Propaganda for homosexualism therefore must be banned by a specially designed law because it will increase the amount of "non-traditional sex" in society by recruiting young people to its pleasures.[28]

[28] A bill promoted by nationalist deputy Alexander Chuev to ban the organization of "public events insulting public morality" was rejected by the Duma on first reading on November 2, 2005, by a wide margin, after a subcommittee recommended its rejection. The target of the bill was the proposed Gay Pride Parade planned for May 2006. Chuev has, since 2003, proposed draft bills to ban "propaganda for homosexualism" on public morality and religious grounds and has recently said he is still working on a draft law; see http://www.gayrussia.ru/en/news/detail.php?ID=2616 (accessed March 9, 2006).

At the time Enikeeva wrote her book, the age of consent, then 14, was in the process of being raised to 16. She wants it to be 18, and again, this is to ensure that youthful sexuality is not awakened by malign agents of non-traditional sex (401). "Teenage homosexualism" is a transitory phenomenon that requires careful handling by the sexologist and pedagogue; unprotected teens risk falling into the hands of "pedophiles" and "ephebophiles" who will groom them for same-sex relations. Enikeeva is adamant that 9 out of 10 of Russia's homosexuals are that way as a result of devious grooming by confirmed homosexuals—thus the majority of Russia's "sexual minority" are not authentic homosexuals at all but the innocent victims of a minuscule percentage of genuine psychosexual predators (107–8). They constitute an army of "ex-straights" who in turn "seduce other heterosexuals" and prey upon "mentally immature, subordinated, dependent people" (109). Heterosexuals need to staunch this infection by clamping down on the artificial stimulation of sexual desire in youngsters and by putting post-pubescent teens out of the legal reach of predators.

Finally, Enikeeva intimates a series of non-legislative changes she would like to see in Russia's culture to deter the spread of non-traditional sex. The influence of so-called "gay censorship" in the media is something she says should be "impermissible" (400), although how she proposes to make it so is left unsaid. Considering the many stories she tells of her own sexological journalism spiked by spiteful queens, and of traditionally minded sexologists abused by swanky television presenters on air, the inference is that editors and media managers ought to fire, demote, and refuse to hire overtly gay and lesbian journalists and presenters. They should also suppress positive statements and portrayals of same-sex love. Given that most of the media is owned by the Kremlin—Enikeeva is evidently asking for a presidential initiative in this regard. (It's worth noting that she covers herself by mentioning that the current leadership of the country is unequivocally part of the "heterosexual majority" [244-45] and that the influence of gays is obnoxious only in the middle-ranks of authority—Enikeeva is no fool. The tsar is a good man but his officials are malignant.)

She also believes that anyone claiming expertise as a sexologist must be heterosexual and trained in medicine. The danger of the "gay-sexologist juggling terminology and garbling scientific data" to prove that homosexuality "is not a sexual deviation but only one variant of normal sexual behavior" is plain (387). Such a person, and she has Igor Kon in her sights here, is not "helping" but creating an environment where more and more people can express same-sex feelings and turn their backs on traditional sex for good.

"The homosexual path exists, but it ends in a cul-de-sac."

So the confident sexopathologist concludes, in a pithy slogan that updates Maxim Gorky's 1934 declaration, "Destroy the homosexuals—and fascism will disappear."[29] As a result of the reforms of 1993, Enikeeva must accept the right to existence of homosexuals, but she cannot ascribe to these fellow citizens a future, any more than Gorky could some seventy years ago. What else is "Soviet" now in the rhetoric of the contemporary scourge of Russia's gays and lesbians?

Nostalgia for a constellation of lost Soviet values and conditions is vividly evident in Enikeeva's ideas. Among these lost values is arguably the ideal of the medical expert to diagnose maladies and prescribe self-evidently (because they are scientific) beneficial solutions for a paternalistically conceived, and uniform, "public good." These technocratic solutions were often intended to reduce the differences between disparate populations in the Soviet Union, raising everyone to a "modern" standard of public health.[30] We can appreciate how important technical uniformity was in the Soviet pantheon of values when we recall that a pavilion devoted entirely to *standardizatsiia* (standardization) graced the central avenue of Moscow's Exhibition of Economic Achievements.

There is nostalgia here, too, for the lost power of the expert, a value perhaps indulged most fully only in the Brezhnev era, when technocracy was given its greatest freedom. Then, if the sexopathologist was a slightly dubious expert operating behind the scenes to manage problematic and primarily biological anomalies, at least the claim to expert knowledge had acquired recognition and a niche in the medical system was won. There is reason to think that this cautious plumbing-and-mechanics version of sexology was in fact flourishing by the Brezhnev era. As long as it stayed away from the question of normal sexuality and focused on pathology, late Soviet sexological science could build modest empires and wield influence.[31]

Now however the sexological expert is thrown to market forces. The need to sell expertise to earn a living forces the medical sexopathologist into the public

---

[29] Enikeeva, *Gei i lesbiianki*, 396; Maksim Gorkii, "Proletarskii gumanizm," *Pravda*, May 23, 1934, 3; on Gorky's article, see Healey, *Homosexual Desire in Revolutionary Russia*, 189–90.

[30] See, for example, Paula A. Michaels, *Curative Powers: Medicine and Empire in Stalin's Central Asia* (Pittsburgh: University of Pittsburgh Press, 2003).

[31] The management of transsexuals and intersexuals was one "empire" erected by Aron Belkin in the 1970s–80s; another was the sexopathological clinic opened in Leningrad in 1973 by Avram Sviadoshch. Note also the latter's manual on female sexual pathology, issued in a staggering print-run of 100,000 copies: A. M. Sviadoshch, *Zhenskaia seksopatologiia* (Moscow: Meditsina, 1974). For a sardonic view of the discipline's late-Soviet development, see Kon, *Seksual'naia kul'tura v Rossii*.

arena (and the graphomanic Enikeeva has acquitted herself here with a vast range of advice-manuals for all aspects of love and sexuality, in addition to her detective fiction). Moreover, and evidently far more disturbing to Enikeeva, is the new "marketplace of ideas" that requires her to compete with liberal sexologists like Kon. Her many ad hominem attacks on Kon are laced with the condescension of the professional disdaining the amateur, the *samouch*. Not only is "Kon's sexology" (*konskaia seksologiia*) worthless because of his supposed pro-gay stance and perceived homosexual orientation, it is also impermissible because Kon is not a physician by training but instead comes to sexology from a philosophical and historical background. Disciplinary boundaries, the bulwarks of modernist scientific thought, must be maintained at all costs. The Soviet system for the classification of knowledge, so familiar to any user of a Russian library card catalogue, lives on, and not only in wooden drawers.

Enikeeva's views hint at a nostalgia for the moral certainties supplied by ideology. Always the Soviet-trained scientist, she never refers to religion in her moralizing against homosexuality, but the form of her text implies regret for the lost ideological framework of Marxism-Leninism. Although vast tranches of her prose are light-years from Soviet language in their chatty informality, vulgar turns of phrase, and gossip-mongering, they are punctuated with axioms in boxes and slogans distinguished by bold type that are a catechistic device to arouse "simple Russians" to action. Moreover, the insistent resort to medical science as the correct arbiter of *moral* and social values recalls the aspiration felt by Soviet doctors to extend their influence beyond the clinic, laboratory, and operating theatre.

There are notes of nostalgia here that seem sympathetic, too. Without entirely embracing a rosy interpretation of the Brezhnev era, the retrospective view of "traditional sex" is not devoid of its discreet charms. It is not just a question of an ageing population of *semidesiatniki*, "people of the 1970s," mistily recalling the personal experience of sexual awakening.[32] The positive feature of discursive silence for many thoughtful people was a kind of public decency, the absence of a culture utterly drenched in superfluous and market-driven sexuality. The (admittedly controversial) positive reading of *beskonfliktnost'* might be, for those who were fortunate enough to experience them, the lived experience of "happy families" in a world of apparently clearly prescribed gender norms. As for *zhizneradost'*, the secret, intimate joys of private life might be related in the nostalgic post-Soviet mind to the public value of

[32] For a thoughtful reassessment of the Brezhnev era, including an allusive contrast between the *shestidesiatniki* (people of the 1960s, the often-supposed "liberal" Khrushchev generation) and the *semidesiatniki*, see Edwin Bacon and Mark Sandle, eds. *Brezhnev Reconsidered* (Basingstoke: Palgrave Macmillan, 2002), 205–6.

letting nature take its course—or, to the opposite: the joy of finding private happiness that the state could not touch.

I have also indicated that longer legacies, pre-dating Soviet experience, permeate Dilia Enikeeva's critique of the homosexual problem in contemporary Russia. The parallels with anti-Semitism in her homophobia, the myth of a sexually innocent Russia, and the antiliberal responses to the appearance of a "sexual minority" in society are significant cultural threads that the sexopathologist draws together in her analysis. In combination with Enikeeva's pervasive nostalgia for Soviet values and conditions, these pre-revolutionary elements show that Russians have a rich arsenal of responses at their disposal when approaching the dilemma of same-sex love. Enikeeva's dangerous new discourse condenses these responses in a sophisticated yet folksy blend of neo-nationalist and neo-conservative rhetoric, and shows Russian politicians a series of resonant arguments for containing the gay and lesbian threat.

The Social Promise:

Rights, Privileges, and Responsibilities in Russian Welfare State Reform since Gorbachev

Andrea Chandler

Russia began the transition from communism with a fairly comprehensive social welfare system inherited from the Soviet Union.[1] Postcommunist leaders have never made a holistic, proactive effort to reexamine Russia's social welfare system in its entirety, but in the last ten years they have introduced social policy reforms that present dramatic departures from the assumptions and values of communism. For example, the social welfare benefits available to a citizen now depend less than previously on that individual's work history and more on her earnings and income. Not all of Russia's social welfare reforms have been well received. Indeed, governments that attempt to reform social welfare programs can expect political opposition from affected groups in society, according to a well-developed literature.[2] In some post-communist countries, declining social welfare eroded support for market reformers, contributing to electoral victories for opposition parties.[3]

The author would like to acknowledge the support of a Standard Research Grant from the Social Sciences and Humanities Research Council of Canada for part of the research in this paper. I would like to thank to the editors, and also Janet Hyer, for their comments and suggestions.

[1] Albeit a flawed and inefficient social welfare system. See Mark G. Field and Judyth L. Twigg, eds. *Russia's Torn Safety Nets: Health and Social Welfare During the Transition* (New York: St. Martin's Press, 2000).

[2] For example, Paul Pierson, *Dismantling the Welfare State? Reagan, Thatcher and the Politics of Retrenchment* (Cambridge: Cambridge University Press, 1994); Salvatore Pitruzello, "Social Policy Implementation of the Maastricht Fiscal Convergence Criteria: The Italian and French Attempts at Welfare and Pension Reforms," *Social Research* 64, no. 4 (Winter 1997): 1589–1636; James J. Rice and Michael J. Prince, *Changing Politics of Canadian Social Policy* (Toronto: University of Toronto Press, 2000).

[3] For example, see Claus Offe, "The Politics of Social Policy in East European Transitions: Antecedents, Agents and Agenda of Reform," *Social Research* 60, no. 4 (Winter 1993): 649–83; David J. Bartlett, *The Political Economy of Dual Transformation: Market Reform and Democratization in Hungary* (Ann Arbor: University of Michigan Press, 1997); Janos Kornai, Stephan Haggard, and Robert R. Kaufman, eds. *Reforming the State: Fiscal and Welfare Reform in Post-Socialist Countries* (New York: Cambridge University Press, 2001).

Social welfare reforms in Russia have also encountered political difficulties.[4] For example, as I have argued elsewhere, pension reform in 2001 was accomplished only through a great deal of effort and compromise, yet the reform has remained politically controversial.[5] In another example, a major reform introduced in 2005 to convert in-kind benefits (*natural'nye l'goty*) to cash payments proved to be so unpopular that the Russian government made compromises to the law's original intent. However, in some areas of social policy, such as child welfare assistance and parental benefits, changes were made quickly and attracted far less attention.

Russia's experience in these two areas of reform suggests that it was much easier to change programs that affected mainly women than in programs whose beneficiaries were veterans and pensioners. The question is why, and the purpose of this article is to explain this puzzling pattern. This empirical question draws on a discrepancy in the literature on postcommunist social welfare reform. The literature cited in the previous paragraph points to the great difficulty in reforming social welfare in general, whether in Western Europe or in postcommunist countries, because of the backlash that spending cuts can inspire. In contrast, much of the literature on gender and social policy in Eastern Europe links social policy reform with the reversal of equality rights for women in the postcommunist context. Some countries have undertaken dramatic changes in policies such as maternity/parental leave and family benefits programs: in examining the factors that made these reforms possible, scholars have variously pointed to the roles of pronatalist ethnonationalism, the dominance of international institutions, or conservative, anti-communist politics.[6] In Russia, rather than supporting the notion that there was a conscious adoption of a radical new social model, the evidence suggests that social policies affecting women were neither radically overhauled nor given high priority.[7]

[4] Linda J. Cook, "The Russian Welfare State: Obstacles to Restructuring," *Post-Soviet Affairs* 16, no. 4 (2000): 355–78.

[5] Andrea Chandler, *Shocking Mother Russia: Democratization, Social Rights and Pension Reform in Russia, 1990–2001* (Toronto: University of Toronto Press, 2004), chapter 8.

[6] See, for example, Peggy Watson, "The Rise of Masculinism in Eastern Europe," *New Left Review*, no. 198 (March–April 1993): 71–82; Susan Gal and Gail Kligman, *The Politics of Gender after Socialism* (Princeton: Princeton University Press, 2000); Joanna Goven, "New Parliament, Old Discourse? The Parental Leave Debate in Hungary," in *Reproducing Gender: Politics, Publics and Everyday Life after Socialism*, ed. Susan Gal and Gail Kligman (Princeton: Princeton University Press, 2000), 286–306; Rachel Alsop and Jenny Hockey, "Women's Reproductive Lives as a Symbolic Resource in Central and Eastern Europe," *European Journal of Women's Studies* 8, no. 4 (2001): 454–71; Lynne Haney, *Inventing the Needy: Gender and the Politics of Welfare in Hungary* (Berkeley: University of California Press, 2002).

[7] See Chandler, "Gender, Political Discourse and Social Welfare in Russia: Three Case Stud-

Below, I hypothesize that divergent discourses in social welfare, dating from Soviet times, structured the possibilities for reform of various social policy sectors. I understand the term "discourse" to mean the ways in which an issue is represented in political debates, law and policy, on the assumption that these representations directly affected the distribution of benefits.[8] It was relatively easy to cut back child care and parental and child benefits in Russia because these services had only a weak basis in law and had never been considered to be social rights to which individuals were entitled. Historically, such benefits were conditional insofar as they were expected to serve the interests of the state. Even when benefits were increased substantially in 2006 legislation, improvements were generally presented as provisional measures rather than permanent entitlements. On the other hand, pensions and veterans' benefits were established on radically different assumptions: they were primarily products of the post-Stalin era, had a stronger legal foundation, and were depicted as being absolute and irreversible.[9] As T.H. Marshall argued, once a particular right becomes established as a norm within a society, it becomes politically difficult to rescind that right, as citizens tend to defend their rights once they have attained them.[10]

In postcommunist Russia, social welfare policy reveals contradictions in values over whether social welfare should be universal (meaning, eligibility for benefits is inclusive and available to *individuals* considered to be *equally* eligible); means-tested (where benefits are primarily oriented toward those who are able to *document* their need for assistance) or meritocratic (where the state offered a greater or lesser degree of *privileges* to certain *groups* considered to be "deserving"). The controversy over social welfare in Russia demonstrates that these three visions have still not been reconciled into a consensus. Furthermore, social welfare policy in the Soviet Union was shaped by the experience of the Second World War II, and there were well-entrenched social benefits that recognized people who either fought or labored in the war. Cutting those benefits is difficult because of the widespread assertion that the

ies" (paper presented to the Annual Meeting of the Canadian Political Science Association, London, Ontario, June 2, 2005).

[8] The general notion of "discourse," as reflecting and shaping political relationships has been well developed by Michel Foucault in works such as *The History of Sexuality: An Introduction*, vol. 1 (New York: Vintage, 1990), 92–8.

[9] See Chandler, *Shocking Mother Russia*, chapters 2 and 7, and also Andrea Chandler, "Democratization, Social Welfare and Individual Rights in Russia: The Case of Old-Age Pensions," *Canadian Slavonic Papers* 43, no. 4 (December 2001): 409–35.

[10] T.H. Marshall, "Citizenship and Social Class," in *Citizenship and Social Class*, ed. Marshall and Tom Bottomore (London: Pluto Press, 1992), 3–51.

Soviet Union's wartime experience must be honored and remembered as a decisive moment in Russian history.

In this article I would like to focus on two policy initiatives: first, the monetization of in-kind benefits (reformed in 2004-2005) and second, reforms of maternity leave, parental leave, and child welfare benefits (reformed incrementally between 1989 and 2004, with a dramatic policy shift in 2006). I will argue that discursive legacies inherited from the Soviet state influenced the process of reform and the political response to that reform. The main goal of this article is to provide hypotheses regarding the influence that Soviet values and assumptions hold in Russian social policy debate. It is not my intent here to provide an exhaustive historical analysis, but rather to draw on historical examples in order to illuminate some of the controversies of the present. I do believe, though, that social welfare is an excellent case study for examining the cleavages that exist in Russian society over the threat that market reform imposes to prevailing values.

The Monetization of Social Benefits (*L'goty*)

As Bernice Madison argued in her classic work, the Soviet social welfare system had complex normative underpinnings. Some of its programs were directed towards the working population, and others were state initiatives to help people with particular needs (such as the disabled or orphans).[11] One aspect of the Soviet social welfare system that is often overlooked in the literature is the notion of privileges, or *l'goty*. This component of the social welfare system involved two principles: the notion that some categories of citizens were "deserving" of special recognition from the state, and secondly, the notion that social welfare benefits were an appropriate form for extending this recognition. I coin the phrase "social promise" in reference to these principles. This phrase differs from the notion of the "social contract" that some scholars (notably Linda Cook and Peter Hauslohner) have used to describe the increasing social benefits offered by the Soviet state to its citizens after the death of Stalin.[12] I consider the notion of a "social contract" to be a useful term to describe the regime's social welfare regimen for workers, implying a rational, mutual exchange between state and society. However, the concept is less useful to describe social

[11] Bernice Q. Madison, *Social Welfare in the Soviet Union* (Stanford: Stanford University Press, 1968), 50.

[12] Linda J. Cook, *The Soviet Social Contract and Why It Failed: Welfare Policy and Workers' Politics from Brezhnev to Yeltsin* (Cambridge, MA: Harvard University Press, 1993); Peter Hauslohner, "Politics before Gorbachev: De-Stalinization and the Roots of Reform," in *Politics, Society and Nationality Inside Gorbachev's Russia*, ed. Seweryn Bialer (Boulder: Westview, 1989), 41–90.

welfare benefits extended to veterans and pensioners. For these groups of people, and select others considered by the regime to be especially deserving, the Soviet "social promise" assumed that honor and valor obliged the state to make absolute, irreversible commitments for social protection. Increasingly, such commitments were written in law and used unequivocal language affirming the state's obligation to extend firm social rights to defined groups.

To be sure, the Soviet system always allowed for special privileges, or *l'goty*, to be available to certain individuals at the discretion of the regime authorities. As Sheila Fitzpatrick argued, the shortages common in the planned economy created the logic for granting privileges to a select few, and she used the phrase "institutionalized hierarchy of access" to describe the special services available to the Soviet elite.[13] According to Julie Hessler, the Soviet practice of giving food parcels, consumer goods, and special services to valued workers and officials expanded during and after the Second World War. These benefits were intended to reward those who had served well and to encourage others to follow their example.[14] Similarly, privileges (*privilegii* and *l'goty*) were available to certain groups who were represented as deserving supplementary social welfare provisions. For example, so-called "personal pensions," which were relatively high, were granted on a case-by-case basis when the state chose to recognize "individuals having special merits before the Soviet state in the field of revolutionary, state, social, and economic activity, or meritorious contributions in the fields of culture, science, or technology."[15]

The use of social welfare benefits as a form of rewarding dedication to socialist values always existed in the USSR, but after the Second World War, *l'goty* expanded to encompass veterans of combat or workers who had particularly assisted in the war effort. Given the massive social problems that confronted the USSR's postwar reconstruction effort, the state made an effort to recognize the pressing need for demobilized soldiers to find housing and to assist those who were disabled, widowed, or orphaned because of casualties in the armed forces.[16] From the end of the war to the mid-1960s, various kinds of *l'goty*, such as free transportation, subsi-

[13] Sheila Fitzpatrick, *Everyday Life in Extraordinary Times: Soviet Russia in the 1930s* (New York: Oxford University Press, 1999), 96.

[14] Julie Hessler, *A Social History of Soviet Trade: Trade Policy, Retail Practices and Consumption, 1917–1953* (Princeton: Princeton University Press, 2004), 301–2.

[15] "Ob utverzhdenii Polozheniia o personal'nykh pensii," November 14, 1956, *Sobranie postanovlenii pravitel'stva SSSR*, 1957, no. 2: 72–80.

[16] See for example in M.L. Zakharov and V.M. Piskov, eds. *Sotsial'noe obezpechenie i strakhovanie v SSSR: sbornik ofitsial'nykh dokumentov i kommentarii* (Moscow: Iuridicheskaia literatura, 1972), 474.

dized prescription drugs, visits to rest homes, or housing benefits, were extended to disabled veterans, pensioners, and survivors of soldiers who lost their lives in battle.[17] Increasingly, *l'goty* became part of an open and institutionalized system of recognizing categories of people rather than an ad hoc, closed system of recognizing individuals.

These benefits were often defined *in relation to* the benefits enjoyed by the population as a whole: as supplementary cash benefits (more than what average people received), as discounts (*skidki*) for rent and utilities or free-of-charge transportation; or as preferential access (the all-important *vneochered'naia* status, i.e., the ability to "jump the queue"). Hence, *l'goty* could be conceived as the right to claim more, sooner, and to pay less, compared to other people. This notion of preferential treatment was at odds with the socialist principle of equality. In the late 1980s, perestroika opened up a whole debate on the legitimacy of privileges in society, as the principle of equality before the law was finding increasingly vocal defenders. On the one hand, Mikhail Gorbachev promised to improve conditions for veterans, linking social benefits with the state's demonstration of respect towards those who served in the armed forces. Said Gorbachev at the First Congress of People's Deputies, "It is our moral duty and responsibility to constantly care for veterans of war and labor, those who defended the independence of our Motherland in the Fatherland War, who in difficult times supported the country's economy, strengthened its industrial capacity, to whom we owe everything we have."[18] At the Congress, plans to expand welfare benefits for veterans were announced.[19]

On the other hand, under Boris Yeltsin, Russia launched a campaign to eliminate the privileges enjoyed by the *nomenklatura*, decrying those who received "undeserved and unearned comfortable conditions."[20] At the same time, *l'goty* were extended to a new category of people, those whom the state had an obligation to

[17] For example, Resolution of the USSR Council of Ministers, "O rasshirenii l'got invalidam otechestvennoi voiny i chlenam semei voennosluzhashchikh, pogibshikh v Velikoi Otechestvennoi Voine," March 6, 1965, in Zakharov and Piskov, *Sotsial'noe obespechenie i strakhovanie v SSSR*, 481–3.

[18] M.S. Gorbachev, "Ob osnovnykh napravleniiakh vnutrennei i vneshnei politiki SSSR," First USSR Congress of People's Deputies, May 30, 1989, *Stenograficheskii otchet*, vol. 1 (Moscow: Izdatel'stvo Verkhovnogo Soveta SSSR, 1989), 447.

[19] N.I. Ryzhkov, "O programme predstoiashchei deiatel'nosti Pravitel'stva SSSR," First USSR Congress of People's Deputies, June 7, 1989, *Stenograficheskii otchet*, vol. 3 (Moscow: Izdatel'stvo Verkhovnogo Soveta SSSR, 1989), 17–19.

[20] Resolution of the RSFSR Supreme Soviet Presidium, "O privilegiiakh v RSFSR," *Vedomosti Soveta Narodnykh Deputatov RSFSR i Verkhovnogo Soveta RSFSR*, no. 8, July 26, 1990, 159.

compensate for undue suffering. Laws passed under Yeltsin's watch defined social welfare *l'goty* as among the responsibilities that the state owed to Chernobyl victims and rehabilitated victims of Stalin-era repressions. These *l'goty* were similar to those available to veterans.[21] Although the erosion of socialism had brought debate about how social welfare should be redistributed, the "social promise" survived intact into the post-Soviet era: the state still affirmed that it was obliged on moral grounds to provide special social welfare benefits to particular groups.

As the economic reform of "shock therapy" proceeded in Russia after the Soviet collapse, the left-leaning legislature passed a series of measures intended to alleviate the situation of particular groups, including veterans and pensioners. Furthermore, the budgetary crisis of the state provided a temptation to expand in-kind benefits (delivered as access to services) rather than cash benefits, which constituted a direct net cost to the state. Key examples of service-oriented measures include the Law on Veterans, passed in 1994, and the Law on the Disabled (Invalids), passed in 1995. The Law on Veterans made absolute commitments to provide social welfare benefits to veterans, with little direct consideration of the costs or the mechanism for delivering these benefits. Said the preamble of the law, "This federal law establishes legal guarantees for the social protection of veterans in the Russian Federation with the goal of creating the conditions to guarantee them an adequate life, activity, *honor and respect in society*" (emphasis added).[22] Thus, social welfare benefits were regarded as a direct means of demonstrating the status and esteem accorded to veterans, and were represented as rights. The law divided veterans into subcategories of eligibility for varying degrees of benefits, such as housing discounts, free city transportation, free medicine, and access to medical care. Similarly, the Law on the Disabled also established various in-kind *l'goty* for subcategories of disabled people and posited that these benefits were rights.[23]

To summarize, both laws offered substantial in-kind benefits to their target groups; both laws created complex hierarchies of *l'gotniki* (those who were eligible for privileges); and both laws framed these benefits as permanent rights. A particularly noteworthy feature of the Law on Veterans was the way it gave carte blanche

---

[21] Zakon, "O sotsial'noi zashchite grazhdan, podvergshikhsia vozdeistviu radiatsii vsledvstvie katastrof na Chernobyl'skoi AES," *Vedomosti Soveta Narodnykh Deputatov RSFSR i Verkhovnogo Soveta RSFSR*, no. 21, May 23, 1991, 725–49; Zakon, "O reabilitatsii zhertv politicheskikh repressii," *Vedomosti Soveta Narodnykh Deputatov RSFSR i Verkhovnogo Soveta RSFSR*, no. 44, October 31, 1991, 1690–96.

[22] Zakon "O veteranakh," passed December 16, 1994 (Moscow: Izdatel'stvo Akt, 2000), 1.

[23] Zakon, "O sotsial'noi zashchite invalidov v Rossiiskoi Federatsii," *Rossiiskaia gazeta*, December 2, 1995, 5.

for these benefits to be paid irrespective of their cost to the state: according to article 11.3, "Rights and privileges, and also other measures of social protection for veterans and members of their families, earlier established by USSR legislation and Russian Federation legislation cannot be repealed without replacements of equal value."[24] The existence of this provision meant that any attempt to repeal it could create the appearance of reneging on a firm commitment.

While perhaps expedient as a temporary measure, the expansion of *l'goty* incurred substantial costs that were difficult to measure, thus complicating the federal budgetary system. The Russian government attempted to initiate a reform of the benefit system in 1997, but it failed in the State Duma.[25] In 2004, monetization became a priority of the new Prime Minister, Mikhail Fradkov, and the new Minister of Health and Social Development, Mikhail Zurabov, who as the former head of the Pension Fund had ushered in Russia's 2001 old-age pension reform. The rationale for monetization was that the existing system was expensive, inefficient to administer, and opaque.[26] The monetization reform was intended to replace in-kind benefits with cash benefits. Reformers noted that existing law provided no way to limit or control the costs of *l'goty*.[27]

The monetization reform, insofar as it attempted to address the inchoate distribution of responsibilities for social welfare within the various levels of government in Russia, must be seen within the context of a larger plan to rationalize the federal system. Vladimir Putin has attempted a variety of reforms purportedly intended to strengthen federal governance, although some Western experts have been fairly critical of these efforts.[28] One glance at the monetization law will reveal a substantial

[24] Zakon "O veteranakh" (1994), 4.

[25] "Duma Rejects Cuts in Social Welfare," *Moscow Tribune*, June 18, 1997, 2.

[26] Remarks of Minister of Health and Social Development Mikhail Zurabov and Minister of Finance Aleksei Kudrin, to the State Duma, Gosudarstvennaia Duma, *Stenogramma zasedanii*, biulleten' no. 39, July 2, 2004, http://wbase.duma.gov.ru/steno/nph-sdb.exe (accessed February 8, 2006).

[27] Andrei Isaev, head of the social policy committee in the Duma, quoted in Marina Kalashnikova, "Repressive Bookkeeping: No One Wants to Pay Stalinist Regime's Bills," *Vremia novostei*, January 13, 2005, 1–2, translated in *Current Digest of the Post-Soviet Press* 57, no. 5 (March 2, 2005): 13–14.

[28] For example, Fiona Hill, "Governing Russia: Putin's Federal Dilemmas," *New Europe Review*, January 2005, http://www.brookings.edu/views/articles/hillf/20050104.htm (accessed January 12, 2007); Donna Bahry, "The New Federalism in the Paradoxes of Regional Sovereignty in Russia," *Comparative Politics* 27, no. 2 (January 2005): 127–46; C. Ross, "Putin's Federal Reforms and the Consolidation of Federalism in Russia: One Step Forward, Two Steps Back," *Communist and Post-Communist Studies* 36, no. 1 (2003): 29–47.

part of the reason why it was so controversial: the law was long and complex, and much of it consisted of repeals and substitutions to existing laws. Indeed, some State Duma deputies raised concerns about the difficulty considering the law because of its voluminous detail.[29]

The law was passed fairly speedily in the State Duma in the summer of 2004, despite various protests from society.[30] It took effect January 2005, following an effort in the autumn to prepare local governments and the population for the effects of this reform. This endeavor would prove to be difficult. While it is understandable that a reform must change existing laws rather than simply superimpose new ones, this particular law was so complicated that it is difficult to comprehend in its entirety unless one is prepared to track down and compare the original laws. As a result, it would be difficult for the average citizen to read the law for herself to find out how it would affect her, which was at odds with the law's original intent to create more transparency.[31]

Because of the breathtaking length and complexity of the monetization law, I will discuss here only the changes to laws on social benefits for veterans, Chernobyl victims, and politically repressed persons. Essentially, the law established that most in-kind benefits were to be replaced with cash benefits. *L'gotniki* would now receive a monthly payment from the state and would no longer receive benefits such as local transportation free of charge. The monthly payment would be indexed regularly.[32] The law, although adopted quickly, was to be phased in over time. For the first year, recipients who registered in advance would be able to receive a "social package" of

---

[29] Ol'ga Tropkina, "Gosudarstvennaia Duma primet zakonoproekt o monetizatsii l'got v pervom chtenii," *Izvestiia*, July 3, 2004, 3.

[30] Tropkina, "Gosudarstvennaia Duma primet zakonoproekt," 3; n.a., "Zakhvachen i razgromlen kabinet ministra Zurabova," *Izvestiia*, August 3, 2004, 1–2.

[31] Russia's Minister of Finance, Aleksei Kudrin, told the Duma in the first reading that existing law was vague, and that monetization would provide clarity: citizens would be able to better inform themselves of their eligibility for benefits. Gosudarstvennaia Duma, *Stenogramma zasedanii*, biulleten' no. 39, July 2, 2004, http://wbase.duma.gov.ru/steno/nph-sdb.exe (accessed February 8, 2006).

[32] Federal law, Zakon No. 122-FZ, "O vnesenii izmenenii v zakonodatel'nye akty Rossiiskoi Federatsii i priznanii utravshimi sily nekotorykh zakonodatel'nykh aktov Rossiiskoi Federatsii v sviazi s priniatiem federal'nykh zakonov 'o vnesenii izmenenii i dopol'nenii v Federal'nyi zakon 'ob obshchikh printsipakh organizatsii zakonodatel'nykh (predstavitel'nykh) i ispol'nitel'nykh organov gosudarstvennoi vlasti sub'ektov Rossiiskoi Federatsii i 'ob obshchikh printsipakh organizatsii mestnogo samoupravleniia v Rossiiskoi Federatsii," (hereafter, Law No. 122-FZ, 2004), *Rossiiskaia gazeta*, August 31, 2004, 1–21.

vouchers for services instead of the cash benefits.[33] Rather than abolishing all in-kind benefits, the monetization was to occur gradually, starting with transport benefits, prescription drugs, and visits to sanitaria.[34] The monthly payment was supposed to be sufficient to cover the cost of the previous *l'goty*. So although veterans would now have to pay bus fare, the monthly benefit that they received from the state was supposed to cover that.

There are several striking features of the law. First of all, since it was a law that was oriented towards repealing and replacing parts of existing laws, it by definition was reducing benefits. The law considerably narrowed the scope of in-kind benefits that were offered to various groups, replacing them with monthly cash payments. The law also in a number of instances removed statements implying absolute state commitments to benefits, instead affirming that benefits would be offered within budgetary parameters. For example, the monetization law repealed the section of the Law on Veterans that stated that no benefits guaranteed in the law could be repealed. Even more striking, the monetization law deleted many references to "rights and privileges" to social benefits and replaced them with the phrase "measures of state support." It also used language that weakened the state's commitment to compensate Chernobyl victims and victims of political repression.[35]

Clearly, the government was trying to limit its obligations by reconfiguring the discourse on social policy. But curiously, the law cut back the number of *l'goty* while maintaining intact the notion of *l'gotniki*; the government continued to affirm that particular groups were entitled to special social benefits. In fact, the law further reified and stratified the list of recipients. For example, in its amendments to the Law on Veterans, the monetization law differentiated the cash value of monthly benefits offered to various categories of eligible people. Meanwhile, the federal government gave the regions responsibility for "labor veterans" and "rear workers," meaning that their value could vary from one region to the next.[36] In fact the law upheld the norm that certain categories of citizens deserved special social benefits, and the state in effect continued to rank these categories of citizens. The government also maintained the idea of the "social promise," by reassuring *l'gotniki* that they would not be left worse off as a result of the changes.[37] But at the same time, the reform would give

---

[33] Irina Nevinnaia, "Vam paket. Sotsial'nyi," *Rossiiskaia gazeta*, November 5, 2004, 30.

[34] Irina Nevinnaia, "Sotspaket uzhe gotov!" *Rossiiskaia gazeta*, December 31, 2004, 31.

[35] Law No. 122-FZ (2004), articles 3 (p. 1), 6 (p. 2), and 44 (pp. 8–9).

[36] "Labor veterans" were specially recognized workers. "Rear workers" were people who performed valued industrial work during World War II. Law No. 122-FZ (2004), 8–9.

[37] Mikhail Vinogradov, "L'goty obeshchaiut vozmozmestit' sotsial'nym paketom," *Izvestiia*,

the regions more responsibility and leave the federal government with little control over the cost of services such as local bus fares. Furthermore, there were direct cuts in some benefits to some groups, such as students.[38]

The reform was introduced in January 2005, and provoked a nation-wide crisis as protests spread across Russia. Incidences of scuffles, police actions against protesters, and acts of alleged civil disobedience attracted attention from the media.[39] Some State Duma deputies from the Motherland Party went on hunger strike to protest the law.[40] In St. Petersburg, a large protest included calls for an "Orange Revolution,"[41] invoking the successful protests against contentious Ukrainian presidential elections the previous fall. In particular, pensioners and veterans seemed to be objecting to the requirement that they now had to pay local bus fares. Some claimed that they had been inadequately informed in advance about the implications of the law. Others claimed that their cash benefits were insufficient to cover the new costs of services. Still others objected that they were no longer eligible for local transport privileges outside of their home locality, an issue that was central when Moscow oblast residents discovered that they could no longer afford transportation within Moscow city limits.[42] Concerned about the course of events, Putin himself spoke on the monetization crisis, criticizing insufficient preparation by government officials and local authorities.[43] In a compromise move, the government agreed to provide funds to help support monetization, while most regional governments agreed to sell

---

August 5, 2004, 2. As Finance Minister Aleksei Kudrin admitted to the Duma, "we did not succeed to prevent the worsening of the situation for some groups." Ol'ga Tropkina, "Kudrin i Zurabov priznali svoi oshibki," *Izvestiia*, 24 January 2005, 3.

[38] Nevinnaia, "Vam paket. Sotsial'nyi," 30.

[39] Anatolii Gusev, "Rossiia bez l'got," *Izvestiia*, January 11, 2005, 1–2; Konstantin Frumkin, Natal'ia Granina, Nikolai Morozov, Sergei Zhdakaev, and Il'ia Stulov, "Zurabova ia otpustil. Prem'er ministr razbiraetsiia s monetizatsiei," *Izvestiia*, January 14, 15, and 16, 2005, 1–2.

[40] "Patriotic Duma Faction Goes on Hunger Strike," *Moscow News*, January 26–February 1, 2005, 3.

[41] Elena Rotkevich, "Peterburzhtsy trebuiut otmeny zakona o monetizatsii l'got." *Izvestiia*, January 17, 2005, 2.

[42] "Ne zhdali: kak rabotaet zakon, zamenivshii natural'nye l'goty den'gami," *Rossiiskaia gazeta*, January 12, 2005, 2; Elena Lashkina "I na 16-ye den' reform," *Rossiiskaia gazeta*, January 18, 2005, 1.

[43] Ekaterina Grigor'eva and Konstantin Frumkin, "Eti voprosy gluboko i vsestoronne ne byli produmannyi," *Izvestiia*, January 18, 2005, 1; "Pensionerves: President and Government Think of Ways to Calm Benefit Recipients," *Vremia Novostei*, January 18, 2005, 1–2, translated in *Current Digest of the Post-Soviet Press* 57, no. 3 (February 16, 2005): 1–2.

low-cost transportation passes to the *l'gotniki.*[44] The government also increased the base old-age pension 36 percent.[45] These measures helped to defuse the crisis but undermined the original intent of the law, which was to streamline the *l'goty* system in order to introduce economies. Even after the reforms were well underway, monetization continued to inspire debate. Reports claimed that there was ongoing controversy over the way the reform was carried out, that it had cost considerably more money than anticipated, and that many citizens continued to prefer in-kind benefits to cash.[46]

In short, the monetization reform proved to be so politically unpopular that the government modified its stance. Clearly, the obstacles were daunting from an administrative perspective. As the title of the law indicates, it was intended to be not just a reform of social benefits, but a sweeping rationalization of the budgetary relationships between the federal government, the regions and localities: not an insignificant problem in a federal system comprising eighty-eight units. But the main reason for the controversy was that political and legal discourse had structured *l'goty* as entitlements for groups largely defined on the basis of an emotionally resonant patriotism. In introducing monetization, the state did not reevaluate the assumption that social welfare benefits are an appropriate means to recognizing intangible, meritorious acts from its citizenry. For example, a Khimki demonstrator was quoted in the media as saying "I am a pensioner, a war veteran, and a labor veteran. Yet as of January 1, my past services became absolutely worthless."[47] Said another *l'gotnik*, who had been awarded the title of Hero of the Soviet Union, "Benefits should be given to Heroes,

---

[44] Ekaterina Grigor'eva and Konstantin Frumkin, "Pozdno i nedostatochno," *Izvestiia*, January 25, 2005, 1, 3.

[45] Konstantin Frumkin and Anna Kaledina, "Ruchnaia nastroika monetizatsii," *Izvestiia*, January 28, 2005, 2.

[46] "Russian Official Slams Benefits Reform," Interfax, February 8, 2006, in World New Connection (online), February 8, 2006, document number 200602081477.1_020800277d6e826; Yuriy Politov, "Monetization Law was Lesson for Duma and Government," *Izvestiia,* August 3, 2005, translated in Foreign Broadcast Information Service, World News Connection (on-line), August 3, 2005, document number 200508031477.1_248c007c4ca622b0; Yelena Shishkunova, "Benefit Recipients are Turning Down the Money," *Izvestiia*, May 12, 2006, translated in *Current Digest of the Post-Soviet Press* 58, no. 18 (May 31, 2006); Emilia Kazumova, "Government Sclerosis. Hundreds of Thousands of Chronically Ill Russians May Be Left without Medicines," *Novye Izvestiia*, August 30, 2006, 3, translated in *Current Digest of the Post-Soviet Press* 58, no. 35 (September 27, 2006).

[47] Yelena Starovoitova, "They Didn't Surrender Moscow," *Russkii kur'er*, January 11, 2005, 2, translated in *Current Digest of the Post-Soviet Press* 57, nos. 1–2 (February 2–9, 2005): 1–2.

not as a form of support but as the population's gratitude for extraordinary service. It would be shameful for the government if its heroes needed social assistance."[48] A speech that Putin made in January 2005, at the height of the crisis, is illustrative. On the one hand, he claimed that nobody's position should be worsened as the result of the reform, but on the other hand, he said that *l'goty* had mushroomed well beyond the point of affordability because of the extension of benefits beyond veterans and the disabled to other groups.[49] It is easy to find Putin's remarks confusing. Is he implying that pensioners and veterans, but not other groups, deserve benefits? And if the scope of benefits offered is too broad to be supported with existing funds, how could the system be reformed without cutting benefits? In this context, repealing benefits could be interpreted as second thoughts about the state's commitments. One observer noted that pensioners had voted in large numbers for Putin and United Russia.[50] As a result, monetization was disadvantageous in a Russia where political discourse has become wholeheartedly patriotic.

Reforms of Maternity Leave, Parental Leave, and Child Welfare Benefits

In contrast, we can now examine postcommunist social welfare reforms primarily affecting women and children, which have been adopted rapidly amidst a very different historical context. It is important to consider the origins of the state's narrative on policies for women and children. In 1936, under Joseph Stalin, a Soviet government resolution was passed that is best known for its sweeping ban on abortion, a move intended to promote increased births.[51] This resolution also planned the expansion

---

[48] Valerii Anatolevich Burkov, Hero of the Soviet Union, quoted in Sergei Zhakaev, Leonid Novikov, Il'ia Stulov, Ol'ga Timofeeva, and Aleksei Ukkone, "Ne meshaete nam dozhit' do dnia pobedy," *Izvestiia*, July 3, 2004, 3.

[49] Putin speech, "Chto skazal prezident o monetizatsii l'got," *Izvestiia*, January 18, 2005, 3.

[50] Georgy Satarov, "Forecast," *Moscow News*, February 9–15, 2005, 7. Similarly, political scientist Andranik Migranyan noted that the government compromised because it was reluctant to alienate the *l'gotniki*. Migranyan quoted in Kirill Zhrenkov, Oksana Prilepina, and Guell' Fazullina, "Oni ne proidut: novoe pokolenie pensionerov vybiraet miting," *Ogonek*, 2005, no. 4: 19.

[51] See David L. Hoffman, "Mothers in the Motherland: Stalinist Pronatalism in its Pan-European Context," *Journal of Social History* 34, no. 1 (2001): 35–54; Susan Gross Solomon, "The Demographic Argument in Soviet Debates over the Legalization of Abortion in the 1920s," *Clio Medica* 23 (1993): 140–70; Wendy Goldman, "Women, Abortion and the State, 1917–1936," in *Russia's Women: Accomodation, Resistance, Transformation*, ed. Barbara Evans Clements, Barbara Alpern Engel, and Christine D. Worobec (Berkeley: University of California Press, 1991), 243–66.

of maternity leave benefits, child welfare benefits, nurseries, and daycare spaces in anticipation of an expected increase in the numbers of children. There are several features about the resolution that are striking. First, it showed a patronizing view of women, who were depicted in need of support and enlightenment from the state. Women were considered to have an obligation before the state to raise children. According to the document, the Soviet woman "bears a great and responsible duty to give birth to citizens and raise them."[52] As an article in *Pravda* claimed at the time, "We alone have all the conditions under which a working woman can fulfill her duties as a citizen and as a mother responsible for the birth and early upbringing of her children.…We must safeguard our family and raise and rear healthy Soviet heroes."[53] Second, the document spoke of child care resources and family benefits in conditional terms, emphasizing short-term planning and funding goals. Finally, the resolution put responsibility for daycare not with government but with the enterprises, on the assumption that the state would continue to provide the necessary funding through the planning system.[54] Hence, the resolution did not construct social welfare benefits for women and children as being based on the notion of social rights, but instead to enhance the goals of the state on the basis of women's obligations. In subsequent years, and especially during the Second World War, pronatalist measures increased. Bonuses were granted to women who bore seven or more children (and eventually to mothers of three or more children), while women who bore five or more children were eligible to receive medals. Maternity leaves were lengthened; pregnant and breastfeeding women were allowed flexible working conditions; and single mothers were given additional monthly allowances.[55]

---

[52] "Postanovlenie TsIK i SNK o zapreshchenii abortov, uvelichenii maternal'noi pomo shchi rozhenitsam, ustanovlenie gosudarstvennoi pomoshchi mnogosemeinym, rashirenie seti roditel'nykh domov, detskikh iaslei i detskikh sadov, usilenii ugolovnogo nakazaniia za neplatezh alimentov i o nekotorykh izmeneniiakh v zakonodatel'stve o razvodakh." *Sobranie zakonov i rasporiazhenii Raboche-Krest'ianskogo Pravitel'stva SSSR*, no. 34, July 21, 1936, 509.

[53] "Public Discussion on the Law on the Abolition of Legal Abortion—leading article from *Pravda*, May 28, 1936," in *The Family in the USSR: Documents and Readings*, ed. Rudolf Schlesinger (London: Routledge, 1949), 254.

[54] "Postanovlenie TsIK i SNK o zapreshchenii abortov" (1936), 511–15.

[55] Postanovlenie SNK "Ob utverzhdenii instruktsii o poriadke naznachenii i vyplaty gosudarstvennogo posobiia mnogodetnym materiam," *Sobranie zakonov i rasporiazhenii*, no. 35, June 1, 1937, 330–4; "Decree of the Presidium of the Supreme Soviet of the USSR on increase of state aid to pregnant women, mothers with many children and unmarried mothers; on strengthening measures for the protection of motherhood and childhood; on the establishment of the title Heroine Mother and on the Institution of the Order 'Motherhood glory' and the "motherhood Medal, July 8, 1944," in Schlesinger, *The Family in the USSR*, 367–77;

For pragmatic reasons, the ban on abortion was reversed after Stalin's death, in a decree that explicitly mentioned the need to prevent the negative health outcomes that resulted when abortions were performed outside of hospitals.[56] However, apart from abortion, other basic aspects of policy outlined in the 1936 decree continued; as Bernice Madison argued, policy towards child benefits did not change much after Stalin's death.[57] Consistent with existing policy, a 1970 resolution (*polozhenie*) affirmed women's right to 16 weeks of paid maternity leave, as well as monthly benefits for mothers of three or more children and for single mothers. The state granted a one-time subsidy for the birth of a newborn baby, which could be collected by either parent; this was a small departure from previous policy, which had largely left fathers out of social benefits.[58] In the 1980s, the Soviet government showed a new interest in expanding benefits for mothers and children. At the 26th CPSU Congress in 1981, Prime Minister Nikolai Tikhonov declared that in the upcoming five-year plan, the state would allocate 9 billion rubles to allow mothers of babies one year of paid parental leave, with the goal of increasing this leave to eighteen months in the second half of the decade. He also announced a number of increases in other benefits, noting that "The task of children, of mothers in our country is truly a matter of state importance."[59] Women would be able to take an additional six months of unpaid leave until their child reached the age of eighteen months, and the child benefit payment was extended.[60] In the late 1980s, Gorbachevian reforms further required

"Polozhenie o poriadke naznacheniia i vyplaty gosudarstvennoi posobii i predostavleniia l'got beremennym zhenshchinam, mnogodetnym i odinokim materiam," *Sobranie postanovlenii i rasporiazhenii Pravitel'stva SSSR*, 1944, no. 11: 214–24.

[56] Ukaz Prezidiuma Verkhovnogo Soveta SSSR, November 23, 1955, 'Ob otmene zapreshchenie abortov," in Zakharov and Piskov, *Sotsial'noe obespechenie i strakhovanie*, 576. See also Michele Rivkin-Fish, "Sexuality in Russia: Defining Pleasure and Danger for a Fledgling Democratic Society," *Social Science and Medicine* 49, no. 6 (September 1999): 803; Hoffman, "Mothers in the Motherland," 35–54; Solomon, "The Demographic Argument," 140–70; Goldman, "Women, Abortion and the State," 243–66.

[57] Madison, *Social Welfare in the Soviet Union*, 208.

[58] "Polozhenie o poriadke naznacheniia i vyplaty posobii, beremennykh zhenshchinam, mnogodetnym i odinokim materiam," resolution of USSR Council of Ministers, August 12, 1970, in Zakharov and Piskov, *Sotsial'noe obespechenie i strakhovanie*, 576–85.

[59] N.A. Tikhonov, "Osnovnye napravleniia ekonomicheskogo i sotsial'nogo razvitiia SSSR na 1981–1985 gody i na period do 1990 goda." *26-oi S"ezd KPSS. Stenograficheskii otchet* (Moscow: Izdatel'stvo politicheskoi literatury, 1981), 12.

[60] Ukaz Prezidiuma Verkhovnogo Soveta SSSR, "O merakh po usileniiu gosodarstvennoi pomoshchi sem'iam, imeiushchim detei," *Vedomosti Verkhovnogo Soveta SSSR*, 1981, no. 36: 863–4.

employers to grant working mothers more flexible working conditions, and followed through on the intention to extend paid parental leave to eighteen months. They also charged the Soviet government with the task of drafting a more comprehensive and coherent system for family-oriented social welfare benefits,[61] a task pre-empted by the collapse of the USSR.

The point here is that Soviet policies towards mothers' and child benefits were generally presented in the form of economic plans and short-term resolutions, not as laws. Therefore, they had a conditional, provisional character because unlike laws, they offered no firm or lasting commitments. Benefits were intended to serve the interests of the state and to enable women to fulfill their duties to the state. Women were not presented as individual citizens with rights, but as a collective of vulnerable people. As a result, with a lack of funding or attention, these benefits could simply disappear.

Under perestroika and in the postcommunist environment, there were steps towards universality in parental and child welfare benefits. In 1989, the Soviet Union extended parental leave benefits to non-working mothers, establishing the new principle that "the payment of this benefit should not depend on whether the mother works or not. It is given out to the child."[62] This was a powerful step towards creating a universal benefit available to all citizens, but it also reduced the visibility of the working mother in policy. In 1995, under Yeltsin, maternity and parental leave benefits were enshrined in a law as being "rights" available to citizens, including allowing fathers equal access to parental leave.[63] But established by a weak state during an economic crisis, this law came too late to establish a norm. Since mothers' and child benefits had never been regarded as universal rights, there was little basis in law for a defense of social welfare benefits.

Moreover, the rhetoric on maternity leave, parental leave, and child benefits from 1989 on became increasingly focused on the needs of children, their health and well-being, rather than on working mothers. Since babies and children by definition

[61] Ukaz Presidiuma Verkhovnogo Soveta SSSR. "O rasshirenii l'got rabotaiushchim beremennym zhenshchinam i zhenshchinam, imeiushchim malodetnykh detei," *Vedomosti VS SSSR*, no. 36, September 9, 1987, 660–1. Postanovlenie Verkhovnogo Soveta SSSR, "O ne otlozhnykh merakh po uluchsheniiu polozheniia zhenshchin, okhrane materinstva i detstva, ukrepleniiu sem'i," *Vedomosti SND SSSR I VS SSSR*, no. 16, April 18, 1990, 330–4.

[62] As argued by head of the USSR Supreme Soviet Committee on Women's Issues, Protection of the Family, Motherhood and Fatherhood, V.I. Matvienko, in Verkhovnyi Sovet SSSR, *Stenograficheskii otchet*, biulleten' 22, April 10, 1990, 5.

[63] Zakon, "O gosudarstvennykh posobiiakh grazhdanam, imeiushchim detei," May 19, 1995. Website of the Russian Federation State Duma, http://wbase.duma.gov.ru/ntc/vdoc.asp?kl=964 (accessed December 13, 2005).

had not yet had time to make a contribution to society, they lacked any claim to have earned their benefits. As a result, it was relatively easy to limit these benefits without a great deal of debate. Means-testing was introduced in 1998 to the child welfare benefit. Formerly a universal benefit available to parents with children,[64] it would now be available only to families who on average had an income equivalent to no more than double the monthly subsistence minimum.[65] Eligibility was further reduced to one subsistence minimum in 1999.[66] These reforms faced relatively little debate in the State Duma and met with little reaction from society. The law on social benefits monetization, discussed above, created an important change in the child benefit system: it turned responsibility for establishing and funding the benefit over to the subjects (regions) of the Russian Federation. Effectively, it is no longer a federal responsibility, thereby ending its last remaining claim to be a universal benefit.[67] In a separate reform, new limits were imposed on maternity leave benefits.[68] Yet these changes attracted little attention from the media and society.

Similarly, child care facilities dramatically declined in Russia after the collapse of communism. Although there was never a formal centralized child care system, the Soviet Union did consider daycare for working parents to be an important part of the Soviet social welfare system, and increasing the spending on daycare centres became a point of pride in Soviet propaganda. This propaganda presented the image of a generous state choosing to make short-term decisions to fund child care, and although there was the aspiration to make child care increasingly accessible for those who needed it, there was no firm commitment to a universal system.[69] After the

---

[64] "Polozhenie o poriadke naznacheniia i vyplaty gosudarstvennoi posobii grazhdanam, imeiushchim detei," *Rossiiskaia gazeta*, September 13, 1995, 4–5.

[65] Zakon "O vnesenii izmenenii i dopol'nenii v Federal'nyi Zakon 'o gosudarstvennykh posobiiakh grazhdanam, imeiushchim detei,'" July 29, 1998, Website of the Russian Federation State Duma, http://wbase.duma.gov.ru/ntc/vdoc.asp?kl=5139 (accessed December 13, 2005).

[66] Zakon "O vnesenii izmeneniia v stat'iu 16 Federal'nogo zakona 'o gosudarstvennykh posobiiakh grazhdanam imeiushchim detei,'" July 17, 1999. Website of the Russian Federation State Duma, http://wbase.duma.gov.ru/ntc.vdoc.asp?kl=6758 (accessed December 13, 2005).

[67] Law No. 122-FZ (2004), 9.

[68] Zakon, "Ob otdel'nykh voprosakh ischisleniia i vyplaty posobii po vremennoi netrudosposobnosti, po beremennosti i rodam i razmerakh strakhovogo obespecheniia po ob'iazatel'nomu sotsial'nomu strakhovaniiu ot neschastnykh sluchaev na proizvodstve i professional'nykh zabolevanii v 2006 godu," December 22, 2005, http://wbase.duma.gov.ru/ntc/vdoc.asp?kl=16132 (accessed March 14, 2006).

[69] For example, Maria Kovrigina, "Public Health and Mother and Child Welfare in the USSR,"

Soviet Union collapsed, there was a lack of a state commitment to a national child care program and little institutional basis to protect daycare resources, which had been concentrated in the responsibility of the enterprises. With the economic blows of "shock therapy," maintaining daycares became unaffordable, and centres simply deteriorated or closed altogether.[70] Russia's family policy program of 1995 discussed the importance of preventing or alleviating poverty in families, sustaining parental leave benefits, and helping women to realize their equality in the workforce, but was virtually silent on the question of daycare for children of working parents.[71] The same held for Yeltsin's presidential "Children of Russia" program, which was primarily oriented towards children with health problems, orphaned children, and pregnant women.[72] There was only a vague intention "to strengthen state guarantees to free-of-charge and generally accessible preschool, general, and elementary education."[73] As the idea of hierarchy in the overall social welfare system was restored, women and children fell to the bottom because they were never seen as having claims that could "jump the queue" (*vneocherednye*).

The conditionality in this part of the social safety net is in striking contrast with the discourse on pensioners and *l'goty*, which for decades has used the language of absolute rights, hard-earned privileges, and state commitments to recognize citizens' sacrifices. Here I invoke the concept of the state's "social promise" to pensioners, but especially to veterans—the "social promise" was based on vague but compelling notions of a state bound by a code of honor to recognize the valorous acts of particular citizens who deserved *vneocherednye* social benefits. As such, the existence of benefits (*l'goty*) for veterans and others contained an implicit but engrained hierarchy. There was no social promise for women and children, who were

---

in *Equality of Women in the USSR*, ed. L. Petrova and S. Gilevskaya (Moscow: Foreign Languages Publishing House, 1957), 215–18.

[70] See for example Natal'ia Radulova, "Nekuda devat'," *Ogonek*, November 7–13, 2005, 20; "Vse v sad," interview with Iurii Rosliak, first deputy mayor of Moscow, *Ogonek*, November 7–13, 2005, 23; Mariia Ermakova, "V detskikh sadakh rastut tol'ko tseny," *Rossiiskaia gazeta*, February 14, 2005, 1, 4; Albert Motivans and Jeni Klugman, "Single Parents and Child Welfare in the New Russia," in *Single Parents and Child Welfare in the New Russia*, ed. Jeni Klugman and Albert Motivans (Houndsmills, UK: Palgrave, 2001), 15.

[71] "Gosudarstvo nachinaetsia s sem'i, a sem'ia—s kazhdogo iz nas: osnovnye napravleniia gosudarstvennoi semeinoi politiki," *Rossiiskaia gazeta*, May 21, 1995, 4.

[72] "Prezidentskaia programma 'Deti Rossii' na 1996-7 gody," *Rossiiskaia gazeta*, February 28, 1996, 4.

[73] "Osnovnye napravleniia gosudarstvennoi sotsial'noi politiki po uluchsheniiu polozheniia detei v Rossiiskoi Federatsii do 2000 goda (natsional'nyi plan deistvii v interesakh detei)," *Rossiiskaia gazeta*, September 21, 1995, 5.

perceived as having yet to make their contribution to society. There can be no *vne-ocherednyi* status without a queue (*ochered'*), and women with children were the mainstay of the queue.

As we have seen, throughout the 1990s social welfare benefits for parents and children declined, reflecting the relatively little attention that political actors paid to the issue. The weak legal status of these benefits facilitated this decline. However, the second half of 2006 saw a sudden about-face in social welfare policy, which showed the potential for tangible changes in the benefits available to working parents. Inspired by concern about postcommunist Russia's continuing population decline, Putin's annual address to the State Duma proposed various state measures, including policies intended to encourage an increase in the national birthrate. Putin noted that the economic insecurity of families, and the difficulties that working mothers faced in balancing their responsibilities, were factors that discouraged many people from having more than one child. He posited that it was therefore in the state's interest to increase funding for social benefits to families.[74] Putin's remarks met with a generally positive response. As a result, a comprehensive package of social welfare reforms proceeded smoothly through the State Duma and was signed into law by the end of December 2006.

The most important features of these reforms may be summarized briefly as follows. First, a large lump-sum benefit, the "base maternal (family) capital," was established, to be granted primarily to mothers of a second child. It is anticipated that after the child's third birthday, the mother can invest the funds in her children's education, improved family housing, or her future pension benefits.[75] Second, the parental leave benefit system was extended to unemployed women and students.[76] Many parents can now expect increases in the size of parental leave benefits, as well as a

[74] President Vladimir Putin, "Poslanie Federal'nomu Sobraniiu Rossiiskoi Federatsii," May 10, 2006, http://www.kremlin.ru/text/appears/2006/05/105546.shtml (accessed May 12, 2006).

[75] This is assuming that the mother continues to care for the child directly. In some cases, for example, if the mother dies, the child's father can access the benefit. Russian Federation federal law, No. 256-FZ, "O dopolnitel'nykh merakh gosudarstvennoi podderzhki semei, imeiushchikh detei," *Rossiiskaia gazeta*, December 31, 2006, http://www.rg.ru/2006/12/31/roditelyam.dok.html (accessed January 2, 2007).

[76] Russian Federation federal law, No. 207-FZ, "O vnesenii izmenenii v otdel'nye zakonodatel'nye akty Rossiiskoi Federatsii v chasti gosudarstvennoi podderzhki grazhdan, imeiushchikh detei," December 5, 2006, Gosudarstvennaia Duma, Pravovoe Upravlene Informatsionno-Poiskovaia sistema, http://ntc.duma.gov.ru/bpa/docctrol.phtmol?bpaid=1&code=129659&rdk=0&nv=0 (accessed January 2, 2007), article 1-12.

greater benefit for leave taken after the birth of the second child than for the first.[77] Third, more social benefits were made available to adoptive parents and legal guardians to make them comparable with many of the benefits enjoyed by birth parents.[78] Finally, daycare reforms provided limits on the fees that daycares are permitted to charge to parents and offered partial fee rebates to parents, especially for the second or third child in daycare.[79]

What do these reforms illustrate about the theses outlined in this article? In the first place, the recent changes clearly demonstrate that benefits for parents and children changed because they became a matter of higher priority for the state. Like pensioners and veterans before them, families and children became perceived by top political actors as symbols: healthy families symbolize a healthy nation. The state's motivation was concern about the future of the polity rather than the importance of empowering women. And certainly the reforms do inspire a certain amount of caution. The focus on cash benefits, rather than on improving institutions and workplaces, continues the tendency for the state's efforts to be limited by its budgetary capacity. For example, the base maternal capital benefit is limited to parents of children born before 2017.[80] And although parents' daycare costs have been alleviated, the availability of sufficient funds to allow nation-wide access to quality daycare over the long term remains in question.

Nonetheless, these reforms are significant insofar as, more so than previously, they establish a clearer legal foundation for family benefits rather than conditioning these benefits on short-term funding allocations and resolutions. Could the state's relationship with parents be redefined as a "social promise?" Increasingly, these laws use the language of "rights" to describe parents' entitlements. We saw above that this process was evident in 1995, but that at that time the benefits were too frail to be significant. However, now that parents' benefits have increased and expanded, the notion that mothers and fathers have rights to state benefits carries more weight. This notion could be an important resource for parents in the future, in the same way that pensioners' and veterans' legal rights became significant issues earlier in the transition. Finally, the reforms of 2006 show a tendency for parents' benefits to become more universal, as they have been extended to include groups beyond the working class. But it should be kept in mind that they have been primarily oriented towards achieving population goals rather than advancing the rights of women.

[77] Law No. 207-FZ (2006), article 1-15.

[78] See Law No. 207-FZ (2006), article 1-5, 1-6, 1-11, and Law No. 256-FZ (2006), article 3.

[79] Law No. 207-FZ (2006), article 3

[80] Law No. 256-FZ (2006), article 13.

Conclusion

Social welfare reform in Russia became a politically loaded subject, where different perspectives of what is "fair" and "realistic" contended. In Soviet times, social welfare benefits were not, strictly speaking, based on universal citizenship; most of them were based on class, gender, place of residence, and occupation. As Sheila Fitzpatrick argued, people outside the boundaries of recognized categories had no claim to rights or benefits from the state.[81] However, after Stalin's death there was an increasing emphasis on universality: in particular, old-age pension laws demonstrated recognition of the norm that every person should be included in a nationwide system on the same legal basis, and this notion gained greater currency under Yeltsin.[82] Gorbachev and Yeltsin continued to advance this idea, but not consistently, because they both still continued to reinforce the notion that certain social programs should be directed primarily at particular groups. In post-Soviet times, universality clashed with the government's inclination to contain spending, as well as with the persistently-voiced demands to protect groups from the deprivations associated with economic reform.

In the pension reform, but also especially in the monetization reform, the government shows a desire to make public policy more transparent and funding more predictable. Measurable, money-related units and concepts became the terms of reference in social welfare. Value was measured in relation to earnings, incomes, taxes paid, and revenue generated. As a result, other measures of value were downgraded (time spent in the workforce, meritorious accomplishments, loyalty to a single workplace, altruistic service). It would be obvious to say that monetization is controversial because people have lost trust in the value of money given the inflation that accompanied "shock therapy."

But it goes further than that. Post-Soviet social welfare reforms were unpopular partly because they were impersonal and ahistorical; benefits were increasingly reduced to monetary terms, rendering the notion of the individual person's multiple identities and contributions to society more and more irrelevant. The new emphasis on money reduces everyone to their individual, material self-interest, as a participant in a mutual exchange. For example, one *l'gotnik* was quoted in *Izvestiia* as saying "The repeal of privileges debases and insults us. Benefits were not just given to us, they can never be replaced by any sum of money … we will only be able to go and

[81] For example, she cites prostitutes and "kulaks" during the Stalin period. Fitzpatrick, *Everyday Life in Extraordinary Times*, 116–27.

[82] Chandler, *Shocking Mother Russia*, chapters, 2, 3, and 8.

throw our stars at the feet of deputies."[83] In her study of the impact of privatization in a baby food factory in postcommunist Poland, Elizabeth Dunn argued that workers took exception to the notion that under market reform they were becoming simple inputs of production. Instead, people needed to see themselves as individuals whose contributions to a community were valued.[84] Similarly, the monetization debate in Russia reveals a widespread belief that the state should recognize in ongoing, visible, regular, and material ways certain categories of groups that gave active service to the nation. Thus, social welfare becomes a way of commemorating history. Social benefits for women and children, on the other hand, are more fragile because, in political discourse, these social groups represent the future: a future that is all too uncertain.

[83] Sergei Nikitich Reshetov, Hero of the Soviet Union, quoted in Sergei Zhakaev, Leonid Novikov, Il'ia Stulov, Ol'ga Timofeeva, and Aleksei Ukkone, "Ne meshaete nam dozhit' do dnia pobedy," *Izvestiia*, July 3, 2004, 3.

[84] Elizabeth C. Dunn, *Privatizing Poland: Baby Food, Big Business and the Remaking of Labor* (Ithaca: Cornell University Press, 2004), 170–2.

Social Welfare or Wasteful Excess?

The Legacy of Soviet Tuberculosis Control Programs in Post-Soviet Russia

Michael Z. David

In no field have the differences in the medical care and public health systems of the FSU and the United States become more controversial, perhaps, than in the control of tuberculosis (TB). Both the United States and the USSR had largely contained TB by 1970, and both regions experienced a recurrence of the disease in the century's final decade in a severe form—multidrug resistant TB (MDR-TB). The miniature epidemic was contained successfully but at enormous expense in the United States.[1] Although the incidence of new cases slowed in the Russian Federation after 1998, MDR-TB continues to spread in an epidemic of thousands of cases centered in penal institutions, the consequences of which remain potentially catastrophic for the FSU and the world.[2] Policies for containment of the MDR-TB epidemic in Russia have elicited condemnatory statements about the Soviet TB control system from many foreign experts and organizations, in part because of apparent resistance to reform from post-Soviet TB experts.

The Soviet TB control system that has been so criticized has roots in the pre-revolutionary TB control programs, which centered around the dispensary, a distinctive sort of clinic that served the social and medical needs of impoverished TB patients. After 1917, the dispensaries were reinvented as part of the larger, holistic project of Soviet medicine. As a practical consequence, the anti-TB infrastructure in the FSU still serves as both a focus of state-subsidized medical care and a source of social welfare for those most in need. If this system is dismantled, alternative social service providers will be needed.

Comparing the medical practices of health care workers in the two political superpowers of the twentieth century reveals many differences and raises intriguing questions. How do differing medical cultures develop? How do political and cultural milieus influence medical practice, research, and tradition? Effective answers require a detailed analysis of the points of intersection of institutional, professional,

[1] Lawrence Geiter, ed., *Ending Neglect: The Elimination of Tuberculosis in the United States* (Washington, D.C.: National Academy Press, 2000), 5–45.

[2] For a review of studies on MDR-TB in the FSU see O.S. Toungoussova, G. Bjune, and D. A. Caugant, "Epidemic of TB in the Former Soviet Union: Social and Biological Reasons," *Tuberculosis* (Edinburgh) 86, no. 1 (2006): 1–10.

epidemiological, political, and scientific history. The present work is a preliminary description of some of these intersections in the history of tuberculosis control in late Imperial and early Soviet Russia and an assessment of their legacies in the successor states of the former Soviet Union (FSU). In short, it is an exploration of what is Soviet now in TB control.

The evidence base for the practice of biomedicine derives from two sources. The first is the world's biomedical literature and the second is medical tradition, which in turn derives from local custom, the continuing practice of training by apprenticeship, and historical, economic, and political constraints. In various geopolitical settings, medical anthropologists, historians, and international health workers have repeatedly discovered the often overriding importance of medical tradition and the politicization of the medical literature.[3] The result is that the practice of biomedicine varies greatly from country to country.

The nature of Soviet TB programs remains an unspoken player in the debates between foreign public health experts and their counterparts in the FSU. An understanding of the history of the ideals undergirding dispensary-based TB care in the Soviet era may open new arenas for discussion and increase the potential for successful reform initiatives.

Tuberculosis

TB is a communicable bacterial disease usually caused by *Mycobacterium tuberculosis*. The most common source of infection is the respiratory droplet, coughed into the air by a TB patient. Bacteria are inhaled by a potential victim. In the lung, if the bacteria make a foothold, they elicit a destructive immune response. Most frequently, the initial encounter of the TB bacilli with the immune system results in a flu-like illness known as primary TB. After the initial infection of the lung, the TB bacteria typically continue to reside there in an uneasy stand-off, encased in structures called granulomas.[4] Up to at least 1930 in Russia, and to about 1910 in Western Europe and North America, approximately 70 to 90 percent of the adult population would be in this position at any given time, most of them infected by the age of

---

[3] See, for example, Robert A. Hahn, *Sickness and Healing: An Anthropological Perspective* (New Haven: Yale University Press, 1995), an exploration of obstetrics as it developed in the United States; and William Johnston, *The Modern Epidemic: A History of Tuberculosis in Japan* (Cambridge, MA: Council on East Asian Studies, Harvard University, 1995).

[4] For an account of the contemporary understanding of the bacteriology, pathogenesis, epidemiology, and treatment of TB, see David Schlossberg, ed., *Tuberculosis & Nontuberculous Mycobacterial Infections*, 5th ed. (New York: McGraw-Hill Medical Publishing Division, 2006).

fifteen.[5] For example, in Vladivostok in 1928, 74.2 percent of 12-year-olds tested positive for exposure to TB by the tuberculin skin test.[6] Approximately 10 percent of infected people, months or years later, develop the condition now called reactivation TB, which may be brought on by an insult to the immune system resulting from starvation, certain dietary deficiencies, stress, cancer, and some infectious diseases. Alternatively, reactivation can occur with no obvious predisposing event. Patients with reactivation TB experience night sweats, weight loss, and a cough, often with blood in their sputum. Secondary TB has long been associated with destitution, and with it all of the prejudices and stigmata associated with poverty, appropriate to each era and cultural milieu.[7] Without antibiotic treatment, reactivation TB usually ends in death over the course of years. Today infection is rare in developed countries, but worldwide over two billion people have been infected and about 1.7 million die each year from TB, particularly in the poorest nations of the world.[8]

It is likely that isolation of patients in sanatoria, the pasteurization of milk, artificial pneumothorax, and programs for early detection of the disease did decrease the rates of TB infection in many places between 1850 and 1952, when effective antibiotics were introduced widely,[9] although improved nutrition and living conditions certainly contributed.[10] MDR-TB, defined as TB resistant to at least two antibiotics (isoniazid and rifampin), arises when infected people are treated with too few or incorrect antibiotics; it is exclusively a product of human actions.

[5] Anne L. Davis, "A Historical Perspective on Tuberculosis and Its Control," in *Tuberculosis: A Comprehensive International Approach*, ed. Lee B. Reichman and Earl S. Hershfield, 2nd ed. (New York: Marcel Dekker, 2000), 13–16; Asim K. Dutt, "Epidemiology and Host Factors," in *Tuberculosis: A Comprehensive International Approach*, 1–3.

[6] G. I. Blankov, "Tuberkulez sredi shkol'nikov Vladivostoka," *Voprosy tuberkuleza*, 1928, no. 9–10: 242–4.

[7] Susan Sontag, *Illness as Metaphor* (New York: Farrar, Strauss & Giroux, 1978); Thomas Dormandy, *The White Death: A History of Tuberculosis* (London: Hambledon Press, 1999; repr., New York: New York University Press, 2000).

[8] Matthew Gandy and Alimuddin Zumla, eds., *The Return of the White Plague: Global Poverty and the "New" Tuberculosis* (London: Verso, 2003).

[9] Amy L. Fairchild and Gerald M. Oppenheimer, "Public Health Nihilism vs Pragmatism: History, Politics, and the Control of Tuberculosis," *American Journal of Public Health* 88 (July 1998): 1105–17; and Leonard G. Wilson, "The Rise and Fall of TB in Minnesota: The Role of Infection," *Bulletin of the History of Medicine* 66 (1992): 15–52.

[10] Thomas McKeown, *The Role of Medicine: Dream, Mirage, or Nemesis?* (Princeton: Princeton University Press, 1979), 3–65, 71–8.

"Soviet Methods" of TB Treatment

During the Soviet era, public health experts constructed a massive anti-TB infrastructure, which successfully contained the disease. TB had been the leading cause of death among adults in Soviet cities in the late 1920s, but was a rare cause by the late 1970s. This remarkable feat was made possible by a multifaceted approach to treatment and prevention, including isolation; BCG vaccination; antibiotic, dietetic, and surgical therapies; and mass screening by chest x-rays for active case-finding. In the post-Soviet era, TB became a new threat, with a doubling in the incidence of new cases diagnosed in Russia between 1990 and 1998 in an era marked by a collapse of the infrastructure for social services, rising unemployment, malnutrition, internal migration, and rampant alcoholism.[11] As noted, a rapid rise in infections with MDR strains of TB, concentrated in the prison system, was especially concerning.[12]

Physicians in the FSU use some methods of TB treatment routinely that were all but abandoned in the West by 1970.[13] In the West, tuberculosis is treated with antibiotics alone and almost exclusively in outpatient settings rather than in the hospital; this was a major change from the pre-antibiotic era, when patients were isolated in sanatoria.[14] In contrast, the Soviet-era norm of therapy for TB was, "a complex of various methods of treatment," mainly while patients were confined to institutions. The standard Soviet handbook for physicians published in 1988 was edited by Aleksandr Grigor'evich Khomenko (1923–99), Director of the Central TB Institute of the Russian Academy of Medical Sciences and editor of the Soviet/Russian TB journal *Problemy tuberkuleza* from 1981 until his death.[15] His handbook described this complex therapy.

[11] See Mark G. Field and Judyth L. Twigg, eds., *Russia's Torn Safety Nets: Health and Social Welfare During the Transition* (New York: St. Martin's Press, 2000); R. Coker, M. McKee, R. Atun, et al., "Risk Factors for Pulmonary TB in Russia: Case-Control Study," *British Medical Journal* 332 (2006): 85–7; and E.M. Krupitsky, E.E. Zvartau, D.A. Lioznov, et al., "Co-Morbidity of Infectous and Addictive Diseases in St. Petersburg and the Leningrad Region, Russia," *European Addiction Research* 12 (2006): 12–19.

[12] Alexey Bobrik, Kirill Danishevski, Ksenia Eroshina, and Martin McKee, "Prison Health in Russia: The Larger Picture," *Journal of Health Policy* 26 (2005): 30–59.

[13] Robert F. Johnston and Kenneth H. Wildrick, "State of the Art Review: The Impact of Chemotherapy on the Care of Patients with TB," *American Review of Respiratory Disease* 109 (1974): 636–64.

[14] Dormandy, *The White Death*, 147–86.

[15] On Khomenko, see obituary, *Problemy tuberkuleza*, 1999, no. 5, front endsheet; and Lee B. Reichman and Janice Hopkins Tanne, *Timebomb: The Global Epidemic of Multi-Drug Resistant Tuberculosis* (New York: McGraw-Hill, 2002), 74–5.

In addition to antibiotics, other measures, seemingly anachronistic or bizarre to the Western European and North American doctor, were also in use. The Soviet handbook states, "[i]t is wrong to assume that it is possible to cure a TB patient only with the help of medications and pathogenetic methods. The outlook on life of the patient [and] the character of his nourishment play a very important role in the process of the cure."[16] Contemporary American medical textbooks have no counterpart to this statement. Russian physicians also routinely perform surgery on TB patients to remove ribs or parts of the lung. Approximately five hundred TB surgeries were performed per year in one Moscow hospital, while surgery is reserved for only the most resistant and severe cases in the United States.[17] Frequent surgery was still regarded as necessary by many tuberculosis experts in the FSU in 2005, who lamented the drop in the number of lung TB patients under dispensary surveillance who had undergone a surgery from 5.6 percent in 1985 to just 3 percent in 2003.[18]

The use of specialized TB hospitals and sanatoria in the Soviet Union was a distinctive characteristic of the TB control system, as the author of the handbook continued,

> Abroad, in developed countries, on the whole, only out-patient treatment is conducted. In recent years, this tactic has gradually spread even in the economically highly developed countries of Western Europe...This practice is not supported in our country, in that, in accordance with the doctrine held in our country, hospital and out-patient treatment do not contradict one another, but are stages in the protracted treatment of TB patients.[19]

TB patients in Moscow were kept in institutions for longer periods of time as the decades progressed, reversing the trend in the West after 1954. For example, the average patient was in a Soviet sanatorium or hospital for 43.2 days in 1939, for 49 days in 1945, 98.4 days in 1961, and 117 days in 1976.[20] A final difference was

[16] A.G. Khomenko, ed., *Tuberkulez organov dykhaniia: Rukovodstvo dlia vrachei* (Moscow: Meditsina, 1988), 359.

[17] Reichman and Tanne, *Timebomb*, 165.

[18] M.V. Shilova, T.S. Khruleva, and E.B. Tsybikova, "Sostoianie khirurgicheskoi pomoshchi bol'nym tuberkulezom organov dykhaniia," *Problemy tuberkuleza i boleznei legkikh*, 2005, no. 5: 31–6.

[19] Khomenko, *Tuberkulez organov dykhaniia*, 359.

[20] S.D. Poletaev, I.A. Flit, Ia.M. Gurtovoi, E.I. Ianov, and L.M. Kusikova, "Epidemiologicheskie i klinicheskie sdvigi po tuberkulezu za 40 let (po materialam protivotuberkuleznogo dispansera)," *Problemy tuberkuleza*, 1978, no. 10: 5. In the United States, the average hospitalized patient had a length of stay decreasing from 299 days in 1952, to 200 days in 1962, to 87 days in 1972. The average daily census in these institutions dropped from

that in Western nations, the 1988 textbook author claimed, an identical treatment was offered to all TB patients, while in Soviet practice, there were a variety of regimens offered, which would be tailored to the needs of each patient.[21] These included air and diet therapy, "which have not lost their import even in our day," according to Khomenko. He also noted the continued use of "methods of physiotherapeutic force,"[22] such as light and water. These methods and beliefs were supported by a vast Soviet literature of experiment and clinical experience.[23] They were not advocated only during the Soviet era; nearly the same text on therapies for TB was included in a 1996 edition of the handbook edited by Khomenko[24] and this remains the basis for TB treatment in the FSU a decade later.[25]

Conflict: TB Control Strategies in the Soviet Union and the West, 1991–2006

The former Soviet anti-TB system in the Russian Federation is a large, crumbling system, which in 2002 included 502 dispensaries and 182 sanatoria employing 9,000 physicians and 38,000 other medical personnel.[26] Public health experts have been engaged by international NGOs and foreign governments to address the growing epidemic of TB in Russia both in an effort to support the economy and to prevent the spread of resistant organisms to other nations.[27] It quickly became clear to foreign health reform workers that Russian TB experts were resistant to the introduction of many techniques successfully practiced in the West to contain the disease.[28] This

---

93,000 in 1952 to 10,700 in 1972. See Johnston and Wildrick, "State of the Art Review," 657.

[21] In fact, drug treatment regimens in the United States had long been tailored to the antibiotic resistance pattern of the bacteria in a given patient. Khomenko here presumably referred to other factors, such as employment, diet, and lifestyle, which have been completely rejected in American practice.

[22] Khomenko, *Tuberkulez organov dykhaniia*, 404.

[23] See ibid., 568–71, as well as the monthly Soviet journal *Problemy tuberkuleza*.

[24] A.G. Khomenko, ed., *Tuberkulez* (Moscow: Meditsina, 1996), 316–66.

[25] B. Jacobs, C. Clowes, F. Wares, et al., "Cost-Effectiveness Analysis of the Russian Treatment Scheme for TB Versus Short-Course Chemotherapy: Results from Tomsk, Siberia," *International Journal of Tuberculosis and Lung Disease* 6, no. 5 (2002): 396–405.

[26] M.I. Perel'man, "Novyi etap bor'by s tuberkulezom v Rossii," *Problemy tuberkuleza*, 2002, no. 6: 4.

[27] "The Health Crisis in Russia: Countries in the EU and G8 Must Help Russia Tackle Its Health Crisis," *British Medical Journal* 331 (2005): 1418–19.

[28] For a thoughtful assessment of the current system of care and barriers to its improvement,

resistance has led to tensions and the failure of several international partnerships.

Since the 1980s, representatives of the World Health Organization (WHO) and others have advocated the worldwide implementation of a TB control strategy called Directly Observed Therapy – Short Course (DOTS). This approach entails the use of a standard regimen of four drugs for two months and then two drugs for four additional months to treat patients sick with TB, administered under the observation of a public health worker. This is to ensure compliance with the medications and to prevent the emergence of antibiotic resistance. To obtain certification by WHO as a DOTS-employing country, each country must demonstrate a political commitment to the WHO program, implement direct observation of drug administration, have an effective drug supply, institute standardized drug regimens, and have an acceptable monitoring system in place to evaluate the program.[29] DOTS involves the diagnosis of patients by their symptoms and the presence of the bacteria in the sputum, rather than by annual x-ray screening of the population, which was the method used in the Soviet era. DOTS was not well received in the mid-1990s by TB experts in the FSU when representatives of WHO and the Soros Foundation presented it as the best solution to the rising incidence of TB. Russian experts resisted the strategy perhaps in part because it flew in the face of Soviet approaches and because the FSU lacked an infrastructure and adequate funding to implement directly observed therapy.[30] Nevertheless, pilot DOTS programs were started in Ivanovo oblast and elsewhere after 1994,[31] and some studies have shown promise in cost and efficacy compared with the

---

see R. J. Coker, B. Dmitrova, F. Drobniewski, et al., "TB Control in Samara Oblast, Russia: Institutional and Regulatory Environment," *International Journal of Tuberculosis and Lung Disease* 7, no. 10 (2003): 920–32.

[29] See "Tuberculosis," World Health Organization, http://www.who.int/tb/en/ (accessed January 16, 2007).

[30] M. E. Kimerling, "The Russian Equation: An Evolving Paradigm in Tuberculosis Control," *International Journal of Tuberculosis and Lung Disease* 4, no. 12 (2000): S160–7; and Gene Bukhman, "Reform and Resistance in Post-Soviet TB Control" (PhD diss., University of Arizona, 2001), 59–175. Bukhman examines the conflict between the foreign advisors and the TB experts of the FSU from 1994–2000 using the methods of anthropology, but he does not address the historical context of Soviet TB control substantially. Journalists and foreign experts have commented widely on this resistance. See Reichman and Tanne, *Timebomb*; Natalya Shulyakovskaya, "WHO Warning on TB Ignored," *St. Petersburg Times* (Russia), March 27, 1998, 8; Carlotta Gall, "The Death Stops Here," *Moscow Times*, January 17, 1998, 7; and Masha Gessen, "Tuberkulez: Pobednyi marsh pobezhdennoi zarazy," *Itogi*, September 16, 1997, 44–9.

[31] A.G. Khomenko, "Strategiia DOTS i ee rasprostranenie v Rossii," *Problemy tuberkuleza*, 1999, no. 1: 4–8.

traditional Russian methods.[32] Other studies have shown less positive results.[33]

While DOTS proved successful and inexpensive as a method to contain TB in developing nations, it unfortunately is not effective at controlling the disease in regions with high rates of MDR-TB, such as the FSU.[34] In fact, DOTS likely drives up the rate of MDR-TB cases in those regions.[35] As this came to light, the earlier wariness of Russian TB experts seemed quite justified, although modifications in the DOTS strategy since 1998, resulting in the DOTS-Plus strategy, have improved the efficacy of the program in regions with a high incidence of MDR-TB.[36] DOTS-Plus requires expensive testing of bacteria recovered from sputum for antibiotic resistance patterns; it resembles the state-of-the-art treatment used in the United States. Even with these improvements, the WHO program still was not accepted by leading Russian TB experts, who preferred at least to add on the "Soviet" style treatments.[37] One study demonstrated that in those regions employing DOTS in 2001, the number of bed-days per patient was not different when compared to regions not employing DOTS because the Soviet-era system remains largely intact; most patients continued to receive in-patient care even in areas with DOTS programs.[38] WHO programs had spread to over 20 regions of Russia by 2004, covering about 45 percent of the popu-

[32] Jacobs, et al. "Cost-Effectiveness Analysis"; T.A. Grishina, "Itogi primeneniia DOTS v Rossii," *Problemy tuberkuleza*, 1999, no. 1: 9–12.

[33] I. Danilova, M. Stoyunin, E. Repina, et al., "Primary Multi-Drug Resistant Tuberculosis—Ivanovo oblast', Russia, 1999," *MMWR Morbidity and Mortality Weekly Report* 48 (1999): 661–3.

[34] F. Drobniewski, Y. Balabanova, V. Nikolayevsky, et al., "Drug-Resistant Tuberculosis, Clinical Virulence, and the Dominance of the Beijing Strain Family in Russia," *Journal of the American Medical Association* 293 (2005): 2726–31.

[35] I. Bastian, L. Rigouts, A. Van Deun, and F. Portaels, "Directly Observed Treatment, Short-Course Strategy and Multidrug-Resistant Tuberculosis: Are Any Modifications Required?" *Bulletin of the World Health Organization* 78, no. 2 (2000): 238–51; M. Bonnet, V. Sizaire, Y. Kebede, et al., "Does One Size Fit All? Drug Resistance and Standard Treatments: Results of Six TB Programmes in Former Soviet Countries," *International Journal of Tuberculosis and Lung Disease* 9 (2005): 1147–54.

[36] V. Leimane, V. Riekstina, T.H. Holtz, et al., "Clinical Outcome of Individualized Treatment of Multidrug-Resistant TB in Latvia: A Retrospective Cohort Study," *Lancet* 365 (2005): 318–26.

[37] WHO, *Global TB Control* (Geneva, 2005), 120–1.

[38] Florian M. Marx, Rifat A. Atun, Wieslaw Jakubowiak, Martin Mckee, and Richard J. Coker, "Reform of Tuberculosis Control and DOTS within Russian Public Health Systems: An Ecological Study," *European Journal of Public Health* 2006, advance access publication July 12, 2006.

lation[39]; "adapted to conditions" there, DOTS-Plus was shown to be successful at curing TB.[40] The conflict between the "Soviet" and the "Western" treatment for TB is often framed as a conflict surrounding DOTS, but I believe that the divide is more complex.

Why Russian TB Experts Support Soviet-Era Methods: Russian and Foreign Opinions

Both Russian and foreign physicians have offered their opinions as to why there is resistance to reform of TB control strategies in Russia. A U.S. Centers for Disease Control and Prevention (CDC) official involved in DOTS programs in Russia hypothesized that the Russians' "intellectual pride" was central and that "they see their system as equal and separate from the West."[41] An official from Abt Associates and Sandy Michaels from the CDC both described the Soviet method as not being "cost-effective" in comparison with foreign models.[42]

Shock at the distinctive post-Soviet TB control system has been almost universal among Western observers visiting Russian TB treatment facilities for the first time. American TB expert Lee Reichman, on visiting a leading Moscow institute in July 1997, was surprised when he

> saw a young girl of 16 who had been flown across Russia's nine time zones from Vladivostok, a port in the Far Eastern region of Russia on the Pacific Ocean, to undergo drastic surgery to remove parts of both her lungs at the Priimak Institute... We were stunned… Back home in New Jersey, I would have treated such a young woman with drugs to which her TB was sensitive for 6 months or so. She would probably never have been hospitalized and almost certainly would not have needed surgery.[43]

Reichman referred to Russia's TB establishment as "long out of touch with Western

---

[39] V.V. Erokhin, "Osnovnye itogi i perspektivy raboty sotrudnichaiushchevo tsentra VOZ po bor'be s tuberkulezom v Rossiiskoi federatsii," *Problemy tuberkuleza*, 2004, no. 8: 3–7. For data on 2004 DOTS coverage, see "Russian Federation," WHO Report 2006, http://www.who.int/globalatlas/predefinedReports/TB/PDF_Files/RU_2004_Detailed.pdf (accessed January 16, 2007).

[40] L.P. Kapkov, V.V. Punga, M.I. Vasil'ev, et al., "Vliianie vnedreniia adaptirovannykh k Rossiiskim usloviiam rekomendatsii VOZ po bor'be s tuberkulezom na otechestvennye statisticheskie pokazateli po tuberkulezu," *Problemy tuberkuleza*, 2004, no. 8: 15–19.

[41] Bukhman, "Reform and Resistance in Post-Soviet TB Control," 166–8.

[42] Ibid., 178.

[43] Reichman and Tanne, *Timebomb*, 72.

advances in treatment, which clung to the old largely unnecessary and ineffective ways."[44] He concluded that the major differences between the West and Russia arose not only from Cold War tensions and variations in approaches to treatment, but perhaps more importantly in an understanding of the pathophysiology of TB:

> To this day, many Russian scientists believe that directly or indirectly, TB affects every part of the patient's body, not just the lungs…TB drugs are often supplemented by "pathogenetic therapy," a sort of therapy that may include anti-inflammatory drugs, agents thought to improve the immune system, vitamins, detoxifying agents, drugs to improve the circulation, liver tonics, exposure of the blood to ultraviolet rays (the blood is removed from the patient, exposed to ultraviolet light, and then returned to the patient by transfusion), and many other treatments as the doctor decides…Such scientifically unproven therapy is virtually never done in other countries.[45]

Experts inside the Russian system have expressed resistance to change in print. In a 1995 article, Dr. Aleksei Priimak, then the head TB doctor of Russia, called for a "new conception" of TB control for Russia, choosing radical fiscal restraint within the traditional Soviet system rather than acceptance of the DOTS reform proposals.[46] In 1999, Reichman interviewed the TB surgeon Mikhail Izrailovich Perel'man (b. 1924), the chief TB doctor at the Russian Ministry of Health. Perel'man "argued forcefully for the rebuilding of the former Soviet system, with some modifications." He continued to reject DOTS, as had Priimak before him. He said, "DOTS couldn't be implemented here. It's a social problem," to which Reichman responded in his book, "as if our TB patients in New Jersey did not have similar problems."[47] Perel'man later, at least in theory, accepted DOTS adapted to Russian conditions and maintaining adjunctive therapies.[48]

Russian experts have often supported their distinctive anti-TB system using broad historical references to bolster their arguments. For example, in an article in 2000 on TB control, the Russian Minister of Health, Iu.L. Shevchenko, wrote, "even before the antibiotic era, our national anti-TB service, primarily through preventative and organizational means, was able to keep the TB epidemic in check under the most unfavorable economic conditions." He called for a preservation and renovation

---

[44] Ibid., 99.

[45] Ibid., 114–15.

[46] Ibid., 113.

[47] Ibid., 123–4.

[48] M.I. Perel'man, "'DOTS', 'DOTS +', i nauchnaia terminologiia," *Problemy tuberkuleza*, 2004, no. 10: 4.

of the "basic structure of the anti-TB service of the Russian Federation," noting that there were 76,526 beds for TB patients in the country although 15 percent of them were "wrecked."[49] In an interview in 2000, Priimak also turned to history to support the Russian system, linking the disease to wars and other traumatic events of the twentieth century.[50]

The Dispensary and the Origins of the Soviet TB Infrastructure

The TB dispensary is a medical clinic that has a long history; it was central to and was altered by each successive period of Russian/Soviet history during the twentieth century. The Soviet TB dispensary was founded on a pre-revolutionary model adapted by members of the Pirogov Society (the most prominent pre-revolutionary Russian physicians' organization[51]) from an original French institution, the *dispensaire* of Dr. Albert Calmette (1863–1933). Dr. Filip Maksov Bliumental' (b. 1859) was a member of the Pirogov Society's Temporary Tuberculosis Commission[52] and the foremost authority on popular tuberculosis education in pre-revolutionary Russia. At a seminal meeting of the Commission in 1903, when there were very few TB treatment institutions in Russia for the poor, he argued for the adoption of the French and Belgian model of the tuberculosis *dispensaire* as the central pivot about which all tuberculosis control should revolve. Fedor Aleksandrovich Get'e (1863–1938), another Moscow physician with an interest in tuberculosis and one of Lenin's physicians after 1917,[53] clashed with Bliumental' at the meeting, insisting that the French model was not appropriate for Russia.

Bliumental' described Calmette's clinic, which opened in Lille in February 1901, as having the following purposes:

> to track down consumptives (*chakhotochnykh*) from the poor working class, especially in the beginning stages of the disease; render the patients medical assistance and material support, improve their housing conditions and protect

[49] Iu.L. Shevchenko, "Bor'ba s tuberkulezom v Rossii na poroge XXI veka," *Problemy tuberkuleza*, 2000, no. 3: 2–6.

[50] Reichman and Tanne, *Timebomb*, 113.

[51] Nancy Mandelker Frieden, *Russian Physicians in an Era of Reform and Revolution, 1856–1905* (Princeton: Princeton University Press, 1981), 118–22 and passim.

[52] R.B. Kaganovich, *Iz istorii bor'by s tuberkulezom v dorevoliutsionnoi Rossii* (Moscow: AMN, 1953), 24. Bliumental' founded the first bacteriological institute in Moscow in 1887.

[53] Get'e after the Revolution became the senior doctor at the Khimki tuberculosis sanatorium outside of Moscow. On his career, see V.M. Vasil'ev and V.N. Rozanov, "K iubileiu F.A. Get'e," *Moskovskii meditsinskii zhurnal* 8, no. 10–-11 (1928): 286–8.

> those nearby (healthy people) from the danger of infection by the making-healthy (*ozdorovlenie*) of housing, its disinfection, the laundering of clothes, and the distribution of necessary hygienic information.[54]

Insisting that the French *dispensaire* (not yet a common Russian term, although there had been institutions for poor relief called *dispensarii* in St. Petersburg founded in 1804[55]) be adopted for Russia, he continued, "In the absence of special treatment establishments (sanatoria and others) for tuberculosis patients, out-patient care is the first real step of the public struggle with tuberculosis."[56] This contrasted with earlier commonly held views that sanatorium treatment, often in what was regarded as a salubrious locale, was the gold standard therapy.

Calmette's facility enrolled all patients who had tuberculosis and were poor. The physician, after a physical examination of the patient and a home visit, decided if that patient needed food, rent payments, or clothing. The *dispensaire* remained in permanent contact with its patients, with periodic visits to their homes, providing advice to them in simple language about medical advances, and sponsoring popular educational programs for the general public. [57] This all-inclusive TB clinic and paternalistic monitor would provide one-stop care for patients, as well as a rather invasive intrusion into their personal lives, in an effort to change behaviors and to decrease the infectious potential of patients' homes and belongings. By 1905 there were at least 17 similar dispensaries in French cities, most based directly on Calmette's model.[58]

---

[54] F.M. Bliumental', "O znachenii ambulatorii v dele bor'by s tuberkulezom," in Obshchestvo russkikh vrachei v pamiat' N. I. Pirogova, *Trudy postoiannoi komissii po izucheniiu tuberkuleza: Zasedaniia komissii 17–19 maia 1903 g. s uchastiem priglashennykh lits* (Moscow, 1904), 24–5.

[55] The term *dispensary* had long been applied to institutions for the treatment of the poor in England and Anglo-America. See "Social Class and Medical Care in Nineteenth Century America: The Rise and Fall of the Dispensary," in Charles E. Rosenberg, *Explaining Epidemics and Other Studies in the History of Medicine* (Cambridge: Cambridge University Press, 1992), 155–77; "Dispanser," *Bol'shaia meditsinskaia entsiklopediia*, 1st ed., vol. 9 (Moscow, 1929), 298–9.

[56] Bliumental', "O znachenii ambulatorii."

[57] A. Calmette, "The 'Émile Roux' Antitubercular Dispensary at Lille," in *Transactions of the British Congress on Tuberculosis for the Prevention of Consumption. London, July 22nd to 26th, 1901*, Report of the State Section, vol. 2 (London: William Clowes & Sons, Limited, 1902), 447–61.

[58] "Lille, Préventorium Émile Roux," *Congrès International de la Tuberculose tenu à Paris, du 2 au 7 octobre 1905*, vol. 3 (Paris: Masson et Cie, Éditeurs, 1906), 360–70. In 1905, Calmette published a report on the cumulative work of his Lille *dispensaire*, where over 1000 patients had been identified.

Dr. Get'e, responding to Bliumental's spoken and earlier published views,[59] proposed an alternative approach for Russia—the use of specialized TB hospital wards as treatment facilities. Get'e objected to the central figure of the visiting nurse, called by Calmette the *assistant-ouvrier* (assistant-worker), who also acted as inspector of homes, protector of families, and instructor in hygiene. While the *dispensaires* were very useful in the West, Get'e argued that the work of the *assistant-ouvrier* required a certain combination of talents and attributes which would be difficult to find in any Russian. He suggested that there were few people capable of social engagement of both the common man and the intelligentsia. Furthermore, Get'e insisted that the cost of maintaining those workers who needed food and housing improvements would be impossible to fund if Calmette's model were brought to Russia. The financial limitations reflected the relative paucity of resources provided by the state and civil society for charity medical care in Russia.[60]

Despite Get'e's concerns, the French *dispensaire* was accepted as the ideal type of outpatient clinic for TB care. The number of Russian *dispensary* began to multiply after the foundation of the All-Russian League for the Struggle with Tuberculosis in 1910.[61] The year 1913 was the high point for dispensary treatment of tuberculosis in Imperial Russia. In that year, approximately 35,808 patients made 355,567 visits to Russia's TB clinics. Estimates vary, but in 1913 there were probably 59 out-patient TB clinics run by 53 organizations in the Russian Empire. The number decreased sharply as the First World War began, and the downward trend continued through 1918.[62]

In the autumn of 1918, while civil war, famine, and typhus ravaged Russia, the People's Commissariat of Public Health, Narkomzdrav RSFSR, was founded in Moscow. The leaders were guided by principles that were entirely novel for a national health program, namely, that all health care in the new state would eventually be

---

[59] F.A. Get'e, "Oznachenii sanatorii i ambulatorii v dele bor'by s tuberkulezom," in *Trudy postoiannoi komissii po izucheniiu tuberkuleza: Zasedaniia komissii 17–19 maia 1903 g.*, 25–30. The book cited in this article was F.M. Bliumental', *Ob ambulatoriiakh dlia legochnykh bol'nykh v Germanii, Frantsii i Bel'gii i o znachenii ikh v dele bor'by s tuberkulezom* (Moscow, 1902).

[60] For a history of charitable giving in imperial Russia, see Adele Lindemeyr, *Poverty is Not a Vice: Charity, Society, and the State in Imperial Russia* (Princeton: Princeton University Press, 1996).

[61] I.N. Al'tshuller, "Sovremennoe polozhenie tuberkuleznykh popechitel'nost' v Rossii," *Tuberkulez* (St. Petersburg), 1914, no. 2: 146–9.

[62] Kaganovich, *Iz istorii bor'by s tuberkulezom*, 64–5.

centralized, governmental, preventative, free of charge, and "generally available."[63] TB in peace-time imperial Russia and during NEP was the single most common cause of death among adults, killing on the order of 3,000 Muscovites each year and an estimated 41,724 of them in the period 1912–21, far surpassing any other disease.[64] Doctors working in Section for the Struggle with TB of Narkomzdrav spent the three difficult years from 1919 to 1921 devising and inaugurating a new, Soviet anti-TB infrastructure. They adopted many of the concepts used by the All-Russian League, which was formally disbanded in 1918. The Soviet version of the TB dispensary, they felt, would be a mechanism to link society with science in order to reshape people with backward lives, ruined (but not irredeemably) by capitalist economic relations, into new, Soviet citizens. TB dispensaries had been opened in many other countries, but the Narkomzdrav model was different, its founders believed, because it would be integrated into the world's first socialized medical system.

The Soviet dispensaries were to be distinctive in several ways. First, in the ambitious plans of Narkomzdrav's Tuberculosis Section of 1919–21, a dispensary would cover every district of every Soviet city or region, and would be responsible for the diagnosis of, observation of, and assistance to all tuberculosis victims, actual and potential, in its district. When the patients became too ill to work, they were to be sent to sanatoria. For the very ill, the Section planned specialized tuberculosis hospitals. Second, the new dispensaries would have full state financial support. Soviet accounts of the dispensary's origins in Russia usually cite the work of the All-Russian League's 67 clinics as a precursor to Soviet dispensaries. Soviet authors invariably asserted that these dispensaries were a model, but one doomed to failure as merely charitable institutions embedded in a capitalist society.[65]

The third innovation was the Council of Social Assistance, with representatives from the medical staff and from local housing, health, educational, and labor bureaucracies. The Councils, renamed Committees for the Making Healthy of Labor and Daily Life (KOTIBs) in the mid-1920s, were ideally to help patients in each relevant sphere of their lives—with knowledge, rest, necessary medical care, and better food, housing, or work. The roots of tuberculosis would thereby be extirpated, making life healthy and ultimately contributing to the creation of a new, Soviet form of

[63] "Ocherki po teorii organizatsii sovetskogo zdravookhraneniia," in N. A. Semashko, *Izbrannye proizvedeniia*, 2nd, corr. and exp. ed., ed. N. I. Kal' (Moscow: Izdatel'stvo meditsina, 1967), 55–96.

[64] Henry Beeuwkes, *American Medical and Sanitary Relief in the Russian Famine, 1921–1923* (New York: American Relief Administration, 1926), 48.

[65] For example, "Dispanser," *Bol'shaia meditsinskaia entsiklopediia*, 301.

daily life. The KOTIBs would intervene on behalf of patients at work, at school, and even at home. Staff members, especially "specialized teaching nurse-investigators,"[66] would visit, inspect, and report on patients' homes and teach them and their family members rules of hygiene, just as in Calmette's *dispensaire* of 20 years before.

Dispensaries would have cafeterias featuring nourishing food for patients, among other interventions. Doctors would examine and, if necessary, treat close contacts of the patients. In order to understand and alter the socio-cultural forces acting on patients that might influence their health, Soviet TB experts devised various exhaustive questionnaires and medical forms.[67] Doctors, finally, would provide medical treatment, and the dispensary would act as a clearing house for patients in need of a sanatorium or hospital stay. The treatment function was lacking at most Western European dispensaries at the time because of objections from physicians in private practice, sometimes on grounds that they would lose paying patients,[68] a fact frequently noted by Soviet propagandists.

In 1922, Moscow's eight dispensaries began to carry out systematic examinations of employees at industrial enterprises. By October 1, the physicians had examined 33,213 people, about 3.2 percent of the city's population. Of these, 23,643, or 71 percent, were tuberculous or at high risk, and they were added to the growing list of patients to be kept under surveillance by the dispensaries.[69] The TB dispensary was the inspiration for other institutions in Moscow during NEP, expanding the use of the model to encompass venerological, narcological, and occupational dispensaries.[70]

Social hygienists in the Moscow Health Department, led in 1919–29 by Dr.

---

[66] Ibid.

[67] One of them, published in the 1920 handbook of the Section, included 84 detailed medical and biographical questions. *Materialy po ustroistvu dispanserov dlia bor'by s tuberkulezom*, Spravochniki sektsii bor'by s tuberkulezom, vyp. V (Moscow: Izdanie Narodnogo komissariata zdravookhraneniia, 1920), 11.

[68] For example, in 1934, at the Ninth International Conference of the International Union Against Tuberculosis, the Parisian pioneer of the dispensary, Leon Bernard, noted that objections from professional medical organizations would have to be addressed in order to introduce the new therapy of artificial pneumothorax widely to dispensaries. See Leon Bernard, *L'utilisation des dispansaires pour le traitement des tuberculeux* (Warsaw, 1934); and IX Conference de L'Union Internationale contra la Tuberculose, *Co-rapports: L'utilisation des dispensaires pour le traitement des tuberculeux* (Warsaw, 1934).

[69] *Tuberkuleznyi trekhdnevnik: Pervaia proletarskaia belaia romashka* (Moscow: Izdanie komiteta po provedeniiu tuberkuleznyi trekhdnevnika pri M. S. R. i K. D.), 26–31.

[70] See, for example, on the first venerological dispensary's social assistance council: A.P. Kushelevskii, "Praktika 2-letnei raboty komissii ozdorovleniia truda i byta," *Moskovskii meditsinskii zhurnal* 6, no. 3 (1926): 74–80.

Vladimir Aleksandrovich Obukh (1870–1934), rapidly devised an ambitious, comprehensive system of examination and surveillance for all illnesses in the population, which came to be known as *dispanserizatsiia* (dispensarization), further building on the TB dispensary model. In 1925, the Moscow Soviet officially approved this system.[71] Other Soviet cities initiated similar programs on a smaller scale. Dispensarization was a theory of public health, a fusion of epidemiology, social hygiene, primary care medicine, occupational health, and social work unprecedented in scope.[72] Teams of doctors visited hundred of institutions—schools, factories, institutes, and others—where they examined people and interviewed them to correlate physical illnesses with environmental and living conditions. A "sanitary journal" for each individual was created to track changes in health and exposures over time.[73] The experiment of dispensarization was promising, but it ultimately failed. There were too few doctors to see and treat the entire population of Moscow in 1924–29. The nearly half-million people examined in almost 1,000 institutions in the city by 1929 could not be kept under regular medical surveillance. Perhaps most importantly, however, general dispensarization in Moscow was ended ungracefully, a victim of the Cultural Revolution. It was denounced as a "mechanist" project, not attending particularly to the working class, and was replaced by a new doctrine of industrial medicine during the First Five-Year Plan.[74]

In 1929–32, Soviet state policies effectively downgraded general public health programs by decreasing their funding. Under pressure from the central leadership of the state, the Party, and trade unions, budgets for public health were concentrated

---

[71] "Rezoliutsiia, priniataia po dokladu tov. Obukha o deiatel'nosti Moszdravotdela na plenume Mossoveta ot 27 oktiabria 1925 goda," *Moskovskii meditsinskii zhurnal* 5, no. 11 (1925): ix–x. On the adaptation of the methods of the TB dispensary to the larger program of dispensarization, see N. Vvedenskii, "Ocherednye sotsial'no-profilakticheskie zadachi moskovskikh tuberkuleznykh dispanserov," ibid. 5, no. 4 (1925): 87; and the statement by Shvaitsar on May 7, 1925, reproduced in "Nauchnoe obshchestvo moskovskikh vrachei 'Leninizm v meditsine'," ibid. 5, no. 7 (1925): 107.

[72] By late 1932, a bibliography on dispensarization (*not* including articles on TB, venereal, narcological, or other dispensaries associated with just one medical field) listed 279 publications in Russian and Ukrainian. R.I. Al'perovich, V.M. Borovskaia, S.Iu. Veisberg, and B.A. Ivanov, "Bibliografiia po voprosam dispanserizatsii s vkliucheniem po granichnykh oblastei organizatsii zdravookhraneniia," *Tsentral'nyi meditsinskii zhurnal*, 1933, no. 5–6: 395–418.

[73] A review of the project is provided in "Dispanserizatsiia," *Bol'shaia meditsinskaia entsiklopediia*, 1st ed., vol. 9 (Moscow, 1929), 303–19.

[74] See "Obukh, Vladimir Aleksandrovich," *Bol'shaia meditsinskaia entsiklopediia*, 1st ed., vol. 22 (Moscow, 1932), 53–4.

on the short-term needs of industry.[75] TB control was among the programs that suffered from this drastic shift in focus. The Soviet TB control infrastructure, as well as social hygiene[76] and other labor-intensive medical movements of the 1920s meant to contain disease through mechanisms of social change, were threatened almost with extinction. The TB dispensary lost prominence.

In the early 1930s, local health departments opened poorly staffed TB departments in giant, multispecialty unified dispensaries and other large medical facilities, sometimes replacing older dispensaries.[77] The framers of the TB dispensary model in Moscow, however, never stopped agitating from within the bureaucracy to reinstate the 1920s model. For example, between January and September 1934, the staff of Narkomzdrav generated a blunt and boldly negative report on the status of TB control in the RSFSR.[78] The authors complained that the TB system had suffered since December 1929.[79] With this internal report, the new Commissar of Narkomzdrav, G. N. Kaminsky (1895–1939), took action, writing a memo to the Council of Peoples Commissars RSFSR (Sovnarkom).[80] In December 1934, Sovnarkom passed a decree based on a draft submitted by Kaminsky,[81] which included provisions to promote TB dispensaries. Although this decree and a second one in 1936 were honored more in the breech than in practice, the number of TB treatment facilities and the quality of

[75] The initial Five-Year Plan for public health was revised in July 1930 to reflect this change. Christopher M. Davis, "Economics of Soviet Public Health, 1928–1932: Development Strategy, Resource Constraints, and Health Plans," in *Health and Society in Revolutionary Russia*, ed. Susan Gross Solomon and John F. Hutchinson (Bloomington: Indiana University Press, 1990), 146–72.

[76] Susan Gross Solomon, "Social Hygiene and Soviet Public Health, 1921–1930," in Solomon and Hutchinson, *Health and Society in Revolutionary Russia*, 175–99.

[77] In 1932, the 226 dispensaries in the RSFSR were supplemented by 76 TB departments and 46 rural and industrial TB stations. See I.I. Liudvinovksii, "Bor'ba s tuberkulezom v RSFSR," *Problemy tuberkuleza* 14, no. 3 (1936): 309.

[78] In 1935, the Director, Munblit, and Senior Inspector Rozanov were the only two physicians employed in the TB Sector ("tubsektor") of NKZ. "Shtaty lechprofupravleniia Narkomzdrava," [1935], State Archive of the Russian Federation (hereafter GARF) f. 482, op. 24, d. 454, l. 24.

[79] "Tezisy k dokladu 'meropriiatiia po bor'be s tuberkulezom," n.d. [between January and September 1934], GARF f. 482, op. 24, d. 517, l. 131.

[80] To Predsedatel' Sovnarkom RSFSR, Sulimov from Commissar of NKZ Kaminskii, No. 643/630, September 14, 1934, f. 482, op. 24, d. 176, ll. 10–13.

[81] "Proekt. Postanovlenie Soveta narodnykh komissarov RSFSR [...] 1934 g. 'O meropriiatiiakh po usileniiu bor'ba s tuberkulezom,'" [September 14, 1934], f. 482, op. 24, d. 176, ll. 14–17.

their work did rise in their wake. By 1938, many of the fundamental structural elements of the Civil War era plans of the TB Section of Narkomzdrav were enforced once again. Some of the "formal" TB departments in unified dispensaries, with no social assistance programs, were closed between 1935 and 1937.[82]

The number of TB dispensaries operating in the RSFSR increased steadily beginning in 1923.[83] At the conclusion of the First Five-Year Plan in 1932, however, the number of dispensaries in the RSFSR had dropped from 1928 by more than one-fifth, to just 226. After 1933, health authorities began to open new TB dispensaries once again. By 1941, the number of dispensaries in the Soviet Union had increased to 562. After the Second World War, the dispensary model of the 1920s remained at the center of anti-TB efforts in the Soviet Union and expanded with increasing financial support. By 1960, there were 1,377 Soviet dispensaries in operation, almost double the number in 1950. Many continue to operate into the post-Soviet era along with TB sanatoria and specialized hospitals.[84]

Conclusion: Why Is the Soviet TB System Still Valued?

The dispensary method was a powerful conceptual tool for doctors specializing in TB in the Soviet Union between 1922 and 1941. It provided a mechanism for interaction between state and society, mediated by a small group of experts, with the goal of reforming everyday life to cure and prevent the spread of a fatal disease. After the Second World War, the dispensary was the institutional embodiment of the idealistic goals of the founders of Soviet medicine; it broadly addressed the social and medical problems of the neediest members of society. The ideal function of Soviet

---

[82] N.E. Vvedenskaia et al., "20 let bor'by s tuberkulezom v SSSR," *Problemy tuberkuleza*, 1937, no. 11: 6–8.

[83] By 1926 this figure had grown to 206, 16 of which were in Moscow guberniia and 11 in the city of Moscow. E.G. Munblit, ed., *Tuberkulez i bor'ba s nim: Spravochnoe rukovodstvo dlia tuberkuleznykh uchrezhdenii, zdravotdelov, vrachei i rabotnikov po ozdorovleniiu truda i byta trudiashchikhsia* (Moscow: Izdatel'stvo Narkomzdrava R.S.F.S.R., 1926), 485, 490, 534, 541.

[84] *Desiat' let sovetskoi meditsiny: Diagrammy* (Moscow: Gosudarstvennoe meditsinskoe izdatel'stvo, [1928]), 17; V.L. Einis, *Tuberkulez: Klinika, profilaktika i lecheniia*, 2nd corr. and exp. ed. (Moscow: Gosudarstvennoe izdatel'stvo biologicheskoi i meditsinskoi literatury, 1937), 278; M.D. Kovrigina, ed., *Sorok let sovetskogo zdravookhraneniia* (Moscow: Gosudarstvennoe izdatel'stvo meditsinskoi literatury, 1957), 165; Narodnyi komissariat zdravookhraneniia RSFSR, *Statisticheskii obzor sostoianiia zdravookhraneniia i zabolevaemost' zaraznymi bolezniami v RSFSR za 1927 g*. (Moscow: Gosudarstvennoe meditsinskoe izdatel'stvo, 1931), 392; *Voprosy tuberkuleza* 5, no. 4 (1927): 87; *Bor'ba s tuberkulezom* 13, no. 6 (1935): 35; *Problemy tuberkuleza* 14, no. 3 (1936): 309; ibid. 15, no. 11 (1937): 6; ibid. 25, no. 5 (1947): 28; ibid. 80, no. 6 (2002): 4.

dispensaries continued largely unchanged throughout the Soviet era and beyond, as demonstrated by a review of 31 separate editions of Soviet and post-Soviet tuberculosis textbooks and handbooks for physicians spanning the seventy years from 1926 to 1996. The same structures and goals for the dispensary were also described in the Russian medical press after 1991.[85]

Atun and colleagues published a study of hospital use by pulmonary TB patients in the Samara region of Russia, studying records for 1999–2002 and finding that 8,427 patients were hospitalized in 14,823 TB-related stays. The average stay was 84 days. Over four years, the average patient had 1.8 stays and an average total of 145 days in the hospital. Unemployed and disabled adults were more likely to be hospitalized for TB and were likely to have longer average lengths of stay in hospitals.[86] A second study from Volgograd identified homelessness, status as a pensioner, and unemployment as strongly associated with death from the tuberculosis in 2000–02. Homelessness increased the risk of death from tuberculosis by 92 times over the general population.[87] These findings suggest that the elimination of TB control structures centered at dispensaries might leave homeless the poor or disabled TB patients who are now given increased access to hospital beds by dispensary health care workers. Russian TB dispensaries, hospitals, and sanatoria likely serve as shelters of last resort for a population of TB patients with no other resources. Atun and colleagues concluded that there was no close relationship between the medical and the social service sectors of state administration in Russia, and this led to an increased burden on the anti-TB infrastructure and the health care system.[88] However, this provision of an "extra-medical" social service fits well with the original goals of the TB dispensary as it was planned by the idealistic doctors in the All-Russian League in 1910 and reformulated by the doctors of Narkomzdrav in the 1920s. Unfortunately, the TB infrastructure is underfunded; it may no longer be receiving adequate funding

---

[85] For example, see E.S. Ivanova and N.M. Rudoi, "Zadachi protivotuberkuleznogo dispansera v sovremennykh usloviiakh," *Problemy tuberkuleza*, 1994, no. 2: 4–5; N.M. Rudoi, E.S. Ivanova, Iu.Ia. Fisher, et al., "Dispanserizatsiia grupp povyshennogo riska zabolevaniia tuberkulezom, ibid., 17–18; A.N. Grishko, "Mediko-sotsial'nye aspekty profilaktiki tuberkuleza v usloviiakh mnogomillionnogo goroda," ibid., 1994, no. 3: 13–16.

[86] R.A. Atun, Y.A. Samyshkin, F. Drobniewsi, S.I. Kuznetsov, I.M. Fedorin, and R.J. Coker, "Social Factors Influencing Hospital Utilisation by TB patients in the Russian Federation: Analysis of Routinely Collected Data," *International Journal of Tuberculosis and Lung Disease* 9 (2005): 1140–6.

[87] N.A. Frolova, "Mediko-sotsial'nye factory, vliaiushchie na smertnost' bol'nykh tuberkulezom," *Problemy tuberkuleza i boleznei legkikh*, 2004, no. 3: 10–13.

[88] Atun, et al., "Social Factors Influencing Hospital Utilisation."

to provide even proper nutritional support for its patients,[89] much less the expensive medications needed to treat MDR-TB.

It is likely that along with professional inertia and national pride, the mystique of the distinctly Soviet tuberculosis dispensary, with its original focus on universally available care, preventative goals, care for the poorest citizens, and its association with an era of greater prosperity for the medical system before 1991 all contribute to the nostalgia for the Soviet TB control system and the observed sustained resistance to change. That the dispensary system persists nearly unchanged in structure sixteen years after the fall of the Soviet Union also reflects the desperation of the poor at a time when many of the other safety nets of the social welfare system have become frayed. Unfortunately, the TB infrastructure now lacks the political support it enjoyed during the Soviet era.

[89] R.J. Coker, B. Dmitrova, F. Drobniewski, et al., "Health System Frailties in Tuberculosis Service Provision in Russia: An Analysis Through the Lens of Formal Nutritional Support," *Public Health* 119, no. 9 (2005): 837–43.

Continuities in Penal Russia:

Space and Gender in Post-Soviet Geography of Punishment

Judith Pallot

Mikhail Khordokovsky's dispatch in October 2005 to a penal colony in Chitinsk oblast—3,774 miles from Moscow—is a reminder that sending people to the peripheries is a deeply sedimented response to deviancy in Russia. To visit her husband, Inna Khordokovskaia has to undergo a six-hour flight, followed by a ten-hour train and car journey. She is fortunate in that she can afford the journey. For the majority of people with relatives serving custodial sentences, the remote extra-urban locations of Russia's penal colonies mean that visits are prohibitively expensive, time consuming, and physically challenging. Research in the West has shown that the maintenance of contacts with family and friends is an important factor in the successful rehabilitation of offenders, and for this reason, but with varying degrees of success, Western penal systems attempt to place prisoners close to their homes. Post-Soviet Russia has declared itself to have a similar aim, but it is hampered by a physical infrastructure of prisons inherited from the Soviet era and a penal culture that continues to select peripheral locations as sites of punishment.

In a previous article I have written about the Soviet Union's distinctive penal geography that was forged during the post-Stalin rationalization of the GULag.[1] It consisted of a discontinuous arc of colonies stretching from the north of Arkhangelsk oblast in the European north through the Komi republic, Kirov oblast, and Mordovia, into the northern Urals and further on to northern Kazakhstan and western and eastern Siberia. In this heartland, places (sometimes covering large territories that embraced one or more rural districts) emerged that were characterised by a particularly close integration of penal and civilian economy and society, where the prison service as the principal employer took responsibility for maintaining social and physical infrastructure and for the production of services for the civilian population.[2] Second and third generation officers and guards together with prisoners who

---

[1] Judith Pallot, "Russia's Penal Peripheries: Space, Place and Penalty in Soviet and Post-Soviet Russia," *Transactions of the Institute of British Geographers* 30, issue 1 (March 2005): 98–112.

[2] See, for example, the description of the forging of such a penal region in the North of Perm oblast in Judith Pallot, "Forced Labor for Forestry: The Twentieth Century History of Colonization and Settlement in the North of Perm' oblast'," *Europe-Asia Studies* 54, no. 7 (2002): 1055–83.

stayed on after release swelled the population of these regions, which were largely confined to the peripheries of oblasts. Under the command administrative system, peripherally located penal regions may have had an economic rationale, but this has dissolved since 1991, when high transport costs and the loss of orders for the products of penal labor have meant that many colonies can no longer cover their costs, with negative consequences for prisoner welfare. The current problems are exacerbated by the strict sentencing practices of the courts, which have kept the prison population consistently above the three-quarter of a million mark and limited the scope the federal penal service has for restructuring its network of colonies to bring prisoners closer to their home areas.[3] As in the Soviet period, therefore, there is an enormous gap between oblasts in the number of penal colonies they host and rates of incarceration. The Komi republic heads the list with approximately 1,620 prisoners per 100,000 population. This is eight times the number in Moscow city and Moscow oblast, both of which have about 200 prisoners per 100,000 population. Among the top ten regions both in terms of the relative and absolute numbers of prisoners are the traditional oblasts and republics of the penal heartland: Mordovia, Arkhangelsk, Perm, Sverdlovsk, and Irkutsk oblasts and Krasnoiarsk krai.[4] Together with Komi, these six regions have 228 of all the Russian Federation's 760 correctional colonies, 30 percent of the total. Moscow city and oblast, meanwhile, have just five correctional colonies for adults and two juvenile colonies, despite having sixteen pre-trial facilities. This distribution of penal facilities is testimony to the continued existence in Russia of "donor" and "recipient" regions for prisoners and of the practice of displacing deviancy to the peripheries.

There were 55,400 women in penal colonies or in pre-trial facilities in Russia in April 2006. They constitute a small minority of the prison population, although at 6.5 percent of the total, their share has increased from the 1989 figure of 4.6 percent.[5] Women's experience of the penal system goes beyond their role as prisoners,

[3] With 532 prisoners per 100,000 population, Russia is second only to the United States in terms of its rate of imprisonment. The United States has 714/100,000; England and Wales, 142/100,000; and Canada, 116/100,000. The Russian figures do not include military prisons, which would increase the Russian rate since prisoners held in Ministry of Justice administered colonies account for around only 90 percent of the total prison population. Roy Walmsley, ed., *World Prison Population List*, 6th ed. (London: King's College, International Centre for Prison Studies, 2005).

[4] The Federal Prison Service does not publish a regional breakdown of prisoners. Estimates of the regionally differentiated population have been calculated for the end of the 1990s by the Moscow Center for Penal Reform (*Tsentr sodeistviia reforme ugolovnogo pravosudiia*), http://www.prison.org/facts/human_4.htm (accessed March 31, 2003).

[5] Roy Walmsley, ed., *World Female Imprisonment List* (London: King's College, Interna-

however, as vast numbers are drawn into it by virtue of their relationship with the vast population of male prisoners. The pre-revolutionary tradition of family members making the trek to the peripheries to be reunited with their husbands, sons, and brothers, captured in the phrase "*gde muzh, tam zhena*" (where the husband is, so is the wife), has survived into the twenty-first century, albeit in modified form. Compared with their forebears, travellers in penal Russia today have the advantage of modern transportation, so that instead of taking weeks or months, journeys to prisons can be completed in under a week or, for the fortunate, in a day. As in the past, the journey to visit their incarcerated relatives is both an act of reaffirmation of familial or friendship ties and a means of improving the quality of life of prisoners, who, especially in the most remote regions, can suffer from material deprivations, including shortages of food, associated with the crisis in the penal economy since 1991. The women queuing up to hand in their parcels at the reception center (*priemnyi punkt*) of the pre-trial prison in *Zona* (the Zone), the controversial soap opera on Russian television in 2005, belong to Russia's vast population of "quasi-prisoners," people who, while not prisoners themselves, have their lives shaped by the penal system.[6] In what follows, I explore the myriad ways in which the continued use of peripheral regions as "sites of punishment" impacts upon Russian women.

Women Prisoners in Contemporary Russia

Feminist scholarship in the West has found that penal systems are not gender neutral, but that legal practices, sentencing, and imprisonment forms discriminate against women and reproduce gender stereotypes.[7] The Russian penal system is similarly gender-biased. Reforms in the penal correction code introduced in the early 1990s that aimed to bring Russian practice in line with international minimum standards included provisions that reflected women's "special needs."[8] Women, for example,

tional Centre for Prison Studies, 2006), 5.

[6] I am using the concept of quasi-prisoner in the same way as Megan Comfort who describes how relatives of detainees in California are forced to submit to the disciplinary control of the penal system, including over the choices they can make about how to spend their weekends to what they wear and what they eat when they make prison visits. Megan L. Comfort, "Still Booming: Prisons in California," *Footnotes*, December 2003, 1–3.

[7] For example, Mary Bosworth, *Engendering Resistance: Agency and Power in Women's Prisons* (Aldershot, UK: Ashgate, 1999).

[8] For a general discussion of the reforms, see Roy D. King, "Russian Prisons after Perestroika: The End of the Gulag?" *British Journal of Criminology* 34, no. 1 (1994): 62–81; Alexander S. Mikhlin and Roy D. King, "The Russian Prison System: Past, Present and Future," in *Prisons 2000: An International Perspective on the Current State and Future of Imprisonment*, ed. Roger Matthews and Peter Francis (Houndsmills, UK: Macmillan, 1998), 219–39.

are exempt from the death penalty and benefit from special provisions in the penal correction code relating to their role as mothers. Today, courts are able to give suspended sentences to pregnant women and to women with young children found guilty of crimes carrying a sentence of less than five years. Women with custodial sentences can apply to take their children with them to the penal colony up to the age of three, and such women are entitled to superior rations, can keep half their earnings they make in the prison workshops, and cannot be placed in punishment cells or subjected to "enhanced severity" punishment regimes. These concessions can come at a price. According to Liudmila Al'pern of the Moscow Center for Prison Reform, attitudes of rank-and-file prison officers can be patronising, from accusations that women get pregnant in prison in order to win themselves a lighter regime to the insistence that prison nurses are better able to "give the children a childhood" than their biological mothers. In all but one of the eleven colonies with kindergartens that Al'pern surveyed, women's contact with their children is limited, often no more than an hour a day, and the number of women granted leave to enable them to settle their children in children's homes or with relatives is very small.[9] Al'pern argues that women find themselves in the disciplinary and isolation cells more often than men and for more trivial offences against internal discipline. She attributes this to society's intolerant attitude towards women's crimes, especially when they involve violence that "contradicts their nature" and, therefore, needs immediate correction. Whereas disciplinary cells in men's penal colonies are reserved for the most serious infractions, women are put in disciplinary cells for offences as trivial as smoking in the wrong place or swearing, and for homosexual relationships.[10] The organisation in some women's colonies of beauty contests and fashion displays in the past decade can be understood as an attempt on the part of penal authorities to "feminize" women's experience of a penal system that, otherwise, is characterised by military-style regimentation, collectivism, and the absence of private space. These efforts also underline how gendered are attitudes to women prisoners.[11]

If, albeit in ways that reinforce gender stereotypes, the Russian penal service

---

A different, and more pessimistic, view of post-Soviet changes is given in Laura Piacentini, *Surviving Russian Prisons: Punishment, Economy and Politics in Transition* (Cullompton: Willan, 2004).

[9] Liudmila Al'pern, *Zhenshchiny v rossiiskoi tiur'me. Problemy, svidel'stva vzgliad iznutri. Sbornik materialov* (Moscow: Tsentr sodeistviia reforme ugolovnogo pravosudiia, 2001), 63–9.

[10] Liudmila Al'pern, *Son i iav' zhenskoi tiurmy* (St. Petersburg: Aleteiia, 2004), 27.

[11] For a description of such a beauty contest in the women's colony near Novosibirsk see M. Yatskova, "Crime and Beauty," *Marie Claire*, September 2006, 135–40.

is making some concessions to women, little has been done to ameliorate the impact on them of Russia's penal geography. Table 1 shows the regional distribution of pre-trial adult and juvenile women's penal colonies in the Russian Federation at the end of 2006. The table groups colonies by federal district and within these the location in relation to the regional capital and the type of colony (pre-trial, correctional, and juvenile) is given. The Central Federal Region, which contains 26 percent of Russia's total population, has just one correctional colony for women (this is the large women's colony at Mozhaisk in Moscow oblast), one pre-trial prison for women located in the capital city itself, and two of the country's three juvenile colonies for women. By contrast, 65.9 percent of all women's colonies are located in the Volga and Urals Federal Districts, which have just 43.5 percent of Russia's population. Colonies are further concentrated within this broad region; the Mordovian and Chuvash republics and Perm, Sverdlovsk, and Cheliabinsk oblasts together have one quarter of the country's 40 women's correctional colonies. Mordovia has a strong association for Muscovites as a place of women's imprisonment because many women sentenced in the capital are sent to IK-2 and IK-14 in Iavas. During the Soviet era, Mordovia was in the "middle rank" of regions for the size of its GULag population. In the 1930s, around 4,300 women were held together with men in Temlag and Dubravlag, but they were subsequently moved to other camps. In 1953, there were only 47 women in Mordovia's camps. Women were brought back to Mordovia later in the Soviet period, and today they probably count for between 15 and 20 percent of all prisoners in the republic.[12]

In broad outline, the geographical distribution of women's penal colonies imitates that for men, except for their absence in the extreme north. Their concentration in Russia's penal heartland together with their overall small number means that women face a higher probability than men of being sent "out of oblast" to serve their sentences. This is confirmed by a 1999 census of prisoners conducted by the penal service, the result of which are summarised in Table 2.[13] As the table shows, whereas

[12] The numbers of women in particular camps varied over time—at the end of the GULag there were particular complexes and regions where the numbers of women prisoners were particularly significant (that is, between 2,000 and 10,000). These included Tavda, Novosibirsk, Vorkuta, Karpinsky, Nizhni Tagil, Nyrob, and Karaganda. In 1953, the largest concentrations of women prisoners were in Sverdlovsk, Vologda, Viatka, Krasnoiarsk, Omsk, Magadan, Perm, Irkutsk, and Saratov. *Sistema ispravitel'no-trudovykh lagerei v SSSR* (Moscow: Zven'ia, 1998).

[13] The census was conducted by the Federal Prison Service and funded by the Ford Foundation. It consists of two volumes, the first on pre-trial prisoners and the second on convicted prisoners. Unfortunately, the census has not been repeated. *Kharakteristika osuzhdennykh k lisheniiu svobody. Po materialam spetsial'noi perepisi 1999 g.*, vols. 1 and 2 (Moscow: Iurisprudentsiia, 2001).

Table 1:

The Distribution of Women's Penal Institutions in the Russian Federation

(PC= penal colony; JC = juvenile colony; PreC = pre-trial prison)

Federal region	Oblast, krai or republic in which colony located	Type of institution	Distance from regional capital (in kms)	Number of prisoners
Central Percentage of total Russian population = 26.2%	Moscow	PC	89	1100
	Moscow city	PreC	-	n/d
	Belgorod	JC	30	400
	Riazan	JC	91	300
Volga Percentage of total Russian population = 21.5 %	Kirov	PC	148	n/d
	Mordovia	PC	160	820
		PC		700
		PC		n/d
	Nizhegorod	PC	-	1350
	Perm	PC	73	300
		PC	168	1700
		PC	-	n/d
		PC	-	n/d
	Samara	PC	-	850
		PC	28	380
	Saratov	PC	110	n/d
	Udmurtia	PC	55	350
	Chuvashia	PC	149	1100
		PC	73	1500
		PC	31	1200
Southern Percentage total Russian population = 15.8%	Adigeia	PC	-	50
	Dagestan	PC	56	250
	Kabardino-Balkaria	PC	46	400
	Krasnodar krai	PC	59	1600
	Rostov	PC	28	60
	Stavropol krai	PC	169	1150

North Western Percentage total Russian population = 9.6%	Vologda	PC	-	700
	Kaliningrad	PC RC	29 29	600 15
	Komi	PC	-	n/d
	Leningrad	PC	53	-
	St. Petersburg	PreC	-	-
Urals Percentage total Russian population = 8.5%	Kurgan	PC	-	n/d
	Sverdlovsk	PC RC	130 -	n/d 1100
	Tiumen	PC	193	300
	Cheliabinsk	PC PC	- 23	1000 1500
Siberian Percentage total Russian population = 13.8%	Ust-Ordynsky-Buratia	PC	n/d	n/d
	Kemerovo	PC	143	1260
	Krasnoiar krai	PC PC	- 221	1200 n/d
	Novosibirsk	PC	20	1240
	Tomsk	JC	-	300
	Khakasia	PC	25	500
Far Eastern Percentage total Russian population = 26.2%	Kamchatka	PC	188	n/d
	Primorsk krai	PC	?	1500
	Khabarovsk	PC	?	n/d

Sources: *Arestant*: Informatsionno-analiticheskii proekt (http://www.arestant.msk.ru); Population data for 2002 available online from Eastview Information Services at http://www.eastview.com.

Table 2.

The Distribution of Prisoners in Relation to their Oblast of Origin, 1999

		Place of Incarceration				
As a percentage of the total prison population:		**Prisoners of no fixed abode**	**In settlement where prisoner registered**	**In region where prisoner resident (but not in settlement)**	**In region other than that in which prisoner sentenced**	**In region other than that in which prisoner resident or sentenced**
All prisoners in census years	1989	8.9	8.3	41.5	8.1	33.2
	1999	1.8	17.0	66.8	2.2	12.2
Men's penal colonies by regime:	general	1.9	18.0	68.8	2.3	9.0
	strict	4.8	13.3	67.5	2.2	12.2
	Special	4.9	4.9	33.0	3.2	54.0
	For life prisoners	4.7	8.8	23.4	2.1	61.0
	Total	3.3	15.4	66.2	2.3	12.8
Women's penal colonies by regime:	general	3.4	11.0	38.8	2.2	44.6
	strict	5.0	20.0	21.4	27.2	26.4
	Total	3.5	11.5	37.9	3.5	43.6
Juvenile colonies		0.7	15.3	67.7	1.3	15.0
Penal settlements		1.8	7.0	47.9	1.9	41.4
Cellular prisons		4.1	8.2	23.4	3.0	61.3

Source: *Kharakteristika osuzhdennykh k lisheniiu svobody. Po materialam spetsial'noi perepisi 1999 g.*, vol. 2 (Moscow: Iurisprudentsiia, 2001), 56

12.2 percent of all prisoners were held outside the republic, oblast or krai in which they were normally domiciled or sentenced, for women prisoners the figure was 43.6 percent. This figure was exceeded only for men convicted of the most serious crimes held in prisons with single cell rather than dormitory accommodation or "special regime" colonies. Also above average were penal settlements (*kolonii poseleniia*). These are supposed to be the least severe type of penal institution, reserved for people convicted of relatively minor or "accidental" offences, first offenders on short sentences, and prisoners nearing the end of their sentences, but they are among the most remote of Russia's penal institutions, many having being remodelled out of the *spetsposeleniia* to which kulaks and ethnic minorities were deported during the 1930s and 1940s. Women held in penal settlements are generally transferees from "general regime" colonies who have served most of a sentence for a serious crime. The improvement for all categories of prisoner in 1999 compared with 1989 was achieved largely as a result of more careful planning of prisoner placement at the center and by mixing regime types in existing colonies. In the case of women prisoners, the two "strict regime" colonies to which serious offenders were sent in the past have been recategorized to "general regime." This has reduced the average distance women are taken to serve their sentences but at the expense of women who have committed less serious offences being held with serious offenders and recidivists. Any further reduction in the distances women and men are sent to serve their sentences would require the state to embark on an ambitious rebuilding programme, which is not currently on the cards.

One measure of the differential impact of the distribution of penal colonies on men and women prisoners is the length of time it takes for them to be transferred to their final destination once sentence has been passed. In the penal correction code, the target time for transportation is ten days, but as Table 3 shows, it takes longer in the case of one-third of all women prisoners and 20 percent of men. Prison transports run to set timetables and long distance transfers are punctuated by periods when prisoners are kept in transit colonies while arrangements are made for onward transit. The journey from Moscow to Berezniki women's colony in the north of Perm oblast, for example, involves two or three transit points and can take anything from two weeks to two months. The last leg of transfer in the case of some men prisoners in the north is by helicopter. Even transfers over relatively small distances between oblasts in the European Center can take a long time, while vacancies become available in receiving institutions.

Table 3.

The Average Length of Time Taken in Transporting Women and Men Prisoners, 1999

Length of journey time to colony (in days)		**Under 10 days**	**10 days to one month**	**Over one month**	**Total**
Men's penal colonies by regime:	General	81.4	10.0	8.6	100.0
	Strict	81.0	9.9	9.1	100.0
	Special	49.5	30.1	20.4	100.0
	For "lifers"	14.7	25.5	59.8	100.0
	Total	79.3	10.8	9.9	100.0
Women's penal colonies by regime:	General	67.2	21.9	10.9	100.0
	Strict	46.1	30.9	23.0	100.0
	Total	66.0	22.4	11.6	100.0
Juvenile colonies		74.6	15.0	10.4	100.0
Penal settlements		53.8	21.5	24.4	100.0
Cellular prisons		37.5	34.2	28.3	100.0
All convicts		77.2	12.2	10.6	100.0

Source: *Kharakteristika osuzhdennykh k lisheniiu svobody. Po materialam spetsial'noi perepisi 1999 g.*, vol. 2 (Moscow: Iurisprudentsiia, 2001), 16

The penal service still uses Stolypin carriages[14] to transfer prisoners and conditions during transit are poor: food can be in short supply and cells on the transports and in the transit colonies are usually overcrowded and unhygienic, the mixing of sick and healthy prisoners serves to spread TB and other infectious diseases. Women are separated from men in the transit cars, but only by the bars of the cages in which they are held. When they set out on their journeys, prisoners do not always know their precise destination and they are denied contact with relatives and friends during transit. The destination colony is not required to inform relatives of a prisoner's arrival for another ten days. The *etap* is an integral and degrading element of women prisoners' experience of Russia's penal geography reinforcing their isolation and distorting their sense of distance.[15]

Making Prison Visits in Twenty-First Century Russia

Since the end of the Soviet period, the Russian state has greatly extended the rights of prisoners with respect to the contacts they can have with the outside world.[16] Prisoners are now entitled to unlimited correspondence by post and to 15-minute telephone conversations, they can receive and "bank" money from relatives and send any money earned in the colony home, and they can receive a limited number of parcels and small packages. Additionally, prisoners have the right to a limited number of visits, which can be short (up to four hours) or extended (lasting up to three days, with provision in special circumstance of this to be increased to five). Prisoners in penal settlements can apply to live outside the colony in rented accommodation with their spouse. Prisoners can request compassionate leave and, as already observed, women can be granted a two-week exeat to settle their children with relatives or in a children's home. These are important advances in the human rights of Russian prisoners, but unfortunately, their full impact is often negated by the location and distance of penal colonies. The communication costs, whether for personal travel or parcel delivery, and technical deficits in the communications network conspire to make contact with the outside world difficult, especially when prisoners are held in remote places.

Some sense of the difficulty can be obtained from postings on *Arestant*, a

[14] Prison railway carriages of the Tsarist era.

[15] There are first hand description of prison transports in Liudmila Al'pern, *Vsego lish' desiataia chast'. Zhenshchiny i deti v rossiiskoi tiur'me. Zametki posetitelia tiurem* (Moscow: Tsentr sodeistviia reforme ugolovnogo pravosudiia, 2001) and A.G. Borisov, E.A. Gordeeva and I.M. Dziadko, eds., *Ostorozhno, tiur'ma …* (Moscow: Tsentr sodeistviia reforme ugolovnogo pravosudiia, 2005).

[16] O.G. Perminov, *Ugolovno-ispolnitel'noe pravo* (Moscow: Iurisprudentsiia, 1999): 130–1.

remarkable self-help Internet site established to support prisoners and their families in 2001.[17] I have drawn narratives about prison visits from this website posted by people, mainly women, recently returned from visits to their relatives in penal institutions all over Russia. The postings provide a unique source of factual information about penal institutions in Russia, including where they are situated, how to get to them, and their visiting rules. The *Arestant* website confines itself to practical advice for visitors—comments on the conditions in which prisoners are held in different colonies are discouraged—but nevertheless it gives a unique insight into the experiences of the many women who make visits to prisoners and in so doing continues a long standing tradition in Russia of labor camp testimony. The testimonies are in the public domain so, necessarily, their authors disguise their identities by using their first names only, initials, or pseudonyms. The choice of the latter—for example: "a Decembrist's wife," "Floggin," "A Rambler," "Tribune," and "I won't forget"—provide insights into the authors' understanding of their own situation and sense of history. Entries are organised for each region under colony number and type and the date of the posting. The majority of users of the *Arestant* site are Muscovites and, necessarily, they have to have access to a computer. This means that the results from the site are skewed towards the better off and computer literate, and geographically to those regions where Muscovites are held, that is, in European Russia, the Urals, and western Siberia.

Women travellers in penal Russia have to be physically and psychologically strong, as Tatiana's journey to visit her common-law husband in the penal settlement in Iangory, Arkhangelsk oblast, illustrates. She describes the last section of her journey, which began in Moscow:

> To get there is complicated, actually unrealistic. First, you have to take the train to Pelsetskaia station and then catch a bus … to the settlement of Severoonezhsk … Arriving there you have to find your way to the main administration and get a pass for the "train" to the regime zone … If everything goes well [with the documentation] you are given a pass and you can go to the station to await the "train" to the colonies. The station is a small room without glass in the windows, no heating, and one bench … The train is supposed to set off at 8:40 pm, but sometimes it doesn't come in until 9:30 or 10:00 pm. It's best to arrive a bit early so you can get a seat. I've put "train" in quotation marks because this isn't really a train at all—it's a single wagon … a Stolypin of the old design, but with the internal cages removed. Moreover, the track isn't the ordinary sort—it's narrow gauge, so that you feel like you are on an American roller coaster. Sometimes, the train comes off its tracks … [and] simply comes

[17] *Arestant Koloniia RF*, http://www.arestant.msk.ru.

> to a stop in the grass … Prison guards travel with the driver; they check your passport and ask where you are going and whom you are visiting … they didn't always ask for my documents, but this is probably because I went there three times in four months and everyone remembered me … The journey takes 4-5 hours and sometimes the "train" also pulls wagons with felled timber and provisions … so it can sometimes arrive at 1 or even 4 or 5 o'clock in the morning. A vehicle waits at the destination … it takes you to the visiting room in the colony … very few people go there for visits; mainly mothers and sometimes a wife. When I went there, the whole zone was in shock; they said that it was the first time a young woman had visited … The convicts in Iangory need everything: warm clothes (it's cold even in the summer), blankets, medicines, kettles, utensils, and, in the summer, anti-mosquito cream—there are so many flying insects there that it's impossible to see more than 3 meters in front of your face. On maps this place is shown as uninhabited.[18]

Tatiana's "heroic" journey to the regime zone is not exceptional for people visiting more distant colonies; the *Arestant* website is full of similar stories. Maria, who visited her husband in Krasnyi Bereg in the penal region north of Solikamsk in Perm oblast, for example, has good advice for other women undertaking a similar journey:

> How to get there? From Perm to Solikamsk there is a bus every hour. It leaves at 11.30 am—don't be late. It costs 167 rubles one way. You arrive at four o'clock in the afternoon in Solikamsk … and here in the square you will see a PAZ [commercial bus] waiting. It usually goes at 4:30 pm … the ticket to Krasnyi Bereg costs 65 rubles … The length of time the journey takes depends on the weather and the state of the road. In the winter when there is a blizzard … the bus can get stuck, but there are all-weather timber trucks on the road that you can hitch a lift with. The locals … are very friendly and curious … but they always will guess who you are, because you have large bags and look lost. They are afraid to have dealings with the "prisoner's relative" and this makes them withhold their normal hospitality. They won't offer you a bed for the night … but they will tell you how to get to Auntie Anya's place: she puts you up for a symbolic price … only take your own bed linen because she is so poor she doesn't have any … Getting home is more of a problem. You have to make sure you get back to Solikamsk by 8:00 pm. It's best to stay the night at Auntie Anya's—she will wake you up at 6:30 am to get the bus. The alternative is on the day of your meeting to try to hail a passing timber truck.[19]

[18] Arkhangelsk, KP-27, Tatiana, November 4, 2004, http://www.arestant.msk.ru/guin-arhang-det.html.

[19] Perm, IK-5, Maria, January 25, 2005, http://www.arestant.msk.ru/guin-perm-det.html.

The journey to less remote colonies is not always easy because many have extra-urban locations, as Maria visiting one of the colonies outside Berezniki, also in Perm oblast, describes:

> The bus from Perm is comfortable with TV and video and costs 150 rubles one way. It takes about three to three and one-quarter hours. The bus stops on the way at the settlement of Chelva, where you will find aunties from the village selling the most delicious pies that cost 10 rubles each. They are very tasty with potatoes. Don't worry about the money—buy one for your *zek*.[20] In order not to miss your stop, after about two hours ask the driver to drop you at the turning for zone 38. And now the difficult bit begins—you've got about five miles to walk (an asphalt road with no pavement) … If you thumb a lift they will put up the price because they know you are the relative of a prisoner. Lots of military vehicles go past but they never pick you up—they are not allowed to mix with prisoners' families.[21]

As these narratives show, during the journey to the penal colonies women are reminded of their "quasi-prisoner" status and vulnerability because of this. The contributors to the *Arestant* website continually remind other women to conceal their identity during the journeys to the colonies. In setting out for the first time, women are travellers in unfamiliar territory which the Russian penal service leaves them to navigate alone.

One hazard which women have to contend with is the possibility that, after the long journey to a colony, a visit will be denied. Remarkably few women appear to apply in advance for the visit, but even those that do can find that circumstances have changed by the time they arrive: "their" prisoner, for example, may have been placed in the punishment cell or transferred to a different colony or to hospital, and every colony seems to have its own rules governing meetings with common-law partners and non-relatives. *Arestant* contributors warn against making complaints. Maria, whom we have already met describing her visit to her husband in Krasnyi Bereg includes the following advice: "Don't be concerned when the guards are polite to you, especially if you have experience of rudeness in other colonies. They will smile at you and ask how the journey was and whether you have any complaints. Don't complain—remember that your loved one will be blamed for telling tales and as soon as you leave will be punished … in Krasnii Bereg they are masters at punishment … (sorry for the emotion)."[22]

---

[20] Slang for prisoner in the GULag from *zakliuchennyi*, or incarcerated.

[21] Perm, IK-38 Maria, January 28, 2005, webpage n/a.

[22] Perm, IK-5, Maria, January 25, 2005, http://www.arestant.msk.ru/guin-perm-det.html.

In order to respond to the center's new commitment to support contacts between prisoners and their families, some penal colonies have built "hotels" within the compound, which allow the prisoners to spend time with their families. These hotels are also a source of much needed income for cash-strapped colonies. Rooms can be rented for the visits and, depending upon the rules of the particular colony, the prisoner spends all or a portion of the time with his or her family. The rates charged for the rooms, the range of facilities provided, what products can be brought in for the duration of the visits, and the frequency and type of searches made are subject to large variation. Room charges for 24 hours, for example, range from 100 to 750 rubles, the latter would be for what the users of *Arestant* describe as a "luxury" room in a more centrally-located colony. Olya, whose partner is in a colony in Rostov oblast, gives general advice to women embarking upon their first extended visit to a colony:

> Dear girls, don't take too much with you. Take bed linen, a towel, all the hygiene items needed for two people so that your husband doesn't have to bring these from the zone ... take his favorite bright clothes, especially if in the zone they make them wear a uniform. Don't go to a meeting with any gold jewellery, with bottles of perfume—these will be confiscated. Take a notebook and pencil—they'll be useful. Any money in excess of what you need to pay for the room will be taken off you at the entrance (you get it back when you leave). In some colonies, they allow you to take a photograph with your husband as a keepsake ... usually the hotel in the colony [consists of] ... small rooms each with a bed, table, a pair of stools, a shared kitchen and bathroom, and sometimes a communal fridge. The cleanliness and comfort of the hotel depends upon the colony boss. I know that in Rostov the conditions in IK-2 and 5 are very good ... Naturally, take fresh and tasty food. Bear in mind that you can cook. In the kitchen there are usually saucepans, plates, spoons, forks, and cups. I advise you to move like a bullet and grab the best utensils as soon as you arrive. A special deficit is forks—only made of aluminium. Also remember that you will be searched ... they can look through your provisions. Generally they open all boxes, Pepsi-Cola bottles, and packets ... take with you your favorite videocassettes—there may be a player or a TV in the common room ... I advise you all to prepare everything at home so you don't waste time cooking. Always there is a crowd of mothers and sisters in the kitchen chatting half the day ... the wives tend to spend more time in the rooms with their husbands. But that's to be expected.[23]

[23] Rostov, IK-5, Olya, 2005, http://www.arestant.msk.ru/guin-rostov-det.html.

Judging from other descriptions of visits, there are colonies where the administration has made considerable efforts to provide a pleasing environment for extended visits, but these may be the exception. *Arestant* contains numerous complaints about overpricing for the facilities; the women's acceptance of the conditions in return for being able to see their "loved ones" underlines the inequality in their relationship with the colony. Olesiya, returned from the first visit to her husband in a colony in Riazan oblast in October 2005, writes,

> I went to see my darling husband … [in the colony hotel] there is a shared kitchen, two hot plates, utensils, but mice running around like horses. But I didn't meet any cockroaches. In the room there were two beds, one in which we slept. It was terribly cold. The central heating didn't work and there were only two blankets. We slept in our tracksuits. The mice kept me awake all night—but my husband was used to them. The shower was communal and it ran permanently with tepid Riazan water. But this is all trivial compared with the fact that I was able to see him!!! Even in such a godforsaken place, I was in heaven to be with him. My husband had lost weight terribly … we reminisced about our life together, and I showed him photos of our son … When the visit was over, they returned my valuables to me and body-searched my husband.[24]

Similarly, Maria, writing about the extended visit she was permitted after she had married her husband in a colony in Voronezh oblast, did not begrudge the 600 rubles:

> In the room there was a double bed that dated from the time of the NKVD—it was all lumpy and hard, a small table … washbowl, a cupboard with its doors off. Later because it was so cold and because [having just got married] we were privileged guests, we were given a small heater. The toilet, shower, and kitchen were clean enough … There was a children's room, but it was locked, and a common room with TV and ashtrays made of the lids of coffee jars … in the kitchen were utensils for general use. In general, I was happy with what I found … The guards only came once a day to escort prisoners and visitors. The hotel supervisor saw that I was frying potatoes and mushrooms and asked if she could have little—I gave her some. She was starving poor thing … they came for my dear one at one o'clock and he took with him all the bed linen I had brought, the utensils, soaps, books, photographs, manicure scissors, coffee, tea, meat paste, apples, silver ring … After the meeting I understood that our feelings had become stronger than before and that no material problems could

[24] Riazan, IK-1, Olesiya, October 18, 2005, http://www.arestant.msk.ru/guin-ryazan-det.html.

detract from my happiness. This was the first extended visit in four years. He has only 2 1/5 years to go.[25]

One month later, Maria was back on the web reporting that her new husband had contracted TB and was transferred to a prison hospital.[26] Olga also has a husband in a colony in Voronezh oblast, but is less compromising about the 2,000 rubles for a three-day visit she had to pay for herself and her son, twice what she would have to pay in an ordinary hotel in the town. She writes, "The cold in the room is just unbearable; you have to go to bed fully clothed and … you are not allowed a heater. What it's like in the zone itself, I can't imagine—my husband doesn't say much about it. Probably it's a scandal like everywhere elsewhere."[27]

The physical difficulties and costs involved in maintaining contact with prisoners is the context within which the figures shown in Table 4 have to be interpreted. The table shows that whereas more than half of male and female prisoners received parcels in 1999, the frequency of visits and telephone conversations is much lower, with over 70 percent of all women prisoners and 50-61 percent of men reporting that they received no visitors and 85 percent that they had had no telephone contact with anyone. These figures suggest that for prisoners for whom there is an interested relative on the outside, the location of colonies may be an obstacle to realising their right to be visited. The estimated costs of extended visits to out-of-region colonies can run into several thousands of rubles once all the associated expenditures—train, bus, and taxi fares, hotel accommodation, and provisions—are included. Likusha calculated that the round trip from Moscow to a penal colony in Dagestan involving three nights in a colony hotel cost her 15,000 rubles[28] at a time when the average monthly wage in Russia was 3,360 rubles.[29]

The provision in the penal correction code for relatives of certain categories of prisoner held in penal settlements to cohabit with their partners is rarely taken up. In remote regions, where there is plenty of cheap accommodation, there are no jobs to be had, while in more central locations rents can be prohibitively high. In Oktiabrasky in Riazan oblast, for example, the rent for a "decent two-bedroom

---

[25] Voronezh, IK-2, Maria, October 16, 2005, webpage n/a.

[26] This link has since disappeared from the website (ed.).

[27] Voronezh, IK-9, Olga, December 15, 2004, http://www.arestant.msk.ru/guin-voroneg-det .html.

[28] Dagestan IK-7, Likusha, October 14, 2005, http://www.arestant.msk.ru/guin-dagestan-det .html.

[29] According to Levada Center figures. See *Izvestiia*, April 25, 2006, 2.

Table 4.

Frequency and Types of Contacts Maintained by Prisoners in Colonies, 1999

Type of social contact	Frequency of contact	Female average	Male average
Receipt of parcels	Maximum number	16.5	28.7
	Fewer than maximum	39.8	40.9
	None	43.7	30.4
Long visits	Maximum number	6.8	17.0
	Fewer than maximum	14.0	21.9
	None	79.2	61.1
Short visits	Maximum number	9.2	21.1
	Fewer than maximum	19.7	29.5
	None	71.1	49.4
Telephone conversations	One-more than five	14.9	15.5
	None - for technical reasons	17.5	36.2
	None - lack of money	7.9	1.7
	None - nobody to speak to	7.9	3.8
	None - no desire	52.0	56.3

Source: *Kharakteristika osuzhdennykh k lisheniiu svobody. Po materialam spetsial'noi perepisi 1999 g.*, vol. 2 (Moscow: Iurisprudentsiia, 2001), 6, 63, 67

apartment" is 1,500 rubles per month, beyond the purse of most.[30] In the case of telephone conversations, distance makes itself felt in the absence, or low density, of land lines. Some prison governors are reluctant to install telephones because of expense and staff shortages. Where there are telephones, arranging for calls can be complicated and involve the prisoner telegraphing ahead and enduring hours waiting for lines to become free. Ira describes some of the frustrations in attempting to talk by phone with her partner in Kotlas: "I have managed to speak with my husband by phone (we're allowed four calls a year). This is humiliatingly little. They listen to the conversations on a parallel receiver so, as a result, absolutely nothing can be heard. You have to ask the same question a hundred times and instead of the fifteen minutes, they generally cut you off after ten. These phone calls are only for people with nerves of steel."[31]

One important area over which a colony's governor evidently exercises discretion is whether to allow conjugal visits with common-law wives, and on what terms. Partners seeking a conjugal visit normally have to provide evidence that the relationship is serious, which can be in the form of a certification from the district housing authority, militia, or neighbours that the couple has been cohabiting for two years or a birth certificate where there are children. Common-law wives may be required to provide colonies with medical certificates showing that they are free of TB, AIDS, and sexually transmitted diseases. Correctional colony IK-2 in Voronezh is among those doing its bit for Russia's marriage statistics by requiring common-law partners to marry if they wish to have an extended visit: "Partners are allowed a single conjugal visit, but they have to marry before another one is allowed. I got married to my husband in the colony … I had to pay for the notary to come … I collected her from the Palace of Weddings in town … the ceremony took five minutes and we were allowed a conjugal visit straight afterwards."[32] In contrast, a penal settlement also in Voronezh was not permitting any visits, either short or extended, with common law partners and other non-relatives in 2005.[33]

Statistics on the rate of marriage and divorce among prisoners are not encouraging, given the new found desire to support the family. According to the 1999 census, 31.5 percent of married men divorced while in prison, with 47.7 percent as the equivalent figure for women. The authorities' explanation for the higher rates

[30] Riazan, IK-3, T July 27, 2005, http://www.arestant.msk.ru/guin-ryazan-det.html.

[31] Arkhangelsk, IK-4, Ira, July 5, 2004, http://www.arestant.msk.ru/guin-arhang-det.html.

[32] Voronezh, IK-2 Natalia, August 5, 2005, http://www.arestant.msk.ru/guin-voroneg-det .html.

[33] Voronezh, KP-10, Anna, October 18, 2005, http://www.arestant.msk.ru/guin-voroneg-det .html.

of marital breakdown among women prisoners and their generally poorer record for maintaining contacts with the outside explanation is negative societal attitudes towards women's criminality: "In society women fulfil the role of mothers and maintain the family unit. Once they are in prison women cannot continue to fulfil these roles. The husbands of women in prison, as a rule, are not prepared to wait and do not worry how their wife is doing. They are not able to come to terms with their wife's criminality, seeing it as shameful".[34] Al'pern, by contrast, argues that the explanation is more likely to be located in women's rejection of patriarchal society and the development of relationships within the colony.[35] Both arguments are plausible, but, at the present time, are not easy to test.

Conclusion

In his seminal work on penality, Michel Foucault argued that the discipline of the prison does not stop at the prison gate.[36] Borrowing and extending Solzhenitsyn's metaphor, he described modern disciplinary society as the "carceral archipelago," seeing in the regimentation of the workplace, schools, and hospitals and in taxonomy another expression of the power exercised in the modern prison. Foucault's argument rests in part on the proposition that power flows from the organisation of bodies in space. Foucault, of course, had in mind the micro-geography of the prison, but his insight can be applied to higher spatial scales. The current distribution of prisons in Russia, which confines prisoners to the peripheries of regions, has repercussions on the whole of Russian society, not just in what it says about the nature of Russian democracy, but in the roles it constructs for people. The argument of this article has been that Russia's geography of penality impacts upon women in very specific ways that reproduce gender stereotypes. By sending women to isolated colonies, far from public gaze, difficult questions about the origins of women's offending behavior are removed from the center of debate and its marginal interest confirmed in Russia's general crisis of criminality. In this respect, the fact that women are such a small minority of the total prison population is not helpful to them. The women who make their sacrificial journeys to the support the tens of thousands of men in Russia's penal peripheries are a different matter for, in contrast to their "offending sisters," they fulfil a more recognisable role in Russian society, albeit one that also reproduces their subordinate status. The Russian Penal Service takes for granted that the woman is

[34] *Kharakteristika osuzhdennykh k lisheniiu svobody*, vol. 2, 364.

[35] Al'pern, *Son i iav' zhenskoi tiur'my*, 27.

[36] Michel Foucault, *Discipline and Punish. The Birth of the Prison* (London: Penguin, 1987).

pivotal in maintaining the family, but this is in the context of an extremely conservative understanding of "family." "Non-traditional" families, including, for example, same-sex relationships, are not are not included in the definition. The descriptions of rooms, prices, and lists of permitted produce and other "travellers' tips"—down, as we have seen, to which pies are worth buying en route—that women post on the *Arestant* website confirm their domestic role and reinforce pre-existing gender stereotypes, as well as indicate how successful the Russian penal complex has been in mobilizing women's labor to help it overcome its current economic problems. But there is another side to this. The existence of the *Arestant* website can be read not just as a practical guide to visiting Russia's prison, but also as an attempt on the part of the women to contest their powerlessness when faced with the formidable penal bureaucracy. By sharing with others how to navigate penal Russia, contributors to *Arestant* are forcing debate about Russia's prisons into the public arena and insisting that newly conferred rights are translated into practice. Considering the history of penality in Russia, this is an achievement indeed.

IV. Landscape after the Future

Post-Post-Communist Sincerity

Pioneers, Cosmonauts, and Other Soviet Heroes Born Today

Alexei Yurchak

New Sincerity

In the past several years, a curious shift has been taking place in the Russian art world: increasing numbers of artists and art critics have been turning in their work to Soviet topics and aesthetics. Although this trend may have something in common with the much discussed "postcommunist nostalgia," some features of this phenomenon make nostalgia, as a concept, quite inadequate to describe it. For example, among the artists who turn to the Soviet topics and aesthetics today, some are too young to remember the Soviet period well, while others belonged to the subculture of the artistic and intellectual "underground" during the Soviet period, which was hardly sympathetic of the Soviet system and often explicitly sabotaged it. The artists' interest in Soviet topics and aesthetics has more to do with their attempt to engage with the present context of Russian life rather than a nostalgic gaze into the Soviet past. This aesthetic shift can be seen as a form of what Dominic Boyer calls postcommunist "politics of the future."[1] To understand how engaging with the Soviet past may enable an aesthetic construction of the future, we must first consider what artistic forms are developed to address that past, and what is said about this trend by the artists themselves and by art critics and art historians who are close to this movement.

One concept that they frequently invoke when speaking about this trend is sincerity. Sincerity in this case has two related but distinct meanings—a particular attitude employed by the artists to explore Soviet socialist life and an intrinsic characteristic of that life itself. In both these senses, sincerity is further related to a set of other terms: idealism, romanticism, humanism, purity, friendship, comradeship, self-sacrifice, etc. Whereas much of the Russian art scene of the late 1980s and early 1990s was dominated by the aesthetics of absurdist irony and *stiob*[2], in today's scene

---

[1] Dominic Boyer, "Beyond *Algos and Mania*: The Politics of the Future in Postsocialist Eastern Europe" (paper presented at the Institute of Slavic, East European, and Eurasian Studies, University of California, Berkeley, April 13, 2007).

[2] In fact, cynicism and sincerity were always linked in much informal art in the late Soviet period. For example, the unique Soviet postmodern genre of *stiob* incorporates a remarkable mix of sincerity and irony directed at the subject that is treated with this attitude. For an extensive discussion see chapter 7 in Alexei Yurchak, *Everything Was Forever Until It Was No More: The Last Soviet Generation* (Princeton: Princeton University Press, 2006) and idem.

sincerity has become the dominant aesthetic form.

This turn to sincerity is often connected to a growing interest in the ethics and aesthetics of the Soviet period, and to a perceived lack of sincerity today, but it may also be related to the broader contemporary trend in global popular culture of turning to what is known as the "new sincerity." Although this term has different meanings in these different contexts, it usually signals a departure from the pervasive political cynicism and alienation that have been common in postmodern culture.[3] Broadly speaking, new sincerity takes the form of a close and interested attention to the subject matter; cynicism or sarcasm are avoided.[4] In the Russian context, the term new sincerity (*novaia iskrennost'*) was originally used in the early 1990s by poet Dmitry Prigov and literary critic Mikhail Epstein, members of the unofficial Soviet artistic community.[5] According to them, new sincerity in this context first appeared in literary and poetic texts around 1990, and was a backlash against the postmodern absurdity and ridicule that dominated the informal culture of the late Soviet and early post-Soviet periods marked by the crisis of the Soviet state.

Although the aesthetics of new sincerity implies avoidance of cynicism in relation to the subject matter, this does not mean that new sincerity lacks irony. Quite the contrary, as a post-postmodern phenomenon it is acutely self-aware and self-ironic. However, this is a particular brand of irony, which is sympathetic and warm, and allows its authors to remain committed to the ideals that they discuss, while also

---

"Gagarin and the Ravekids: Transforming Power, Identity and Aesthetics in the Post-Soviet Nightlife," in *Consuming Russia: Popular Culture, Sex, and Society since Gorbachev*, ed. Adele Barker (Durham: Duke University Press, 1999).

[3] In the United States, the turn to post-postmodern sincerity happened at about the same time as in Russia. While in Russia this turn is usually associated with the crisis of state socialism in the early 1990s, in the United States it is associated with the events of 9/11. One may argue, however, that the collapse of the state-organized "communist project" was the initial inaugural event of the global regime change, of which the events of 9/11 were one element. In the United States, the term "new sincerity" has been popularized since 9/11 by some youth media (for example, by Jesse Thorn, the host of a popular music program *Sound of Young America*, on New York's National Public Radio station WYNC).

[4] Art critics have argued that the aesthetics of new sincerity is found today in such contemporary media and art forms as reality television, Internet blogs, diary style "chicklit" literature, personal videos on You-Tube, neorealist cinema (for example, Danish *Dogma*, Aki Kaurismäki, Lars von Trier, Pedro Almadovar). See Aleksandr Burenkov, "Novaia iskrennost'," *Be-in journal*, 2007, http://www.be-in.ru/journal/index.php?phenomena/9 (accessed September 26, 2007).

[5] Dmitrii Prigov, "Novaia iskrennost' (katalog obrashchenii)," *Krizis tsivilizatsii*, 1991, no. 2; Mikhail Epshtein, "Katalog novykh poezii," *Sovremennaia russkaia poeziia posle 1966. Antologiia* (Oberbaum Verlag, 1990), 359–67.

being somewhat ironic about this commitment.[6] In Russia, the shift from cynicism to new sincerity, with a touch of warm irony, is manifested today in many art forms, especially in youth culture. I will describe two examples that are symptomatic of this aesthetic turn and discuss the phenomenon in greater detail, focusing on what it tells us about the meaning that Soviet socialism has acquired in Russian life today.

My first example is an Internet cartoon character Masyanya, a product of St. Petersburg computer artist Oleg Kuvaev. Making her first appearance on the Internet in 2001, Masyanya has achieved the status of a cult celebrity in Russia. In the spring of 2002, "Masyanya" became the most frequently used search term on the main Russian-language internet search engine, Yandex.ru[7], and Oleg Kuvaev won awards for the best Russian cartoon of the year, the best Russian web site of the year, etc.[8] After just a year, the cult cartoon character even became a regular participant in a cultural program on the NTV television channel. The original Internet cartoons that made Masyanya popular are organized into short (two to three minutes long) episodes that Kuvaev created on his home computer and then circulated online. Like her creator, the cartoon character lives in St. Petersburg and is known for her sarcastic remarks about life in the city and her talent for doing nothing in particular. And yet, behind her sarcasm and laziness Masyanya is sincere and vulnerable. It is the combination of counter-cultural sarcastic attitude with warmth and sincerity that has made Mas yanya so popular. Writing in the English-language *St. Petersburg Times*, a Western expatriate commented on the explosion of Masyanya's unlikely popularity:

> She's a foul-mouthed, dope-smoking idler with a skirt that's much too short and far too few teeth in her mouth. She has no job, no respect for authority and sports a cackle so piercing that it's painful to the unaccustomed ear. And yet Masyanya, for that is her name, is the talk of the northern capital. Locals have begun speaking Masyanya-speak. Children write her fan mail. Internet cafes are filled with people glued to computer screens watching her latest adventures, bending in spasms of uncontrolled laughter. And at the end of every working day, the city's white-collar workers feverishly log on to the net for a

[6] This distinction between warm irony and cynicism is similar to a Susan Sontag description: irony implies a serious and sincere relation to the world; cynicism does not. Responding to the question on what ought to be characteristics of a good writer Sontag said: "Be serious. By which I meant: never be cynical. And which doesn't preclude being funny." Jenny Diski, "Seriously Uncool." *London Review of Books* 29, no. 6 (March 22, 2007).

[7] Dawn Nafus, *Time, Sociability, and Post-Socialism* (DPhil diss., Department of Anthropology, Cambridge University, 2003).

[8] Elena Petrovskaia, "Dusha pautiny: Masiania i 'novaia' iskrennost'," *Vliianie interneta na soznanie i strukturu znaniia* (Moscow: Institut filosofii RAN, 2004), 175–81.

> glimpse into her life … A simple, urban girl from the dawn of the 21st century, Masyanya is blessed with a set of traits that anyone who has spent some time in this country is bound to recognize: a bit of impulsiveness, a handful of irresponsibility, a pinch of laziness and a healthy dose of *dushevnost'*, or soulfulness.[9]

A Russian philosopher, Elena Petrovskaia, contemplating the reasons for Masyanya's quick rise to the cult status, writes that it is symptomatic of the post-postmodern turn to authenticity and idealism, which in the Russian context has been exacerbated by the fall of the Soviet state and the experience of the first post-Soviet decade marked by pragmatism, disintegration of social solidarity, and erasure of common history. In this context, Masyanya has become a symbol of the lost impracticality, sincerity, and warmth of the pre-market social world. Petrovskaia writes, "despite her vulgar speech and openly bad habits, [Masyanya] is kind, good, and vulnerable. She is full of irony, and yet behind this irony one senses *sincerity* … Sincerity which we have always suspected was there, but which only today sounds like a plea … We have fallen in love with Masyanya because this element of Masyanya is in everyone of us."[10]

Masyanya is not a success story of the market reforms; on the contrary, she is poor, unemployed, and uninterested in success. Her total lack of ambition and a mixture of sincerity and irony make her quite different from the cynical cartoon characters on American TV shows such as Beavis and Butthead and South Park, which are well known in Russia. Indeed, adds Petrovskaia, Masyanya is "the Russian answer to Beavis and Butthead."[11]

The shift to sincerity is also manifested today in unlikely genres of youth culture such as the notoriously jaded cosmopolitan nightclub scene and electronic music.[12] An example is a young band from St. Petersburg called Kim & Buran, which has become popular on the club scene in the past few years. The band samples soundtracks from Soviet 1970s animated science fiction cartoons for children and writes its own material that imitates this style. To preserve the authentic sound of the period the band plays only real Soviet synthesizers produced in the 1970s. The band's name also comes from two characters in a popular animated cartoon of

[9] Ana Uzelac, "Sassy Cyber-Chick Puts the City on the Map," *St. Petersburg Times*, no. 758, Tuesday, April 2, 2002, http://www.sptimes.ru/index.php?action_id=2&story_id=6843 (accessed September 26, 2007).

[10] Petrovskaia, "Dusha pautiny."

[11] Ibid.

[12] In Russia this scene first developed in the early 1990s, having grown out of the informal rock music subculture of the 1980s. See Yurchak, "Gagarin and the Ravekids."

that period, "Mysteries of the Third Planet" (*Tainy tret'ei planety*), based on books by Soviet science fiction writer Kim Bulychev adapted for children, in which heroic bearded scientists, their adventurous children, and good-natured robots make intergalactic voyages through communist space.[13] At first glance, the group's style might seem as an ironic postmodern reinterpretation of a Soviet children's classic performed by members of a post-Soviet cosmopolitan youth culture. However, this interpretation would miss the peculiar sensibility of sincerity and warmth towards the Soviet past that lies at the heart of this aesthetic and that is responsible for the group's tremendous appeal to young audiences.

It is instructive, for example, to consider how art publications and critics explain the reasons for the band's success. According to them, this popularity is based not on the band's music per se, but on its successful revival of sincerity, romanticism, and futurism that were present in Soviet life in the 1970s and that are today experienced as lacking. One publication wrote that the band's success can be explained "not by their technique of sampling or art of stylizing, but, first and foremost, by the genuine lyricism and heartfelt sincerity" with which they build bridges to "the Soviet world of the 1970s, where space exploration was part of everyday life."[14] Another praised the band for the explicit use of music and footage from 1970s Soviet science fiction films in its live performances, which allows the band to recreate that period's atmosphere of "purity and kindness" and to celebrate the achievements of "Soviet engineers and scientists … without a trace of cynicism … a drop of fakeness, a shadow of scorn."[15] According to a third, when Kim & Buran—then an unknown band—appeared at the 2005 Stereo Leto music festival, they overshadowed famous foreign guests because their music revived the atmosphere of the Soviet dream and "made even skeptics believe in the Bright Future."[16] And a fourth called Slava Zavialov, the group's leader, "an incorrigible romantic who believes … in the romanticism of space exploration, and who composes music that is radiant, very kind, and

[13] References to Soviet science and space exploration have been common in Russian rave and night dance scene from the beginning. The first Russian electronic music group, *Novye kompozitory* (New Composers), which emerged in Leningrad in the early 1980s, incorporated in their compositions real-life recordings of the conversations between the Ground Control and Soviet cosmonauts orbiting the Earth. Around 1990, when the Soviet state was undergoing its final crisis, the first massive rave parties in Russian history took place in the Leningrad Planetarium and at the Cosmos Pavilion at Moscow's VDNKh (Exhibition of Soviet Economic Achievements). See discussion in Yurchak, "Gagarin and the Ravekids."

[14] "Kim i Buran," Time Out Petersburg, December 2004.

[15] Maria Shul'rufer, "Kim i Buran," *Afisha*, December 17, 2004.

[16] Review by *Special Radio*, http://www.specialradio.ru/rec3/index.php?top=27 (accessed September 26, 2007).

nostalgically immerses us into the great past of Soviet films about pioneers who are dreaming to follow in Gagarin's footsteps." The band's music, continues the review, brings back "a kind of untainted perception of life that is characteristic of a child. This is what *new sincerity* is all about!"[17]

What is the meaning of this growing fascination in contemporary Russian youth culture, media, and art with the alleged Soviet traits of idealism, sincerity, and futurism? How is it linked with the general trend in Russia today of turning away from postmodern irony and cynicism? And what does this aesthetic turn tell us about the ideological shifts in contemporary Russia? To answer these questions we must analyze the context of ideological and geopolitical transformations in which younger generations of Russian cultural producers have found themselves in the past twenty years. To analyze these changes, I turn to interviews with Russian artists, art historians, and other members of the artistic scene.

Global Context and Local Identity

Today, when the Soviet past is sufficiently distant and a whole new post-Soviet generation has come of age, it is perhaps easier than before to contemplate Soviet socialism in more complex ways without stirring too much pain and emotion. It is also easier to discuss ethical commitments and idealist dreams associated with socialist life without necessarily linking them to the oppression, alienation, or boredom that were also part of that life. The historical distance from the Soviet period may explain why it is possible to turn to these topics today, but it does not explain the reasons for this retrospective gaze performed by young artists and musicians. Therefore, it is important to consider in greater detail what specific features of the contemporary post-Soviet context have become associated with this trend a decade after state socialism ended. In the case of the artists I discuss several features of that context are particularly important.

In the 1990s, following the collapse of the Soviet state, the opening up of the borders, and the entry of Russian art in the global art market, many formerly unofficial Soviet artists discovered that after a short period of great international interest in their work, their status in the West had changed in unexpected ways. During the Soviet period, they experienced themselves as culturally internationalist, despite being isolated from the outside world geographically and politically. Soviet socialism was presented as a global project and, for better or worse, unofficial artists saw themselves and their art in global historical terms. However, with the collapse of state socialism the Soviet Union was no longer seen as a powerful maker of modern

[17] Alexandr Luchistyi, "Slava Zav'ialov, gruppa Kim i Buran," *Be-in zhurnal*, February 2007, http://www.be-in.ru/journal/index.php?people/47 (accessed September 26, 2007).

history. As a result, during their early travels to the West many formerly unofficial Soviet artists learned that in the eyes of Western curators and audiences, their identity had shrunk from something global, international, and historically important to something local, ethnic, and intensely parochial. They discovered that to be seen as an "international artist" one had to come from the West, and that the only identity available to post-Soviet artists now was "Russian" (or, in the case of other former republics, "Georgian," "Ukrainian," and so on).

To the artists from Soviet Russia this newly found "Russianness" sounded unfamiliar and exotic.[18] Moscow artist Oleg Kulik remembers that during Western art shows in the early 1990s, the question "Are you Russian?" , sounded humiliating to him and his fellow artists, like the question "Are you a country bumpkin?"[19] What these artists experienced was a new set of relations between Russians and Westerners that appeared to have certain neo-colonial traits. Art critic Ekaterina Degot described that experience with a metaphor: with the collapse of the Soviet state, Russia had moved "from the Third Rome to the Third World."[20] Sociologist Boris Kagarlitsky described the same experience with another metaphor: Russia was like an airplane whose passengers were still being told that they were flying to Paris or London although the airplane had landed a long time ago in a third world country and was parked on a reserve landing strip.[21]

In the 1990s, Russian artists also discovered that the only international identity they could retain in the eyes of the West was that of "Soviet dissident artists"—members of some heroic artistic underground that struggled with the "oppressive state" and exposed its evils to the "free world." This reduction of their art and identity to a politicized image of resistance fighters made many artists resentful. Even Ilya Kabakov, the most successful post-Soviet Russian artist on the international art scene, who has made his name by creating installations about the alienation of the Soviet

[18] In Soviet times, the term *russkii* (Russian) in Russia proper was rarely used as a marker of identity and had an unfamiliar ethnic ring to it. The widespread Western tradition of referring to all Soviet people as Russians was still unfamiliar to them and, when encountered, seemed strange and misconstrued.

[19] See Ekaterina Degot' and Oleg Kulik, "Russkii–eto sotsial'naia kategoriia" [Russian is a social category], *Kriticheskaia massa*, 2003, no. 1.

[20] Ekaterina Degot, "Russia: Third Rome or Third World?" *Watch Out! Art from Moscow and St. Petersburg*. Exhibition Catalog (Oslo: The National Museum of Art, Norway, 2004), 33–49. See also Degot', "Kak poluchit's pravo na postkolonial'nyi diskurs?" [How to obtain the right for post-colonial discourse?], *Moscow Art Magazine*, 1998, no. 22.

[21] Boris Kagarlitsky. 2005. "Toward the 'Organic Intellectual'," *Moscow Art Magazine*, Digest 1993/2005. See: http://xz.gif.ru/numbers/moscow-art-magazine/toward/ (accessed October 21, 2007)

experience, refused this interpretation of his artistic work. When Kabakov first arrived in the United States in the late 1980s, he was interview for a U.S. publication entitled *Soviet Dissident Artists*. The interviewer started the conversation by asking Kabakov to describe his dissident past, to which Kabakov retorted: "I was not a dissident. I did not fight with anything or anybody. The word does not apply to me."[22] Kabakov was clearly not a supporter of the Soviet system, however, the response shows his resentment of a simplified binary view of socialism, Soviet life, and his subject position in it that was implicit in the question.

The experience of encountering dominant Western interpretations of their Soviet past, argues Ekaterina Degot, made many Russian artists turn to Soviet topics and aesthetics and contemplate that history in more complex terms. This interest in the past has little to do with being nostalgic for a lost world, let alone wanting to reconstruct it. And yet, it is inspired today by the recognition that the non-Stalin periods of Soviet history—both, the early revolutionary period (1920s and early 1930s) and the late Soviet period (1970s and 1980s)—can still offer an "enormous human, intellectual, educational and even democratic potential that has not been appropriated in post-Soviet Russia."[23]

Dasha Fursei

The interest in considering some aspects of the Soviet past for the purposes of imagining an alternative future is not limited to the artists who grew up in the Soviet Union. Many younger artists, who were children when the Soviet Union collapsed, turn to the theme of "Soviet sincerity" today, as we saw in the case of the band Kim & Buran. Another example is the work of a young St. Petersburg artist, Dasha Fursei. Until recently, Dasha, who was born in Leningrad in 1978, never reflected much on her Soviet childhood and did not think of the Soviet system in positive terms. In fact, as she mentioned to me in an interview: "I used to resist everything Soviet; I tried to run away from it as something false and imposed from above."[24] To her own surprise, she has been drawn to Soviet topics and aesthetics in the past couple years. This became possible to some extent, explains Dasha, because "the past is no longer

[22] Ilya Kabakov, "Interview," in *Soviet Dissident Artists: Interviews after Perestroika*, ed. Renee Baigell and Matthew Baigell (New Brunswick, NJ: Rutgers University Press, 1995), 142. See also Matthew Jesse Jackson, "Ilya Kabakov and the Concentrated Spectacle of Soviet Power," *Art Margins*, 2001, http://www.artmargins.com/content/feature/jackson.html (accessed September 26, 2007).

[23] Ekaterina Degot', "Sotsrealizm okazalsia nad divanom" [socialist realism ended up above the sofa], *Ogonek*, no. 44, October 31–November 6, 2005.

[24] Author interview, summer 2005.

an object of hostility" and her attitude to it has become "more complex." She started thinking of what she calls "untaintedness and sincerity" (*neisporchennost' i iskrennost'*), which she claims were part of her Soviet life but have disappeared during the post-Soviet period.

In 2005, when Dasha spent a few weeks living and painting in Paris, she was provoked to turn to Soviet topics in her art by what she describes as "misconceptions of the Soviet past" in Western media and public discourse. That interest developed into a series of pictures called *Pionerki* (Pioneer girls), in which Dasha explores the feelings and dreams that she associates with her Soviet childhood. Dasha was among the last cohort of Soviet children to be a member of the Pioneer organization[25]: in 1991-1992 (when she was 14, the top age for a Pioneer), the Soviet Union disintegrated and with it most state-run and ideological organizations, including the Pioneers.

For Dasha, *Pionerki* is "my honest attempt to return to my actual feelings in those years. I wanted to recover the feeling of romanticism and idealism that was a real part of my life then and that was not simply naïve, but that has been forgotten since." The Pioneer organization "actually encouraged you to aspire for heroism (*nastraivala na podvigi*), and this aspiration was never cynical." The first post-Soviet decade was dominated by a hostile attitude towards any idealism. According to Dasha, "in the 1990s, the image of a young romantic girl had become equated with a fool. A man was no longer supposed to idealize her. He was supposed to despise her, because she, like a simple fool, fell in love with him and let him control her. One was supposed to despise sincerity. Since then a whole new cynical generation has grown up."

This pragmatic, anti-idealist ideology gradually rendered life devoid of meaning, argues Dasha, which is why today pragmatism is loosing its appeal. Many of Dasha's young friends, she explains, are growing tired of it, "missing something that is not based on pure calculation." According to her, "today once again, there is a need for sincerity, romanticism, ability to give yourself up completely to something (*polnost'iu otdat'sia chemu-to*), beyond just pragmatism … One is getting tired of the image of a pragmatic young woman who is constantly calculating how much things cost and with whom it is useful to keep friendship, and whose ultimate dream is to marry a 'New Russian' man." Comments of this type would be considered banal in the informal culture of the 1980s and 1990s, but today they are increasingly common even among successful young artists, suggesting a certain shift in the ethical parameters of informal art practice.

---

[25] A youth Communist organization for schoolchildren ages 10 to 14, in which most Soviet children participated.

Dasha explores this link between romanticism, sincerity, and a refusal of cynicism and pragmatism in the picture "Girl with a Book" in her *Pionerki* series (Picture 1).

Picture 1
"Girl with a Book"
(*Devochka s knigoi*)

A Pioneer girl is reading Pushkin's *Eugene Onegin*. She identifies with Tatiana Larina, says Dasha, Pushkin's heroine and perhaps the utmost Russian (and Soviet Russian) symbol of inner purity, sincerity, and untainted love, which is opposed in the poem to the cynicism and jadedness of the world around her. Mixing historical figures and contexts, Dasha assigns these features to her Pioneer girl. She says that the airplane folded out of the newspaper *Pravda* is Tatiana's letter, which may convey several messages at once. The word "pravda," or truth, suggests the sincerity of this character. The title "Pravda" of the main Soviet newspaper links Tatiana's sincerity with that of a Soviet Pioneer girl of Dasha's generation. In Dasha's view, many Soviet girls were just as sincere and pure as Tatiana and were in love with that character. However, the pragmatic post-Soviet society, like the high society of Onegin's times, "is laughing at Tatiana; they see her as a total fool who does not know how to behave properly," says Dasha. Tatiana and the Pioneer girl are both symbols of unconditional pure love, opposed to the cynicism, pragmatism, and calculation that came to dominate the 1990s: "Pure truth (*chistaia pravda*), pure *Pravda*, is Tatiana's message to the world."

And yet, it would be too simplistic to reduce Dasha's picture to this romantic interpretation. As the rest of the *Pionerki* series suggests, this young romantic heroine, not unlike Pushkin's Tatiana, is full of erotic dreams and unexplained yearnings. The theme of purity, romanticism, and sincerity, and the theme of unexplored eroticism of a young Lolita-esque Pioneer girl are not in contradiction, argues Dasha. They are all irreducible elements of the idealism that she wants to explore. And, like Kim & Buran, they are linked with the Soviet futurist utopia, science fiction, and space exploration. In "City of the Sun" (Picture 2), Dasha linked the idealism of her pionerki with early Soviet utopia of the Bright Future.

Picture 2
"City of the Sun"
(*Gorod solntsa*)

The picture's name is taken from Tommaso Campanella's famous utopian novel and refers to the dream of a socialist city. Another picture, first displayed at an exhibition in Paris, is of a woman cosmonaut modeled on Valentina Tereshkova. To be close to the material—that is, to be authentic and sincere in treating the past—Dasha interviewed Tereshkova about her experience of being a woman in space. She also incorporated unique materials of the Soviet space program into the picture—"fragments of real meteorites and real Moon dust to create a landscape relief on the picture," which she obtained "from the scientists at the Research Institute of Space Exploration." Another picture in the series, "Dreaming of Cosmos" (Picture 3), shows a young, dreamy Pioneer girl next to a portrait of Yuri Gagarin, who since Soviet times has played a particularly important role in youth culture as a cultural symbol linking idealism, futurism, and romanticism.[26] For adolescent Pioneer girls,

[26] Gagarin remains a key symbol of the utopian ideal of socialism. In a recent special issue devoted to "Soviet nostalgia," the weekly *Ogonek* quoted a romanticized picture drawn by a collector of Soviet cars: "I adore Soviet cars: like Soviet sausage, which cost 2.20 for a kilo,

explains Dasha, Gagarin was "the most heroic and attractive man, who was beautiful and moral. It was pleasant that such a person was the first one to go into space. He was an appropriate image for a hero. He was a myth for all Soviet girls."

Picture 3
"Dreaming of Cosmos"
(*Mechta o kosmose*)

Indeed, although her heroine "thinks that she is dreaming about outer space and Yuri Gagarin," adds Dasha, "in fact, she is experiencing her first adult feelings. She is unconsciously dreaming about love and about a man."

Every picture in the series mixes the feelings of idealism, sincerity, and eroticism. In addition to legendary heroes like Gagarin, there are other abstract male figures around which the ideals and dreams of Pioneer girls become eroticized. When I asked Dasha to describe the picture of a girl and her father at a May Day parade (Picture 4), she replied with surprise: "But this is not her father! This is a man, just a man (*prosto muzhchina*)." In this picture and the next, "Induction into the Pioneers" (Picture 5), the figures of men are strong, big, and abstract. They are much larger than the Pioneer girls and are never visible in full. This is a general idea of heroic masculinity that links sincere socialist ideals with first romantic dreams.

Abstract heroic masculinity is also represented by other forms. In "Bathing a Red Horse" (*Kupanie krasnogo konia*) (Picture 6), Dasha's reworking of Petrov-Vodkin's revolutionary avant-garde classic from 1912, the naked peasant boy of the original picture is replaced with a young Pioneer girl wearing a red Pioneer scarf. For Dasha, the powerful horse is a masculinized and eroticized metaphor of the revolution that drives her heroine into the future, transforming her life.

---

they symbolize the time when everyone was 'kind and happy' and when Gagarin flew into space." (Dmitrii Oktiabr'skii, "Kto i kak prodaet Rodinu," *Ogonek*, 2005, no. 44; see also http://www.ogoniok.com/4918/2/ (accessed October 21, 2007).

Picture 4
"Peace, Labor, May!"
(*Mir, trud, mai!*)

Picture 5
"Induction into the Pioneers"
(*Priem v pionery*)

Picture 6
"Bathing a Red Horse"
(*Kupanie krasnogo konia*)

Dasha demonstrates in her pictures and argues in her interviews that in Soviet life "sincerity and revolutionary idealism were always linked with pure and untainted eroticism. These feelings were indivisible, even though we did not consciously realize this at the time ... For all their eroticism, these characters remain first and foremost good and sincere, not vulgar or dirty ... I am not ashamed that in these characters heroism and sexuality are linked. There is nothing to be ashamed of, because this is how it really was then. These feelings were pure and they were truly linked in life."

The emphasis on the eroticized aspect of revolutionary idealism is Dasha's attempt to counter the currently dominant representations of Soviet socialism that reduce it to operations of totalitarian power. Instead, she attempts to uncover the revolutionary romanticism that was sustained in that life, with its devotion to ideal beauty, self-sacrifice and dreams about the future. The world of Dasha's Pioneer girls seems anything but drab, boring, or oppressive.

Neither Sots-Art nor Socialist Realism

Dasha's approach is dramatically different from ironic representations of Soviet reality that have been famously practiced by Moscow conceptualists of the Sots-Art movement of the 1970s and 1980s (for example, Komar and Melamid, Erik Bulatov, and Alexander Kosolapov) and by their contemporary followers (for example, Ivan Razumov and Konstantin Zvezdochetov). An example of a contemporary ironic treatment of the Soviet past is the work of Moscow conceptualist artist Ivan Razumov. In the late 1990s, Razumov created his own graphic series entitled "Pioneer Heroes" (*Pionery-geroi*). Although Razumov, like Dasha, addresses the link between young Pioneers' devotion to an ideal and their budding eroticism, for him this link is about blind fanaticism and sexual perversion. In the most famous picture in his series called "Lena," a young Pioneer girl lustfully embraces the statue of Lenin (Picture 7). The picture ridicules not only the sacred core of Soviet ideology, represented by Lenin, but also a young naïve girl who is seduced by that ideology.

An additional problem with this approach, argues Dasha, is that creating such negative images today, many years after the fall of the Soviet state, is neither original nor risky from political and aesthetic standpoints. This is not art but pragmatically calculated "political caricature, whose effects are not artistic but moralistic." In other words, the effect of this work is similar to that of "politically correct" art—the kind of art that Jacques Rancière criticized for its representation of the dominant view and therefore its inability to produce new understandings and create palpable political effects.[27]

[27] Jacques Rancière, *The Politics of Aesthetics: The Distribution of the Sensible* (London: Continuum, 2004), 63.

Picture 7
"Lena" (Ivan Razumov)

Dasha explicitly distances herself from this conceptualist work because it is based "on open criticism and negative judgment" and because "these artists have a negative attitude to their heroes, they are openly sarcastic about them, and one instantly feels this in their pictures … One senses that they are portraying evil even in their choice of openly somber colors and in their depiction of faces as unpleasant and grotesque. Their Pioneers are also unmistakably negative characters." In contrast, Dasha feels affinity to her characters: "I share their idealism and do not want to ridicule them." Her Pioneers are different from both the official representations of the Pioneers during the Soviet period (as heroic supporters of the Party) and from the new post-Soviet ridicule of these characters (as brainwashed automatons). Her heroines neither blindly support the Party rhetoric nor explicitly oppose it. Instead they occupy a third position, in which they remain devoted to the ideal but their devotion is not reduced to the Party diktat. Dasha says: "I would like to distance myself completely from Sots-Art, including the Sots-Art of the Soviet and post-Soviet periods. That genre represented a clear struggle against Soviet ideology. It performed a division of the world into two parts, putting Soviet ideology on one side and us on the other. I do not feel any affinity for this view of the world (*mne eto ne blizko*), and don't want to have any traces of this division in my work. I see my work differently. I do not struggle against anyone."[28] Note that Dasha's last sentence is

[28] Another example of this turn to the aesthetics that draws on socialist realism is the work of the Moscow duo Vinogradov and Dubossarsky. Dasha says: "They take from socialist realism and from Soviet aesthetics in general something good, they try to see positive aspects of

almost identical to Ilya Kabakov's statement, quoted above, about not fighting "with anything or anybody."

Unlike Sots-Artists, Dasha strives not only to portray the contradictions, ambiguities, and ironies of the Soviet world, but also to maintain that despite the oppressive character of that system, it contained authentic idealism that should be reclaimed today for post-Soviet Russia. This point becomes even clearer in Dasha's recent response to an American art historian who attempted to interpret her work as another example of the familiar ridicule of the Soviet system conducted in the tradition of Sots-Artists. Commenting on this interpretation, Dasha told me:

> That art historian thought my work continued in the tradition of Komar and Melamid because, as she recognized, we are investigating similar topics. However, each of us is portraying their own Soviet experience, and is doing this in their own context. From the work of Komar and Melamid you clearly learn that Soviet ideology was evil, and that one must expose that evil. The work of conceptualist artists often contained a hidden message: that we [Soviet people] were all idiots, that we were simply fooled, that there was nothing good in our life, that we followed Stalin as a herd of asses, that "we had no sex"[29], and so on. It is not by chance that this work often includes the aesthetics of political cartoon. This is felt in the works of older conceptualists and in the work of their current followers. I do not agree with this artistic treatment of ideals. I cannot agree with caricaturing the dream of a better future and one's pure and sincere devotion to that dream. Especially when this is done after the fact, when everything is safe and sound. In my work I want to express something different—the idea that, yes, perhaps we were naïve and inexperienced, but we were also sincere and we were not stupid. I have no desire to be cynical about that life and that past. I would rather try to understand it, treating it with the same sincerity and respect that were present in that life then.

---

that life. They are ironic but not angry. They are kind and positive. They are closer to how I feel" (author interview).

[29] This idiomatic phrase entered common usage after being uttered by a Soviet participant in a live broadcast of the "Leningrad-Seattle televised bridge" in 1989, during perestroika. In that experimental program, the audiences in Soviet and US TV studios were linked by satellite to have a live conversation on various topics of common interest, including social problems in each country. During a discussion of pornography and its effects on children, one Soviet participant (a middle-aged woman in conservative attire) exclaimed: "We do not have sex!" implying that in the Soviet Union, unlike the West, pornography or prostitution practically did not exist and were not problems. However, the literal meaning of her words (that Soviet people never practice sex) produced an uproar in both studios. It became an instantly popular catch-phrase in Russia symbolizing a stereotypical view of a Soviet human devoid of all human pleasures. Dasha refers to this stereotypical misinterpretation.

The attempt to distance oneself from both the anti-Soviet dissident position and the Soviet state's political ideology, while also redeeming the original ideals of the socialist project, has led Dasha and other new artists and art historians to start experimenting again with the official Soviet art of socialist realism. They argue that it is necessary to distinguish between earlier works of socialist realism that were idealistic and sincere, and later works of the Stalinist and post-Stalinist periods, when idealistic dreams became replaced with Stalin's cult of personality. As Dasha points out, earlier socialist realist works "seem much closer to me. I like the pictures of Deineka, which remind me of the image of life that I had as a child. What is good about socialist realism, at least about many of these works? You instantly see that they are sincere! They contain a dream of a hero (*mechta o geroe*), a kind of dream from which postmodernists later ran like from fire."

Moscow art historian Ekaterina Degot, whom we encountered earlier, similarly argues that the socialist realism of the earlier period (1920s and early 1930s)[30] should be freed from the political baggage of the later periods and allowed to be seen again for the authentic values, sincerity, and artistic innovation that it represented to its authors. Unlike the ideological art of mature Stalinism, argues Degot, early socialist realism shared sincere ethical commitment with the revolutionary avant-garde and therefore should be understood as a particularly innovative example of twentieth-century modernism: "the level of innovation in early Soviet art was comparable with, and perhaps even greater than, parallel trends in Western modernism. The conceptions developed in this art anticipated many radical art practices of today. However, to appreciate the contribution that the Soviet artists of that period made to the global historical process, one must first abandon many widespread prejudices [about Soviet socialism]."[31] To stress the point, Degot has suggested calling early socialist-realist style "Soviet Idealism" or "Second Russian Avant-garde."[32]

A similar view has been voiced by another celebrated artist and the leader of the Neoacademism art movement in St. Petersburg, Timur Novikov. In the mid-

---

[30] This movement included such artists as Deineka, but not Stalin's courtly painters of the late 1930s and early 1950s such as Reshetnikov. Degot', "Sotsrealizm okazalsia nad divanom."

[31] Milena Orlova, "Kon"iuktura proletariata," *Kommersant*, no. 197, October 19, 2005. See also Ekaterina Degot', "Sotsrealism, angely istorii i razminka pered nastoiashchei kar'eroi" (Socialist idealism, Angels of History, and Warming up before a Real Career), *ARTFon*, September 3–28, 2005, http://www.artinfo.ru/ru/news/main/Sarkisyan-3.htm (accessed September 26, 2007).

[32] Recently Degot organized an art show, *Soviet Idealism: Painting and Cinema of 1925–1939* (Museum of Wallon Art in Liege, Belgium, 2005–06), in which some parallels are drawn between early socialist realism and unofficial Soviet art of the 1950s to the 1980s. See also Degot', "Sotsrealizm okazalsia nad divanom."

1990s, Novikov surprised many observers when he announced that the Western art world had betrayed the authentic purpose of art to search for idealism and beauty. According to Novikov, the only form of modernism in the twentieth century that preserved this calling was early socialist realism. Novikov's claim was designed to provoke, but it was not simply ironic. The Neoacademism movement that he founded has attempted to connect classical art with the communist aesthetics of early socialist realism as a means of reclaiming for Russian history a place in global modernity.[33]

These artists and art historians claim that despite the Soviet state control over art there was always a certain core of idealist aesthetics that remained free, sincere, and positive in its search for a utopian ideal. More broadly, they argue that political regimes can never fully predict what effect the form of aesthetics that they develop, sponsor, and utilize for their own purposes will have. Aesthetics is not secondary to politics, but rather has its own political potential, and no aesthetic form can be completely reduced to being a tool of political manipulation. Even the official aesthetic forms of a highly controlling political regime are capable of acquiring meanings that the regime can neither control nor predict.

This view explains Dasha's desire to revisit Soviet socialist aesthetics. She wants to isolate the idealist values that inspired these aesthetic forms from the negative associations with Soviet history that they later acquired, and to redeploy them for a new, postcommunist project. Making a similar point, Georgy Gurianov, a famous member of the Neoacademist movement, goes even further in his comments on the art created in the contexts of the two most notorious totalitarian regimes of the twentieth century, Nazi Germany and the Soviet Union of the Stalinist period: "I like the art of Arno Breker, Leni Riefenstahl, and also Deineka, Samokhvalov, and Mukhina [early Soviet socialist realism]. They created great art, although they happened to live during particular totalitarian regimes."[34] Gurianov separates the regimes from the idealism that was present in some of the aesthetic forms developed by them. When a journalist asked Gurianov how can aesthetics be free from politics, when it is clear that under Soviet political regime art was unfree, Gurianov retorted:

---

[33] In fact, interest in early socialist realism (especially such artists as Deineka and Samokhvalov) existed among unofficial Soviet artists already in the late 1980s and early 1990s. This style became very popular among unofficial Russian artists in the 1990s. One example is the artwork and texts of Timur Novikov, who wrote about socialist realism with great respect and called on experimental artists of his circle to learn socialist realist techniques and devotion to an ideal.

[34] Liubov Nevolainen, "Georgii Gur'ianov. Idealist i conformist?" (Georgy Gurianov: Idealist and Conformist?), *Krasnyi*, 2004, no. 4 (12): 60. See also Arkadii Ippolitov, "Proekt Georgiia Gur'ianova. Petersburgskaia Florentsiia," *Zhurnal Festivalia*, 2000, no. 1: 7–8.

"Of course it was free!"[35]

From these examples it becomes clear that these post-Soviet artists, despite their different styles and philosophies, share one artistic project: to recover the idealist aesthetic core of utopian art, while simultaneously separating it from concrete political agendas and regimes that enabled it. Both Novikov and Degot have argued that performing such a separation is the only important project that art can play today, and that the specific postcommunist context of Russia provides artists with a unique opportunity for doing this. Today's Russian artists have come to recognize, argues Degot, that the Soviet past is Russia's most valuable cultural capital in the global context.[36] Turning to the explorations of that past may become an important artistic strategy for reintegrating Russian art into the global art scene.

Indeed, a peculiar mix of sincerity, irony, and eroticism in Dasha's work allowed it to attract very different audiences and make it successful in different segments of the Russian and international art markets. Her St. Petersburg *Pionerki* show received very positive reviews in the Russian press, and the entire series was bought for a considerable price by the Sandretti fund of contemporary Russian art at the MART Museum in Italy. Dasha was invited to participate in the international Biennale Art-Moscow in 2006 and 2007, and to work in Paris and Venice. This encouraged her to continue developing her mix of idealism, eroticism, and irony as a strategy of self-presentation to the public and journalists, as attested, for example, by her promotional photos, in which she herself clearly performs the role of a Lolita-esque Pionerka (Picture 8).

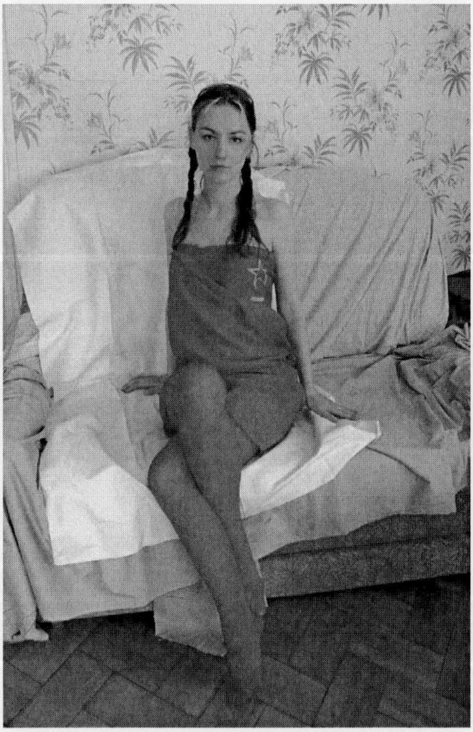

Picture 8
Author as provocative Pionerka (promotional photo)

[35] Ippolitov, "Proekt Georgiia Gur'ianova."

[36] Ekaterina Degot', "Why we must remember Soviet values, or does the world need an alternative to capitalism," *Razgovorchiki*, no. 34, October 9, 2006, http://www.razgovorchiki.ru/arkhiv/degot.htm (accessed September 26, 2007).

This strategy is also seen in the organization of her art exhibitions. For example, a recent show of the *Pionerki* series was organized on International Worker's Day, May 1, in Sigmund Freud Museum of Dreams in St. Petersburg[37], where the pictures hang next to the room that displayed accounts of famous dreams interpreted by Freud. The announcement of the show explained: "A series of pictures devoted to young Pioneers, explorers, and space travelers, dreams and spring, bright future and expectations of first love." Thus, although Dasha rejects an outright ridicule of the Sots-Art approach, she is aware of the irony and eroticism of her idealist heroines and is willing to engage with them, without ridiculing her subjects.

Ultimately, Dasha and other artists and critics of this new trend argue that the aesthetic core of utopian art, including some varieties of totalitarian art, can be freed from the political manipulation of its era precisely because pure and sincere aspirations for an ideal transcend immediate political agendas. Instead, this aesthetics bears its own political potential—what Jacques Rancière calls "the politics of aesthetics"[38]—which is based on the redeemed categories of sincerity and idealism. It follows from this claim that one can draw on the idealized core of the socialist realist aura while distancing it from both the political regime of the socialist state that made use of this art and the neoliberal market that has turned this art into a fashionable commodity. In other words, these artists' search for sincerity cannot be reduced to either nostalgia for the Soviet system or pragmatic considerations of an art market demand (indeed, their search for "Soviet sincerity" predates their market success[39]). Rather, their interest in exploring the past sincerity and a popular demand for such explorations are both instances of the same contemporary phenomenon of reassessing the history of Soviet modernity, exploring its meaningful aspects, and separating the original ethical aspirations of that modernity from the political regime which relied on them for its ends. The utopian world that discourse envisions is neither Soviet nor neoliberal; it belongs to a different system altogether. If this sentiment can be compared with nostalgic yearning, it is yearning "not for the Communist past, but rather for what that past might have been, for the missed opportunity of creating an alternative world."[40]

[37] The show was organized by art critic Viktor Mazin, director of the Museum of Dreams.

[38] Rancière, *The Politics of Aesthetics*, 63.

[39] Dasha and all her colleagues was surprised when her *Pionerki* attracted rich buyers in Russia and abroad. As for the Neoacademists, Gurianov, for example, had worked on his own "Soviet heroes" (sailors and workers) since 1990, almost without any change in style of topic, but achieved real success only in the past few years and was able to sell his canvases for high prices.

[40] Slavoj Žižek, "Lenin Shot at Finland Station," *London Review of Books*, August 18, 2005.

Finding the Soviet in Post-Soviet Space

An Excavation of the Post-Soviet City of Nizhni Novgorod

Heather DeHaan

Urban space reflects the course of time—changing aesthetics, changing socio-economic and political organization, and changes in the environment. The cityscape affects the pattern of day-to-day movement, and it reflects new societal goals, ambitions, technologies, and power. In space, past dialogues with present: contemporary life builds on historic layers of time, sometimes masking history and at other times adapting historic spaces, events, and ideas to modern life. A city is both society's body and its clothing. On the one hand, urban space provides the very skeleton upon which the flesh, blood, and clothes of the city are placed: the city has a bone structure (geographically defined layout), a circulatory system (roads), a metabolic system (spaces for energy production and use), a waste disposal system (today's garbage or recycling services), a respiratory system (greenery), and skin (buildings, the protective covering for its inhabitants). On the other hand, a city's statues, monuments, street names, and architecture function like fashionable outerwear, donned and doffed as a means of redefining and updating society's sense of self.[1]

Because a city's skeleton, sinew, and basic organs resist rapid alteration, urban space adapts slowly and incompletely to revolutionary change. Monuments can be removed, buildings torn down, or roads renamed, but roads, bridges, and developed areas cannot easily be changed—not without great economic and social loss. Redesigning infrastructure requires decades of "surgical" interventions, and the basic form of the city usually remains at least partially intact. A city's garments might change dramatically, redefining urban space by emphasizing or deemphasizing the city's

---

[1] In his *Understanding Media,* Marshall McLuhan borrows Lewis Mumford's concept of the city as clothing—a protective covering for society. See Marshall McLuhan, *Understanding Media, The Extensions of Man* (New York: McGraw-Hill, 1964), 47. Using a similar metaphor, Daniel Brower describes Imperial Russian cities as "extensions" of the imperial self—a means through which imperial power and identity were manifested. See Daniel R. Brower, *The Russian City Between Tradition and Modernity, 1850-1900* (Berkeley: University of California Press, 1990), 9–10. The notion that roads, bridges and transportation infrastructure constitute the "skeletal structure" of a city comes from A.E. Gutnov, "Strukturno-funktsional'nyi analiz gradostroitel'noi sistemy s ispol'zovaniem kolichestvennykh kharakteristik (na primere goroda Moskvy)," *Goroda i sistema rasseleniia* 18, no. 3 (1981): 45. Also see O.V. Orel'skaia, "Arkhitektura gorodov Gor'kovskoi aglomeratsii 1920kh–1930kh godov (Gor'kii, Balakhna, Dzerzhinsk)," (PhD diss., Arkhitekturnyi institut Moskvy, 1982), 17.

various elements, but the city consists of more than fashionable attire.[2] Contrary to what Orthodox Marxists once claimed, urban space is not purely derivative—that is, not a passive receptacle through which power manifests itself. Rather, urban space reflects and perpetuates old cultural patterns and ideas, frustrating human dreams of unfettered urban renewal or transformation.[3]

Because of the interaction between space and human events, the urban landscape represents a profitable area of research. Recognizing this, Viktor Buchli recently conducted an "archaeological" study of socialism. In his study, he examined the aesthetic, technical, and ideological development of Moscow's Narkomfin building (Moisei Ginzburg, 1928–1930), treating the building as a material artifact of Soviet culture.[4] Inspired by his focus on material history, this article will also conduct an archaeological study. But rather than examine a single building, this article will excavate an entire city—in this case, Nizhni Novgorod, Russia. Paying attention to both skeletal structure (morphology) and societal garments (architectural edifices), it will not only uncover the Soviet past, but also explore the dialogue between the Soviet, pre-Soviet, and post-Soviet eras.

The city to be excavated, Nizhni Novgorod, consists of two main sections, which are separated by the Oka River. On the right bank of the Oka, the medieval part of the city perches on a steep promontory overlooking the confluence of the Volga and Oka rivers. Appreciating the military and economic advantages of this site, Prince Iurii Vsevolodovich opted to establish a kremlin (a walled city) here in the early thirteenth century, a time of constant warfare involving the princes of Rus', Finno-Ugric tribes, and Mongol warriors. For almost two hundred years, the city's

[2] To oppose philosophers who claimed that their philosophy grounds itself in some *fundamental* truth, Derrida employed an architectural metaphor to suggest that philosophy, like architecture, defines its own foundation by delineating the ground in such a way as to appear to arise out of it. Although Derrida meant to discuss philosophy, not urban space, his comments on architecture's power of definition may prove useful to urban historians. On the architectural metaphor in Derrida's thought, see Mark Wigley, *The Architecture of Deconstruction: Derrida's Haunt* (Cambridge, MA: MIT Press, 1996).

[3] This approach to urban space was first advanced by Henri Lefebvre in his *The Production of Space*. For the most recent edition, see Henri Lefebvre, *The Production of Space* (Oxford: Blackwell, 1991). Edward Soja used Lefebvre's theories to critique traditional Marxist urban theory for ignoring the way in which spatial configurations of power can inhibit social and political change. See Edward W. Soja, "The Socio-Spatial Dialectic," *Annals of the Association of American Geographers* 70, no. 2 (June 1980): 207–25.

[4] Victor Buchli, *Materializing Culture: An Archaeology of Socialism* (Oxford: Berg, 1999); Victor Buchli, "Moisei Ginzburg's Narkomfin Communal House in Moscow: Contesting the Social and Material World," *The Journal of the Society of Architectural Historians* 57, no. 2 (June 1998): 160–81.

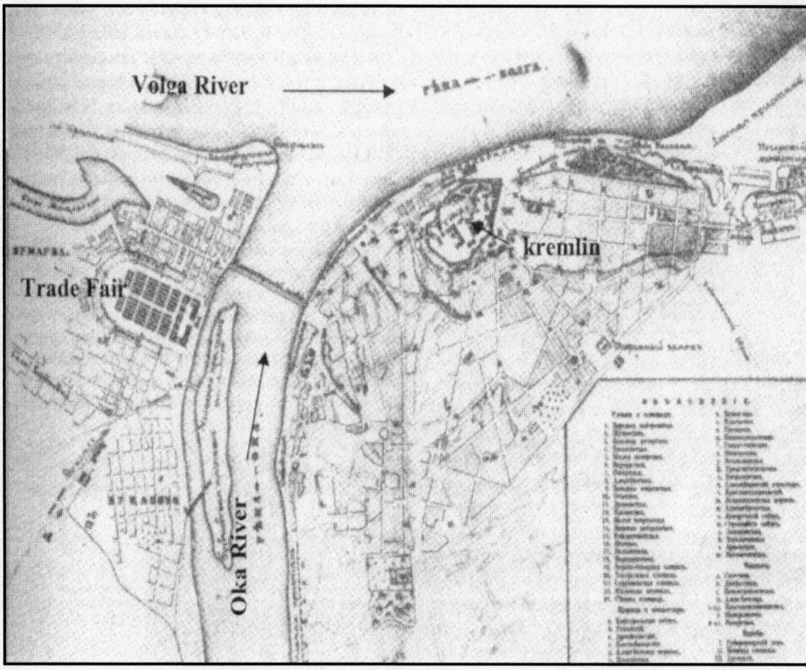

Image A. Nizhni Novgorod and the Trade Fair (c. 1877)

ruling princes fought to retain and expand their power, resisting subordination to Moscow until the late fourteenth century. Moscow's tsar, not a local prince, funded the construction of the current kremlin in the sixteenth century in preparation for an attack on Kazan, a Tatar stronghold. As Muscovy expanded, Nizhni Novgorod's commercial strength grew.

In the early nineteenth century, the city spread to the left bank of the Oka. This expansion can be attributed to the relocation of the Makariev Trade Fair to Nizhni Novgorod in 1817. This annual fair drew merchants from Western Europe as well as from Khiva and Bukhara.[5] Its growing commerce attracted port and transportation facilities, and these helped promote nascent industry. By 1928, the left-bank region had developed such extensive industry that Soviet authorities decided to incorporate the area, creating "Greater Nizhni Novgorod." The left-bank zone—consisting of Kanavino, Sormovo, and the small working-class settlements that encircled them—merged with Nizhni Novgorod in 1928. Avtozavod, the site of a factory town built in

[5] A complete history of the trade fair can be found in Anne Lincoln Fitzpatrick, *The Great Russian Fair: Nizhnii Novgorod, 1840–90* (London: Macmillan, 1990). For information on the facility's architectural design and construction by August Betancour, see N.F. Filatov, *Nizhnii Novgorod: Arkhitektura XIV–nachala XX vv. Entsiklopediia Nizhegorodskogo kraia* (Nizhnii Novgorod: Nizhegorodskie novosti, 1994), 68.

the early 1930s, became part of the city by the end of the decade. Through continued economic and population growth on both banks, post-Soviet Nizhni Novgorod has

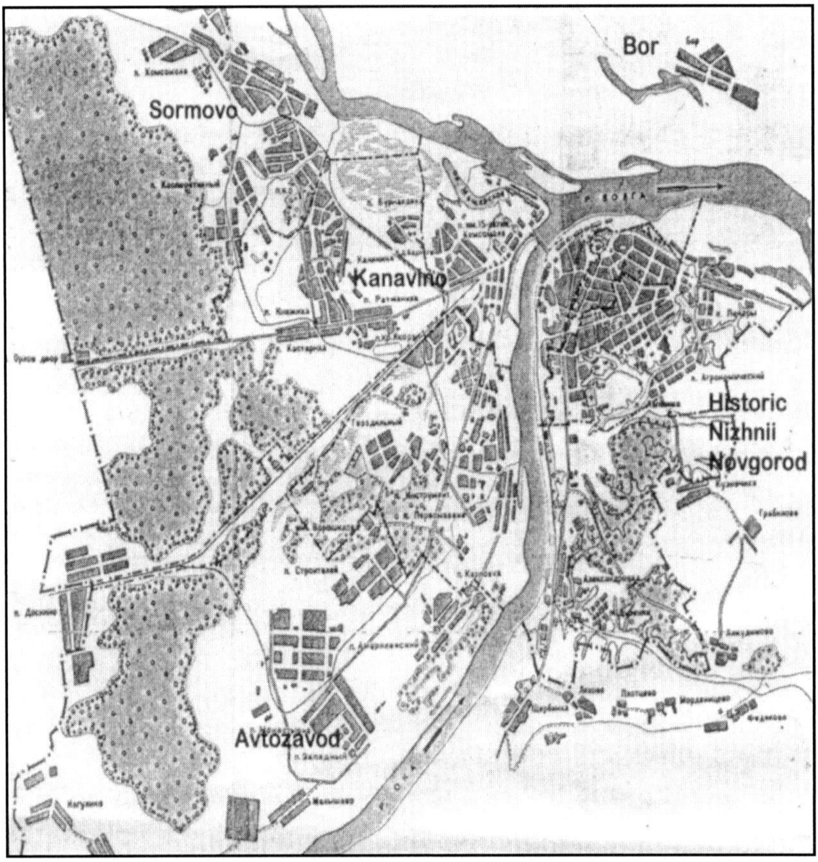

Image B. Districts of Nizhni Novgorod

become the third largest city in European Russia and an important center for education, industry, government, commerce and the arts.

Through its chronological development (from fortress-city to trade-city to industrial city to post-industrial commercial and cultural center), Nizhni Novgorod inherited a number of competing traditions—local and national, religious and secular, Soviet and anti-Soviet. Its post-Soviet space reproduces these divergent traditions, particularly insofar as two competing architectural trends have emerged: "contextualized architecture" and "generic modernism." Both styles embrace some aspects of Soviet modernism and both articulate a distinct sense of city and place, but their responses to city, place, and tradition differ greatly.

Contextualized architecture emerged in the 1990s, when post-Soviet Russia rediscovered its pre-Soviet past. Eschewing Soviet uniformity in design, the soon-to-be masters of contextualized architecture united the grace of simple, rational form (as embraced by constructivists) with an appreciation for the city's architectural her-

Image C.
Nizhnii Novgorod State Bank (1913)

Image D.
"Contextualized Modernism":
"Garantiia" Bank (1993–94)

itage, particularly its pre-Soviet treasures. They produced powerfully avant-garde and yet local works of architecture—buildings that modernized the urban landscape without diminishing its historically distinct (and diverse) aesthetic.[6]

Alongside such experiments, architects also perpetuated what might be called generic modernism. Although these architects shunned the standardized designs and the low-quality workmanship typical of Soviet construction, their work sustained the city's modernist architectural legacy—the constructivism of the 1920s and the post-Stalin period. They produced highly innovative designs, projects that can only be called "generic" insofar as they would suit almost any industrial or post-industrial

[6] For more on the post-Soviet development of the city, particularly on the tension between "contextualized" and "generic modern" architecture and the politics fostering the relative predominance of one or the other, see Sandra Frimmel, "The Miracle of Nizhny Novgorod, or How a Russian Provincial City Became the Country's Architectural Capital," *Kultura* 2 (February 2006): 3–7. For more on "contextualized modernism," also see *Project Russia,* no. 4 (1997), 15–88. Finally, see O.V. Orel'skaia, *Arkhitektura epokhi sovetskogo avangarda v Nizhnem Novgorode* (Nizhnii Novgorod: Promgrafika, 2005), 158–65.

Image E. Project for Residential Building in Avtozavod (1999)

Image F. The Socialist City of Avtozavod (c. 1932)

city. Such projects celebrated the aesthetic thrill of modern rational form, not the particularities of local space. Although such modernist works can be found on both sides of the city, generic modernism blends most harmoniously with the modernist architecture of the left-bank area.

Architects of both schools merit praise for bold creativity in reinventing Russian architecture, yet their differences reflect the tension between the local, the national, and the global. Contextualized modernism emerged in the early 1990s, when local control over architecture and governance climaxed; generic modernism predates it and has continued to flourish, irrespective of decreasing local autonomy. The former articulates what is unique to local history, whereas the latter delights in modern, global progress and innovation. Both grapple with the relationship between locality and (post)modernity.

Soviet cultural and political leaders grappled with these same forces, and the Soviet system therefore became known both for its grandiose celebration of modernity (Moscow, the subway, urbanization, factories, etc.) and for its recurrent embrace of historic and folk architectural motifs. In the Soviet period, sentiments favoring architectural preservation warred with those seeking to destroy the imperial architectural heritage. Boris Groys locates this tension between traditional and revolutionary elements, particularly as manifested in socialist realist architecture, in the Marxist dialectic.[7] But, one might also root this tension in the problem of place—in the challenge of translating ideology into practice, making it meaningful and applicable to local experience.[8] In Nizhni Novgorod, the Soviet future had to negotiate its place in a pre-Soviet present—a process that both extended and destroyed the legacy of tsarist predecessors.

Image G. Alexander Nevsky Cathedral (on the Strelka) (c. 2000)

Visitors to Nizhni Novgorod unknowingly witness the legacy of this battle whenever they travel down the hill from the kremlin to the bridge over the Oka. As they cross the river, their eyes are generally drawn to a rather enigmatic scene—a tall cathedral standing in the midst of loading cranes. In the early 1920s, authorities had tentatively designated the site on which the cathedral stands as the new city center. Not only did they plan to move municipal offices to the area at the foot of the bridge,[9] but they also proposed to annex Bor, which lies on the opposite side of the Volga River.[10] To highlight the symbolic centrality of this site, they drafted plans

[7] Boris Groys, "The Art of Totality," in *The Landscape of Stalinism: The Art and Ideology of Soviet Space,* ed. E.A. Dobrenko and Eric Naiman (Seattle: University of Washington Press, 2003), 96–124.

[8] Without translating abstract ideology into a real context, the Soviet regime could not legitimize its rule. For a study of the Soviet state's appropriation of the Russian imperial past as a means of legitimization, see David Brandenburger, *National Bolshevism: Stalinist Mass Culture and the Formation of Modern Russian National Identity, 1931–1956.* Russian Research Center Studies, 93 (Cambridge, MA: Harvard University Press, 2002).

[9] The city administration currently resides in the kremlin, but in the 1930s planners referred to the site of the current trade fair as "city council square," because they intended to build a new city council building on the site. See State Archive of the Russian Federation (hereafter GARF), f. A-314, op. 1, d. 7509, ll. 38–39.

[10] This plan was only one of four proposals for Nizhni Novgorod, as drawn up between 1928 and 1931. These four proposals are discussed in V.G. Davidovich and T.A. Chizhikova, *Aleksandr Ivanitskii* (Moscow: Stroiizdat, 1973), 73–80; O.V. Orel'skaia, *Arkhitektura epokhi Sovetskogo avangarda v Nizhnem Novgorode* (Nizhnii Novgorod: Promgrafika, 2005), 26. For more about the proposal discussed in this article (and about local support for it), see Heather DeHaan, "From Nizhnii to Gor'kii: The Reconstruction of a Russian Provincial City in the Stalinist 1930s" (PhD diss., University of Toronto, 2005), 186–215. Aspects of the plan

for a riverside architectural ensemble that would have culminated in a large lighthouse on the *strelka*, the arrow-shaped (or *strelka*-shaped) patch of land on which the cathedral stands. The cathedral threatened to lose its place as the city's riverside beacon.[11]

These Soviet plans to relocate the city center to the *strelka* reflected the ideological and architectural challenge posed by the formation of Greater Nizhni in 1928. Ideally, the creation of "Greater Nizhni Novgorod" would have given historic "merchant Nizhni" a truly industrial, Soviet identity, while facilitating the modernization of the left-bank district, which lacked sufficient public transportation, paved roads, schools, street lights, and cultural facilities. In honor of the geographic and industrial dimensions of the new city, Soviet planners sought to establish a new city center somewhere on the left bank, in the quintessentially Soviet (i.e., industrial) zone. They initially selected the *strelka,* because of its prominent location on the left-hand side of the confluence, opposite the kremlin—a site far too important to be dominated by the Alexander Nevsky Cathedral.

Image H. Alexander Nevsky Cathedral (under restoration) (1999)

Despite these plans, Soviet authorities never destroyed the cathedral on the *strelka.* In 1929, they closed the church and began making plans to reconstruct the area. By the mid-1930s, however, they no longer envisioned the *strelka* as the new city center. And so, the Alexander Nevsky Cathedral became a fish storehouse to serve the surrounding wharf facility. Large outer segments of the building were torn away to accommodate newly laid service roads. By 1976, local authorities regretted their abuse of the building, which they came to view as an architectural treasure, and they

are also discussed in the file of Ivanitsky, the head planner at the time, as found in the Russian State Archive of Literature and Art (RGALI), f. 2991, op. 1, d. 26, ll. 23–24.

[11] For the debate over later alterations to this proposal, see GARF, f. A-314, op. 1, d. 7509, ll. 39–40.

permitted architectural students to begin restoring the church. Thanks to the collapse of Soviet power, the cathedral has regained its religious purpose, and it also hosts an icon-painting school. Nevertheless, a riverside line of loading cranes continues to mar its silhouette, reminding visitors of the early Soviet distain for the edifice.[12]

Having cast aside plans to center the city on the *strelka,* Soviet planners continued to search for a new city center. After careful thought (and a change in planning teams), they selected the Oka.[13] The river literally divides historic Nizhni Novgorod from the city's modern industrial regions, providing an undeniable "middle line" in the city. Insofar as the river's ports and waterways sustained local industrial development, the new center seemed appropriate for an industrial city. Besides, like the Volga, the Oka River represented the vital, "primordial" force of the Russian people—an appealing symbol for a self-proclaimed "socialist democracy" that shrewdly co-opted patriotic sentiment in the 1930s. In addition, the Oka arguably embodied "rationalized" nature—a sort of civilized and yet animate force, for its waters would soon be walled up behind a shoreline dam to prevent flooding. In this, it represented Soviet-style harmony between man and nature.[14]

Image I. Sketch of Plans for Gorky Monument on the Right Bank (1936)

[12] For the history of restoration, see M.S. Kudriavtsev, "Vozrozhdenie sobora Aleksandra Nevskogo," in *Rossiia i Nizhegorodskii krai: aktual'nye problemy istorii*, ed. T.I. Pelevina and I.I. Soina (Nizhnii Novgorod: Nizhegorodskii gumanitarnyi tsentr, 1998), 269–71.

[13] GARF, f. A-314, op. 1, d. 7509, ll. 28–29, 39.

[14] For more on this ambitious architectural plan, see GARF, f. A-314, op. 1, d. 7501, ll. 3–4; GARF, f. A-314, op. 1, d. 7509, l. 99. Also see DeHaan, "From Nizhnii to Gor'kii," 249–52.

To center the city on the Oka, planners aimed to construct a series of five permanent bridges over the river. The bridges would have facilitated movement from the historic city to the new industrial regions, more fully integrating these distinct zones. The bridges would have been placed at the most scenic locations along the river, and each would have been sculpted architecturally, often with the support of new statues and monuments. On the slope above the bridge near the *strelka* (at the time, the only permanent bridge over the Oka), they hoped to place a large statue of the writer Maxim Gorky (after whom the city was named from 1932 to 1991). From this statue, viewers would have been able to look out over the Oka and its bridge to an enormous, new city square. Planners claimed that the new square would accommodate a parade ground with stands, a Lenin monument, and a row of fountains with enough splendour to rival that of Versailles.[15]

The new plan would have required the "skeletal" reconstruction of both sectors of the city. In the upper city, architects proposed to remove the entire eastern wall of the kremlin, a modification that would have enabled inhabitants to view the Oka from the main city square, located east of the kremlin wall.[16] Throughout the left-bank sector, planners aimed to rationalize the city's roads, which had sprouted up in a rather haphazard fashion around individual settlements. Some roads had to be straightened, and new highways had to be built out from the bridges into the left-bank interior. Had the plan been realized, it would have resulted in the destruction of a large portion of the existing housing stock on the left bank, where two-storey wooden construction lined roads destined for elimination or "straightening." In its place, planners promised to provide modern, multi-storey apartment buildings, particularly along the major transportation routes.[17]

Subterranean forces conspired to undermine this grandiose vision. Just under the surface of the city's right- and left-bank soils, underground streams pulsed out

[15] Central Archive of Nizhnii Novgorod Oblast (hereafter TsANO), f. R-78, op. 2, d. 304, l. 21.

[16] For a description of these plans, see A.F. Zhukov, "Kak rekonstruirovat' Sovetskuiu ploshchad'," *Gor'kovskii rabochii* 48 (February 28, 1936): 2; Nikolai Ushakov, "Kreml' i Sovetskaia ploshchad'," *Gor'kovskii rabochii* 40 (February 21, 1936): 2. For the decree approving the destruction of the kremlin wall, see "Ob osnovnykh polozheniiakh po sostavleniiu general'nogo plana rekonstruktsii goroda Gor'kogo," *Gor'kovskii rabochii* 164 (July 19, 1936): 1.

[17] Such plans elicited strong opposition from the Director of Construction at the Sormovo Park of Culture and Relaxation. This director, Kokushkin, objected to the proposed destruction of existing housing in the name of realigning roads. See Ia. Kokushkin, "Realen li proekt planirovki Sormova, razrabotannyi Giprogorom?" *Krasnyi Sormovich* 278 (December 4, 1936): 2; GARF, f. A-314, op. 1, d. 7508, ll. 12ob, 13ob.

to the Oka and Volga rivers, destabilizing the ground along the waterfront. On the left bank, such streams frequently swelled up, flooding the surface and damaging building foundations. On the right bank, they eroded the soil, leading to frequent landslides. The proposed monuments (in particular, the Gorky monument) would prove too heavy for this delicate soil structure, and the entire riverfront would have required extensive hydrogeological engineering prior to bridge construction. Such engineering would have cost more time, money, and know-how than the Soviet system could afford in the 1930s. Thus, a second bridge was not built until the 1970s, and the road grid on the left bank remained largely unreformed. Large patches of swampland (which should have been eliminated) remain and landslides (which also should have come to an end) reportedly riddled the right-bank slope in the 1970s.[18]

Thanks to this "subterranean conspiracy," as well as shortfalls in economic and material resources, Soviet authorities failed to center the city on the Oka; in fact, even planners' concept of the city resisted change. Throughout the period, they referred to the left-bank region as the *Zaoch'e*, the "land beyond the Oka" (as opposed to the historic center, which remained the "land on this side of the Oka"). Their political patrons seemed no more eager to change the status quo, for they quickly occupied the impressive architectural edifices located on the right bank. In doing so, they symbolically usurped power from their predecessors, and they avoided the expense of building new facilities. At the same time, they helped preserve the pre-Soviet form of the city, so that the city's main cultural and administrative bodies remained on the right bank.

Image J. Main Trade Fair Building (1999)

Just as the Alexander Nevsky Cathedral and the language of the *Zaoch'e* survived the Soviet era, so did several elements of the city's nineteenth-century trade fair complex. Because plans for reconstruction along the waterfront failed, the area near the *strelka* includes neither a lighthouse nor a mass square for demonstrations. Rather, the city's main trade fair building, unchanged since the nineteenth century, occupies the site. Even the old trade fair cathedral, tucked behind the main building, remains fully intact after years of Soviet power.

[18] Lev Liudvigovich Trube, *Naselenie goroda Gor'kogo* (Gorky: Volga-Viatskoe, 1982), 23.

Image K. Trade Fair Booths

These trade fair buildings testified to the pre-Soviet base of Soviet power—something that Soviet authorities preferred not to acknowledge. In the nineteenth century, the trade fair's grounds overflowed with buyers, sellers, entertainers, and sightseers. Just before the annual fair opened, booths and pavilions sprang up all across the area around the main buildings. This concentration of economic activity fostered local development—the construction of roads, bridges, ports, banks, and a railway. The new industrial regions of "Greater Nizhni" owed their initial industrial development to the economic impetus provided by this fair. In fact, Soviet power relied upon the commercial and transportation facilities that the fair had attracted to the region.

Nevertheless, to Soviet authorities, this trade fair complex was a "contaminant." Just as archaeologists define all items carried upward from one archaeological layer of history to the next as contaminants, so the trade fair would have been viewed as a contaminant, for it belonged to an earlier historical period, one that supposedly had no place in the subsequent, Soviet layer.[19] Wishing to obliterate this relic of the past, Soviet leaders had closed the fair, removed the stalls around the main building, and filled in the canals that once provided water, sanitation, and drainage to the site. Hoping to replace the trade fair complex, they sponsored

Image L. Lenin Monument (on Lenin Square)

[19] The cathedral bears an uncanny resemblance to St. Isaac's in St. Petersburg, for it was also designed by August Montferran. For more on the cathedral's design, see S.M. Shumilkin, "Nizhegorodskaia iarmarka," *Arkhitekturnoe nasledstvo SSSR* 29 (1981): 80–9.

designs for the remaking of the site.

Yet, the trade fair "contaminant" still stands, and the area did not undergo significant reconstruction until the 1970s, when municipal leaders funded the construction of a new city square. The new square did not displace the trade fair, and it was much smaller than the square proposed in the 1930s. Located slightly to the south of the current trade fair site, this new square—known as Lenin Square—features the city's long-promised Lenin monument. Lenin faces the Oka River, with his arm outstretched as if to hail the socialist future and welcome visitors to the industrial, left-bank districts of Nizhni Novgorod.[20] Situated toward the foreground of the square, his seventeen-meter high monument expresses the force and power of a great leader. Yet, the site lacks the visible dominance of the *strelka* or the area at the foot of the bridge (i.e., the location of the trade fair building). Also, Lenin's hand points toward a nearby hotel, one reportedly frequented by the local, post-Soviet mafia—the very sort of ambitious capitalists whom Lenin had despised. Lenin and the Soviet history that he represents appear to be squeezed between pre- and post-Soviet capitalism, between the old fair and the new capitalists.

However, the future for which Lenin fought has not entirely disappeared. About twenty kilometers up the Oka, in the direction in which Lenin points, one will find the Gorky Automobile Factory (GAZ), the pride of Soviet-era Nizhni Novgorod. Built with technical assistance from the Ford Motor Company, the factory produced the Soviet equivalent of the Ford Model-T. Its first automobile, the GAZ-A, rolled off the assembly line in 1932. Built with the latest technology, the new vehicle embodied the Soviet vision of the future—modern, efficient, scientific, powerful, and fast.

Image M. The First GAZ-A (1932)

Being somewhat enchanted by modern industrial processes, planners proposed to apply assembly-line rationalization to

[20] The sculptor was Iu.G. Neroda, and the architects of the square were V.V. Voronkov and Iu.N. Voskresensky. For more on this monument, see S.L. Agafonov et al., eds., *Pamiatniki istorii i kul'tury g. Gor'kogo* (Gorky: Volga-Viatskoe, 1977), 22.

the factory's domestic production. In plans for the nearby factory town, they divided housekeeping into discrete tasks that could be carried out by specialized state institutions (laundry services, public baths, dining halls, nurseries, etc.), thereby freeing women to work in the factory. Domestic life revolved around housing combines, clusters of seven multi-storey buildings. Each complex included public services and "self-improvement" facilities, such as reading and study rooms. The original

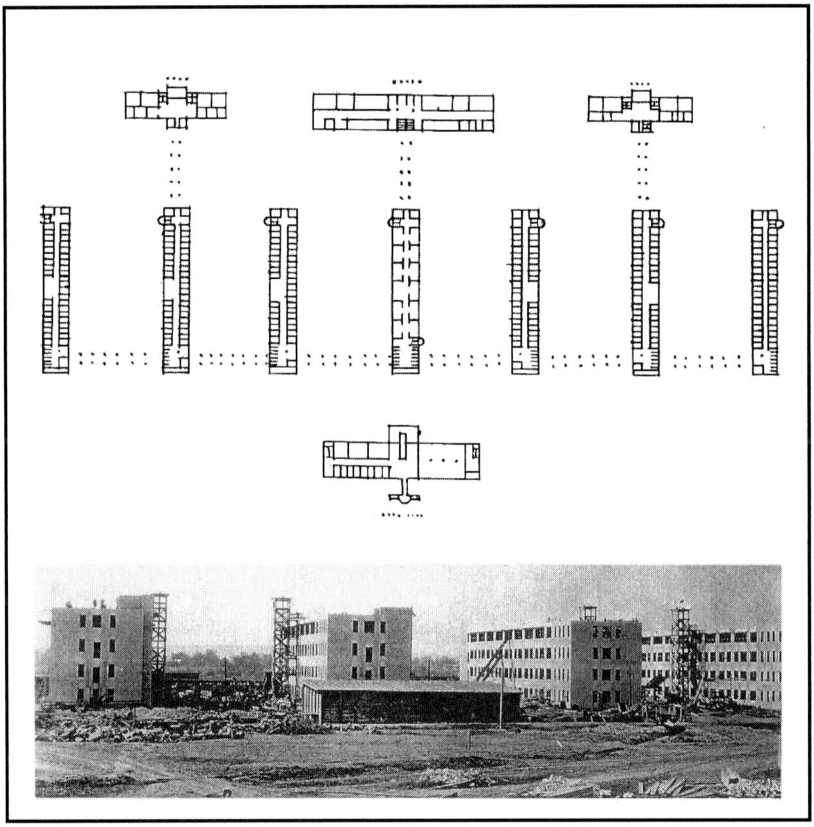

Image N. Design for Housing Combine (MVTU, 1929)

plans did not include family apartments (which might have fostered "unspecialized" domestic arrangements), but separated different age categories, allotting each age group its own residential space. All buildings included red corners (corners with "icons" of Soviet leaders as well as propaganda materials). In addition, to ensure that all units would be flooded with natural light, designers spaced the buildings far apart on a north-south axis, so that all rooms would receive either full morning or full afternoon sunshine.

The GAZ complex fuelled the utopian dreams of architects, mechanical engineers, social engineers, and Soviet political leaders for it promised to restructure all dimensions of human life; yet, both the factory and factory town failed to meet the expectations of their founders. The factory complex suffered from regular production shortfalls, which resulted from hasty, shoddy construction and the lack of properly trained workers. As for the factory's "socialist city," common workers rejected the proposed living arrangements. They shunned the housing combines' communal services and refused to forego family-based domestic arrangements—not only because of their loyalty to the family structure, but also because communal services were either poor quality or non-existent. Soviet authorities seemed to foresee these problems, for in 1930 they criticized plans to communalize domestic life. In response, architects proposed "transitional combines," which made "temporary" concessions to the family unit.[21] Yet, even these failed. Thanks to housing shortages, entire families moved into single rooms.[22] Constructed without proper plumbing or kitchen facilities, the new units proved to be rather inconvenient dwellings. Even today, the complexes serve as administrative buildings and hotel rooms, not as residential facilities.[23] In addition, due to the scarcity of readily available land on which to build cheaply (for the surrounding area was swampy and required costly hydrogeological amelioration prior to construction), later residential construction ceased to be so widely spaced.[24]

Although planners failed to meet their initial goals for domestic production, GAZ remains a powerful symbol of Soviet industrial might. Until the end of the Soviet period, GAZ was the "bastion" of socialism. Its automobiles represented modern speed and power, its production spawned further economic growth, and its plants could be used to produce weaponry if need be. To this day, the automobile factory remains the Gorky Automobile Factory and has not altered its name to become the Nizhni Novgorod Factory, for it owes its origin, fame, and significance to the

---

[21] N.A. Miliutin outlined the decree as well as his proposals for the transitional combine in N.A. Miliutin, *Problemy stroitel'stva sotsialisticheskikh gorodov* (Moscow, 1930), 124.

[22] For more on the socialist city at GAZ, see O.V. Orel'skaia, "Arkhitektury gorodov Gor'kovskoi aglomeratsii," 65–8; O.V. Orel'skaia, "Eksperiment prodolzhaetsia: iz istorii sovetskoi arkhitektury," in *Zapiski kraevedov*, ed. N.I. Kuprianova and I.V. Sidorova (Gorky, 1981), 39–48; A.N. Muravlev, "Sotsgorod avtozavoda im. Molotova (k 10-ti letiiu so dnia osnovaniia)," *Biulleten' arkhitektury* (Gorky, 1940), 24.

[23] For the history of this complex, see Orel'skaia, *Arkhitektura epokhi,* 60–3.

[24] Marina Ignatushko, a trained architect and local journalist, pointed out this design flaw to me in 2001, when we were discussing contemporary planners' attitudes to the old socialist city.

Image O. Avtozavod District, Residential Quarter No. 4 (1936–38)

Soviet past (when the city was known as Gorky). With the collapse of the Soviet system, GAZ, which had not been designed to compete nationally or internationally, underwent a painful period of lagging production and layoffs. It had been a truly Soviet product—one that could easily have crumpled together with the Soviet system.

In spite of Soviet setbacks and post-Soviet disappointments, Soviet power can take credit for modernizing the left bank. Broad paved thoroughfares, heavyset buildings with bold-lettered signs, as well as a multitude of trees and parks define left-bank urban life. All major roadways are now lined with modern construction. In the GAZ settlement, despite the failures of communal settlement, architects successfully oversaw the construction of large, monumental apartment blocks—buildings designed to communicate the Soviet system's durability and majesty. In the 1960s and 1970s, these were joined by five- to fourteen-storey buildings, mostly built according to standardized designs that economized on construction costs. These buildings, and some of the more experimental designs of the late Soviet period, celebrated industrial power, and they transformed the appearance of the left-bank area, turning scattered, pre-Soviet settlements into an aesthetically unified and modern city.[25]

Although GAZ struggled to survive post-Soviet global competition, the technology that GAZ first introduced to the city remains vital to urban life. Traversing post-Soviet Nizhni Novgorod requires a car or, at the very least, a space on a city bus or taxi, for the city's dimensions exceed those of a pre-modern city, which one might have crossed on foot. To cross from GAZ to the right bank, visitors need to enter a thick line of traffic over the bridge to the opposite bank of the Oka. All along the route, foreign and Russian cars, buses, taxis, and taxi-buses crowd city roads, squeezing past familiar, Soviet-era buildings and a host of new stores—mostly, local branches of Moscow-based chains.

From the right bank, one can look back over the Oka to the left bank—over

[25] For a discussion of local architectural development in late Soviet period, see Orel'skaia, *Arkhitektura epokhi,* 152–6. Also see O.V. Orel'skaia, *Arkhitekturnyi duet: Aleksandr Kharitonov i Evgenii Pestov* (Nizhnii Novgorod: Promgrafika, 2001), 10–67.

to GAZ, the Lenin monument, the trade fair, and the *strelka*. All along the bank on top of which the onlooker stands, there are trees lining the slope—in some areas, so thick and dense that they seem to offer an escape from urban life. To the east of these trees, a long highway links this area near the city's outskirts to the city center. The closer one draws to this city center, the greater the historic variety of architecture. On this bank, too, the past "contaminates" the present; but here, many of these "contaminants" derive from pre-modern periods of history.

The very placement and position of this right-bank city reflects the city's origins as a fortress-town. Established in 1221, medieval Nizhni Novgorod served as the outpost for Prince Iurii Vsevolodovich, who sought to expand his realm eastward, into lands inhabited by Finno-Ugric tribes. The original kremlin, like the sixteenth-century kremlin that now dominates the site, took advantage of the site's steep slopes and natural ravines, incorporating these into its defense structure. On its northern and western sides, steep slopes led down to the riverfront, flanking the kremlin walls and protecting them from assault from the ground; along the kremlin's southern and eastern sides, dense woodlands and ravines limited the number of approaches to the city, making the city easier to guard. To enhance the natural advantages of the site, kremlin defenders built two outer defense walls, each with watchtowers and guarded entrances.[26]

Visitors to this city stumble across this early defense structure whenever they traverse the upper city. Throughout the upper city, the main traffic arteries radiate outward from the kremlin. These often follow the lines of ancient ravines and many likely perpetuate former pathways into the walled city. These arteries are intersected by two ring roads, which apparently follow the lines of the former defense perimeters. (One can even see a section of the inner defense perimeter on Piskunov Street.)[27] Many city bridges lead over ravines, not rivers, and the overall terrain is uneven, marked by the dips and crevices that had once proved so beneficial for defense. One can still walk the road through the kremlin, which once served as the city's only land-based traffic artery. And of course, one can also view and travel along the two rivers—the medieval city's most convenient roads.

The city's contemporary structure also includes two medieval monasteries: Annunciation Monastery, which is located to the south of the city along the Oka, and

---

[26] L. Trube, *Naselenie goroda Gor'kogo* (Gorky: Volgo-Viatskoe, 1982), 21.

[27] Filatov, *Nizhnii Novgorod*, 14, 64; T.I. Pelevina et al., eds., *Ulitsy goroda Gor'kogo. Spravochnik* (Gorky: Volgo-Viatskoe, 1972), 99. For a description of the kremlin and its fortifications, also consult S.L. Agafonov, *Kamennaia letopis' goroda* (Gorky: Volgo-Viatskoe, 1971); S.L. Agafonov, *Nizhegorodskii kreml': arkhitektura, istoriia, restavratsiia* (Gorky: Volgo-Viatskoe, 1976).

Pechersky Monastery ("The Monastery of the Caves"), which is located to the east of the city along the Volga. Although these were not founded by imperial or princely fiat and lacked the towers, trenches, and advanced technology of the kremlin's defenses, both monasteries contributed to urban defense: their thick, stone walls protected inhabitants from attack, and both could serve as outposts warning the local kremlin of any impending threat. In addition, each carried out a variety of urban functions, showing as much complexity and variety in purpose as the kremlin in this early period: each conducted religious services, offered healing and poor relief, and also included a *posad* (a settlement for trade and handicraft production), located just outside the gates. (Nizhni Novgorod had its own *posady*—one outside the eastern gate and another outside the southern gate.)

Although the city's skeletal system retains these early modern features, its clothing has changed radically and even its skeleton has been significantly restructured. The city has outgrown the kremlin, which is now just an administrative and cultural facility, not a city within walls. Although a symbol of defense, the kremlin no longer serves any military purpose. New traffic arteries extend outward from the kremlin, and even the historic part of the city has a distinctively modern feel. Catherine II, Alexander I, and Nicholas I invested ample funds into modernizing this city: their engineers filled in swamps, redirected existing water flows, stabilized the slopes of both riverbanks and ravines, and straightened and paved roads. They imposed laws banning wooden construction in the city center, and they banished residential buildings from the kremlin. Nicholas I also banned non-pedestrian traffic from the kremlin, although the kremlin road used to be the sole link between the upper-city zone, the kremlin, and the Oka.[28] Soviet authorities contributed their own alterations, by widening streets, paving roads, and further modernizing the transportation and public service infrastructure.[29]

Despite these "skeletal" changes, even Soviet leaders preserved the essential features of the structure. As already noted, their plans to tear down the eastern kremlin wall floundered, largely because local authorities lacked the time and funds required for reconstruction. Besides, the eastern kremlin wall served as the focal point for upper city streets, and its removal would have left an aesthetic and functional gap in the upper city's road grid. Local residents valued the kremlin's historicity, and they protested the wall's proposed destruction.[30] Also, by the late 1930s, Soviet

[28] Filatov, *Nizhnii Novgorod*, 25–6, 70.

[29] These plans are outlined in Kazin, "Rekonstruktsiia ulitsy Sverdlova," *Gor'kovskii rabochii* 43 (February 22, 1936): 2. Also see G. Fedorov, *Sotsialisticheskii gorod Gor'kii* (Gorky: OGIZ, 1939), 51–2. On Culture Street, see GARF, f. A-314, op. 1, d. 7501, l. 4.

[30] A.A. Iakovlev, Jr., "Sleduet li snosit' kremlevskuiu stenu?" *Gor'kovskii rabochii* 48 (Feb-

authorities began to pose as successors of the Russian state tradition—a stance that precluded the ready dismissal of historic architectural treasures. Thus, sentiment, economics, and political manoeuvring connived to keep the kremlin system intact, even as the sediment of time buried many of its old features and functions.

Soviet authorities did, however, refashion the city, covering it with a host of new monuments, street names, and architectural edifices and styles. In particular, they delighted in symbolic inversions: Prison (Ostrog) Square became Freedom Square, and the former seminary became a pedagogical institute. Streets named in honor of churches (e.g., Pokrovka, Varvarskaia, Alexeevskaia)[31] were renamed in honor of revolutionary figures and events (e.g., Sverdlov, Figner, and October). New Bazaar Square, where radicals had once held demonstrations, became May 1st Square.[32] To plot revolutionary history in local space, Soviet leaders sponsored the preservation and commemoration of buildings and sites associated with local, supposedly "Soviet" heroes, particularly Maxim Gorky. All buildings visited by Vladimir Ilich Lenin merited plaques as a form of commemoration.

The very morphological form of Nizhni Novgorod posed a challenge, however, for its structure celebrated the Orthodox story of salvation. Thanks to the city's soteriological structure, the city became a stage through which Orthodox belief could be symbolized and enacted. Developing without a plan, through the actions and decisions of various individuals at different points in time, this soteriological layout gradually embedded itself in urban space. By the end of the seventeenth century, the city's spatial plan reached its maturity, allowing for the figurative, spatial "enacting" of the Orthodox drama of redemption.

The monasteries, the kremlin, and the road connecting them all played a crucial role in this latent drama. The city's soteriological stage began at the westernmost point in the city—Annunciation Monastery—and proceeded through the kremlin to the easternmost point—Pechersky Monastery. Urban space provided the acts in the drama, for urban toponyms and architecture provided references to biblical events. Since only one road passed through the kremlin, and only the kremlin road linked the

ruary 28, 1936): 2; A.I. Velikorechin, "Kreml' nado sokhranit'," *Gor'kovskii rabochii* 48 (February 28, 1936): 2.

[31] All the major radial streets in the upper city—Bol'shaia Pokrovka, Alekseevskaia, and Varvarskaia—as well as the two main streets in the lower city—Il'inka and Rozhdestvenskaia—began or ended with the church after which the street was named. See N.F. Filatov, *Nizhegorodskoe zodchestvo XVII–nachala XX veka* (Gorky: Volga-Viatskoe, 1980), 83–4; Filatov, *Nizhnii Novgorod*, 64.

[32] See Pelevina, *Ulitsy goroda Gor'kogo*, 89, 102; Iu.N. Bubnov and O.V. Orel'skaia, *Arkhitektura goroda Gor'kogo* (Gorky: Volga-Viatskoe, 1986), 36–7.

Image P. Annunciation Monastery

two monasteries, all visitors to the city engaged some element in this structure, whether or not they were aware of the overall composition.

There were six key elements in this structure. Through its name, the first "element," Annunciation Monastery, celebrated the announcement of Christ's coming birth, namely, the Angel Gabriel's visit to Mary, the soon-to-be mother of the Christ. From here, travelers moving toward the city followed Nativity Street, passed Nativity Church, and then entered the kremlin through the Ivan Gate. Thus far, they would have figuratively witnessed Christ's birth (the nativity) and Christ's baptism by Ivan, or John the Baptist. Insofar as Christ's baptism launched his earthly ministry, the kremlin interior can be viewed as a symbol of Christ's years of preaching and performing miracles on earth. Having entered the kremlin, travelers had to climb a steep hill—a veritable *Via Dolorosa* for the weary. At the top of the hill, they reached Cathedral of the Transfiguration, a symbol of the high point in Christ's earthy ministry, namely, Christ's transfiguration, when Christ's divine glory transformed his human body, awing his disciples and demonstrating his heavenly power. (For the Orthodox, this story of the Transfiguration offers hope for human redemption, the promise of transformation through union with Christ.) At this point, the road leveled off and a short path led to the eastern gates of the kremlin, which represented the end of Christ's years on earth. Outside these gates, people came to the Chapel of the Exaltation of the Cross, from where the road dipped down to the Monastery of the Caves, which arguably represented the church of the martyrs.[33] Thus, simply by traversing the entire city, the traveler could take a Chris-

Image Q. The Kremlin's Ivan Gate

[33] Most historians rightly stress that the monastery's name, as given to it by its founder Dionisii in the fourteenth century, is a reference to Kyiv's Pechersky (Cave) Monastery. However,

tian pilgrimage, revisiting key events in Christ's life on earth.[34]

This pre-Petrine city structure invited visitors and travelers to revisit Christ's life in contemporary urban space, and it clearly identified Nizhni Novgorod and its inhabitants with Eastern Orthodox Christianity. Even those who did not entirely identify with "pure" Orthodoxy fit into the landscape: Yarila Hill, the site of pagan festivals, was located to the southwest of Annunciation Monastery, outside the city at what might be dubbed a "pre-pilgrimage site"—the perfect location for a site that represented paganism.[35] And so, in this structure, earthly space served to represent sacred time.

Image R. The Kremlin Road

Image S. Cathedral of the Transfiguration (built 1652)

given its place in the city's religious and symbolic landscape, the name can surely be understood as a reference to both the Kyivan Monastery (a symbol of Slavic Orthodox piety) and to the catacombs (cave-like structures) of ancient Rome. First-century believers met, worshipped, and prayed in such catacombs. And so, the Monastery of the Caves can be viewed as a metaphorical reference to Christ's church, viewed as a living symbol of his resurrection.

[34] Such spatial-soteriological urban structures were not unique to Nizhni Novgorod or Russia, but were common to all pre-modern cities. See Lewis Mumford, *The Culture of Cities* (New York: Harcourt, Brace, & Co., Inc., 1938), 61–2. For a discussion of how England's seventeenth-century utopias (that is, writings about the ideal city) envisioned spaces that were as much spiritual as political, see Robert Appelbaum's *Literature and Utopian Politics in Seventeenth-Century England* (Cambridge: Cambridge University Press, 2002).

[35] No monograph discusses this soteriology, although information about the construction of individual elements in this structure can be found in the following sources: Filatov, *Nizhnii Novgorod*, 95; Sergei Ivanovich Arkhangel'skii, ed., *Nizhnii Novgorod v XVII veke: sbornik dokumentov. Iz materialov k istorii Nizhnego Novgoroda i ego okrugi* (Gorky: Gor'kovskoe knizhnoe izdatel'stvo, 1961), 96–7.

Image T. The Descent to Pechersky Monastery

Soviet texts make no mention of this pre-modern layout, perhaps because their urban historical narratives identified "urbanity" with progress and "sacred spaces" with eastern backwardness. (Scholars tend to identify the "sacred city" with Asia and the Far East, particularly India, not with western urban sites.) In addition, there appears to have been no tradition of organized or official pilgrimages through this space. Yet, Soviet authorities seemed to recognize the meaning of this early modern space, for in their attempts to symbolically "occupy" imperial space, they inverted this soteriological structure and imposed on it their own narrative, one about redemption from poverty and pain through secular modernization.

The Soviet soteriological narrative also began at Annunciation Monastery, where Soviet authorities turned Alekseevskaia Church—a nineteenth-century construction with a large central cupola—into a planetarium, effectively substituting the Big Bang (the beginning of evolution) for the Annunciation (the beginning of the story of the Messiah). Nativity Street, which had paid tribute to the birth of Christ, became Mayakovsky Street, in honor of a radical, avant-garde poet whose works celebrated the fires of Revolution as a regenerative force. Nativity Church temporarily became a Museum of Municipal Development, a change that suggested that the new source of human hope lay not in a Christ child, but in the birth of modern urban technologies. The Ivan Gate was allowed to decay, and the Cathedral of the Transfiguration was replaced by a constructivist House of Soviets. In this way, a building that celebrated the revolutionary power of workers' unity and modern rationality covered over the city's cathedral, a symbol of spiritual transformation through unity with Christ, embraced as God Incarnate.[36] Authorities closed the Monastery of the Caves, turning the nearby shores of the Volga into a recreational zone, as if to suggest that "life everlasting" consisted of health, rest, and vitality. Thus, Soviet Nizhni Novgorod, like pre-modern Nizhni Novgorod, set the stage for the symbolic reenactment of a cosmic drama, except that the Soviet drama stressed secular modernization, not spiritual transformation.

Through these changes, Soviet leaders dressed the city in revolutionary garb—not changing skeletal structures, but rather altering its self-defining cover. The new clothing pledged change through modernization, identifying Soviet power with a promise that had yet to become a reality. These "clothes" redefined local priorities and identity, highlighting the transformational impulse that lay at the core of the Soviet project. In the Soviet Revolution, they sought not just new spaces, but new men—to be created through these spaces. In this sense, the Soviet restructuring of the seventeenth-century soteriological structure proved emblematic. In reclothing the city, authorities voiced their commitment to the inner and spiritual transformation of society through material change and development—that is, through modernization.[37]

Image U. House of Soviets (1929–31)

[36] On these changes (discussed individually, without comment on the overall structural result), see Filatov, *Nizhnii Novgorod*, 24, 32; S.L. Agafonov, *Nizhegorodskii kreml'* (Gorky, 1971), 40.

[37] Janet Ward discusses such "modernist hope" in the power of architecture to play an "ethical, transformational role" in bettering society. See Ward, *Weimar Surfaces Urban Visual Culture in 1920s Germany*. Weimar and Now, 27 (Berkeley: University of California Press, 2001), 53.

Although the Soviet modification of the city's symbolic landscape clearly voiced the state's ideological commitments, few residents would have walked the space of the Soviet soteriological narrative. In fact, inhabitants rarely followed the kremlin road from one gate to the other, for Nicholas I had arranged for the construction of four roads around the kremlin in the early nineteenth century. Nicholas I's roads were designed to accommodate the high traffic volumes produced by the opening of the Nizhni Novgorod trade fair, and upon their completion, Nicholas I banned vehicular traffic from the kremlin.[38] Thereafter, only pedestrians walked the kremlin road, and even pedestrians had the option of taking another path.

Moreover, long before 1917, the city's Orthodox soteriological plan had deteriorated. First of all, it was missing a key element—namely, the Chapel of the Exaltation of the Cross. Second, society itself had changed, westernizing and secularizing to such an extent that residents may have been quite oblivious to the absence of the chapel. Westernization and imperial expansion had become as central to local and national identity as Orthodoxy. Already under Peter I, authorities showed insensitivity to the city's early modern "drama," approving the construction of a new, Annunciation Square outside the kremlin's eastern gate.[39] Any reference to the Annunciation belonged near the monastery, not in the middle of the city—at least, according to the city's pre-Petrine soteriology. Thus, when Soviet authorities inverted the "pilgrim structure" of the city, they inverted a defunct space—a space with "iconic" meaning, but largely irrelevant to day-to-day life.[40] The Soviet modification to this space unequivocally identified Soviet power with secular modernization, but Soviet rulers were hardly the first to modernize and weaken the structure.

---

[38] Filatov, *Nizhnii Novgorod*, 15–16 (time of Catherine II), 80 (time of Nicholas I).

[39] The chapel is not mentioned anywhere in the literature on architecture, possibly a sign that it decayed or burned down long before the coming of Soviet power. The Chapel of the Exaltation of the Cross was probably torn down, but the chapel was given a substitute in 1809—a woman's monastery, the Monastery of the Source. Nicholas I banished this monastery to the crest of the hill just above the site where one of the new Nicholas-era boulevards began its descent down to the pontoon bridge. At that time, the monastery was given its current name: the Monastery of the Exaltation of the Cross (Filatov, *Nizhnii Novgorod*, 41). The monastery served as a concentration camp in 1918 (L.M. Smirnova, *Nizhnii Novgorod do i posle: istoriko-literaturnye ocherki* [Nizhnii Novgorod: Begemot, 1996], 103). For more on the monastery, see William G. Wagner, "Paradoxes of Piety: The Nizhegorod Convent of the Exaltation of the Cross, 1807–1935," in *Orthodox Russia: Belief and Practice under the Tsars*, ed. Valerie A. Kivelson and Robert H. Greene (University Park: Pennsylvania State University Press, 2003), 211–38.

[40] Katerina Clark identified Soviet-era Moscow as an "iconic space"—that is, a material realm mean to manifest immaterial Soviet truths. See Katerina Clark, "Socialist Realism and Sacralizing of Space," in *The Landscape of Stalinism*, 3–18.

Yet, Soviet authorities differed from imperial authorities in their demand for the total transformation of society—spiritual and material. In their soteriology, Soviet authorities articulated active hostility to religion as a supposed hindrance to modernization. The constructivist House of Soviets most clearly expressed this, for its design rejected historic architectural traditions, producing a building defined by harmony between function and form. By contrast, imperial authorities had accommodated the sacred. Although they had also insisted that crooked streets be straightened and that cities have plans,[41] their newly paved boulevards frequently led to churches, following earlier sacralizing traditions.[42] Also, although their engineers might sometimes have gathered holy springs into underground collector pipes in order to prevent erosion, they showed sensitivity to popular faith. Nicholas I, in fact, provided a chapel at the site where a holy spring exited the river bank through a new, engineer-provided tube.[43]

Despite Soviet hostility to the imperial legacy, pre-Soviet Nizhni Novgorod survived the onslaught of Soviet power. Whatever garments the Soviets cast over the city could easily be cast off. And so, post-Soviet leaders "unclothed" the city, shedding the garb of the Soviet past. In 1991, the city shed its Soviet-era name, Gorky, in favor of its pre-Soviet identity, Nizhni Novgorod. Soviet toponyms disappeared as streets regained their pre-Soviet designations. Old churches reopened, and the streets once named after these regained their pre-revolutionary names. Annunciation Monastery reopened and, after years of juridical battle, the planetarium was removed from its premises. Nativity Street and Nativity Church were restored, as was the Monastery of the Caves. Soviet utopian ambitions, including the soteriological space that expressed these, were thrown aside or buried.

Yet, post-Soviet society has also accommodated the Soviet past. Lenin's monument remains on Lenin Square, and cranes continue to mar the silhouette of

[41] For instance, they banished residential dwellings surrounded by high fences and marked by side entrances. Seeking to create a harmonious, attractive street front, they mandated the construction of western-style, classical buildings with street-front entrances. See Filatov, *Nizhnii Novgorod*, 66–7; E.I. Kirichenko and E.G. Shcheboleva, *Russkaia provintsiia, Kul'turnoe nasledie Rossii* (Moskva: Nash dom; L'Age d'Homme, 1997), 60.

[42] Thanks to the founding of this monastery, three of Nicholas I's new boulevards down the Volga slope began with a church. (The other two began with churches located near the kremlin.)

[43] The waters feeding the holy spring near Annunciation Monastery were gathered into a collector pipe and forced to exit from the hillside further down the slope, nearer to the Oka. There, a chapel was built to sacralize the holy water (which now flowed out of a pipe). The original spring and its chapel had first been consecrated in the fourteenth century. See Filatov, *Nizhnii Novgorod*, 33, 95.

the Aleksander Nevsky Cathedral. The House of Soviets remains, for the building has rightly been deemed an architectural treasure—an impressive sample of early Soviet constructivism. A new Cathedral of the Transfiguration will likely never replace it. Outside the eastern gates of the kremlin, one now finds a monument to Kuzma Minin, a seventeenth-century merchant who organized the forces that helped bring the Romanov dynasty to the throne. A symbol of popular patriotism, his legacy was first embraced by Imperial authorities and then by Soviet and post-Soviet leaders. Soviet rule made the construction of this monument possible, for Soviet leaders removed the churches from the square outside the kremlin. Those churches have not been restored, not just because of the Minin monument, but because the square has become a major traffic center, a site far too busy to be narrowed and constrained by church construction.

In general, the current institutional geography of the city represents not only the end of the Soviet Revolution, but also its permanence. The imperial-era Commercial Club remains the Theatre for Youth (TIuZ).[44] The Rukavishnikov Mansion, an architecturally grandiose and elaborate building, remains the Museum of Local History.[45] The imperial-era archbishop's residence remains the site of the music conservatory, although church institutions have reclaimed other buildings in the Archbishop's administrative complex.[46] The Nobles' Meeting House (Dvorianskoe sobranie), which became the Sverdlov District House of Culture, is now a site for public exhibitions. The old Peasant Land Bank, which became the House of Pioneers, is still the "Pioneer building," although the Young Pioneers are now obsolete. In other words, while sites and symbols of worship have been revived, Soviet economic and political policy has clearly made some "counter-revolutions" unimaginable.

In fact, the very skeletal form of the city has changed, remaining impervious to changes in political style. Avtozavod, born as a Soviet socialist city, plays in indelible role in local economic and cultural life, and the new bridges over the Oka have facilitated movement through the city. The roads, waterlines, infrastructure, and public transportation systems installed in the Soviet era provide the infrastructure for post-Soviet development. Soviet factories, industries, housing projects, and infrastructure have reshaped urban patterns of movement and subverted old socioeconomic structures. Although spaces of worship and piety, including pilgrimages to holy springs and monasteries, have become important features of post-Soviet life, the legacy of Soviet industrial modernization remains.

[44] "Vpechatleniia o gorode," *Gor'kovskaia kommuna* 107 (May 11, 1936): 4; *Gorod Gor'kii: Putevoditel'* (Gorky: Volga-Viatskoe, 1964), 301–2.

[45] Fedorov, *Sotsialisticheskii gorod Gor'kii*, 7.

[46] Filatov, *Nizhnii Novgorod*, 91.

These Soviet artifacts will likely remain embedded in the post-Soviet landscape, for contemporary Russia lacks the strong, transformational and utopian impulse of Soviet times. "Modernist hope" in the power of spatial change to realize spiritual renewal has died, even if the House of Soviets remains. No longer conflicted by the need to realize total revolutionary transformation in change-resistant social and material spaces, post-Soviet leaders have fitted altered garments on an altered urban body. Nizhni Novgorod has outgrown its old clothing, but its current blend of old and new—or rather, its reinvention of historic traditions of trade, religion, and local pride—articulates a new identity and attempts to fit this identity on an ever changing urban landscape. Just as Soviet culture found itself shaped by the culture that preceded it, so post-Soviet life incorporates and reshapes its Soviet past. Local, national and international forces will continue to war with multiple pasts and a complex present, slowly and often irrevocably shaping the development of urban life.

Sources for Images

A. This map was taken from N.F. Filatov, *Nizhnii Novgorod: arkhitektura XIV-nachala XX vv.* (Nizhnii Novgorod: Nizhegorodskie novosti, 1994), 75.

B. The districts are plotted on the 1938 map of the city. For the original map (without English-language labels), see GARF, A-314, op. 1, d. 7510, l. 74.

C. The architect of this building was V. Pokrovsky. Maksim Dmitriev took this photograph at the turn of the 20th century. The photograph was printed in Tat'iana Pavlovna Vinogradova and Valerii Prokop'evich Mashkovtsev, *Tsarstvenno postavlennyi gorod: Nizhnii Novgorod v staroi otkrytke* (Vladimir: Posad, 2000), 103.

D. Architects E.N. Pestov and A.E. Kharitonov designed this building. The original photograph was published in *Project Russia*, no. 4 (1997): 33.

E. This design was produced by A. Kornilov. The image was printed in O.V. Orel'skaia, *Arkhitektura epokhi sovetskogo avangarda v Nizhnem Novgorode* (Nizhnii Novgorod: Promgrafika, 2005), 161.

F. This image was taken from Orel'skaia, *Arkhitektura epokha*, 62.

G. This image was taken from *Welcome: Nizhnii Novgorod Reference Guide Book* (Nizhnii Novgorod: Begemot, 2000), 9.

H. The church was designed by R. Kilevin and built between 1868 and 1881. This particular photograph was taken by Viktor Ivanovich Borodin and published in N. V. Morokhin, ed., *Nizhnii Novgorod. Predaniia . . . Istoriia . . . Novye vremena . . .*, with images and text compiled by V. I. Borodin and I. V. Sidorov (Nizhnii Novgorod: Nizhnii Novgorod Press, 1994), n.p.

I. This sketch was produced by the Leningrad State Institute for City Planning in 1936. This sketch can be found in Orel'skaia, *Arkhitektura epokhi*, 150.

J. The building was designed by A. von Gogen, G. Trambitsky, and K. Treiman in 1890. The photograph comes from Deirdre Shelley, n.p.

J. The building was designed by A. von Gogen, G. Trambitsky, and K. Treiman in 1890. The photograph comes from Deirdre Shelley, n.p.

K. Maksim Dmitriev appears to have been standing in the Main Trade Fair Building when he took this photograph. The image was printed in V.V. Koliabin, ed., *Na rubezhe dvukh vekov: Nizhegorodskoe povolzh'e i Volga v fotografiiakh M. P. Dmitrieva* (1985), 2nd edition (Gorky: Volgo-Viatskoe, 1988), 65.

L. Deirdre Shelley, n.p.

M. This photograph was taken by Viktor Ivanovich Borodin and published in Morokhin, *Nizhnii Novgorod*, n.p.

N. The design was produced by the Moscow Higher Technical Institute, as part of an international competition for this socialist city. To view the source of this image and to learn more about both the competition and the construction of the settlement, see Orel'skaia, *Arkhitektura epokhi*, 61.

O. This building was produced by the Vesnin Brothers' Architectural Workshop. The architects were N. Krasilnikov and P. Poliudov. For the photograph, see *Project Russia*, no. 4 (1997): 60.

P. Deirdre Shelley, n.p. The planetarium was housed in the large, domed church in the foreground of the monastery ensemble. When taking this photo, the photographer was standing on the bridge over the Oka River.

Q. The original photograph can be found in Vinogradova and Mashkovtsev, *Tsarstvenno postavlennyi gorod*, 162.

R. This road leads upward from the Ivan Tower, which can be seen on the right-hand side of this photograph. This image was taken by Maksim Dmitriev and can be found in Koliabin, *Na rubezhe dvukh vekov*, 35.

S. This photograph was taken by Maksim Dmitriev in Nizhnii Novgorod in 1911. This particular image was printed in Vinogradova and Mashkovtsev, *Tsarstvenno postavlennyi gorod*, 153. This cathedral, built in 1652, replaced an earlier edifice, which was first built in 1225 (Filatov, *Nizhnii Novgorod*, 23).

T. Author's photograph.

U. The building was designed by A. Grinberg. For the photograph, see Selim O. Khan-Magomedov, *Pioneers of Soviet Architecture: The Search for New Solutions in the 1920s and 1930s* (1983), trans. Alexander Lieven (London: Thames and Hudson, 1987), 414 (figure 1085).

Decay or Endurance? The Ruins of Socialism

Thomas Lahusen

> Put aside their negative image, so sensationalized by a self flagellating media, and view them, for a moment, as you might one of the celebrated ruins of the world. Then you may come to understand why I call them *The Fabulous Ruins of Detroit.*
>
> *Lowell Forest Boileau*

From Szoborpark, on the outskirts of Budapest, displaying statues of Karl Marx, Friedrich Engels, and Béla Kun, as well as monuments celebrating Soviet-Hungarian friendship and other "specters of Communism," to the Soviet banners, medals, and busts sold on Arbat Street or at the Izmailovsky flea market in Moscow, socialism has undoubtedly become part of the heritage and nostalgia industry.[1] Similar examples include the pop version of "The East Is Red" purchased at the Beijing Friendship Store, the Che Guevara key chain sold in a Cuban resort for Canadian vacationers, and Wolfgang Becker's much celebrated film *Good Bye Lenin!* (2003). Not all such objects or places, however, can compete in this new market of *lieux de mémoire* (sites of memory), to use Pierre Nora's term.[2] There are those that engage in rearguard resistance to preserve the "real environments of memory" (*milieu de mémoire*), that is, memory embedded in the everyday habits, traditions, and social interactions of "real socialism."

I believe that this resistance originates in the very *foundations* of real socialism, in its utopian impulse to build the people's home based on the overcoming of human alienation. The conditions in which this project took place meant that the building of socialism, in its concrete and metaphorical sense, was in a state of constant decay—in ruins—from the very beginning. As for the people, they endured. But it is precisely this endurance that explains the resistance, by both people and the

---

This article first appeared in *Slavic Review* (65, no. 4 [Winter 2006]: 736–46), published by the American Association for the Advancement of Slavic Studies. It is reprinted with the permission of the publisher.

[1] See Régine Robin, "The Past as a Dustbin, or, The Phantoms of Socialist Realism," in *Socialist Realism without Shores*, ed. Thomas Lahusen and Evgeny Dobrenko (Durham: Duke University Press, 1997), 337–55.

[2] Pierre Nora, "Between Memory and History: Les Lieux de Mémoire," in "Memory and Counter-Memory," special issue, *Representations,* no. 26, Spring 1989, 7–24.

landscapes in which they live, to the market. Nostalgia for socialism has become a commodity, but not for those who still live in its ruins, because they are home.

Does the fight to preserve the Palace of the Republic in Berlin represent such resistance? The palace was built in 1976 on Marx-Engels Platz (Schlossplatz today), on the spot where the ruin of the nineteenth-century baroque Hohenzollern palace of the former German royal family was dynamited and cleared away in 1950 by the government of the German Democratic Republic (GDR) to symbolize its break with the Prussian militarist past. The "international-style" architecture of the new palace, made of amber glass, metal, and concrete, was intended to express the achievements of advanced socialism. The building housed the People's Chamber (the GDR parliament); it was the meeting place for East Germany's trade unions, and it hosted many famous cultural events for GDR citizens, who could also get a touch of western atmosphere in its restaurants, bars and cafes, and bowling alley. To use Svetlana Boym's apt formula, it was "a site of power and a place for the people."[3] Closed after reunification due to asbestos contamination, it was stripped down to an empty shell between 1997 and 2002. In July 2002 the Bundestag determined the palace's fate: considered an eyesore in Berlin's historical center, its demolition began in early 2006. The reconstruction of the old palace has been announced for 2008, but funds have yet to be raised. In the meantime, a lawn will take the place of the Palace of the Republic. The website of the Association for the Preservation of the Palace of the Republic, officially created in 1997, argued that the decision to tear down the building was wrong, because "this piece of modern architecture demonstrates that the architects and builders were devoted to the fundamental idea of bringing together state and people." It represents, according to the association, "the continuation of the 'people's house,' an old social democratic tradition."[4]

> History was made in this building. Here the first freely-elected parliament of the G.D.R. paved the way to German unification. For that reason and with regard to the 40-year history of the two separated states, which are now reunited, is it necessary to do everything to preserve the building. During the past few years too much has been lost that is of importance for the citizens east of the River Elbe. Of course, much was destroyed before, but is that any justification for a renewed spirit of destruction?[5]

---

[3] Svetlana Boym, *The Future of Nostalgia* (New York: Basic Books, 2001), 188.

[4] "Palast der Republik," http://www.pdr.kultur-netz.de/ (accessed July 12, 2006). See also "Keeping the Light on at the People's Palace," *Deutsche Welle,* 10.07.2003, http://www.dw-world.de/english/0,3367,1441_A_916784_1_A,00.html (accessed July 12, 2006).

[5] "Palast der Republik." Basic grammar errors have been corrected.

In the years since reunification, the activity of the association has been enhanced, and complicated, by the decision of the Berlin Senate in 2004 to open the palace shell for "temporary" cultural use, including guided tours, concerts, exhibitions.[6] Since then, the struggle to prevent the demolition of the palace has attracted a broad spectrum of supporters, from various political parties to partisans of retaining the building for a depoliticized "creative use" and triggered many protests and demonstrations, as well as thousands of letters from the citizens of the former GDR. Despite the fact that barges began halting at the River Spree to transport the rubble from the impending demolition, the struggle continued: on 6 December 2005, a petition protesting the demolition, signed by more than 10,000, was handed over to Wolfgang Tiefensee, the federal minister of construction, by Claudia Roth, federal chairperson of Alliance 90/The Greens. Roth endorsed the newly created "Alliance for the Palace" (Bündnis für den Palast), whose recent website displayed "voices for an authentic Berlin."[7] As I write this essay, sand and water are being pumped into the basement of the palace, and demolition will start soon, to be documented online.

Things were simpler, and probably less democratic, when the decision was made to rebuild the Church of Christ the Savior in Moscow, at the location of Moscow's open-air swimming pool. The pool had been built in the foundation pit of B. M. Iofan's never-constructed Palace of Soviets, after the original church was blown up in 1931. Even if both sites—Berlin's Palace of the Republic and Moscow's swimming pool—share a place on the losing end of history, the latter cannot pretend to the "sense of loss" and the "powerful melancholic aura" with which the former was endowed.[8] Still it was undoubtedly "a place for the people."

So is the remainder of real socialist architecture. Much of it covers the territory of the former "second world" in the form of decrepit-looking buildings made of precast concrete slabs, from the *khrushchevki* of the 1960s to the unfinished skeletons of the Gorbachev or Ceauşescu era. These buildings come close to what Tim Edensor calls "zero-value rubbish." In his book, *Industrial Ruins: Space, Aesthetics and Materiality,* Edensor writes about the ruins of postindustrial Britain and the erasure of its "derided popular cultures of yesteryear, the objects that emerge out of working-class cultures and the spaces where they are played out."[9] If there has been a tendency to reclaim these ruins, usually by treating them as museumized spaces,

[6] Ibid.

[7] "Stimmen für ein authentisches Berlin," http://berlinpalast.de/ (accessed July 12, 2006).

[8] Boym, *Future of Nostalgia,* 189.

[9] Tim Edensor, *Industrial Ruins: Space, Aesthetics and Materiality* (Oxford: Berg, 2005), 132.

or by repackaging "historical" districts through urban regeneration, "the spaces of working class political action have [. . .] been eradicated from spatial commemoration, the lives of the poor are largely forgotten and those of the wealthy are often celebrated."[10]

The only difference is that in Russia, the former eastern bloc, Cuba, or China these places have no gentrification or exhibition value, and people continue to live in these concrete ruins of socialism. According to recent sources published by *Rossiiskaia gazeta,* khrushchevki make up half a billion square meters, out of the 2.8 billion square meters that constitute the entire housing space of Russia. The state construction committee Gosstroi recently announced that 100 million square meters of housing space need to be demolished in the near future and 300 million must be reconstructed. The task of reconstruction encompasses between 60 and 80 thousand buildings housing approximately 30 million people. In other words, writes *Rossiiskaia gazeta,* between 150 and 200 small cities have to be entirely rebuilt, or three times Moscow.[11] For the time being, the implementation of these plans have an "experimental" character, mostly limited to Moscow, St. Petersburg, or Kiev.[12] The rest of "five-story Russia" (*piatietazhnaia Rossiia*), Ukraine, or other such places will continue to dream the "one-story" dream once slandered by Ilya Ilf and Evgeny Petrov, unless the dream becomes nightmare.[13] A recent article in *Nezavisimaia gazeta* announces that, according to the Moscow authorities, "all 'five-story khrushchevki' will be demolished before the year 2010."[14] Where and how these 30 million inhabitants will be relocated is unclear. The Khabarovsk journalist Irina Stepura writes:

> Lidia Egorovna has lived in her khrushchevka for more than forty years. A long time ago, when her husband was given the flat for his leadership in production, it was a luxury. Today, this splendor is considerably tarnished, and for the two-room apartment Lidia Egorovna will not get more than 20 thousand "standard units" (*u.e.*) from the realtors. To move elsewhere is beyond the means of these tenants: the cost of new housing in Khabarovsk is legendary.[15]

---

[10] Ibid.

[11] "Deshevle skinut'sia na rekonstruktsiiu chem platit' po schetchiku," *Rossiiskaia gazeta,* March 4, 2004.

[12] Sergei Zverev, "'Khrushchevki' budut sneseny" *Ekspert. Ukrainskii delovoi zhurnal* 7 (12), February 27, 2005.

[13] I. Il'f and E. Petrov, *Odnoetazhnaia Amerika* (Moscow, 1937).

[14] Resin, "Vse 'khrushchevki-piatietazhki' budut sneseny k 2010 godu," *Nezavisimaia gazeta,* November 10, 2005.

[15] Irina Stepura, "Regional'nye khrushchevki," *Rossiiskaia gazeta,* March 4, 2004.

One should add here that the "standard unit" (*uslovnaia edinitsa*) can signify anything, from the U.S. dollar to the euro, depending on the current "market." "Today everyone has a specific 'u.e.' and the only way to compare prices is to recalculate them in rubles. As a result, sellers have an ideal instrument for disguising inflated prices."[16]

In the conditions of postprimitive accumulation of capital, as far as aesthetics go, these ruins have nothing to offer that could compare, for example, to "the fabulous ruins of Detroit."[17] But as Edensor correctly states, the commodification of memory includes not only the mediazation and commercial recontextualization of places and objects of the past, but also the participation of "expert" readings of place. Historical expertise plays a particularly important role in the ways a place is remembered and reconstructed. "When 'universal,' rigorous, scientific techniques are applied to the classification of objects and places, archives and archaeological traces, they tend to predominate over local memories or even efface them."[18]

What most obviously comes to the mind are the former cold war histories, privileging the political study of "communist" systems, often reduced to "Kremlinology" and "politburo" studies, over social and regional history. But new histories have yielded new fetishes and new commodities. Out of the rubble of personal documents, such as diaries and autobiographies, new constructs have emerged—reminding us of older ones—such as the "laboratories of the self" that allegedly help the investigator to better understand the "Stalinist soul" and "communist psychology."[19] Overall, academic contribution to the "nostalgia" industry has of course snowballed with the demise of state socialism worldwide. Helmut Dubiel's "Linke Trauerarbeit" (Leftist mourning), published in the wake of the German *Wende*, describes the reasons why leftist intellectuals from the west have failed in their work of mourning the loss of real-existing (state) socialism by engaging in what Sigmund Freud described

---

[16] Renata Yambaeva and Afanasy Sborov, "The Most Standard Unit," *Kommersant. Russia's Daily Online,* February 27, 2004: http://www.kommersant.com/page.asp?idr=1&id=452034 (accessed September 6, 2006).

[17] A website designed and administered by Lowell Boileau, an artist and photographer living in Farmington, Michigan, on the outskirts of Detroit, http://detroityes.com/ (accessed July 25, 2006).

[18] Edensor, *Industrial Ruins,* 129.

[19] Jochen Hellbeck, "Fashioning the Stalinist Soul: The Diary of Stepan Podlubnyi (1931–1939)," *Jahrbücher für Geschichte Osteuropas* 44, no. 3 (1996): 344–73; Igal Halfin, *From Darkness to Light: Class, Conscience, and Salvation in Revolutionary Russia* (Pittsburgh: University of Pittsburgh Press, 2000); Halfin, *Terror in My Soul: Communist Autobiographies on Trial* (Cambridge, MA: Harvard University Press, 2003).

as the two responses to failed mourning: "manic" denial and "melancholia."[20] Arguing for a constructive self-criticism of the left, which understands, for example, that "critical theory" was itself part of "working through," Dubiel proposes to redefine "real-existing capitalism." Reaching back to Marxist theoreticians such as Otto Bauer, Antonio Gramsci and Franz Neumann, Dubiel calls for exchanging final "revolutionary" tactics for gradualist and reformist strategies, whose goal is not the end of capitalism, "but the reinforcement of its inherent democratic, welfare-statist [*sozialstaatlichen*], and ecological counter bearings. Instead of 'final fictions,' the historical possibility clearly exists to 'civilize capitalism beyond recognition.'"[21]

Is Charity Scribner's recent *Requiem for Communism* (2003) an example of leftist "melancholia" (which somehow all too often becomes elitist observation)? Scribner "aims to negotiate the realities of the post-industrial moment [. . . to] enter in the gap left by the disintegration of real socialism and the welfare state by analyzing its aesthetic response to the crisis."[22] Inspired by the works of Oskar Negt and Alexander Kluge,[23] Scribner collects the "cultural residues of collective labor" that inform the alternative "public sphere" of the second world, the "pauses and absences" and "countless hours of dead labor" typical of the second-world factory floor, those "intractable moments of both solidarity and intrafactory arbitration that did not square with the market or the plan."[24] Scribner's "shop-floor romanticism" turns out to be rather elitist when its true purpose becomes explicit: "As factories and plants are shut down, the site of culture becomes an important meeting ground for the collective. Indeed, the end of the Industrial Revolution reveals truths that the left has yet to fully acknowledge: culture's potential for social change exceeds that of the workspace. After the socialist crisis of the eighties and nineties, we can appreciate more than ever the centrality of literature and art to the European public sphere."[25]

One can only wonder how Lidia Egorovna would respond to Scribner's musings. Scribner's book *is* an interesting potpourri documenting various reactions from

---

[20] Helmut Dubiel, "Linke Trauerarbeit," *Merkur: Deutsche Zeitschrift für europäisches Denken* 496, no. 6 (June 1990): 482–91.

[21] Ibid., 491.

[22] Charity Scribner, *Requiem for Communism* (Cambridge, MA: MIT Press, 2003), 5, 9.

[23] Oskar Negt and Alexander Kluge, *Öffentlichkeit und Erfahrung* (Frankfurt: Zweitausendeins, 1972). Trans.: *Public Sphere and Experience: Toward an Analysis of the Bourgeois and Proletarian Public Sphere* (Minneapolis: University of Minnesota Press, 1993); Negt and Kluge, *Geschichte und Eigensinn* (Frankfurt am Main: Zweitausendeins, 1981).

[24] Scribner, *Requiem for Communism,* 6.

[25] Ibid., 158.

western and eastern Europe to the problems and the demise of real socialism. Some of the reactions undeniably qualify as pieces of the "nostalgia industry," while others seem to be more genuine responses "from below." Among the first I would count Chantal Ackerman's 1993 documentary film *D'Est* (From the east), whose display of highways expanding from the former East German border to the snowy streets of Moscow, shot by steady cam, captures little beyond a very western imagination of the "boundless spaces" inhabited by the mythical *âme slave*. As far as the landscapes are concerned, the film could have been shot in any suburban sprawl of North America or Europe. As "responses from below" one could count the pages reporting on the museum of everyday life in the GDR in Eisenhüttenstadt and the Kindergarten Museum of the GDR in Oranienburg; Andrzej Wajda's films *Czlowiek z marmuru* (*Man of marble*, 1977 and *Czlowiek z zelaza* (*Man of iron*, 1981) in the context of Solidarity and its politics; Leslie Kaplan's 1982 prose poem *L'excès-L'usine* (Factory excess); Tony Harrison's poem and film *Prometheus* (1998), and Mark Herman's film *Brassed Off* (1996). Both films react to Margaret Thatcher's "rolling back the state" during the mid-1980s. One chapter is devoted to Christa Wolff's pre- and post-2002 writings, which are, according to Scribner, "a literary bridge [affording] us a keen perspective on Europe's second sex as well as its second world."[26]

Despite Scribner's claim that her book, "at odds with postmodern flux ... fixes its attention upon the local, the concrete,"[27] we have definitely left the precast concrete slabs of real socialism for a more "metaphorical" treatment of its ruins. "When an era crumbles, 'History breaks down into images, not into stories,'" writes Susan Buck-Morss in *Dreamworld and Catastrophe*.[28] This book, in itself a "Benjaminian" composition of discontinuous fragments, is (again) a curious mix of "working through," relevant observations, and irritating passages, at times coming from undigested secondary sources, heavily influenced by the writings of Valery Podoroga and his circle of postcommunist and postmodern Moscow philosophers with whom Buck-Morss created a "working collective" during her many trips back and forth between Moscow and Ithaca, New York. Writing for instance about "cinema and simulacrum" and the "revolution-as-spectacle," she opposes Hollywood's "prosthetic experience of collective desire" to the "prosthetic experience of collective power" of the Soviet screen.

---

[26] Ibid., 160.

[27] Ibid., 5.

[28] Susan Buck-Morss, *Dreamworld and Catastrophe: The Passing of Mass Utopia in East and West* (2000; reprint, Cambridge, MA: MIT Press, 2002), 68. The internal quotation is from Walter Benjamin.

> When later generations "remembered" the October Revolution, it was Eisenstein's images they had in mind. The particular characteristics of the screen as a cognitive organ enabled audiences to see the materiality not only of this new collective protagonist, but also of other ideal entities: the unity of the revolutionary people, the idea of international solidarity, the idea of the Soviet Union itself. Indeed, it is doubtful whether the Soviet experience would have been possible without cinema. [The] impact [of Dziga Vertov's *Shestaia chast' mira* (A sixth of the world, 1926)] was greatest within the Soviet Union, where it gave a simulated immanence to the idea of "socialism in one country" by introducing a pleased public to the myriad of ethnic types as the new Soviet "we."[29]

Here the author of *Dreamworld and Catastrophe* falls victim to the mythologization common to many western admirers of Soviet avant-garde cinema. It is Sergei Eisenstein's *Oktiabr'* (October, 1927) that, indeed, the later generations had in mind when they were picturing the storming of the Winter Palace, but as far the Soviet "collective" of the 1920s and 1930s goes, neither Eisenstein nor Vertov (nor "montage" film in general) had any significant impact on it. On the contrary, the Soviet public at large longed for the "collective desire" provided by American and other "bourgeois" film. *Stachka* (Strike, 1925) or *Chelovek s kino-apparatom* (Man with a movie camera, 1929) were replaced by *Tsirk* (Circus, 1936) and other musical comedies of the 1930s, that were Hollywood in form, socialist in content. In her reminiscences of her time in the camps in the 1930s, Ekaterina Olitskaia recalls a scene in a freight car heading toward a Siberian camp. The prisoners try to cheer themselves up by singing the "Hymn to the Motherland," the famous song by Isaak Dunaevsky and Vasilt Lebedev-Kumach that propels Grigory Aleksandrov's *Circus.* Olitskaia shudders. She cannot understand: "I looked at the singing women, and said to myself: 'They have just been forced to walk naked past a line of male guards. They are being transported like cattle, locked up in a prison car . . . 'Wide is My Beloved Country' . . . Was there no limit to human baseness and stupidity?"[30] For Yuri Slezkine, the singing women prisoners and Olitskaia, "a dispossessed gentry woman who never emigrated and an ascetic revolutionary who never triumphed, [. . .] have nothing to say to each other."[31] Buck-Morss is in good company. She has nothing to say to (most of) the citizens of the former Soviet Union. More convincing, though,

[29] Ibid., 147.

[30] Sheila Fitzpatrick and Yuri Slezkine, eds., *In the Shadow of Revolution: Life Stories of Russian Women. From 1917 to the Second World War* (Princeton: Princeton University Press, 2000), 433. I wish to thank Tracy McDonald for drawing my attention to this passage.

[31] Ibid., 30.

are Buck-Morss's thoughts, comparing machine culture in the Soviet Union and the west: "For the proletariat of the Soviet Union, industrialization was still a dream world when, for workers in capitalist countries, it was already a lived catastrophe."[32] Alexander Gastev's Central Institute of Labor, which imported Taylorist work methods from the United States in 1920 was in fact "run by a poet," and, in the utopian context of the Soviet 1920s, the "scientifically calculated body movements were [indeed] the industrial-age equivalent of a rain dance."[33] Writing about Konstantin Melnikov's "Green City" (the flip side of Taylorist utopia in the Soviet 1920s), Buck-Morss reverts to Marx's manuscripts of 1844, where "the overcoming of human alienation would necessitate a reconciliation between humans and nature." [. . .] "Perhaps not until the ecological crisis at the end of the twentieth century does the young Marx's commitment to a reconciliation with nature appear to be not merely an expression of nineteenth-century romanticism or youthful idealism, but an intensely practical political concern."[34]

This brings us back to our theme. The ruins of real socialism were the product of the dialectic of "Taylorism" versus the "Green City," or, to generalize a bit, of industrialization versus the countryside. James Scott writes about how attempts to rationalize and simplify society caused some of the disasters of the twentieth century, including not only collectivization in the Soviet Union or the Great Leap Forward in China, but also "the history of Third-World development . . . littered with the debris of huge agricultural schemes and new cities . . . that have failed their residents."[35] As far as Russia and the Soviet Union are concerned, Scott's analysis, however, is limited by an exaggerated focus on "authoritarian high modernism," illustrated by the literary example of Evgeny Zamiatin's novel *My* (We, 1920–21), which was, after all, a satirical response to the Taylorist utopia of the 1920s. Far from being implemented, Soviet high modernism was part and parcel of the "duel of utopias" in the 1920s in which urbanists opposed de-urbanists, leading to the eventual demise of both in the grand scheme of things.[36] The metaphor of the "gardening state," which has resurfaced recently, the "aesthetic vision of an unshakeable, well-coordinated

[32] Buck-Morss, *Dreamworld and Catastrophe*. 105.

[33] Ibid.

[34] Ibid., 118–19.

[35] James C. Scott, *Seeing Like a State: How Certain Schemes to Improve the Human Condition Have Failed* (New Haven: Yale University Press, 1998), 3.

[36] Katerina Clark, "Political History and Literary Chronotope: Some Soviet Case Studies," in *Literature and History: Theoretical Problems and Russian Case Studies*, ed. Gary Saul Morson (Stanford: Stanford University Press, 1986), 230–46.

social harmony" tell us only part of the story, that of the utopian planners of the 1920s.[37] On the ground, not gardening, but uprooting was the rule.

A much more accurate (literary) illustration of built socialism, as it emerged from the forced industrialization and collectivization drive of 1929–31 and beyond, is Andrei Platonov's *Kotlovan* (Foundation pit, 1929–30), where the construction of a shelter from the surrounding world and the transformation of the "dead body" of the world into habitable structures for man, are cancelled out by the transformation of the construction site into a grave.[38] In Platonov's novel, building includes decay, because of the general law of entropy: "endurance exhaustedly went on in the world, as though everything living were located somewhere in the middle of time and its own motion: the beginning has been forgotten by everyone and the end was unknown, so there remained only direction."[39] Platonov's formulation captures in a mesmerizing way what so many testimonies from the Soviet construction sites of the early 1930s tell us about what socialism meant for most of its participants, from Dneprostroi to Magnitogorsk to Komsomolsk-na-Amure: a community cemented by "endurance" (*terpen'e*), extraordinary efforts in primitive and chaotic times and conditions. Whether metaphorically understood or *concrete,* built socialism was decaying, or, if you wish, "in ruins," from the very beginning of its existence. The most "nonliterary," immediate reason for this state of affairs can be stated in one word: poverty. Andrei Ikonnikov shows that what plagued the Soviet state's construction plans most prominently during the 1930s was the constant lack of high-quality materials, industrial technology, and skilled laborers, which caused many projects to fail even before their completion. The best metal was used to build machinery and industrial tools, the best cement to construct dams. Housing units were built using the leftovers.[40]

The re-privatization of domestic space, away from *komunalki* and hostels, which took place with the mass construction of separate apartments in the prefabricated blocks of the Khrushchev era and beyond, was limited because it was determined by the same, nonresolved compromise between the norms put forward by the state and the needs of "private life." The Soviet housing crisis was in fact never

[37] Amir Weiner, ed., *Landscaping the Human Garden: Twentieth-Century Population Management in a Comparative Framework* (Stanford: Stanford University Press, 2003), 8.

[38] Andrei Platonov, *The Foundation Pit,* trans. Mirra Ginsburg (Evanston: Northwestern University Press, 1994).

[39] Platonov quoted in Thomas Seifrid, *Andrei Platonov: Uncertainties of Spirit* (Cambridge: Cambridge University Press, 1992), 147.

[40] Andrei Ikonnikov, *Russian Architecture of the Soviet Period* (Moscow: Raduga Publishers, 1988). I wish to thank Mark Laszlo-Herbert for drawing my attention to this passage.

resolved and still remains a pressing concern, as we have seen. Regulations concerning average living space per capita and the "condensation" (*uplotnenie*) of the living space of the former well-to-do after the October Revolution became permanent and universal features of socialist living, with the exception of those who were "more equal than others," to refer to the well-known Soviet joke. Moving from the communal apartment to one of the normed cubicles in a prefabricated housing unit was a cause for boundless joy and sordid machination.[41] As to the space beyond the flat's

Figure 1. Dashkovo-Pesochnia, Riazan, 1996. Photograph by Evgeny Kashirin. Reproduced with permission.

borders, it was, and still is, a no man's land open to all hazards, private and collective, including those of nature. In Figure 1, the presence of a massive flock of birds is due to the garbage and other residues originating from the prefabricated housing blocks that we see on the horizon. Katerina Gerasimova writes about those "privatized" territories that were "nevertheless collective in their form."[42] In this indeterminacy (or "dialectic"?) of unresolved collectivity and privacy the origin of socialism's ruin in progress becomes visible.

[41] Yuri Trifonov's short novel *Obmen* (The exchange), published in 1969 provides a good example of the political economy of private space and its human consequences in the conditions of post-Thaw Soviet socialism.

[42] Katerina Gerasimova, "Privacy in the Soviet Communal Apartment," in *Socialist Spaces: Sites of Everyday Life in the Eastern Bloc*, ed. David Crowley and Susan E. Reid (Oxford: Berg, 2002), 210.

An often-cited illustration of Soviet ruin and decay is Andrei Tarkovsky's film *Stalker* (1979). Harmut Böhme has shown that this film follows the tradition of philosophies of history and nature whose poetic expression is allegory and melancholia.[43] *Stalker* inverts the Hegelian or Marxist philosophy of history: the progress of spirit turns out to be only an episode of natural history. The center of Tarkovsky's poetics is not the construction site, the "principle of hope," the fantasy of the "not yet," but the melancholia of decay, the "no more" of mourning. The gigantic industrial settings at the end of the film function as the "crematoria of civilization."[44] Tarkovky's allegory is of course a symptom of late Soviet "stagnation" and "posthistory" in which the utopian impulse of the early periods is missing. Sheila Fitzpatrick aptly captured this initial impulse in her "enlarged" definition of socialist realism, that is, not just a literary theory, a blueprint for literary production, but "a method of representation characteristic of the Stalin period and the Stalinist *mentalité*. [. . .] In the socialist-realist view of the world, a dry, half-dug ditch signified a future canal full of loaded barges, a ruined church was a potential kolkhoz clubhouse, and the inscription of a project in the Five-Year Plan was a magical act of creation that might almost obviate the need for more concrete exertions."[45]

But the well-known definition of socialist realism, "the truthful, historically concrete depiction of reality in its revolutionary development," encapsulates a lot more than "Stalinism." It captures real socialism. Embodying the contradiction between people's genuine aspirations and the (political, economic, social) reality they lived in, socialist realism was also, metaphorically speaking, a literature in ruins from the very start, with a mechanism of increasing self-destruction that emptied it of its artistic "structures."[46] This mechanism is already present in Platonov's definition of "endurance": "as though everything living were located somewhere in the middle of time and its own motion."[47] As time passed, this difficult balance between "endurance" and "revolutionary development" faded, but did not completely vanish.

[43] Harmut Böhme, "Ruinen–Landschaften: Zum Verhältnis von Naturgeschichte und Allegorie in den späten Filmen von Andrej Tarkowskij, *Natur und Subjekt* (Frankfurt am Main: Suhrkamp, 1988), 334–79.

[44] Ibid., 362–3.

[45] Sheila Fitzpatrick, "Becoming Cultured: Socialist Realism and the Representation of Privilege and Taste," *The Cultural Front: Power and Culture in Revolutionary Russia* (Ithaca, NY: Cornell University Press, 1992), 217.

[46] The rewriting of Fedor Gladkov's novel *Cement* is a classic example of this process. See Thomas Lahusen, "Cement (Fedor Gladkov, 1925)," in *The Novel*, ed. Franco Moretti, vol. 2, Forms and Themes (Princeton: Princeton University Press, 2006), 476–82.

[47] Platonov quoted in Seifrid, *Andrei Platonov,* 147.

Without a doubt, this balance defined the "civilization" that Stephen Kotkin wrote about in *Magnetic Mountain.*[48] It was repeated, for example, in the planning, construction, and decay of East Germany's "first socialist city," Eisenhüttenstadt/Stalinstadt, and other such places.[49] It resurfaced as late as Nina Andreeva's defensive "anti-perestroika" letter to *Sovetskaia Rossiia* on 13 March 1988,[50] or in the struggle to prevent the demolition of the Palace of the Republic in Berlin, especially after it was gutted of its "bureaucratic baroque." As a commentator in the *Frankfurter Allgemeine Zeitung* explained, "What remained was a glassed-in steel and concrete skeleton, full of empty levels, platforms, and terraces that would bring tears to the eyes of any stage designer."[51]

In his famous essay on the ruin, Georg Simmel wrote: "Decay appears as nature's revenge for the spirit's having violated it by making a form in its own image."[52] This testimony to violation is perhaps what makes the ruins of real socialism unbearably unforgettable.

---

[48] Stephen Kotkin, *Magnetic Mountain: Stalinism as a Civilization* (Berkeley: University of California Press, 1995).

[49] See *Utopie zur Gegenwart. Wandel industrieller, regionaler und sozialer Strukturen in Eisenhüttenstadt* (Marburg: Schüren, 1997); Arbeitsgruppe Stadtgeschichte, ed., *Eisenhüttenstadt: "Erste sozialistische Stadt Deutschlands"* (Berlin: be bra verlag, 1999).

[50] Nina Andreeva, "A Manifesto against Restructuring?" *The Current Digest of the Soviet Press* 40, no. 13 (April 27, 1988): 1–6.

[51] Niklas Maak, "Palast der Republik: Schaut in dieses Haus," *Frankfurter Allgemeine Zeitung,* no. 244 (October 19, 2004): 35.

[52] Georg Simmel, "The Ruin," in *Essays on Sociology, Philosophy and Aesthetics*, ed. Kurt H. Wolff (New York: Harper & Row, 1965), 259.

Contributors

Jessica Allina-Pisano is Associate Professor in the School of Political Studies at the University of Ottawa and an associate of the Davis Center for Russian and Eurasian Studies at Harvard University. She received her PhD from Yale University. She is the author of *The Post-Soviet Potemkin Village: Politics and Property Rights in the Black Earth* (Cambridge University Press, 2007). Her research on land privatization, property rights, and informal politics in Eastern Europe has appeared in journals such as *World Politics*, *International Journal of Labor and Working Class History*, *Journal of Peasant Studies,* and *Otechestvennye zapiski,* and as chapters in edited volumes.

Andrea Chandler is Professor of Political Science at Carleton University. She is the author of *Institutions of Isolation: Border Controls in the Soviet Union and its Successor States, 1917–1993* (McGill-Queen's University Press, 1998) and *Shocking Mother Russia: Democratization, Social Rights and Pension Reform in Russia, 1990-2001* (University of Toronto Press, 2004). Her current research focuses on gender and social welfare in post-communist Russian politics.

Michael Zdenek David is a clinical fellow in infectious diseases at the University of Chicago, where he was a Robert Wood Johnson Clinical Scholar (2004–06) and is a PhD candidate in Russian history (exp. 2007). He holds a BA in Russian Language (Amherst College), an MD (Yale University), and an MS in Health Studies (University of Chicago). His historical research focuses on infectious diseases and on the medical profession in Russia, and his biomedical research is on the clinical and molecular epidemiology of antibiotic-resistant bacterial pathogens.

Heather DeHaan received her PhD from the University of Toronto and is now Assistant Professor of History at Binghamton University (a member of the State University of New York). Her dissertation, "From Nizhnii to Gor'kii: The Reconstruction of a Russian Provincial City in the Stalinist 1930s," recently won the Tucker-Cohen Prize for its analysis of the politics of urban planning, and she is currently revising it for publication.

Ben Eklof is Professor of History and Education at Indiana University, whose research and writing has centered upon village life in Imperial Russia before the Revolution, schools, reforms, and Mikhail Gorbachev. He is the author of *Russian Peasant Schools* (University of California Press, 1986) and *Soviet Briefing* (Westview

Press, 1989), as well as editor of six volumes, the most recent being *A Social History of Imperial Russia* (Boris Mironov with Ben Eklof; Westview Press, 2000) and *Educational Reform in Post-Soviet Russia* (F. Cass, 2005).

Dan Healey is Senior Lecturer in History at Swansea University, UK. He is the author of *Homosexual Desire in Revolutionary Russia: The Regulation of Sexual and Gender Dissent* (University of Chicago Press, 2001), a Russian translation of which is forthcoming from Moscow's Ladomir Press. He is co-editor of *Russian Masculinities in History and Culture* (Palgrave Macmillan, 2002), with Barbara Evans Clements and Rebecca Friedman. In addition to articles on gender and sexuality in Russian history, he is currently finishing a book on forensic medicine and sexual disorder in early Bolshevik Russia.

Robert E. Johnson is Professor of History and past Director of the Centre for Russian and East European Studies at the University of Toronto, with research interests in Imperial Russian and Soviet history, demography, and social history. Recent publications have included studies of Russia's war in Chechnya and of the rewriting of twentieth-century Soviet and Cold War history in the light of new archival discoveries. In 2004 he produced a three-hour radio documentary, 'In the Stalin Archive,' for the Canadian Broadcasting Corporation, and in 2006 a sequel entitled 'The Cold War Declassified.' He has visited Russia more than twenty times, beginning in 1970.

Nikolai Krementsov is Associate Professor at the Institute for the History and Philosophy of Science and Technology at the University of Toronto. He has published extensively on the history of Soviet science. Among his publications are *Stalinist Science* (Princeton University Press, 1997); *The Cure: A Story of Cancer and Politics from the Annals of the Cold War* (Chicago University Press, 2002); and *International Science between the World Wars: The Case of Genetics* (Routledge, 2005).

Thomas Lahusen is Canada Research Chair in History, Arts and Culture at the University of Toronto, where he teaches Russian/Soviet cultural history, comparative literature, and film. His publications include *How Life Writes the Book: Real Socialism and Socialist Realism in Stalin's Russia* (Cornell University Press, 1997) and the co-edited volumes *Intimacy and Terror: Soviet Diaries of the 1930s* (New Press, 1995) and *Socialist Realism without Shores* (Duke University Press, 1997), and the special journal issue "Harbin and Manchuria: Place, Space, and Identity," *The South Atlantic Quarterly* (2001). He is currently working on a history of film distribution in the Soviet Union and has co-directed several documentaries.

Alena V. Ledeneva is Reader in Russian Politics and Society at the School of Slavonic and East European Studies, University College London, UK. She studied Economics at the Novosibirsk State University and Social and Political Theory at the University of Cambridge, and has been a postdoctoral Research Fellow at New Hall, Cambridge. She is author of *How Russia Really Works* (Cornell University Press, 2006), *Russia's Economy of Favours* (Cambridge University Press, 1998), and *Unwritten Rules* (Centre for European Reform, 2001); and co-editor of *Bribery and Blat in Russia* (Macmillan, 2000) and *Economic Crime in Russia* (Kluwer Law International, 2000).

Tracy McDonald is Assistant Professor of History at McMaster University. She is currently working on a manuscript on peasant-state relations in Riazan province in the 1920s. She co-edited (with Lynne Viola, Sergei Zhuravlev, and Andrei Mel'nik) a volume of documents on collectivization entitled *Riazanskaia derevnia v 1929–1930 gg.: khronika golovokruzheniia* (The Riazan Countryside, 1929–1930: A Chronicle of Spinning Heads) (Rosspen, 1998). Her articles on peasant rebellion and on banditry in Riazan have appeared in the *Journal of Social History*, *Canadian-American Slavic Studies*, and *Contending with Stalinism: Soviet Power and Popular Resistance in the 1930s* (Cornell University Press, 2002).

James R. Millar is Emeritus Professor of Economics and International Affairs at George Washington University. Professor Millar directed the Institute for European, Russian and Eurasian Studies at George Washington University 1989–2002. He was previously Director of International Studies at the University of Illinois at Urbana-Champaign. Professor Millar was Principal Investigator for the Soviet Interview Project (1979–87). He edited the *Slavic Review* (1975-80) and *Problems of Post-Communism* (1993–2003). He also edited the four-volume *Encyclopedia of Russian History* (2004). Among other awards, Millar held Guggenheim and Woodrow Wilson Fellowships. He received the Award for Distinguished Contributions to Slavic Studies from the AAASS in 2006.

Judith Pallot is University Lecturer in the Geography of Russia at Oxford University. Dr Pallot has an established reputation in the field of Russian peasant studies. More recently, she has developed links with the Federal Penal Service in the Russian Federation Ministry of Justice, negotiating a memorandum of understanding between Oxford University and the Academy of Law and Penal Management in Riazan, which has led on to a collaborative research project. Recent publications include *Russia's Unknown Agriculture: Household Production in Post-Soviet*

Russia (Oxford University Press, 2007) and *Neizvestnaia Rossiia: Bez korovy nel'zia* (You Can't Live without a Cow) (Novoe izdatel'stvo, 2006), both co-authored with Tatiana Nefedova.

Kathleen E. Smith teaches Russian and East European Politics at Georgetown University and is the author of two books on memory and politics in the former Soviet Union, *Remembering Stalin's Victims* (Cornell University Press, 1996) and *Mythmaking in the New Russia* (Cornell University Press, 2002). She is currently writing a history of the year 1956 in Russia, a crossdisciplinary study of the social history, cultural upheaval, and political change beginning with Khrushchev's denunciation of Stalin in the Secret Speech and ending with a retreat from liberalization after the Hungarian uprising.

Peter H. Solomon, Jr., is Professor of Political Science, Law, and Criminology at the University of Toronto, and a Member of its Centre for European, Russian and Eurasian Studies. His writings include *Soviet Criminal Justice under Stalin* (Cambridge University Press 1996), *Reforming Justice in Russia, 1864-1996: Power, Culture and the Limits of Legal Order* (edited, M.E. Sharpe 1997), *Courts and Transition in Russia: The Challenge of Judicial Reform* (with Todd Foglesong, Westview 2000), and many articles on legal reform in post-communist countries. He is an active participant in judicial reform projects, including the Canada-Russia Judicial Partnership and the Canada-Ukraine Judicial Cooperation Project, both funded by the Canadian International Development Agency.

Alexei Yurchak is originally from Leningrad, USSR, where he got a degree in radio physics. In the late 1980s, during perestroika, he was the manager of the Russian rock group/performance theatre AVIA. Having completed a PhD in Anthropology at Duke University, he now teaches in the Department of Anthropology at the University of California, Berkeley. The author of *Everything Was Forever, until It Was No More: The Last Soviet Generation* (Princeton University Press, 2006), he is currently working on a new book that examines the experimental "artistic utopias" that have emerged in the wake of the collapse of the Soviet Union.